MW00803405

Clinical Applications *of the* Personality Assessment Inventory

Clinical Applications *of the* Personality Assessment Inventory

Edited by
Mark A. Blais
Matthew R. Baity
Christopher J. Hopwood

Routledge
Taylor & Francis Group
New York   London

Routledge
Taylor & Francis Group
270 Madison Avenue
New York, NY 10016

Routledge
Taylor & Francis Group
27 Church Road
Hove, East Sussex BN3 2FA

© 2010 by Taylor and Francis Group, LLC
Routledge is an imprint of Taylor & Francis Group, an Informa business

Printed in the United States of America on acid-free paper
10 9 8 7 6 5 4 3 2 1

International Standard Book Number: 978-0-415-99323-4 (Hardback)

For permission to photocopy or use material electronically from this work, please access www.copyright.com (http://www.copyright.com/) or contact the Copyright Clearance Center, Inc. (CCC), 222 Rosewood Drive, Danvers, MA 01923, 978-750-8400. CCC is a not-for-profit organization that provides licenses and registration for a variety of users. For organizations that have been granted a photocopy license by the CCC, a separate system of payment has been arranged.

Trademark Notice: Product or corporate names may be trademarks or registered trademarks, and are used only for identification and explanation without intent to infringe.

Library of Congress Cataloging-in-Publication Data

Clinical applications of the personality assessment inventory / editors, Mark
    A.Blais, Matthew R. Baity, Christopher J. Hopwood.
        p. cm.
    Includes bibliographical references and index.
    ISBN 978-0-415-99323-4 (hardback : alk. paper)
    1. Personality Assessment Inventory.

    RC473.P56C55 2010
    616.85'81--dc22   2009036281

Visit the Taylor & Francis Web site at
http://www.taylorandfrancis.com

and the Routledge Web site at
http://www.routledgementalhealth.com

To my wife Dr. Cathy A. Conboy; my daughters
Mary Catherine and Alice Victoria; my parents
Earlene and Leo; and my sisters Sheila, Lynn, and Shannon

M.A.B.

To my loving wife and our children, who are
a constant source of inspiration

M.R.B.

To Les

C.J.H

Contents

Preface

The idea for this book took hold shortly after the Personality Assessment Inventory (PAI, Morey, 1991) was featured in a special issue of the *Journal of Personality Assessment* (JPA; Kurtz & Blais, 2007). The JPA Special Issue highlighted the growing empirical support and research application of the PAI. While the PAI Special Issue was well received, many colleagues commented that a companion volume focusing on the clinical applications of the PAI would be highly desirable. This volume represents our effort to address this need by bringing together authoritative contributions covering a diverse range of clinical applications of the PAI. Each chapter is written by psychologists with extensive clinical experience in applying the PAI within specific patient populations or specialized clinical settings. To the extent possible, all chapters follow a similar format, making them easy to use as reference sources for busy clinicians and many chapters also contain unique reference data suitable for supplementing standard PAI interpretations.

In Chapter 1, we briefly introduce the development and composition of the PAI. We discuss psychometric and practical strengths of the PAI that may help to explain its rising popularity, and briefly highlight some interpretive strategies for the instrument. In Chapter 2, John Kurtz, who has used the PAI in his research and practice since its inception, provides a general overview for its use in outpatient clinical assessment. He also provides outpatient-specific reference data from the normative clinical sample, as well as interpretive rubrics for clinical predictions involving treatment continuation and risk of harm to self or others. Caleb Siefert and Mark Blais, who have used the PAI for practice and research at the Massachusetts General Hospital for several years, cover its applications for inpatient assessment in Chapter 3. They also provide reference data to facilitate the use of the PAI in other inpatient settings. Radhika Krishnamurthy, a personality assessment expert with several years' experience in adolescent assessment, summarizes the newly released adolescent version of the PAI in Chapter 4. Dr. Krishnamurthy also describes a case that highlights her interpretive suggestions, and provides reference data from one forensic and two clinical samples.

The next six chapters are written by experts in more specific assessment contexts. In Chapter 5, Ali Khadivi and Andreas Evdokas, who have used and conducted research on the PAI for several years with inner-city substance abusers, describe how they have applied the instrument in this setting. Patrick Calhoun, director of postdoctoral training at the Durham Veteran's Affairs, and personality assessment expert, describes the assessment of veterans with the PAI in collaboration with several colleagues in Chapter 6. In Chapter 7, Mark Ruiz and Ezra Ochshorn outline the use of the PAI in forensic assessment settings. Dr. Ruiz has vast clinical and research experience on this topic, including having co-authored the PAI forensic manual and software for the use of the test in correctional settings (Edens & Ruiz, 2005). Amor Correa and Richard Rogers describe cross-cultural research that has been conducted on the PAI in Chapter 8, clarify areas for further work, and provide helpful suggestions for practitioners using the PAI in populations who differ culturally from normative comparison samples. Timothy Clark, Sarah Oslund, and Christopher Hopwood describe applications of the PAI in medical settings based on their clinical and research experiences with medically ill patients in Chapter 9. In Chapter 10, Peter Weiss who, along with his father William Weiss, has conducted the bulk of research on personnel selection with the PAI, describes this research and provides specific, empirically grounded recommendations for the interpretation of the PAI in this context. Finally, Michael Cheng, Jeremy Frank, and Christopher Hopwood describe the use of the PAI for motor vehicle accident claimants, and provide reference data to augment the interpretation of the PAI in this understudied clinical population in Chapter 11.

The final two chapters return to a more general focus on the interpretation and clinical use of the PAI. In Chapter 12, Mark Blais and Christopher Hopwood present a model of personality organization that has proven useful for conceptualizing PAI scores and integrating PAI data with other psychological assessment information. In Chapter 13, Matthew Baity presents a case depicting a therapeutic assessment with the PAI. Together, these chapters present a broad contemporary overview of the PAI, including its research basis and interpretive strategies, as well as specific recommendations for clinicians working in a variety of psychological assessment settings.

Psychological assessment remains a vital element in the training and practice of professional psychology, yet many of our most popular instruments are based on aging technology and outdated constructs. While these venerable tools can be updated and restandardized, they can never be fully retrofitted with all of the theoretical and psychometric advances of the last 50 years. Therefore, the development and application of contemporary assessment instruments such as the PAI are needed to maintain the vitality of the field. We hope that this volume will help practicing psychologists and psychology students appreciate the psychometric and clinical advantages offered by the PAI and also aid them in translating those improvements into better clinical care. Finally, while each chapter presents a specific clinical application of the PAI along with the supporting research, areas in need of further investigation have also been highlighted throughout the book. Our lofty goals were to have this volume become a valued clinical resource and to stimulate new research on the clinical utility and application of the PAI.

REFERENCES

Edens, V.F. & Ruiz, M.A. (2005). PAI interpretive report for correctional settings (PAI-CS). Lutz, FL: Psychological Assessment Resources.

Kurtz, J.E. & Blais, M.A. (2007). Introduction to the special issue on the Personality Assessment Inventory. *Journal of Personality Assessment, 88*, 1–4.

Morey, L.C. (1991). *Professional manual for the Personality Assessment Inventory.* Odessa, FL: Psychological Assessment Resources.

Contributors

Matthew R. Baity received his Ph.D. from the University of Arkansas in 2003 and completed his clinical internship and postdoctoral fellowship at Massachusetts General Hospital, where he later worked as a staff psychologist. Currently, he is an assistant professor within the California School of Professional Psychology at Alliant International University's Sacramento campus, where he teaches courses in personality assessment, neuropsychological testing, and evaluating research on empirically supported treatments. Dr. Baity is a reviewer for several professional journals, as well as a consulting editor for the *Journal of Personality Assessment*, and is a member of both the American Psychological Association and the Society for Personality Assessment. He has co-authored more than 20 articles and book chapters in his areas of interest, which include cognitive and personality assessment, character pathology, psychotherapy process, and treatment outcome.

Jean C. Beckham, Ph.D. is a tenured professor in the Department of Psychiatry and Behavioral Sciences at Duke University Medical Center and a senior veterans' affairs (VA) Career Research Scientist at the Durham Veterans Affairs Medical Center. Dr. Beckham's primary area of interest is the effect of chronic posttraumatic stress disorder (PTSD) on health, with more than 120 publications. She also serves as the research leader of the Genetics Core of the VISN 6 Mental Illness Research Education and Clinical Center, where she is leading an evaluation candidate gene and whole genome association effort in returning veterans. She serves as principal investigator (PI) on several federally funded projects including an investigation of optimal smoking cessation treatment strategies for PTSD, and a study of genetic and metabolomic biomarkers of cardiovascular and metabolic health in early PTSD. She currently serves on several study sections, the VA Tobacco Advisory Group, and is an executive board member of the International Society of Traumatic Stress Studies.

Mark A. Blais, Psy.D. is associate chief of psychology and director of the Psychological Evaluation and Research Laboratory at Massachusetts General Hospital. He is associate professor of psychology (psychiatry) at Harvard Medical School. Dr. Blais graduated from Nova Southeastern University. His research interests are focused on personality, personality assessment, and outcomes measurement. He has published more than 70 research papers, 25 book chapters, and one co-edited volume on psychiatric ratings scales. An award-winning teacher and mentor, he was the 2009 recipient of the Theodore Millon Award in Personality Psychology presented by the American Psychological Foundation. He served as an associate editor for the *Journal of Personality Assessment* from 2007 to 2009.

Loretta E. Braxton received her Ph.D. from the University of North Carolina at Chapel Hill. She is a staff psychologist at the Durham VA Medical Center, where she directs the Psychodiagnostic Laboratory, serves as the director of internship training, and more recently has become the director of psychosocial rehabilitation services for veterans with serious mental illness. Particular interests include multicultural issues and objective personality assessment. She has been teaching assessment to predoctoral interns, practicum students, and postdoctoral fellows for more than 15 years.

Patrick S. Calhoun received his Ph.D. from Vanderbilt University in 1998 and completed a postdoctoral fellowship in health services research at Duke University Medical Center in 2000. He currently serves as an associate director of the VA Mid-Atlantic Mental Illness Research Education and Clinical Center (MIRECC), the director of Psychology fellowship training at the Durham VA Medical Center, a research associate in the VA Center for Health Services Research in Primary Care, and an assistant professor of psychiatry and behavioral sciences at Duke University Medical Center. In his role as a direct services provider, Dr. Calhoun specializes in the assessment and treatment of PTSD. He has co-authored more than 60 articles and book chapters in his area of interest, which has focused primarily on the psychological, behavioral, and health consequences of traumatic stress. His active projects include an examination of the mental health needs and barriers to care for veterans returning from Afghanistan and Iraq. Other current interests include personality assessment and the relationship between PTSD and health risk behaviors including smoking and alcohol use.

Michael K. Cheng, Ph.D. is a registered clinical and rehabilitation psychologist in Toronto, Ontario. He works in a clinic- and hospital-based setting providing assessment and treatment for patients involved in motor vehicle or workplace accidents. He is a member of the Ontario Psychological Association.

Carolina P. Clancy received her Ph.D. from the University of North Carolina at Greensboro in 2003. She currently serves as a staff psychologist at the Durham VA Medical Center and as a research associate of psychiatry and behavioral sciences at Duke University Medical Center. Dr. Clancy specializes in the assessment and treatment of PTSD. She has a strong interest in evidenced-based treatments for PTSD such as Cognitive Processing Therapy and Prolonged Exposure Therapy (PE). Other current interests include personality assessment and coping with chronic medical illnesses.

Timothy S. Clark, Ph.D. is the program director for the Baylor Center for Pain Management's three interdisciplinary pain management programs in the Dallas metroplex. Research interests include outcomes and use of the Personality

Assessment Inventory (PAI) in pain populations. He is a member of the clinical faculty at University of Texas Southwestern Medical Center in Dallas.

Claire F. Collie received her Ph.D. from Texas A&M University in 2004. She is a senior research associate at Duke University Medical Center and serves as a staff psychologist in the Posttraumatic Stress Disorder Clinic and as the evidence-based psychotherapy coordinator at the Durham VA Medical Center. Her clinical and research interests include dissemination of evidence-based interventions for PTSD and the assessment of PTSD and associated behavioral disturbance, including issues surrounding malingering.

Amor A. Correa is completing her master's thesis at the University of North Texas under the mentorship of Dr. Richard Rogers. Her thesis examines issues of validity and acculturation for the Spanish translation of the Structured Interview of Reported Symptoms (SIRS). In addition to her thesis research, she has co-authored three articles and two national presentations.

Andreas Evdokas received his Ph.D. from the New School for Social Research in 1997 and completed his clinical internship at St. Luke's/Roosevelt Hospital in New York City. Currently, he is an assistant clinical professor of psychiatry and behavioral sciences at the Albert Einstein College of Medicine and adjunct professor at the New School for Social Research, where he teaches courses in personality assessment, psychopathology, and psychotherapy. Dr. Evdokas is also the administrative director of adult psychiatry at Bronx-Lebanon Hospital Center in New York.

Jeremy B. Frank, Ph.D. is a registered psychologist in private practice in Thornhill, Ontario in the Greater Toronto Area. His private practice is largely focused on rehabilitation psychology, where he conducts independent psychological evaluations and provides psychotherapy (with a rehabilitation focus) to automobile accident victims and victims of work-related injuries. He is a member of the Canadian Academy of Psychologists in Disability Assessment.

Christopher J. Hopwood, Ph.D. is an assistant professor of clinical psychology at Michigan State University. He is a member of several academic societies including the Society for Personality Assessment and Society for Interpersonal Theory and Research, is president of the Society for Personality Assessment Graduate Students, and is a consulting editor for the *Journal of Personality Assessment*. Dr. Hopwood has published one book and multiple empirical articles and chapters on the PAI, in addition to his research on psychological assessment, personality pathology, and interpersonal processes.

Ali Khadivi received his Ph.D. from the New School for Social Research in 1990 and completed his clinical internship at New York Hospital Cornell Medical Center's Westchester Division in New York. Currently, he is an associate clinical professor of psychiatry and behavioral sciences at the Albert Einstein College of Medicine and adjunct professor at the New School for Social Research and the John Jay College of Criminal Justice, where he teaches courses in cognitive and personality assessment. Dr. Khadivi is also the chief of psychology and the director of clinical and forensic assessment services at the Bronx-Lebanon Hospital Center, Department of Psychiatry, in New York.

Radhika Krishnamurthy, Ph.D. is a professor of psychology at Florida Institute of Technology and a licensed psychologist in Florida. She is president-elect of the Society for Personality Assessment, diplomate of the American Board of Assessment Psychology, and is currently past president of Section IX, Assessment Psychology, of the American Psychological Association's Division 12. She serves as associate editor for the *Journal of Personality Assessment* and consulting editor for *Assessment* and *Psychological Assessment*. She is co-author of two MMPI-A books and several book chapters and journal articles on psychological assessment.

John E. Kurtz received his Ph.D. from Vanderbilt University in 1994. He completed his clinical internship at the Department of Veterans Affairs Medical Center in Ann Arbor, Michigan and a postdoctoral fellowship at Wayne State University Medical School. Currently, Dr. Kurtz is professor of psychology at Villanova University, where he teaches courses in clinical psychology, personality, and psychological assessment. He is also associate editor of the *Journal of Personality Assessment*, a consulting editor for *Assessment*, and a member of both the American Psychological Association and the Society for Personality Assessment. He has co-authored more than 20 articles and book chapters in his areas of interest, which include personality development, stability and change in personality, and the use of informants in personality assessment.

Ezra Ochshorn, MSW, is employed as chief information specialist in the Department of Mental Health Law and Policy at the University of South Florida. In addition to academic papers and book chapters, Mr. Ochshorn has published newspaper articles dealing with mental health and elderly issues.

Sarah Oslund received her Ph.D. from the University of Texas Southwestern Medical Center at Dallas. She is currently the supervising psychologist for a short-term residential treatment program for juvenile offenders in Dallas County. Her research has focused on predictors of interdisciplinary treatment outcome in a chronic pain population.

Richard Rogers, Ph.D., ABPP, is professor of psychology at the University of North Texas. Dr. Rogers is nationally recognized for his contributions to forensic psychology and psychiatry by the American Academy of Forensic Psychologists and the American Psychiatric Association. His achievements in psychological assessment have also been recognized by the Society of Clinical Psychology and by the 2008 APA Distinguished Professional Contributions to Applied Research Award. Dr. Rogers is the principal author of several assessment measures including the SIRS-2 and the ECST-R. He is a prolific writer, with five books and more than 160 refereed articles.

Mark A. Ruiz, Ph.D., received his graduate training in clinical psychology at Pennsylvania State University and New York Presbyterian Hospital. He is currently a staff psychologist at the James A. Haley VA Medical Center in Tampa, Florida.

Caleb J. Siefert, Ph.D. is a staff psychologist in the Psychological Evaluation and Research Laboratory at Massachusetts General Hospital and an instructor of psychology at Harvard Medical School. He obtained his Ph.D. in clinical psychology at Adelphi University in Long Island, New York. He completed both his predoctoral internship and postdoctoral fellowship at Massachusetts General Hospital/Harvard Medical School, focusing on assessment consultation, applied measurement, and inpatient care. He has conducted research on implicit processes (e.g., implicit memory; implicit perception), measurement, psychological assessment, adult attachment, and the impact of depression on neuropsychological functioning.

Peter A. Weiss received his Ph.D. in clinical psychology from Long Island University in 2001. He is currently assistant professor of psychology at University of Hartford, where he teaches courses on psychological assessment, forensic psychology, and psychotherapy. He is the current (2009) president of the Society for Police and Criminal Psychology and is a member of the editorial board of the *Journal of Police and Criminal Psychology*. He is the senior author of *Self-Esteem: A Study of Methods of Measurement* (VDM) and is editor of the upcoming book *Personality Assessment in Police Psychology: A 21st Century Perspective* (Charles C. Thomas). He has published several peer-reviewed articles and book chapters, and has been a regular presenter at the annual meetings of the Society for Personality Assessment and Society for Police and Criminal Psychology.

1

Introduction

CHRISTOPHER J. HOPWOOD,
MARK A. BLAIS, and MATTHEW R. BAITY

*T*he *Personality Assessment Inventory* (PAI; Morey, 1991) is a 344-item multiscale self-report measure of constructs relevant for a wide range of psychological assessment applications. The PAI differs from other well-known self-report multiscale inventories in several important ways that are largely a consequence of the construct validation approach to test construction (Cronbach & Meehl, 1955; Jackson, 1970; Loevinger, 1957) that guided PAI development. This approach combines theoretical and empirical procedures for selecting the constructs to be measured and items reflective of those constructs. One illustrative effect of this underlying philosophy is that PAI scales are clearly labeled with contemporary terms for constructs that are commonly used among practitioners regardless of their theoretical orientation. Other features of the PAI were designed to ease the administrative burden of the test, given the practical obstacles to lengthy assessment practices (Piotrowski & Belter, 1998). For instance, the PAI requires a lower reading level than similar inventories (Schinka & Borum, 1993) and benefits from relative brevity even though all of its scales have non-overlapping items.

Together these practical features of the test, along with the focus in the construct validation method of test construction on measuring constructs with substantial theoretical articulation and empirical support, resulted in an instrument that is adaptable across a range of psychological assessment applications. For example, interpretive software has been developed for clinical (Morey, 2000), personnel selection (Roberts, Thompson, & Johnson, 2000), and forensic (Edens & Ruiz, 2005) applications. The broad relevance of the instrument likely accounts, in part, for the rising use of the PAI in applied settings (Belter & Piotrowski, 2001; Piotrowski, 2000; Lally, 2003; Stredny, Archer, Buffington-Vollum, & Handel, 2006). The PAI is also increasingly used by psychological researchers. Figure 1.1 shows the number of peer-reviewed journal references for the PAI in a PsycInfo

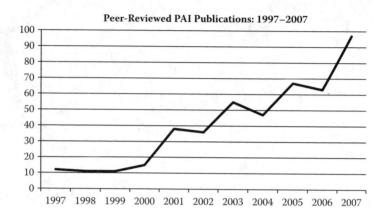

Figure 1.1   Growing popularity of the PAI.

search[*] from 1997 to 2007. The steadily increasing slope characterizing these data clearly illustrates the accelerated adoption of the PAI for psychological assessment research.

Although PAI research has been conducted in a wide range of psychological assessment contexts (see Morey, 2007) and detailed guides for using the PAI in mental health treatment settings have been published (e.g., Morey, 1996; Morey & Hopwood, 2007), systematic reviews and clinical suggestions regarding the use of the PAI for diverse practice applications have been limited. This book is intended to be a resource for practicing assessment psychologists or other professionals and graduate students in a range of settings where the PAI may be used. Chapters have been written by experts who regularly conduct psychological assessments using the PAI across a range of contexts and populations. This chapter will briefly introduce the development, structure, and interpretation of the PAI. More thorough reviews of these issues have been provided elsewhere (e.g., Morey, 1991; 1996; 2003; 2007; Morey & Hopwood, 2007; 2008).

DEVELOPMENT

The construct validation approach recognizes the importance of both adequate theoretical descriptions of constructs that an instrument is intended to measure and empirical methods to refine the items and scales that measure them. Construct validation assumes that focusing narrowly on maximizing any single psychometric characteristic of a test will likely negatively impact other characteristics (Morey, 2003). For example, scales that are designed to differentiate clinical from nonclinical populations may do so adequately, but they may also be more limited in describing individuals from clinical populations who vary in their level of severity.

---

[*] The search criteria were "Personality Assessment Inventory" anywhere and not "Chinese" anywhere, and the search was conducted in October, 2008. This exclusion criterion was used because no research has investigated the PAI in a Chinese population thus far but there is another instrument called the Chinese Personality Assessment Inventory (Cheung et al., 1996).

PAI development began with a consideration of the range of constructs that might be regarded as important for treatment planning and behavioral predictions by psychological assessors. Criteria for this search included the stability of use in the clinical psychology lexicon, extent of use in contemporary practice, breadth of validity evidence, and quality of theoretical articulation (Morey, 1991). This process ultimately resulted in four domains comprising 22 full and 31 subscales, as shown in Table 1.1.

The first of these domains involves the measurement of response style. *Validity scales* were developed to signify random, negative, and positive responding that may affect the interpretation of other scales. *Clinical scales* measure constructs similar to those in the *Diagnostic and Statistical Manual of Mental Disorders* (DSM; APA, 1994), although there are a number of divergences, in part because some current DSM constructs are quite new to the clinical literature and have limited validity evidence, but also because of theoretical differences in the DSM and PAI approaches to measurement (Morey, 1991). *Treatment consideration scales* were designed to supplement clinical scales in predicting client behavior. These include measures of aggression, suicidal ideation, environmental stress and support, and treatment motivation. Finally, *interpersonal scales* assess client personality characteristics that can affect the expression of clinical disorders and are important for developmental hypotheses and treatment planning (Pincus, Lukowitsky, & Wright, in press).

Content Validity

A major focus in developing the PAI, and one of the features that sets the PAI apart from similar instruments, involves content validity. Content validity refers to the degree to which item content is relevant to and representative of the targeted construct (Haynes, Richard, & Kubany, 1995). Adequate content validity requires attention to both the breadth and depth of measured constructs. Breadth involves the coverage of diverse aspects of broad phenomena. To ensure adequate *breadth*, subscales were created for nine clinical scales and one treatment consideration scale (Table 1.1). For example, the Depression scale has subscales measuring depressive affect (e.g., dysphoria), depressive cognitions (e.g., hopelessness), and physiological symptoms of depression (e.g., difficulty sleeping). The composition of these subscales was based on theoretical and empirical descriptions of the structure of psychological syndromes measured by the PAI. Subscales are particularly important because substantial symptomatic heterogeneity can occur even among individuals with the same psychiatric diagnosis. Subscales may also be helpful in considering the effects of treatments. For example, in some instances, subscales correspond to symptoms that are differentially targeted in particular therapies, such as DEP-C with cognitive therapy or DEP-A with psychopharmacology (Morey, 1996). As such, patients may be matched to treatments based on subscale profiles, and different subscales can be used to indicate changes attributable to particular interventions. In some instances, subscale elevations may relate to phenomena that are somewhat independent of their parent scale. For example, the MAN-G scale can often indicate self-esteem independent of a manic episode or bipolar disorder (Morey, 1996).

TABLE 1.1   PAI Scales and Subscales

Scale		Meaning of Elevations
Validity Scales		
ICN	Inconsistency	Concentration or attention problems
INF	Infrequency	Idiosyncratic or random responding
NIM	Negative Impression Management	Pessimism and/or intentional feigning
PIM	Positive Impression Management	Naïveté, lack of insight, or intentional dissimulation
Clinical Scales		
SOM	Somatic Complaints	
SOM-C	Conversion	Unusual medical symptoms
SOM-S	Somatization	Diffuse health-related complaints
SOM-H	Health Concerns	Preoccupation with physical health
ANX	Anxiety	
ANX-C	Cognitive	Ruminative worry
ANX-A	Affective	Tension and difficulty relaxing
ANX-P	Physiological	Sweating, increased heart rate, and other overt signs of anxiety
ARD	Anxiety Related Disorders	
ARD-O	Obsessive-Compulsive	Presence of obsessive compulsive disorder and personality features
ARD-P	Phobias	Fearfulness, particularly with regard to social situations
ARD-T	Traumatic Stress	History of trauma with enduring psychological consequences
DEP	Depression	
DEP-C	Cognitive	Worthlessness and hopelessness, with low scores indicating self-efficacy
DEP-A	Affective	Sadness, lack of interest, and anhedonia
DEP-P	Physiological	Fatigue and sleep or eating problems
MAN	Mania	
MAN-A	Activity Level	Energy and behavioral over-extension
MAN-G	Grandiosity	Inflated sense of self-worth with low scores indicating low self-esteem
MAN-I	Irritability	Impatience and low frustration tolerance
PAR	Paranoia	
PAR-H	Hypervigilance	Suspiciousness, with low scores indicating tendency to trust others
PAR-P	Persecution	Belief that others are actively preventing one's success
PAR-R	Resentment	Tendency to hold grudges and externalize blame
SCZ	Schizophrenia	
SCZ-P	Psychotic Experiences	Unusual perceptions or ideas including positive psychotic symptoms
SXZ-S	Social Detachment	Social isolation and detachment
SCZ-T	Thought Disorder	Concentration difficulties and disorganized thinking

TABLE 1.1   PAI Scales and Subscales (Continued)

Scale		Meaning of Elevations
BOR	Borderline Features	
BOR-A	Affective Instability	Emotional reactivity and difficulties modulating mood
BOR-I	Identity Problems	Feelings of emptiness and being uncertain about one's role or place in life
BOR-N	Negative Relationships	History of chaotic and conflicted relationships
BOR-S	Self-Harm	Impulsivity
ANT	Antisocial Features	
ANT-A	Antisocial Behaviors	History of rule-breaking
ANT-E	Egocentricity	Difficulties with empathy and a tendency to exploit others
ANT-S	Stimulus Seeking	Low boredom tolerance and tendency to seek out exciting activities
ALC	Alcohol Problems	Problems with alcohol use
DRG	Drug Problems	Problems with drug use
Treatment Consideration Scales		
AGG	Aggression	
AGG-A	Aggressive Attitude	Belief that it is appropriate to use violence for personal gain
AGG-V	Verbal Aggression	Assertiveness and verbal abusiveness
AGG-P	Physical Aggression	Tendency to fight or physically aggress
SUI	Suicidal Ideation	Consideration of suicide
STR	Stress	Stress related to sudden or dramatic changes in the environment
NON	Nonsupport	Lack of available social supports
RXR	Treatment Rejection	Low motivation for treatment or openness to the need for personal change
Interpersonal Scales		
DOM	Dominance	Assertiveness and tendency to control others, with low scores indicating interpersonal passivity
WRM	Warmth	Need for closeness and tendency to be empathic, with low scores indicating interpersonal aloofness

Depth refers to the extent to which a scale adequately measures the varying severity levels of a clinical construct. As noted previously, a scale in which all items maximally differentiate people who have or do not have a particular diagnosis is limited in assessing severity among people with the same diagnosis. However, such a differentiation can be critical in certain assessment contexts. For example, people with moderately severe depressive episodes may have a low risk for harming themselves and may be able to function adequately, even if somewhat ineffectively, with the help of outpatient treatment. In contrast, people with markedly severe depression may be at high risk to harm themselves and may require inpatient stabilization.

Three features enhance the construct depth of the PAI scales. The first is the four-point, rather than true-false, item response scale. Likert scaling increases the amount of true score variance captured per item and allows respondents to indicate the severity of each element (i.e., item) of the measured construct. This facilitates acceptable scale reliability with fewer items. Second, large community and clinical samples were gathered for normative data. Comparison of an individual's clinical scale score to the community sample mean and variability can be useful in determining the likelihood of being a member of a diagnostic group; understanding the score in the context of the clinical normative sample is useful for determining severity relative to others in a clinical setting. Third, the use of Item Response Theory to select items that were maximally endorsed at varying levels of construct severity further enhanced the depth of construct coverage. For example, an item that reads "Sometimes I feel sad" might differentiate very happy from somewhat depressed people, whereas an item that reads "I wish my life were over" would likely differentiate depressed from severely depressed people. Each PAI scale includes items that were selected for their ability to indicate varying severity levels of measured constructs.

Discriminant Validity

Discriminant validity, or the degree to which scores on a test do not correlate with scores from other tests that are not designed to assess the same construct (Campbell & Fiske, 1959), is closely linked to content validity. Although various psychopathology and personality constructs tend to systematically relate to one another, measures of those constructs should not correlate more strongly than those variables co-occur in nature. Such measures should also not strongly relate to non-clinical characteristics, such as demography. The more faithful test item content is to the construct of interest, the less likely those items are to unintentionally measure something else.

Several procedures enhanced the discriminant validity of PAI scales. A bias panel that included representatives from several ethnic and cultural backgrounds was asked to identify items they thought might inadvertently indicate a cultural characteristic; identified items were removed from the initial pool. Next, psychopathology and personality assessment experts were asked to sort items onto what they felt were the appropriate scales and incorrectly sorted items were removed. Perhaps most importantly, all scales were constructed with non-overlapping items, because tests with items that load onto more than one scale have inflated scale intercorrelations and obfuscated scale meanings. Finally, Differential Item Functioning methods were used after initial data were collected to further ensure discriminant validity. This method assesses the relation of items to the construct they were intended to measure as well as to other characteristics such as demography, and was used to select items with acceptable convergent (i.e., strong correlations of PAI items with their intended scales) and discriminant (i.e., weak correlations between PAI items and other scales or demographic characteristics) validity.

Relatedly, the PAI is not normed separately for men and women. Gender-specific norms have the potential to complicate interpretation by yielding prevalence rates that are similar across genders, even when the prevalence of the corresponding behaviors differs. A clinical example highlights the importance of this difference. Suppose a woman's gender-specific T-score is 65 on the Alcohol Problems scale, and that her raw score might correspond to 55T relative to men, who, on average, tend to be more likely to exhibit alcohol problems. She could be considered more likely than a man with a gender-specific T-score of 60 to have a drinking problem, even though her score, and thus presumed likelihood, is actually lower than his. In fact, only two PAI scales demonstrate clinically significant mean differences across genders: Antisocial Features and Alcohol Problems both have higher mean scores in men than in women (Morey, 1991), although neither of them show differences as dramatic in magnitude as the above example. Importantly, these differences correspond to epidemiological research showing that men are more likely to be diagnosed with antisocial personality disorder and alcohol use disorders than are women (Sutker & Allain, 2001).

PAI Indicators

Several extra-scale indicators (Table 1.2) were developed after the publication of the PAI that are helpful in making important predictions about behaviors such as dissimulation, suicide, violence, and treatment participation. The approaches guiding the development of these indicators varied, with some being purely empirical (e.g., Rogers and Cashel Discriminant Functions) and

TABLE 1.2   PAI Indicators

Indicator		Developmental Strategy	Meaning of Elevations
Validity Indicators			
MAL	Malingering Index	Theoretical	Pessimism or malingering
RDF	Rogers Discriminant Function	Empirical	Malingering
DEF	Defensiveness Index	Theoretical	Minimization of problems to deceive self or others
CDF	Cashel Discriminant Function	Empirical	Intentional dissimulation that is probably in a defensive direction
ALCe	ALC Estimated Score	Empirical	Deception regarding alcohol use
DRGe	DRG Estimated Score	Empirical	Deception regarding drug use
ACS°	Addictive Characteristics Scale	Theoretical	Deception regarding substance use
BRR	Back Random Responding	Empirical	Random responding on back half of PAI
INF-F°	Infrequency-Front	Conceptual	Random responding on first half of PAI
INF-B°	Infrequency-Back	Conceptual	Random responding on second half of PAI
ICN-C°	Inconsistency-Corrections	Conceptual	Inattention
Predictive Indicators			
TPI	Treatment Process Index	Theoretical	Difficult treatment process
VPI	Violence Potential Index	Theoretical	Enhanced probability of violence
SPI	Suicide Potential Index	Theoretical	Enhanced probability of suicide

° Developed for use in correctional settings (Edens & Ruiz, 2005).

others combining theoretical and empirical developmental strategies (e.g., Malingering, Defensiveness, and Predictive Indicators). The resulting indicators also vary in the kinds of behaviors they are optimized to predict, and can be classified broadly into those related to test validity and those related to dysfunctional behavior.

These indicators can often be used in conjunction with PAI scales to augment predictive accuracy. For instance, the Rogers and Cashel Discriminant Functions have been shown to be sensitive to dissimulation, even though they also have the important property of being mostly unrelated to indicators of psychopathology. As such, they may reflect "pure" measures of test faking that is uninfluenced by the respondent's actual clinical problems. This is very helpful, since most validity scales, including PAI, PIM, and NIM, have substantial correlations with clinical scales, complicating the dissociation of response styles and clinical problems (Morey, 1996). Predictive indicators can also be used in conjunction with clinical scales. For example, whereas the suicidal ideation (SUI) scale asks about the extent to which the respondent is consciously considering ending their life, the Suicide Potential Index (SPI) taps other personality features that are associated with carrying out the act. Research shows that these indicators are both associated with suicidal behavior (e.g., Hopwood, Baker, & Morey, 2008), suggesting their conjunctive use improves the assessment of overall suicide risk level.

Construct Validity

The final step in developing the PAI, assessing the construct validity of scales and indicators, will continue for the life of the instrument. Initial examination of these issues involved correlating PAI scales with previously validated measures and comparing PAI scale scores across individuals from various diagnostic groups. The second edition of the PAI manual (Morey, 2007) describes these initial validation studies as well as research conducted following the development of the test. Some of this research will be highlighted in chapters in this book to the extent that it relates to specific applications of the PAI.

INTERPRETATION

PAI data are typically interpreted in light of one or more referral questions offered by the examinee or a referring party and in the context of other information from interactions with the respondent, interviews with referring parties or collateral informants, record review, and other psychological methods. A model for the integration of PAI data with findings from other assessment instruments is outlined in Chapter 12 of this volume.

Interpretation of psychological assessment data is a complex activity that, among other considerations, is informed by the context of and reason for the evaluation. PAI software reports may be helpful, depending upon this context. Many of the chapters of this book focus on interpretive issues with the PAI in particular settings. This section focuses more narrowly on the psychometric meaning of PAI data, independent of the assessment context. Also, because other resources describe the PAI interpretation process in detail (Morey, 1996, 2003; Morey &

Hopwood, 2007), the current section briefly highlights important and distinct aspects of PAI interpretation regarding the examinee's approach to testing, psychiatric diagnosis, and behavioral predictions, rather than providing a step-by-step interpretive guide.

Response Style

An adequate assessment of the respondent's approach to test materials is critical in psychological evaluations, and its importance can escalate in many settings. For instance, forensic assessment can sometimes be adversarial or create secondary motivations for respondents to either downplay or emphasize certain characteristics (e.g., see Chapters 5, 7, 10, and 11 of this volume). The PAI includes multiple methods to assess response style that can be organized according to the type of response issue they are designed to detect. PAI scales and indicators were designed to indicate random (e.g., INF, ICN), positive (e.g., PIM, DEF, CDF), and negative (e.g., NIM, MAL, RDF) responding. More specific indicators were designed to indicate random responding on one half of the instrument (e.g., INF-B) or denial of particular problems (e.g., ALCe).

As discussed, PAI negative and positive validity indicators are unique in that they vary in their relations to psychopathology. Thus, they hold promise to differentiate overt dissimulation from covert defensiveness or lack of insight (in the case of positive response sets) or exaggeration or negative attributional style (in the case of negative response sets) (Morey & Hopwood, 2007). All of these indicators have shown strong effects (typically > 1 S.D.) in detecting faking, but whereas NIM and PIM are moderately correlated with the clinical scales (but in different directions), the RDF and CDF are mostly uncorrelated with the clinical scales, and the MAL and DEF are modestly correlated with the clinical scales. Thus, NIM and PIM appear to reflect the influences of both overt (i.e., faking) and covert (i.e., subconscious exaggeration) dissimulation, but the discriminant functions are uninfluenced by covert factors and appear to be purer measures of faking. For example, if a respondent had an elevated NIM score but MAL and RDF were within normal limits, they might tend to exhibit the kind of negative perceptual style that is common in disorders such as depression. However, if RDF and NIM were elevated, they are more likely to be purposefully endorsing symptoms they do not have. Morey and Hopwood (2007) present a systematic, quantitative framework for interpreting PAI response style configurations. In addition to examining singular scales and indicators, the PAI software (Morey, 2000) includes methods for interpreting other scales in light of the respondent's approach to testing (e.g., Hopwood, Morey, Rogers, & Sewell, 2008).

Diagnosis

Because PAI scales were designed to measure the depth and breadth of specific constructs with non-overlapping items, each scale or subscale essentially represents a standalone measure of a targeted psychological construct. Therefore the PAI scales and subscales can be interpreted independently of the rest of the profile and without slavish regard to specific score thresholds. This differs markedly from instruments for which only scores above a certain cutoff should be interpreted, or for which only the two or three highest scores form the basis for interpretations. In particular, this means that (a) all PAI information can be used for understanding the respondent and making behavioral predictions and (b) interpretation is rooted in the general scientific literature on a given construct rather than the body of research particular to one measurement method. Although experience and familiarity likely augment facility with the instrument, any licensed professional with a contemporary working knowledge of personality, psychopathology, psychometrics, and their particular assessment setting should be able to adequately interpret the PAI.

All PAI scale scores are represented on the PAI profile in T-score units (i.e., with a normative mean of 50 and standard deviation of 10) relative to U.S. census-matched community normative sample (N = 1,000) distributions. A profile "skyline" is also represented on the profile to indicate a score that would be two standard deviations above average in a combined inpatient and outpatient clinical normative sample (N = 1,246). As discussed, comparing an examinee's score to the community normative sample provides information about the likelihood of certain diagnoses and areas of greatest deviation from average. For example, a psychiatric diagnosis becomes likely as its corresponding PAI scale rises above 70T relative to the community norm group. However, two people with the same diagnosis may differ dramatically in the severity of their disorder. Comparisons with the clinical normative sample can provide important information about the severity and rarity of certain diagnostic phenomena.

Diagnostic interpretation can be further enhanced by considering the respondent's scores relative to his or her personal average clinical scale elevation (Mean Clinical Elevation; MCE). Knowing normative scores as well as the personal MCE on the PAI profile allows assessors to differentiate how the level of a given construct differs from normative community, normative clinical, and personal averages. Thus, an assessor might state: "This patient is more anxious than the average person, but his level of anxiety is average for someone from a clinical population and is one of the least prominent elements of the clinical profile, suggesting that anxiety may be secondary to another primary diagnosis." Such a statement is clearly more useful than "This patient is anxious."

Interpretation also benefits from the existence of mean profiles of known clinical groups in the normative data. The PAI interpretive report (Morey, 2000) includes coefficients of fit of an observed profile with groups such as rapists, suicide attempters, or individuals instructed to fake. Overlays can also be used to compare a given profile with the average profile of such groups, and empirical coefficients of fit of observed profiles with the average profiles of these groups can be used to judge overall similarity. Finally, a number of diagnostic algorithms have been developed that map PAI scale configurations onto DSM diagnostic criteria (Morey, 1996).

Predicting Behavior

Behavioral predictions are the sine qua non of psychological assessment (Wiggins, 1973). Accumulating evidence suggests that the PAI is valid in predicting important client behaviors including feigning (e.g., Hawes & Boccaccini, 2009), suicide, violence, and treatment completion (e.g., Hopwood et al., 2008), substance use (e.g., Schinka, 1995), and recidivism (e.g., Salekin et al., 1998). As discussed previously, predictive indicators were developed and have been shown to augment PAI scales in this regard. However, the level of research, using the PAI and other instruments, on psychological tests and the prediction of behavior does not match the importance of this topic (Kurtz, 2008). As such, the significance of ongoing research using the PAI to predict important respondent behaviors cannot be overemphasized.

SUMMARY

This chapter has briefly outlined the development, structure, and interpretation of the PAI. Practical and psychometric strengths of the PAI were offered as explanations for recent increases in its use and general interpretive suggestions were offered. In the remainder of this book, personality assessment experts who use and conduct research with the PAI in a variety of settings describe strengths, weaknesses, and applications of the PAI particular to their contexts, and in some instances, they provide new validity or reference data for the instrument.

REFERENCES

American Psychiatric Association (1994). *Diagnostic and statistical manual of mental disorders–4th ed. (DSM-IV)*. Washington D. C.: Author.

Belter, R. W., & Piotrowski, C. (2001). Current status of doctoral-level training in psychological testing. *Journal of Clinical Psychology, 57*, 717–726.

Campbell, D. T., & Fiske, D. W. (1959). Convergent and discriminant validation by the multitrait-multimethod matrix. *Psychological Bulletin, 56*, 81–105.

Cheung, F. M., Leung, K., Fan, R. M., Song, W. Z., Zhang, J. X., & Xhang, J. P. (1996). Development of the Chinese Personality Assessment Inventory. *Journal of Cross-Cultural Psychology, 27*(2), 181–199.

Cronbach, L. J., & Meehl, P. E. (1955). Construct validity in psychological tests. *Psychological Bulletin, 52*, 281–302.

Edens, J. F., & Ruiz, M. A. (2005). *PAI interpretive report for correctional settings* (PAI-CS). Odessa, FL: Psychological Assessment Resources.

Hawes, S. W., & Boccaccini, M. T. (2009). Detection of overreporting of psychopathology on the Personality Assessment Inventory: A meta-analytic review. *Psychological Assessment, 21*, 112–124.

Haynes, S. N., Richard, D. C. S., & Kubany, E. S. (1995). Content validity in psychological assessment: A functional approach to concepts and methods. *Psychological Assessment, 7*, 238–247.

Hopwood, C. J., Baker, K. L., & Morey, L. C. (2008). Extra-test validity of Personality Assessment Inventory scales and indicators in an inpatient substance abuse setting. *Journal of Personality Assessment, 90*, 574–577.

Hopwood, C. J., Morey, L. C., Rogers, R., and Sewell, K. W. (2008). Malingering on the PAI: The detection of feigned disorders. *Journal of Personality Assessment, 88*(1), 43–48.

Jackson, D. N. (1970). A sequential system for personality scale development. In C. D. Spielberger (Ed.). *Current topics in clinical and community psychology* (Vol. 2, pp. 62–97). New York: Academic Press.

Kurtz, J. E. (2008). Whatever happened to prediction in personality assessment research? *Society of Personality Assessment Exchange, 20*(2), 3.

Lally, S. J. (2003). What tests are acceptable for use in forensic evaluations? A survey of experts. *Professional Psychology: Research and Practice, 34*, 491–498.

Loevinger, J. (1957). Objective tests as instruments of psychological theory. *Psychological Reports, 3*, 635–694.

Millon, T. (1983). *Millon Clinical Multiaxial Inventory Manual* (3rd ed.). New York: Holt, Rinehart, & Winston.

Morey, L. C. (1991). *Personality Assessment Inventory (PAI) technical manual*. Odessa, FL: Psychological Assessment Resources.

Morey, L. C. (1996). *An interpretive guide to the Personality Assessment Inventory*. Odessa, FL: Psychological Assessment Resources.

Morey, L. C. (1997). *Personality Assessment Screener (PAS) technical manual*. Odessa, FL: Psychological Assessment Resources.

Morey, L. C. (2000). *PAI software portfolio manual*. Odessa, FL: Psychological Assessment Resources.

Morey, L. C. (2003). *Essentials of PAI assessment*. New York: Wiley.

Morey, L. C. (2007). *Personality Assessment Inventory professional manual* (2nd ed.). Lutz, FL: Psychological Assessment Resources.

Morey, L. C., & Hopwood, C. J. (2007). *Casebook for the Personality Assessment Inventory: A structural summary approach*. Lutz, FL: Psychological Assessment Resources.

Morey, L. C., & Hopwood, C. J. (2008). The Personality Assessment Inventory. In Archer, R. P. and Smith, S. R. (Eds.). *Personality assessment*. New York: Routledge.

Pincus, A. L., Lukowitsky, M. R., & Wright, A. G. C. (2008). The interpersonal nexus of personality and psychopathology. In T. Millon, R. F. Krueger, & E. Simonsen (Eds.), *Contemporary directions in psychopathology: Toward the DSM-V and ICD-11*. New York: Guilford.

Piotrowski, C. (2000). How popular is the Personality Assessment Inventory in practice and training? *Psychological Reports, 86*, 65–66.

Piotrowski, C., & Belter, R. W. (1998). The impact of managed care on psychological testing: Preliminary findings. *Journal of Personality Assessment, 70*(3), 41–447.

Piotrowski, C., & Belter, R. W. (1999). Internship training in psychological assessment: Has managed care had an impact? *Assessment, 6*, 381–389.

Roberts, M. D., Thompson, J. A., & Johnson, M. (2000). *PAI law enforcement, corrections, and public safety selection report module*. Odessa, FL: Psychological Assessment Resources.

Salekin, R. T., Rogers, R., Ustad, K. L., & Sewell, K. W. (1998). Psychopathy and recidivism among female inmates. *Law and Human Behavior, 22*, 109–128.

Schinka, J. A. (1995). PAI profiles in alcohol-dependent patients. *Journal of Personality Assessment, 65*(1), 35–51.

Schinka, J. A., & Borum, R. (1993). Readability of adult psychopathology measures. *Psychological Assessment, 5*, 384–386.

Stredny, R., Archer, R. P., Buffington-Vollum, J. K., & Handel, R. W. (2006). *A survey of psychological test use patterns among forensic psychologists*. Paper Presented at the Annual Meeting of the Society of Personality Assessment, San Diego, CA.

Sutker, P. B., & Allain, A. N. (2001). Antisocial personality disorder. In H. E. Adams, & P. B. Sutker (Eds.), *Comprehensive handbook of psychopathology* (3rd ed.). New York: Kluwer Academic/Plenum Publishers.

Wiggins, J. S. (1973). *Personality and prediction: Principles of personality assessment*. Reading, MA: Addison-Wesley.

2

Assessment of Outpatients Using the PAI

JOHN E. KURTZ

PSYCHOLOGICAL ASSESSMENT IN OUTPATIENT SETTINGS

*T*raditionally, it has been assumed that outpatient settings treat less severe forms of mental disorder among patients who come and go on a voluntary basis. However, the growth of community mental health agencies, such as those funded by Medicaid, has added more socioeconomic, ethnic, and clinical diversity to the population seen in outpatient mental health settings. In years past, patients with chronic and severe mental disorders spent most of their time in institutional or inpatient settings. Recent changes in the healthcare system have resulted in many of these patients now seeking help in outpatient clinics. Thus, accurate psychodiagnosis is essential in order to distribute treatment resources in the most efficacious manner. There is also a wider diversity of treatment modalities now offered within the same clinics, including pharmacotherapy. Care providers in contemporary outpatient settings vary greatly in the type and duration of their education and training. The outpatient clinic staff often includes mental health counselors and other paraprofessionals who have received varied amounts of formal training and who use a wide range of interventions.

The realities of outpatient practice pose a number of challenges for psychological assessment. Clinicians working in outpatient settings have less control over what happens to patients. There is less time to observe patients' behavior to validate or reconsider diagnostic hypotheses. Undetected alcohol and drug problems are common here, and they can impede therapeutic progress. Discriminating psychological disorders from medical conditions is a frequent challenge in the outpatient clinic. The type of patient who might walk through the door next is less predictable than in other settings that focus on specific populations or problems. Despite the wider range of problems that are seen in the outpatient clinic, there is less emphasis on diagnosis. Far less time is allocated to intake assessment relative to hospital settings, which can make formal psychological testing impractical, if not impossible. To make matters worse, many members of the treatment staff, especially those who are not psychologists, may view testing as a nuisance and psychological assessment in general as a perfunctory task necessitated by reimbursement requirements. There may be a pervasive attitude among staff that any time spent in testing would be better spent in treatment. Nonetheless, brief testing oriented toward treatment planning can result in faster responses and better outcomes in treatment (Groth-Marnat, 2003).

The Personality Assessment Inventory (PAI) offers a number of advantages to address the assessment challenges of outpatient mental health clinics. Like most self-report inventories, the test can be administered and scored with minimal professional time. A large amount of useful and relevant information can be gained from responses to the 344 items of the PAI. The items themselves are brief and require only fourth-grade reading skills (Schinka & Borum, 1993). This chapter will focus on the use and interpretation of the PAI with special attention to relevant problems of general outpatient practice, such as planning appropriate treatment approaches. The focus will remain on adult assessment issues, as the use of the PAI with adolescents will be addressed in a separate chapter.

PROFILE VALIDITY

In outpatient settings, invalid profiles will be encountered less frequently than they are in inpatient settings or in forensic evaluation contexts. The PAI is useful for distinguishing three principal threats to the validity of self-report questionnaire data. The first, and most basic, of these threats is random or careless responding, which can be effectively identified using both the Inconsistency (ICN) and Infrequency (INF) scales. Figure 2.1 presents the means for the PAI validity scales and index scores from 355 outpatients included in the clinical standardization sample,* showing average elevations on ICN (T = 52) and INF (T = 51). When both ICN and INF are elevated beyond 70T, there is a 99% probability that the items were not answered with the appropriate care and attention. Although this is an unusual result in an outpatient setting, the random or careless approach may arise when the patient is resistant to the assessment process. This resistance often occurs when the patient is coming to the clinic at the insistence of family members or by an order of the court. Alternatively, the patient may have experienced difficulty with comprehension of the items if English is not the native language (see Chapter 8) or if there is an educational deficit. A formal assessment of reading skills is recommended in these cases to ensure that the patient can read at the fourth-grade level.

Response distortion represents a more complex threat to the validity of PAI protocols. Negative response distortion occurs when patients exaggerate their distress or are indiscriminant in selecting the symptoms that best describe their experiences. The result is a profile that is difficult to interpret in terms of the

* I thank Les Morey and Psychological Assessment Resources, Inc., for granting access to the clinical standardization data reported here.

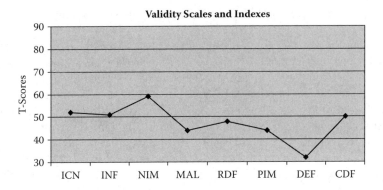

Figure 2.1   PAI Validity Scales and Index Scores for Outpatients (n = 355) from Clinical Standardization Sample. (ICN = Inconsistency; INF = Infrequency; NIM = Negative Impression Management; MAL = Malingering Index; RDF = Rogers Discriminant Function; PIM = Positive Impression Management; DEF = Defensiveness Index; CDF = Cashel Discriminant Function.)

true severity and extent of the patients' problems. The PAI Negative Impression Management (NIM) scale provides an effective means of identifying negative distortion. The nine items on this scale present symptoms that are extreme and unusual, even for clinical respondents. Nonetheless, as shown in Figure 2.1, NIM is the most elevated validity scale among outpatients (T = 59). NIM scores above 70T suggest a degree of exaggeration that warrants added caution in interpreting the elevations on the substantive PAI scales. Morey and Hopwood (2007) describe the use of NIM-predicted profiles as a means of compensating for negative distortion on the PAI. This is a regression-based strategy in which all of the PAI full scales and subscales are statistically predicted solely on the basis of the obtained NIM score. The score profile associated with this NIM score can be plotted and analyzed for discrepancies between the predicted profile and the obtained profile. Obtained scores that exceed the NIM-predicted scores by one or more standard errors of measurement point to scales that the respondent emphasized beyond the level predicted by negative distortion alone. Interpretation may then focus on these discrepant elevations to inform diagnosis or case conceptualization. NIM scores that exceed 92T indicate a profile that is not valid and generally should not be interpreted. Fortunately, such categorically invalid protocols are uncommon among outpatient respondents.

Higher elevations on NIM may warrant the use of NIM-specific scores. This is a strategy for understanding the impact of negative distortion on the PAI results that is similar to the NIM-predicted profile but uses a group-based approach instead. The mean full scale and subscale profiles have been computed for two subsamples of the clinical standardization sample; one group has NIM scores ranging from 84T to 91T and another group has NIM scores of 92T and above (Morey & Hopwood, 2007). For individual cases with NIM scores in either of these two ranges, standard scores can be computed for the full scales and subscales based on the means and standard deviations from a subsample of clinical respondents with comparably elevated scores on NIM. Whereas NIM-predicted profiles can be generated for any score on NIM, the NIM-specific strategy requires elevations of at least 84T.

Negative response distortion can be the result of conscious efforts by some respondents to appear more ill than they know to be the case. Malingering is a rare phenomenon in outpatient assessment because the incentives to engage in such an approach are usually not present. Instead, elevated NIM scores more typically can be attributed to the distorting effects of actual psychopathology on the self-concept. Excess negativity in beliefs about the self is a particularly defining feature of depression (Beck, Rush, Shaw, & Emery, 1979) and borderline personality disorder (Kurtz & Morey, 1998). In other words, the respondent is being straightforward but produces a report that is inaccurate with respect to the degree of pathology. Two other PAI validity measures, the Malingering Index (MAL; Morey, 1996) and the Rogers Discriminant Function (RDF; Rogers, Sewell, Morey, & Ustad, 1996), are useful for making distinctions between these two sources of negative distortion. MAL scores appear to be related to both types of negative distortion and this index must be rather highly elevated (i.e., raw scores > 5; T > 100) to make reasonably confident assertions about malingering. In contrast, RDF scores are uncorrelated with measures of psychopathology but are highly associated with conscious attempts to dissimulate psychopathology. Thus, when NIM elevations are accompanied by elevated scores on RDF (T > 60), the probability of malingering is high. As evident from Figure 2.1, the "true psychopathology" pattern of elevated NIM scores *without* elevations on MAL and RDF is most common in the outpatient setting.

Positive response distortion is less common than negative distortion in the outpatient setting. The Positive Impression Management (PIM) scale is a collection of nine items that inquire about common faults and failings. As shown in Figure 2.1, the mean PIM score among outpatients is below average (T = 44), indicating a general tendency among outpatients to rather freely endorse these common failings. Scores above 57T suggest defensiveness and an unwillingness to admit to problems that may be present. In these cases, PIM-predicted profiles may be plotted in order to identify those scales that are receiving more endorsement than would be expected given the degree of general defensiveness shown by the respondent (Morey & Hopwood, 2007). Alternatively, PIM-specific scores can be computed and compared with the obtained profile. PIM-specific profiles were computed using two subsamples of the clinical standardization sample, one with PIM scores ranging from 57T to 67T and another with PIM scores of 68T and higher. The group-based PIM-specific scores may be more informative about the impact of positive distortion due to greater variance in scores among the PIM-specific groups than is found with the regression-based strategy. On the other hand, PIM-predicted profiles can be generated for any score on PIM, whereas the PIM-specific strategy requires elevations of at least 57T.

Although positive distortion is infrequent among patients presenting for treatment in outpatient clinics, some circumstances give rise to this curious behavior. This response strategy may be seen in reluctant patients compelled by third parties to present for treatment, and it represents a more subtle form of resistance than the antagonist approach of responding randomly. PIM elevations can also occur among patients who are seeking treatment for problems that they see as more circumscribed or situational, such as a stressful life event or medical condition. Defensive approaches to answering the PAI in these cases may be understood as an attempt to compensate for embarrassment about seeking treatment by presenting as extra well-adjusted in all other areas.

Like NIM, elevations on PIM scores may be the result of unconscious self-deception or deliberate attempts to conceal problems with a positive self-presentation (Morey & Hopwood, 2007). Accordingly, two other PAI scores are used to discriminate between these two possibilities, the Defensiveness Index (DEF) and the Cashel Discriminant Function (CDF). DEF and CDF were derived from research studies of respondents making conscious efforts to "fake good" on the PAI under various types of incentive scenarios. When PIM elevations are accompanied by elevations on DEF and CDF, there is a high likelihood of conscious and effortful attempts at positive distortion. Elevations on PIM alone indicate an honest, albeit distorted, perception of the self that may be overly positive but not necessarily suggestive of concealed psychopathology.

DIFFERENTIAL DIAGNOSIS

The great variety of mental health conditions that may be encountered in the outpatient setting creates a staggering array of differential diagnosis situations. To gain some overview of the kinds of PAI profiles that might be seen among these patients, 355 cases from outpatient settings were extracted from the 1,246 cases in the larger clinical standardization sample (see Morey, 2007 for a description of this sample). The mean full scale profile for these 355 cases is presented in Figure 2.2. The Depression (DEP) scale shows the highest elevation among the 11 clinical scales, while Anxiety (ANX) and Borderline Features (BOR) are also elevated above a mean T-score of 60. These outpatient profiles were contrasted with another subset of 255 cases from the clinical standardization sample gathered

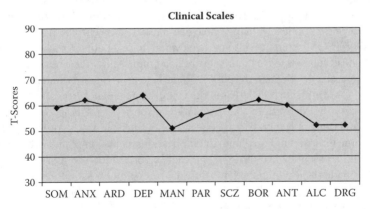

Figure 2.2 PAI Clinical Scale Profile for Outpatients (n = 355) from Clinical Standardization Sample. (SOM = Somatic Complaints; ANX = Anxiety; ARD = Anxiety-Related Disorders; DEP = Depression; MAN = Mania; PAR = Paranoia; SCZ = Schizophrenia; BOR = Borderline Features; ANT = Antisocial Features; ALC = Alcohol Problems; DRG = Drug Problems.)

in inpatient settings (not including inpatient alcohol or drug programs). The largest differences between these two subsamples were observed for Drug Problems (DRG; d = .44) and BOR (d = .43), with all contrasts revealing lower scores in the outpatient sample. The smallest and only negligible effect size was found with the Somatic Complaints (SOM) scale (d = .16). Three common problems of differential diagnosis in outpatient samples are addressed here: the detection of major depressive disorder, somatoform disorders, and substance abuse or dependence.

As indicated in Figure 2.2, depression is a common complaint among patients presenting for treatment in outpatient settings. An important concern is whether this depression represents a major depressive disorder or the more general distress and dysphoria that are secondary to other conditions. The DEP scale contains three subscales measuring Cognitive (DEP-C), Affective (DEP-A), and Physiological (DEP-P) symptoms, and the configuration of these subscale scores can be helpful for identifying major depression. Elevations greater than 65T on all three subscales are characteristic of patient samples diagnosed with major depressive disorder (Kurtz & Morey, 2001; Morey 2007). In contrast, the elevations on DEP commonly seen in patients with non-affective disorder diagnoses, situational stress, and adjustment reactions will tend to be accounted for mostly by elevations on DEP-A, with DEP-C as a secondary elevation. However, DEP-P is less prone to elevation than the other two subscales in most clinical respondents, so its relative suppression should not be taken as a contraindication of major depression. Given the importance of vegetative signs (i.e., appetite and sleep disturbance, loss of energy and libido) for the diagnosis of major depression, DEP-P elevations greater than 65T are strongly suggestive of the disorder when DEP-C and DEP-A are also elevated.

The differentiation between somatoform disorders and actual medical conditions cannot be accomplished with a questionnaire alone. Nonetheless, the PAI, in conjunction with medical records or other historical information, will be useful in cases where these questions arise. Several studies have shown that SOM scores are elevated in respondents with somatoform diagnoses (Morey, 2007) or other medical conditions complicated by psychological factors (e.g., chronic pain; see Karlin et al., 2005). SOM scores are also more elevated among patients with mild or questionable head injuries versus more severe head injuries (Kurtz, Shealy, & Putnam, 2007; Mendella & McFadden, 2005). Nonetheless, it is important to remember that the SOM full scale is called *Somatic Complaints* and not "somatization." Thus, elevations on SOM indicate that the patient experiences a range of discomforts and dysfunctions of the body and concerns about health. In the presence of bona fide chronic illnesses and post-injury complications, such complaints are often warranted and a psychological disorder may not be indicated. The first two subscales of SOM divide these complaints into unusual sensorimotor symptoms (Conversion, SOM-C) and typical complaints of bodily pains, stomach troubles, and a subjective sense of poor health (Somatization, SOM-S). The third subscale, Health Concerns (SOM-H), assesses the level of preoccupation with health matters in the patient as well as frustrations surrounding attending to them with doctors. Elevations greater than 70T across all three subscales are frequently observed in patients with somatoform diagnoses (Morey, 2007), although genuine medical conditions should always be ruled out by physical examination before assigning this diagnosis. Patients with bona fide somatoform disorders are also prone to elevate other PAI subscales that inquire about physical symptoms, such as the Physiological subscales of Anxiety (ANX-P) and Depression (DEP-P) full scales. Such cases serve as a reminder that inspection of the configuration of subscale scores is always important when interpreting full scale elevations.

. The problems that patients present to treatment staff in outpatient settings may be complicated by substance use disorders. When abuse of or dependence on alcohol or drugs is present, this condition often warrants immediate attention, perhaps with inpatient treatment, before other issues can be treated effectively. The PAI contains two scales, Alcohol Problems (ALC) and Drug Problems (DRG), that address the frequency and quantity of use as well as the impairments of social and occupational functioning that may result from alcohol or drug use. PAI users should bear in mind that these scales employ items with considerable face validity. Although research with patients in treatment for substance abuse shows that they are generally forthright in their reports, resulting in high elevations on ALC and DRG (Morey, 2007), patients who attempt to conceal these problems can do so without much difficulty (Fals-Stewart, 1996). This problem may be more prevalent in outpatient settings when patients are seeking treatment for some other problem but do not wish their substance use to be known. To address this concern, Morey (2003) suggests a regression-based strategy for estimating ALC and DRG elevations based on the observed scores for five PAI subscales that are most highly correlated with ALC and DRG scores. When these estimated ALC and DRG scores are 10 T-score points or more higher than the observed ALC and DRG scores, the assessor should give further consideration to the possibility that substance use issues are being denied by the patient. It is also important to remember that some of the items on ALC and DRG are written in the past tense. There are four past tense items on ALC (#95, #255, #334, and #335) and six past tense items on DRG (#23, #62, #102, #103, #182, and #342). Thus, patients with histories of substance abuse or dependence can obtain moderate elevations even if they currently abstain from any use of alcohol or drugs. In this situation, a moderate elevation would necessitate further evaluation to determine the recency and severity of past use, as well as the risk for relapse.

TREATMENT PLANNING

The PAI is more than an inventory of scales that measure personality and psychopathology. From its inception, the PAI was intended to provide useful information for treatment planning and clinical management (Morey, 1991). It is unfortunate that psychological assessment is not practiced more routinely in outpatient settings, because good assessment is a very efficient alternative to even the most highly skilled attempts to figure out what the patient needs over the course of several therapy sessions. Moreover, such understanding of the patient through the ordinary process of therapy is accomplished only for those who remain in treatment for more than a few sessions. Research has demonstrated that nearly 50% of patients do not return after their initial intake appointment, and many others discontinue treatment against the advice of the therapist within the first six sessions (Wierzbicki & Pekarik, 1993). In addition to the 11 Clinical Scales and the two

Interpersonal Scales, the PAI has a set of five Treatment Scales designed to inform the clinician about important considerations for patient intervention. Three will be discussed in this section on treatment planning and the two remaining Treatment Scales, Aggression (AGG) and Suicidal Ideation (SUI), will be discussed in the next section on risk assessment.

Treatment Prognosis

The determination of prognosis for psychotherapy and related psychosocial interventions is a very complex endeavor. Three PAI measures are essential for making these determinations: the Mean Clinical Elevation (MCE), the Treatment Rejection (RXR) scale, and the Treatment Process Index (TPI). MCE is important as a starting point for evaluating prognosis, because it serves as an indicator of the overall severity of clinical symptoms. It is well established in the literature on psychotherapy outcome that patients with more diagnoses and greater severity of symptoms are at risk for deriving less benefit from psychotherapy (for a review, see Clarkin & Levy, 2004). MCE is the mean T-score across the 11 Clinical Scales of the PAI. The MCE has an average value of 61.6 (SD = 10.5) among the 355 outpatient respondents in the clinical standardization sample. Thus, profiles with MCE exceeding 67T exhibit greater severity and diversity of symptoms than are typically seen in outpatient settings. Such cases pose challenges for treatment in part because of the difficulties in selecting the most appropriate target for intervention. MCE values below 52T may indicate a good prognosis for treatment as long as there is at least one elevated score. Such a respondent is able to acknowledge one or a few problem areas that can become the focus for treatment. On the other hand, if a low MCE is the result of a profile without elevations on any Clinical or Treatment scales, then the prognosis is more guarded given the client's disinclination to admit to problems and distress. Further understanding of such cases necessitates consideration of the RXR and TPI scores.

Beyond general severity of clinical problems, a comprehensive understanding of the patient's attitude about treatment and ability to benefit from treatment requires both direct and indirect assessment approaches. The direct approach is accomplished with RXR, which is an eight-item scale that assesses the patient's acknowledgment of personal problems, desire to change the self, and recognition that help from others is necessary to make these changes. As such, RXR scores reflect the patient's explicit attitude about treatment, providing an indication of the patient's own judgment about his or her prognosis to benefit from treatment. RXR is perhaps most meaningful when scores are above average. It has the distinction of being one of two PAI scales (the other is PIM) for which the mean of the clinical standardization sample is lower than that of the adult normative sample. Accordingly, the mean RXR score among the 355 outpatient respondents is equivalent to a community adult T-score of less than 41 (mean = 40.8, SD = 11.1). This reflects the fact that most respondents seen in clinical settings are receptive to treatment and eager to change. Clinicians should thoughtfully explore other possible reasons or incentives for coming to the clinic in a patient with RXR T-scores exceeding 50T. Patients with RXR T-scores exceeding 60T are clearly telling providers there is little they can do to help and that intervention is not desired.

Because most forms of traditional psychotherapy are collaborative, requiring at least as much effort and energy from the patient as from the therapist, an elevated RXR score alone indicates that treatment will be highly challenging due to resistance from the patient. Aside from court-ordered cases, this level of resistance is very uncommon among the voluntary patients seen in most outpatient settings.

RXR scores below 50T are far more common, but they present a more nebulous picture about the prospects for successful treatment. It is certainly not the case that the prognosis continues to improve as RXR scores become lower. In fact, there is some evidence to suggest that the ideal range of RXR scores for patients seen in outpatient settings may be between 40T and 50T. These cases can be classified as sufficiently "motivated," whereas cases with RXR scores below 40T can be classified as "hypermotivated" (Hopwood, Creech, Clark, Meagher, & Morey, 2008). Very low RXR scores (< 30T) suggest a patient who feels desperate for help and holds unrealistic expectations about treatment. Such overly idealized views may cause frustrated patients to terminate treatment prematurely when therapeutic gains are too modest or too slow in coming. These patients may also be excessively passive and expect the therapist to do more of the "work" than is appropriate for collaborative approaches to psychotherapy. In cases with RXR scores below 50T, further assistance in evaluating treatment prognosis is provided by the TPI.

The TPI combines information from several different PAI scales and subscales that are relevant to the patient's capacity to benefit from treatment. Morey (1996) selected PAI scales that are conceptually related to various patient characteristics associated with challenging treatment process. For example, one point is scored if the Paranoia scale is elevated (T > 70), as this finding is taken as an indication of the tendency to make externalizing attributions. The result is a set of 12 configural scoring rules that are scored as 1 if the rule is met or as 0 if the rule is not met. Most TPI items employ multiple alternative rules; thus, lack of empathy is scored as 1 if the patient receives an elevated score on Antisocial Egocentricity (ANT-E), Dominance (DOM), or Manic Grandiosity (MAN-G). As a result, some scales enter into the TPI calculation more than once. For example, elevations on Borderline Features (BOR) score one point on three different TPI items and the Self-Harm subscale of BOR scores on two additional items. Not surprisingly, BOR ends up with the highest correlation with TPI scores ($r = .77$; Morey, 1996). Hopwood, Ambwani, and Morey (2007) propose that the TPI measures treatment "amenability," which distinguishes it from the treatment "motivation" aspect measured by RXR. Morey (1996, 2003) suggests that TPI raw scores of 7 or above forecast a difficult treatment process. Such patients have several personality characteristics that tend to interfere with the formation of an effective therapeutic alliance, and thus pose a greater risk for poor outcome. The patients are difficult to retain in treatment and, if they do remain in treatment, they require longer and more intensive courses of psychotherapy. In light of the fact that the cut-scores proposed for the TPI have not been sufficiently validated, it is advisable to apply flexible judgment in cases with scores close to the recommended cut-scores.

Together, the concepts of problem severity (MCE), motivation for change (RXR), and treatment amenability (TPI) have interacting implications for the overall prognosis of a given patient. Table 2.1 summarizes the prognostic inferences based on combinations of RXR, TPI, and MCE. The structure of the tables reflects

TABLE 2.1   Interpretive Hypotheses for Various MCE, RXR, and TPI Score Configurations

	Low Amenability (TPI = 7+)	High Amenability (TPI < 7)
Unmotivated (RXR T-score > 50)	Resistant; not interested in help with problems; likely mandated case.	Well adjusted; does not acknowledge problems or distress; may have primary somatic or situational focus.
Motivated for Treatment (RXR T-score = 30–50) Moderate Severity (MCE = 52–67)	Fair prognosis; possibly defensive patient; interpersonal problems are challenge to therapist.	Best prognosis for psychotherapy.
Motivated for Treatment (RXR T-score = 30–50) High Severity (MCE > 67)	Guarded prognosis; excess responsibility placed on therapist; longer course of treatment; drop out likely.	Good prognosis, especially if benefits are realized early in treatment.
Hypermotivated (RXR T-score < 30)	Worst prognosis; unrealistic expectations of therapy; challenging case for experienced therapist; high drop out risk.	Fair prognosis; early alliance building may be essential to maintain patient in treatment.

the moderate correlations between MCE and RXR ($r = -.53$), acknowledging that certain combinations are highly unlikely. That is, it is nearly impossible to find high RXR scores concurrently with high scores on the 11 clinical scales. Therefore, qualifications based on MCE are given only for patients with RXR scores in the average range (30T to 50T), as very low RXR scores will tend to co-occur with high MCE and very high RXR scores will tend to co-occur with low MCE.

Patients who are unmotivated for treatment (RXR > 50T) typically do not acknowledge problems with behavior or emotional distress. Thus, a low TPI score is consistent with this report; it is not necessarily indicative of a good prognosis for treatment. The pattern of high RXR and low TPI may indicate defensiveness about matters that should otherwise be shared. Checking for an elevated PIM score (> 57T) or an elevated raw score on the Defensiveness Index (7+) will help to address this possibility. The alternative explanation is that the patient is well-adjusted and treatment is not needed. The distinction between defensiveness and good adjustment is possibly the most difficult discrimination to make in psychological assessment. Patients may view their presenting problem as a highly specific issue, such as a situational stressor or a medical problem. In the less likely scenario in which an elevated RXR is accompanied by a high TPI score (7+), more problems are endorsed and the TPI score indicates a potential for problems in treatment. This pattern of scores may be seen in patients who are court-ordered to receive treatment or have been compelled to the clinic by family members. That is, problems are acknowledged, especially problems with interpersonal relationships, but the patient is resistant to the opportunity to address them through psychotherapy. Regardless of the explanation, the overt lack of interest in treatment indicated by RXR scores above 50T is generally an unexpected result for someone presenting in an outpatient setting.

RXR scores will typically fall between 30T and 50T for patients seen in the outpatient clinic. Within this range, there will be greater variability in symptom severity and the MCE can be included in the determination of treatment prognosis. In cases with low amenability for psychotherapy (TPI = 7+), high severity of symptoms will make a successful course of treatment difficult to achieve. It is a challenge to settle on and formulate realistic goals for therapy when so many problems coexist, and any gains made in treatment may be obscured by these additional problems and the series of crises they generate. If the patient does not drop out of treatment prematurely, a longer course of treatment, preferably with a highly skilled and experienced therapist, will be needed for a successful outcome in this case. When amenability for psychotherapy is favorable (TPI < 7), the prognosis for treatment is optimal for patients with average levels of motivation (RXR 30–50T). Higher symptom severity in these cases may require a longer course of treatment, and keeping the patient in treatment will be easier if he or she perceives improvement after the early sessions.

RXR scores below 30T indicate a "hypermotivated" patient (Hopwood et al., 2008) and symptoms will invariably be numerous and severe for these patients (i.e., MCE > 67). Hypermotivated patients tend to feel desperate about their psychological and situational states, and, as a result, they are more inclined to adopt a passive dependent stance with the therapist. They may need to see quick results in order to maintain their stated motivation to engage in treatment. When amenability is low, the constellation of the three treatment indicators yields the worst prognosis for successful outpatient psychotherapy. The difficulties in forming the therapeutic alliance will be exacerbated by the excess responsibility these patients tend to place on the therapist for a successful outcome. Such a case will be very challenging, even for experienced therapists, and the risk of premature termination is high. If amenability for psychotherapy is high in the hypermotivated patient, then the patient's prognosis is somewhat better. Nonetheless, early alliance building is essential for circumventing the likely disappointment these patients will experience with the inevitably slow progress of therapy. These recommendations are summarized in Table 2.1.

Beyond the original validation data presented by Morey (1991, 1996, 2007), there has been little published research on the validity of RXR and TPI to assess motivation and amenability for treatment. Blais and colleagues (2003) found that RXR was negatively correlated (r = -.63) with the degree to which a sample of inpatients expressed desire for help with five different functional areas (Blais et al., 2003). Hopwood et al. (2007) found that TPI scores effectively predicted non-mutual termination of therapy in a sample of 84 adults seen in an outpatient university clinic (d = .53). This effect was replicated in a subsequent study by Hopwood et al. (2008) in a sample of 309 outpatients being treated for chronic pain (d = .34). Although these findings are encouraging, retention in treatment is just a small part of what the assessor would like to predict regarding the patient's response to treatment. Studies are needed that relate RXR, TPI, and MCE to psychotherapy process variables, such as the quality of the working alliance. Furthermore, patients who complete a prescribed course of treatment still vary with respect to outcome, such as the reduction of symptoms or improvement in role functioning.

Accordingly, the treatment considerations scales discussed here should be correlated with objective assessments of outcome at termination and at follow-up. This type of clinical research would also be useful to refine and improve the treatment scales of the PAI. Using process and outcome correlates, the specific items of the TPI could be individually appraised to direct refinements to the index. Thus, the validity of the TPI might be enhanced significantly if empirical findings suggested the removal of certain scales currently included or the addition of other PAI scales not currently included. For example, research demonstrating that perfectionism has a negative effect on treatment outcome in depression (Blatt, Quinlan, Pilkonis, & Shea, 1995) suggests that the Obsessive-Compulsive subscale (ARD-O) might be a worthy addition to a broad prognostic index like the TPI.

Treatment Selection

The decision to refer a patient for a medication evaluation is one of the more important purposes of assessment in the outpatient setting. Several PAI scales are informative to this question. Prominent elevations (> 80T) on DEP and ANX, especially when DEP-P and ANX-P contribute to these elevations, invariably warrant a consultation with a physician regarding suitability for medication. Similarly high elevations on any of the three subscales of Anxiety-Related Disorders (ARD) also call for a medication consult. Pharmacotherapy is generally considered as essential in the management of bipolar disorders; thus, patients with elevations on the Mania (MAN) scale, especially when accompanied by elevations on all three MAN subscales, may warrant a medical evaluation. Frequent and extreme changes of mood are suggested by highly elevated Affective Instability (BOR-A) scores; a medical consult might also be considered in these cases. When patients with schizophrenia are seen in outpatient clinics, medication regimens are typically already in place. Nonetheless, if PAI assessment reveals the presence of acute psychotic phenomena (SCZ-P) or delusions (PAR-P), then consultation with the treating physician may be helpful to reevaluate the dosage or choice of medication.

In outpatient settings that offer group psychotherapy as an alternative or adjunct to individual treatment, the selection of appropriate patients is an important task for the ultimate success of the group. The PAI offers useful information to guide this selection process. Yalom (2005) cites a number of patient characteristics that may compromise the effectiveness of the group process. First, acutely psychotic thinking and behavior is contraindicated, so elevations of greater than 60T on the Schizophrenia Psychosis (SCZ-P) subscale may be used to exclude patients from groups. The Schizophrenia (SCZ) full scale score should not be used in isolation to exclude patients from groups, especially if the overall SCZ score is driven primarily by an elevated Social Detachment (SCZ-S) subscale. Social withdrawal and awkwardness, in the absence of psychosis, is a very appropriate problem to treat using the group format (Morey, 1996). Yalom (2005) also expresses concern about including patients who might harm the group. Accordingly, elevations on Aggression (AGG), especially Physical Aggression (AGG-P), represent problems that are likely to interfere with the establishment of group cohesion. High scores on Aggressive Attitude (AGG-A) and Egocentricity (ANT-E) indicate that the patient will likely be incapable of expressing empathy and offering support to other group members.

Affective Instability (BOR-A) elevations are associated with patterns of behavior that are likely to be disruptive to the development of group norms and worrisome for individual members.

Groups operate most productively when they attain a strong sense of cohesion, an ability to trust one another, and a general allegiance to the group as a whole. Yalom (2005) noted that group treatment is less effective when patients drop out unexpectedly. As with individual treatment, high scores on the TPI (7+) are indicative of higher risk of early termination. Likewise, patients who see their problems primarily in somatic terms (SOM) are less likely to engage in the interpersonal learning process and acquire the self-understanding offered by the group process. High scores on the Paranoia scale (PAR) may prevent the patient from developing the sense of trust needed to accept honest feedback from members. However, the patient may be an appropriate candidate for a group if these PAR elevations are driven primarily by Resentment (PAR-R), without elevations on the Hypervigilance (PAR-H) and Persecution (PAR-P) subscales, as this configuration suggests interpersonal problems more so than problems with impaired reality testing. Indeed, moderate elevations on PAR-R and BOR-N can result from difficulties in past relationships for which the group format may be helpful.

Many clinicians agree that some degree of heterogeneity in the problems and goals of members can make for very effective group therapy. The PAI may be used to create an appropriate mix of patient characteristics that facilitates the group process. As mentioned above, socially withdrawn persons can benefit from group therapy, but this is more likely to occur if there are models of sociability within the group. Thus, members with relatively lower SCZ-S scores should be selected to complement those with high scores on this scale. A common therapeutic task for groups involves the struggle for leadership of and attention from the members (Yalom, 2005). Although this struggle is both inevitable and ultimately beneficial for the group, a mixture of patients who vary with respect to their needs for interpersonal control (DOM) and admiration from others (MAN-G) may help to keep these struggles from becoming harmful to the group. At least a minimal level of Warmth (WRM), as seen in WRM scores of at least 40T, is probably necessary in all members in order for them to establish a sense of cohesion and identification with the group. Ideally, various configurations of DOM and WRM could be used to assemble a group comprising complementary and anti-complementary dyads.

Morey (1996) offers a number of suggestions about how to use various PAI scale configurations for selecting specific approaches to psychotherapy (e.g., exploratory, cognitive, interpersonal, etc.). Depending on the education, training, and diversity of approaches offered by the clinical staff, these more refined suggestions may be difficult to implement in the typical outpatient setting. If the staff at a particular outpatient facility favors one approach to treatment, then these recommendations may be used to determine the prognosis of various patients to benefit from the services offered at that facility. Alternatively, these hypotheses about the relationship between various PAI configurations and amenability to specific forms of psychotherapy may be useful for understanding why a given patient is experiencing difficulties in treatment or has dropped out of treatment. Finally, the PAI has demonstrated utility as an outcome measure to evaluate the success of treatment in reducing both general levels of distress and psychopathology and specific problem areas targeted by the selected treatment modality (e.g., Harley, Baity, Blais, & Jacobo, 2007).

RISK ASSESSMENT

Although the severity of clinical disorders and the risks for problem behaviors are less acute among outpatients compared with inpatients, it is nonetheless essential to make an accurate determination about dangerousness to self and others for each client. Patients in outpatient settings are more autonomous; the most reliable patients may be seen by treating staff for 1 hour per week or less. Thus, clinicians have less control over the daily activities of outpatients and less knowledge of how they might behave outside the clinic. The PAI addresses the risk of harm to self using both a direct approach, the SUI scale, and an indirect approach, the Suicide Potential Index (SPI). Likewise, the risk of harm to others is addressed using both a direct approach, the AGG scale, and an indirect approach, the Violence Potential Index (VPI). The direct approaches involve presenting the client with face valid items about thoughts and behaviors related to these harmful actions. The indirect approaches gather information about other personality traits and clinical disorders that are conceptually and empirically related to increased risk of suicidal or violent actions. As with any self-report measure, the PAI should never be used in isolation to make clinical decisions about such risks in any patient population.

Suicidal Risk

Suicide is a matter of paramount concern in clinical assessment. The problem is that morbid thinking and passive fantasies about suicide are rather common among persons with mental disorders, but only a small percentage of patients ever act on these ideas. Acute risk of suicide is lower in outpatient settings relative to inpatient settings. Accordingly, SUI scores are significantly lower among outpatients versus inpatients in the standardization sample ($d = -.54$) and this effect represents the largest contrast in PAI scores between these two settings. Nonetheless, the mean SUI score among outpatients is elevated enough (T = 60.6) to indicate that this issue is a matter of concern in the outpatient setting. Indeed, suicidal risk must be routinely evaluated with every patient, regardless of setting.

The mean elevation of SUI scores among outpatients confirms that morbid and self-destructive thoughts are relatively common in outpatients presenting for treatment, and it underscores the need for an additional measure of the patient's capacity to behave in a suicidal or self-harmful manner. This supplementary indirect approach to suicidal risk assessment is accomplished with the SPI. The SPI is a collection of 20 PAI score configuration rules (e.g., Nonsupport T-score is higher than 60) that are more common among respondents presenting with suicide precautions or a history of suicide attempts than among patient respondents in general. A full listing of the 20 score configuration rules and their frequencies in the clinical standardization sample can also be found in Morey (1996). SPI scores of 13 or higher indicate moderate risk of suicide and scores of 18 or higher indicate markedly elevated risk; the T-score equivalent of the latter score is 69 based on the clinical norms.

The SPI score should always be considered in combination with the SUI scale score to get a complete assessment of risk for violence. The correlation between the SUI scale and the SPI is fairly high among clinical respondents ($r = .65$; Morey, 1996). Thus, the incongruent combinations of the two indicators (i.e., low SUI and high SPI; high SUI and low SPI) are less common findings that demand careful interpretation. In these cases, it is important to keep in mind the distinction that SUI is a direct measure of suicidal ideas and behavior, whereas the SPI is an indirect measure aggregating correlates of suicidal behavior. The implications of an elevated SUI score when SPI is not elevated is that the patient's distress has led to morbid thinking that will not be acted upon. Of course, this is a very risky conclusion that is not recommended. Instead, this configuration of findings requires the clinician to conduct a close and careful assessment of the nature of the patient's ideation with regard to whether a specific plan is being considered and the patient's own appraisal of the likelihood of acting on his or her ideas. In any case, a behavioral contract with the patient is clinically indicated when SUI scores exceed 70T. The clinician should ensure that the patient knows how to easily contact the treatment staff and that someone is accessible at all times. Hospitalization should be considered when SUI exceeds 75T, regardless of the level of elevation observed on the SPI. When SUI elevations fall into the subclinical range (60T to 70T), the clinician should attend to the occurrence of life crises or other factors that may increase situational stress. Changes in perceived stress may be accompanied by increases in suicidal ideation; worse, they may precipitate a suicidal attempt or gesture.

Alternatively, a patient with a low SUI score and a high SPI score may be withholding information about suicidal thoughts and plans from the clinician. In this case, a frank discussion with the patient may be necessary to rule out this explanation. A second possibility is that the elements that compose the SPI are artificially inflated due to negative response distortion. Patients with NIM scores higher than 75T are more likely to elevate the SPI and render it less informative about the potential for suicidal behavior. The level of risk associated with low SUI and high SPI is reduced when NIM is elevated (> 75T). When the SPI is elevated but SUI is not, it becomes more important to attend to history in evaluating risk. Of course, a history of self-harming behavior, attempted suicide, or suicidal gestures will always be relevant in evaluating the level of risk, regardless of the test findings. But, the high SPI and low SUI configuration may prompt the clinician to take a second, closer look at the patient's history. If there is a history of suicide attempts or clinical precautions regarding self-harm, then the long range risk associated with this configuration is higher than it would be without such history. The SPI elevation in such a case indicates that suicidal impulses are more likely to be acted upon should the patient experience suicidal thoughts some time in the future. These recommendations are summarized in Table 2.2.

Violence Risk

Risk of harm to others is another paramount concern for assessment of patients in any setting. The AGG scale comprises 18 items and, unlike the other Treatment Considerations scales, it has three six-item subscales: AGG-A, Verbal Aggression

TABLE 2.2   Interpretive Hypotheses for Various SUI and SPI Score Configurations

	Low-Average Suicide Potential (SPI < 13)	High Suicide Potential (SPI = 13+)
Low to Average Suicidal Ideation (SUI T-score < 60)	No special risk precautions are indicated.	Check NIM scale; carefully review history; evaluate for unexpressed intent or plan.
Moderate Suicidal Ideation (SUI T-score 60–70)	Focus treatment on recent crises or situational stresses.	Moderate to high risk; be alert to changes in stress and availability of social supports.
High Suicidal Ideation (SUI T-score > 70)	Moderate risk; evaluate ideation; "contract" with patient is indicated.	High risk of suicidal behavior; inpatient treatment, suicide precautions, and "contract" with patient are indicated.

(AGG-V), and Physical Aggression (AGG-P). AGG-A measures the more enduring characteristics of hostility and anger proneness, whereas AGG-V and AGG-P measure the modalities used to express anger when the person is provoked by the situation. Patients in outpatient settings are not much more aggressive than community adults, as indicated by a mean T-score of 53.4 on AGG. Obviously, in the assessment of violence risk, elevations on AGG-P (> 70T) are associated with increased likelihood of physical harm to others. If this elevated AGG-P score is accompanied by an average or relatively lower score (< 60T) on AGG-V, then the capacity to act out violently may come as a surprise, without the warning provided by threats or yelling. In this case, the treatment staff may not be aware of the patient's inclination to violence until the occurrence of some unpredictable event. In contrast, average scores on AGG-P accompanied by elevations on AGG-V may be seen in patients who are known for a bad temper but are less likely to escalate into physically violent reactions to their anger.

The VPI is a collection of 20 PAI score configuration rules (e.g., DOM is 10 T-score points higher than WRM) that are more common among respondents with a history of violence, such as prior criminal convictions for assault or rape, than among other patient respondents in the clinical standardization sample. A full listing of the 20 score configuration rules and their frequency in the clinical standardization sample can be found in Morey (1996). VPI scores of 9 or higher indicate moderate risk of violence and scores of 13 or higher indicate markedly elevated risk; the T-score equivalent of the latter score is 72 based on the clinical norms.

The VPI score should always be considered in combination with AGG scale scores to get a complete assessment of risk for violence. The VPI is highly correlated with AGG (r = .65) in clinical patients (Morey, 1996), so incongruent combinations are uncommon but possible. As with SUI and SPI, it is useful to bear in mind the direct versus indirect distinction in how these scales are intended to operate. Low AGG combined with high VPI should arouse the clinician's concern that the patient is not disclosing his or her hostile thoughts or violent intentions. A closer evaluation of these issues with the patient may be necessary to alleviate these concerns. Like the SPI, however, the VPI is subject to the effects of negative response distortion. When NIM is elevated above a T-score of 75, a high VPI

TABLE 2.3   Interpretive Hypotheses for Various AGG and VPI Score Configurations

	Low-Average Violence Potential (VPI < 9)	HIGH Violence Potential (VPI = 9+)
Low to Average Aggression (AGG T-score < 60)	No special risk precautions are indicated.	Check NIM scale; carefully review history; evaluate for unexpressed anger, hostility, or history of violence.
Moderate Aggression (AGG T-score 60–70)	Focus treatment on anger management or stress inoculation techniques.	Moderate to high risk; be alert to changes in stress and situational triggers.
High Aggression (AGG T-score > 70)	Moderate risk; consider relative elevation of AGG-P subscale.	High risk of violent behavior; consider more appropriate placement; investigate duty to warn imperatives.

accompanied by a low or average AGG may arouse considerably less concern. If a patient who is so inclined to exaggerate is not endorsing aggressive attitudes or behaviors, then this report may be taken at face value.

At moderate levels of expressed aggression (AGG = 60–70T), anger management may be an important focus of treatment. In this range of AGG scores, an elevated VPI score should increase the clinician's concern about acting out in ways that are harmful to others. The patient's life situation should be carefully assessed, and subsequently monitored, for the presence of highly stressful circumstances (losing a job, divorce or separation, etc.) that can trigger a violent act. High levels of expressed aggression (AGG > 70T) are a matter of particular concern when the patient reports acting on these feelings physically (AGG-P > 70T). Regardless of the configuration of AGG subscales, when elevated AGG scores are combined with VPI scores of 9 or higher, risk of violence becomes a central feature of clinical management. Inpatient treatment may be considered as a more appropriate placement for these patients, and clinicians should investigate whether there is a duty to warn third parties who are a focus of the patient's hostile ideation. These recommendations are summarized in Table 2.3.

INDICATIONS FOR ADDITIONAL MEASURES

The PAI, like any self-report personality inventory, should never be used as the *sole basis* for diagnoses or other important decisions about individuals. At a minimum, the PAI should be accompanied by a thorough and skillful clinical interview that explores the history of the presenting problem, medical history, current relationships, educational and work experiences, developmental history, and family of origin. This chapter provides several examples of how the meaning of specific PAI scores and score configurations can be elucidated with additional information about the patient. For example, a client's history of legal problems related to assault would be relevant information that would help to explain certain discrepancies in AGG and VPI score elevations. Previous experiences with psychosocial treatment and the patient's reactions to these experiences are also helpful guides to current treatment planning. Interpreting elevations on certain PAI scales is easier with some knowledge of the patient's life events and current social context. Thus, although the Traumatic Stress subscale (ARD-T) has produced encouraging evidence for its validity in the identification of posttraumatic stress disorder (McDevitt-Murphy, Weathers, Adkins, & Daniels, 2005; Mozley, Miller, Weathers, Beckham, & Feldman, 2005), an elevated ARD-T score alone is insufficient for the diagnosis. It is still essential to determine whether the past event that is troubling the respondent satisfies the rather specific criteria guiding the definition of traumatic events in the DSM-IV (American Psychiatric Association, 1994).

As mentioned earlier, opportunities for testing may be limited in the outpatient setting. Thus, when additional measures are indicated, they must be chosen with care and attention to the utility of the information given the time costs of administering those tests. Some assessment contexts involve populations with lower base rates for psychopathology (e.g., learning disability evaluations in college students). Patients without psychopathology or behavior disorders will often produce unremarkable PAI profiles. Although some information about normal differences in personality can be gleaned from the interpersonal scales (DOM and WRM), a more detailed assessment of normal personality traits can be accomplished with the revised NEO Personality Inventory (NEO-PI-R; Costa & McCrae, 1992). Even well-adjusted respondents will obtain interesting profile configurations across the five scales and 30 subscales of this instrument, and this information can be effectively applied to referral questions and treatment decisions in outpatient settings. Finally, the PAI can reveal only what respondents are able to see in themselves and their behavior; honesty cannot correct for a lack of insight. That is probably why prodromal symptoms of incipient psychoses are best identified by the Rorschach method than by self-report questionnaires. Concerns about the patient's capacity to report accurately could be addressed by obtaining ratings from collateral informants. The NEO-PI-R and Interpersonal Adjectives Scale (IAS; Wiggins, 1995) are ready to use for this purpose, but these are less helpful for psychiatric diagnoses. It will be useful to develop and standardize informant-rated versions of the PAI. Toward this aim, an other-report version of the Personality Assessment Screener is currently being developed (Christopher Hopwood, personal communication, June 2, 2009).

ADVANTAGES AND DISADVANTAGES OF THE PAI

There is no test that comes close to perfection in the field of personality assessment. In fact, it is most realistic to consider each test as more or less flawed. The diverse approaches to personality assessment all have a mix of advantages and disadvantages. The same feature of a test that is considered an advantage from one perspective may also be seen as a disadvantage from a different perspective. Many writers have cited the brevity of the PAI as an advantage of the test relative to other inventories used in the field, but 344 items and 45–60 minutes may be seen by some outpatient clinicians as a big task for clients and something that is difficult to accommodate into a busy clinic schedule. When the ideal of administering the PAI to all patients at intake cannot be achieved, the value of testing should be reconsidered for that subset of patients who present with unusual complications at intake or early in the treatment process. In settings where great numbers of patients are seen, the Personality Assessment Screener (PAS; Morey, 1997) should prove useful. The PAS contains only 22 items and yields an estimate of the probability that one or more clinical scales of the PAI will be elevated. A full PAI can be administered to patients who show high probability (e.g., greater than .50) for an elevated PAI profile or who endorse content areas of particular concern to clinic staff. It is also possible to estimate the scores on most of the PAI full scales when only the first 160 items on the tests have been answered. The psychometric characteristics support the preliminary validity of this "short form" of the PAI, and norms for these abbreviated full scale scores are reported in the test manuals (Morey, 1991, 2007). However, this practice is not recommended for routine outpatient assessment, because all of the subscales and the STR scale cannot be scored from the short form. As seen in the previous section on Treatment Planning, these measures are critical to the assessment of the treatment prognosis and selection issues that are so important in the outpatient context.

Perhaps the greatest disadvantage in using the PAI lies in the fact that it is a relatively new test in the field of personality assessment. However, the recent introduction of the test is also an advantage, because it enabled its developer to incorporate lessons learned over decades of work in the development and validation of psychological tests. The disadvantage associated with the more recent introduction of the PAI is the relative lack of empirical research on some of the important PAI scales and indexes. Given the increase in research with the PAI each year, this disadvantage will continue to be rectified in the years to come.

COMMUNICATION OF FINDINGS

It is difficult to underestimate the importance of effectively communicating the findings from psychological testing and their implications for treatment. As mentioned, members of the clinical staff in many outpatient facilities vary widely in their education, training, and theoretical or philosophical orientation to treatment and mental health. Thus, the results of psychological testing and assessment must be communicated to referral sources and treating staff in a direct and practical manner. Written reports of psychological evaluations should be free of jargon and references to scores and statistics. The demand for practical and specific guidance to therapists is greater than ever, and the PAI should prove especially useful in this regard.

There is a new appreciation of the importance of communicating results to patients and working collaboratively with them in formulating a treatment plan (Finn & Tonsager, 1997). Morey (2003) presents some specific techniques for soliciting questions from and providing feedback to the patient. The opportunity to answer such questions at the completion of the PAI assessment will have therapeutic benefits for the patient, and it should enhance the clinician's understanding of the case. It is inadvisable to rely too much on computerized narrative reports by quoting them in test reports or sharing them directly with clients or colleagues as a means of reporting the results. These "blind" and mechanical interpretations of a test will inevitably contain a mixture of accurate and inaccurate assertions about the patient. Findings from the PAI, as from all other psychological tests, are most meaningful when considered in the context of the individual respondent's psychosocial history and observable behavior. A reasonably detailed knowledge of the patient's present circumstances and an understanding of the reasons for the referral are essential for knowing what is most relevant to communicate about the patient. In particular, time spent in direct contact with the patient in both interview and testing situations is helpful for narrowing in on the key issues from the array of possible inferences generated by most PAI protocols.

SUMMARY

The PAI offers several advantages to recommend its routine use for clinical assessment in outpatient settings. When supplemented with other clinical and assessment data, the scales of the PAI can assist in common differential diagnostic scenarios, the determination of prognosis for treatment, the selection of appropriate treatment modalities, and the evaluation of suicide and violence risk.

REFERENCES

American Psychiatric Association. (1994). *Diagnostic and statistical manual of mental disorders* (4th ed.). Washington, D.C.: Author.

Beck, A.T., Rush, A.J., Shaw, B.F., & Emery, G. (1979). *Cognitive therapy of depression.* New York: Guilford.

Blais, M.A., Mathews, J., Lipkis-Orlando, R., O'Keefe, S.M., Jacobo, M., Rivas-Vazquez, R.A., et al. (2003). Development and application of a brief multi-faceted tool for evaluating inpatient psychiatric care. *Administration and Policy in Mental Health,* 30, 159-172.

Blatt, S.J, Quinlan, D.M., Pilkonis, P.A., & Shea, M.T. (1995). Impact of perfectionism and need for approval on the brief treatment of depression: The National Institute of Mental Health Treatment of Depression Collaborative Research Program revisited. *Journal of Counseling and Clinical Psychology, 63,* 125-132.

Clarkin, J.F., & Levy, K.N. (2004). The influence of client variables on psychotherapy. In M.J. Lambert (Ed.), *Handbook of psychotherapy and behavior change* (5th ed.). New York: Wiley.

Costa, P.T., & McCrae, R.R. (1992). *Professional Manual: Revised NEO Personality Inventory (NEO-PI-R) and NEO Five Factor Inventory (NEO-FFI).* Odessa, FL: Psychological Assessment Resources.

Fals-Stewart, W. (1996). The ability of individuals with psychoactive substance use disorders to escape detection by the Personality Assessment Inventory. *Psychological Assessment, 8,* 60-68.

Finn, S.E., & Tonsager, M.E. (1997). Information-gathering and therapeutic models of assessment: Complementary paradigms. *Psychological Assessment, 9,* 374–385.

Groth-Marnat, G. (2003). *Handbook of psychological assessment* (4th ed.). New York: Wiley.

Harley, R.M., Baity, M.R., Blais, M.A., & Jacobo, M.C. (2007). Use of dialectical behavior therapy skills training for borderline personality disorder in a naturalistic setting. *Psychotherapy Research, 17,* 351–358.

Hopwood, C.J., Ambwani, S., & Morey, L.C. (2007). Predicting non-mutual therapy termination with the Personality Assessment Inventory. *Psychotherapy Research, 17,* 706–712.

Hopwood, C.J., Creech, S.K., Clark, T.S., Meagher, M.W., & Morey, L.C. (2008). Predicting the completion of an integrative and intensive outpatient chronic pain treatment with the Personality Assessment Inventory. *Journal of Personality Assessment, 90,* 76–80.

Karlin, B.E., Creech, S.K., Grimes, J.S., Clark, T.S., Meagher, M.W., & Morey, L.C. (2005). The Personality Assessment Inventory with chronic pain patients: Psychometric properties and clinical utility. *Journal of Clinical Psychology, 61,* 1571–1585.

Kurtz, J.E., & Morey, L.C. (1998). Negativism in evaluative judgments of words among depressed outpatients with borderline personality disorder. *Journal of Personality Disorders, 12,* 351–361.

Kurtz, J.E., & Morey, L.C. (2001). Use of structured self-report assessment to diagnose borderline personality disorder during major depressive episodes. *Assessment, 8,* 291–300.

Kurtz, J.E., Shealy, S.E., & Putnam, S.H. (2007). Another look at paradoxical severity effects in head injury with the Personality Assessment Inventory. *Journal of Personality Assessment, 88,* 67–74.

McDevitt-Murphy, M.E., Weathers, F.W., Adkins, J.W., & Daniels, J.B. (2005). Use of the Personality Assessment Inventory in assessment of posttraumatic stress disorder in women. *Journal of Psychopathology and Behavioral Assessment, 27,* 57–65.

Mendella, P.D., & McFadden, L. (2005). Personality Assessment Inventory (PAI) profiles in cases of no detectable brain injury, mild brain injury, and severe brain injury. *Archives of Clinical Neuropsychology, 20,* 935–936.

Morey, L.C. (1991). *Personality Assessment Inventory: Professional manual.* Odessa, FL: Psychological Assessment Resources.

Morey, L.C. (1996). *An interpretive guide to the Personality Assessment Inventory (PAI).* Psychological Assessment Resources, Inc.

Morey, L.C. (2003). *Essentials of PAI assessment.* New York: Wiley.

Morey, L.C. (2007). *Personality Assessment Inventory: Professional Manual* (2nd ed.) Lutz, FL: Psychological Assessment Resources.

Morey, L.C., & Hopwood, C.J. (2007). *Casebook for the Personality Assessment Inventory: A structural summary approach.* Lutz, FL: Psychological Assessment Resources.

Mozley, S.L., Miller, M.W., Weathers, F.W., Beckham, J.C., & Feldman, M.E. (2005). Personality Assessment Inventory (PAI) profiles of male veterans with combat-related posttraumatic stress disorder. *Journal of Psychopathology and Behavioral Assessment, 27,* 179–189.

Rogers, R., Sewell, K.W., Morey, L.C., & Ustad, K.L. (1996). Detection of feigned mental disorders on the Personality Assessment Inventory: A discriminant analysis. *Journal of Personality Assessment, 67,* 629–640.

Schinka, J.A., & Borum, R. (1993). Readability of adult psychopathology inventories. *Psychological Assessment, 5,* 384–386.

Wierzbicki, M., & Pekarik, G. (1993). A meta-analysis of psychotherapy dropout. *Professional Psychology: Research and Practice, 24,* 190–195.

Wiggins, J.S. (1995). *Interpersonal adjective scales: Professional manual.* Odessa, FL: Psychological Assessment Resources.

Yalom, I.D. (2005). *The theory and practice of group psychotherapy* (5th ed.). New York: Basic Books.

3

Assessment of Inpatients Using the PAI

CALEB J. SIEFERT and MARK A. BLAIS

*I*npatient psychiatric care has undergone profound changes in the last few decades. The average length for an inpatient hospital stay in the United States decreased from 25 days in 1990 to 10 days in 2000 (Lave, 2003). To qualify for inpatient level of care, patients must suffer from severe psychiatric symptoms with behavioral dysregulation, show significant deficits in self-care and independent functioning, be a danger to self or others, or require complex medication adjustments. Inpatients are more likely to meet criteria for multiple disorders and often have major co-morbid physical illnesses (Miller, Dasher, Collins, Griffiths, & Brown, 2001). With increased patient complexity and decreased time for treatment comes a need for rapid and efficient assessment procedures capable of providing reliable information across multiple domains. As such, inpatient programs are increasingly relying upon multi-scaled self-report instruments like the Personality Assessment Inventory (PAI; Morey 1991, 2007) to meet this need (Marlowe & Wetzler, 1994).

As Boone (1998, pp. 839–840) has noted, the construct validation framework utilized in the PAI's development and the range of construct coverage makes it particularly appealing for use in inpatient settings (for a detailed review of the PAI development process see Chapter 1 of this volume; Morey & Henry, 1994; Morey, 2007). The PAI can be completed relatively quickly (in roughly 45 minutes to an hour), makes minimal demands on staff, and can increase the patients' involvement in treatment (Eisen, Dickey, & Sederer, 2000). The PAI produces 22 *non-overlapping* scales: 4 validity scales; 11 clinical scales, 5 treatment consideration scales, and 2 interpersonal scales. Ten of the full scales are composed of three separate subscales tapping a narrow range of the construct. These subscales aid considerably in PAI interpretation. The PAI also provides information relevant to treatment, such as level of stress, interest in treatment, aggression, and suicidal ideation. Recent data support the psychometric adequacy for the PAI scales in inpatient settings (e.g., Boone, 1998; Siefert, et al., in press). Given the versatility and range of constructs tapped by the PAI it is of little surprise that the measure is being increasingly utilized across a wide range of inpatient settings, such as eating disorder units (e.g., Giorgia, Wood, Demidenko, & Hany, 2002), substance abuse units (e.g., Schinka, 1995), forensic settings (e.g., Edens & Ruiz, 2008), general psychiatric units (Boone, 1998), and medical-psychiatric settings (Siefert et al., in press; Sinclair et al., in press).

This chapter focuses on the application of the PAI to clinical issues that frequently occur in an inpatient psychiatric unit. We first discuss some of the overarching goals of inpatient hospitalizations and provide details on the specific setting in which we make use of the PAI. We then turn to discussing more direct interpretive considerations for the PAI with specific focus on how the tool is used for general assessment of current distress and dangerousness. We also review how data from the PAI can provide important insights into understanding and anticipating how patients will interact with inpatient staff and other patients while on the unit. Inpatient reference data collected exclusively on our unit is presented and we discuss various structural issues (e.g., validity scale considerations) to consider when interpreting the PAI in inpatient settings. Due to space considerations, this chapter is not intended to provide a detailed interpretative approach to the PAI (see Morey, 1996, 2003; Morey & Hopwood, 2007), but rather attempts to provide a view of some of the general ways the tool can be usefully applied in inpatient assessment.

When considering the goals of inpatient admission, it is useful to think in terms of two different levels of goals: primary and secondary. The overarching primary goal of psychiatric inpatient admissions is patient stabilization. Stabilization in this case means a return to near-baseline levels of functioning and emotional stability. Stabilization does not entail the complete amelioration of distress, nor does it imply cure. Instead, stabilization involves reducing a patient's level of distress and risk for dangerousness to the point that he or she is able to engage in some form of outpatient care. Accomplishing this primary goal requires clinicians to accurately assess the patient's baseline level of functioning while rapidly identifying current symptoms, problems, psychosocial stressors, and medical conditions that are contributing to destabilization.

While stabilization is the primary goal of inpatient treatment, there are a number of secondary goals that treatment providers attempt to address. These include diagnostic clarification, increasing patients' involvement and interest in their treatment, increasing awareness of behavior patterns that led to hospitalization, and creating effective discharge plans. Although achieving all of these goals is not necessary for discharge from the unit, inpatient treatment attempts to address as many of these as possible in the hopes of reducing rapid re-admission and increasing compliance with outpatient care.

Our insights regarding the application of the PAI in inpatient units developed from many years of providing clinical (treatment and assessment) services and conducting research on an inpatient psychiatric inpatient unit at a large teaching hospital. The unit is a 24-bed locked psychiatric facility specializing in medical-psychiatric treatment for adults. It is physically divided into two connected sections; an eight-room (single occupancy) intensive care unit (ICU) and a general locked unit. The ICU is typically used to contain patients who are deemed to require a high level of support and monitoring due to disorganization, dangerousness, or as a result of medical complications. The most common diagnoses involve mood disorders (upward of 50% of cases), followed by psychotic, personality, substance, and neurocognitive (e.g., dementia). A substantial portion of our patients are referred, in part, because they have active co-morbid medical conditions that are too severe to be treated in a free-standing psychiatric hospital. Consistent with national rates, the average length of stay is 10 days. Patients are treated by interdisciplinary teams including psychiatrists, psychologists, social workers, occupational therapists, case managers, and nurses. The PAI is typically administered by a staff psychologist or supervised psychological intern within the first 24 to 48 hours of patient admission and the information is used to inform all aspects of the patient's care.

Given the importance of assessment data for treatment decisions and other aspects of inpatient care, the initial assessment process is a critical element of hospitalization. Assessment here refers to a broad range of clinical procedures that yield information regarding the patient's level of functioning and current presentation. These procedures include a clinical interview, information collected from the patient's treatment providers, observation of ward behavior, information from medical records and family or friends (with the patient's consent), and psychological assessment data. Thus, inpatient assessment involves the integration of data from multiple sources. Figure 3.1 outlines this assessment process and highlights that assessment is an ongoing process during hospitalization that continually informs case conceptualization and treatment planning.

In this context, we view self-report measures like the PAI as a means of communication between the patient and the staff. In essence, the PAI provides patients with 344 chances to tell us how they see themselves and how they want us to see them. Scoring these 344 statements organizes and quantifies these communications along a number of known dimensions. This organized and quantified communication can serve many functions—it can help clarify diagnoses, guide treatment selection, and inform discharge plans. It can also be a powerful means of connecting with the patient. In fact, discussing the findings with the patient can represent an important entrée into a therapeutic dialogue (Finn, 2007).

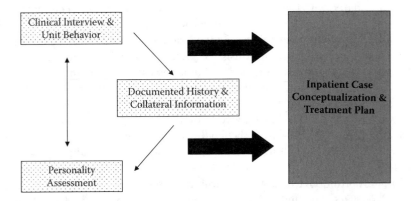

Figure 3.1   The inpatient assessment process.

We are typically asked by the treatment team to answer a number of common referral questions involving issues such as safety risks (to self; to others), underlying psychosis, and co-morbid conditions that may complicate or slow treatment response (particularly drug and alcohol problems or the presence of Axis II psychopathology). Whereas the initial referral question from the treatment team may be vague or generic, we have found that briefly reviewing the case with the requesting psychiatrist usually produces a more focused question. For example, if the psychiatrist requests an assessment for diagnostic clarification, a brief discussion can determine what other conditions are being considered and highlight the information that raised these potential diagnoses. In a similar manner, it is also useful for the psychologist to clarify how the assessment information might impact the course of treatment. For example, if the patient is referred to establish his or her level of depression, it can be useful to know whether the treatment team is trying to determine the appropriateness of an intervention such as electroconvulsive therapy versus other, more conventional treatments, because this suggests that chronicity and severity of depressive symptoms are important to answer the referral question.

Given the time limited nature of inpatient care, we have found that utilizing a collaborative assessment approach (Finn, 2007) that integrates our diagnostic work into the larger body of the patient's treatment maximizes the overall therapeutic impact of the assessment. This broader view informs how we introduce the PAI and assessment to the patient. We suggest starting the assessment with a rapport-building session of approximately 30 minutes. During this interaction we review the patient's adjustment to the unit and staff, closely attend to the patient's view of what has provoked his or her admission, and begin a dialogue about how hospitalization might be helpful. We also attempt to solicit questions patients would like us to help them begin to answer with the assessment data. We stress that we want to *work together with the patient* to learn more about them and gain a better understanding what would be most helpful to them right now. We also discuss the primary referral question with each patient, which overlaps to varying degrees with the patient's questions. At the end of this session, we introduce the PAI as a tool that can help us work toward these goals. We go through the standard test administration, including reviewing the purpose of testing, explaining that results are shared with the treatment team, reviewing the limits of confidentiality, and explaining the patient's right to refuse testing. We then review the instructions with the patients, have them read the first few questions to gauge their comprehension, and leave them to finish the PAI. When we share results with the patients, we try to integrate the PAI and other assessment data in the context of the overall case, generate hypotheses regarding the patients' and the referring party's questions, develop goals, and identify what the patient can do immediately (i.e., while on the unit) to begin to work toward these goals. Our hypotheses are often modified somewhat during the feedback session, where this information can be further contextualized by the patients' view of themselves and response to the test data.

In interpreting PAI data we primarily rely upon the community sample reference norm *t*-scores and the clinical skyline scores (Morey, 1991). However, we also interpret PAI scores in light of how they relate to local reference values obtained from our unit. We find this useful because the clinical composition and treatment philosophy of the unit has remained pretty consistent over the years. Therefore, local reference values allow us to assess how typical a patient is for our unit. Table 3.1 includes mean scores and standard deviations for the PAI full scales for both the full form and the short form (PAI-SF). These references values were derived from 560 valid PAI profiles (Inconsistency [ICN], Infrequency [INF], and Positive Impression Management [PIM], all within the acceptable range as described by Morey, 2007) obtained within 72 hours of admission to the unit. Consistent with the fact that the majority of patients are hospitalized for a mixture of distress *and* safety concerns, the highest mean scores were for the Depression (DEP) and Suicidal Ideation scales (SUI). While reference values are presented for the PAI-SF, it is important to note that the PAI-SF lacks clinical subscales, has

TABLE 3.1   Means and Standard Deviations for the PAI Full Scales in a Psychiatric Inpatient Sample (n = 560)

	Full Form			Short Form		
Scale	Mean	sd	α	Mean	sd	α
ICN	56.82	8.23	n/a	n/a	n/a	n/a
INF	51.46	8.04	.14	49.80	8.66	.05
NIM	62.57	16.30	.72	55.56	14.51	.55
PIM	44.63	11.97	.77	44.89	10.72	.62
SOM	63.64	13.87	.90	65.28	14.13	.86
ANX	65.83	14.59	.93	66.81	16.32	.88
ARD	61.21	15.31	.86	62.45	15.31	.83
DEP	71.54	17.78	.94	72.75	18.46	.90
MAN	49.51	11.45	.83	50.54	11.62	.77
PAR	55.04	12.97	.88	54.83	12.65	.82
SCZ	58.84	14.60	.87	59.00	14.91	.79
BOR	62.98	14.53	.91	63.73	13.82	.85
ANT	52.32	11.39	.84	51.77	11.59	.78
ALC	53.71	14.97	.90	54.72	16.92	.88
DRG	56.57	16.53	.88	56.23	15.85	.82
AGG	51.61	12.30	.88	52.16	12.41	.82
SUI	69.50	23.34	.92	71.83	25.84	.95
STR	62.00	13.79	.80	n/a	n/a	n/a
NON	57.55	14.14	.80	58.57	13.96	.68
RXR	38.20	10.84	.77	37.65	10.11	.74
DOM	45.69	11.37	.79	44.71	10.56	.67
WRM	47.26	11.27	.81	45.98	11.56	.77

Note: Mean = Average t-score for the scale; *sd* = Standard Deviation; α = Coefficient Alpha; n/a = not applicable; ICN = Inconsistency; INF = Infrequency; NIM = Negative Impression Management; PIM = Positive Impression Management; SOM = Somatic Complaints; ANX = Anxiety; ARD = Anxiety Related Disorders; DEP = Depression; MAN = Mania; PAR = Paranoia; SCZ = Schizophrenia; BOR = Borderline Traits; ANT = Antisocial Traits; ALC = Alcohol Problems; DRG = Drug Problems; AGG = Aggression; SUI = Suicidal Ideation; STR = Stress; NON = Non-Support; RXR = Treatment Rejection; DOM = Dominance; WRM = Warmth.

lower reliabilities than the full form, and has a limited research base. Thus, its use should be limited when making important clinical decisions (Morey, 1991, 2007), though there are some specific situations where it may be useful (see Siefert, Kehl-Fie, Blais, & Chriki, 2007; Sinclair, et al., in press).

INTERPRETATION OF PROFILE VALIDITY

The first step in psychological test interpretation is consideration of the likely validity of the profile (Hopwood, Morey, Rogers, & Sewell, 2007; Morey, 2003). Prior research on the PAI suggests that psychiatric inpatients are able to complete the test in a valid manner and tend to produce fewer invalid profiles for the PAI as compared to similar tests of psychopathology (Braxton et al., 2007; LePage & Mogge, 2001). The PAI contains 4 validity scales (ICN; INF; Negative Impression Management [NIM]; PIM) and several other validity indicators that assist in this determination. Elevations in ICN and INF reflect unreliable, inconsistent, or odd responding and elevations above the cutoff scores suggested by Morey (1991, 2007) are taken to indicate that the profile is invalid.

In the inpatient setting, we consider both ICN positive profiles (i.e., a profile where ICN is elevated above the critical cutoff) and INF positive profiles invalid, and do not interpret results directly. However, in many instances we do try to "understand" what factors may have contributed to invalid responding. For example, some patients are unable to respond consistently due to disorientation, a decline in cognitive functioning, or disorganized or accelerated thoughts, all of which may require further assessment. Some patients may have simply failed to maintain focus or interest, at times, due to very high levels of overall distress. We find that discussing invalid profiles with patients can often shed light on the difficulties they had completing the test. In many cases, particularly after a reduction in immediate distress, the PAI can be re-administered to yield a valid profile. In the case of INF positive profiles, we are also interested in signs of any odd or eccentric behavior, as an INF elevation can mark eccentricity or idiosyncrasies that may point to mild psychosis, some personality disorders (PD), or cognitive limitations.

Examination of response styles (impression management) is also important for inpatient assessment. Baity et al. (2007) found that NIM and PIM were effective PAI predictors of psychiatric inpatients' attempts to "fake bad" and "fake good" respectively. PIM elevations are associated with denying or minimizing psychological problems and limited motivation for change. True PIM positive profiles are *rare* on our inpatient units. In a recent analysis of 646 profiles we found only 19 that exceeded the absolute cutoff ($T \geq 68$) for PIM. However, PIM affected (PIM > 57) profiles are somewhat less uncommon. Table 3.1 shows that the mean PIM score for our unit is a t-score of 45 ($sd = 12$), suggesting that a score of 57 may occur in a nontrivial minority of respondents. As PIM exceeds a t-score of 57, there is an increasing possibility that the patient may be less aware, less open, or less forthcoming about problems than is typical for our unit. Inpatients with mildly elevated PIM scores may be at particular risk for elopement, treatment non-compliance, or problematic alliances (also see Morey, 1996). Thus, it is important to make all inpatient staff aware when a patient has even a mildly elevated PIM. The PAI Defensive Index (DEF) is a helpful complement to PIM. In the Baity et al.'s study, psychiatric inpatients instructed to "fake good" as if they were trying to fool their treatment team into letting them leave the hospital, produced significantly higher DEF scores than respondents completing the PAI with standard instructions. Of note, in the case where PIM, DEF, and the Cashel Discriminant Function (CDF) are elevated, defensiveness may be more willful or strategic. A careful review of the clinical history for possible motivations to such behavior should be conducted in light of elevated PIM or DEF. High scores on Treatment Rejection (RXR) in conjunction with elevations in PIM can also suggest a strong desire to leave the hospital and signal an elopement risk. In sum, PIM elevated (*t*-score > 57) profiles *should be seen as a red flag.*

The interpretation of NIM in inpatient settings differs somewhat from traditional settings. As can be seen in Table 3.1, on average inpatients achieve scores of greater than 60*T* on NIM. In a recent analysis of 646 PAI inpatient profiles, 30% had scores of greater than 70*T*. Such results are consistent with previous data for NIM in inpatient settings and with a demonstrated pattern of positive correlations between NIM and the clinical scales (Morey, 1991, 1996). Thus, high NIM scores are common in clinical samples and should not be immediately interpreted as invalidating the profile. On our unit, where the typical patient is willingly hospitalized, elevations on NIM are seen as indicating a highly negative self-view, possibly associated with severe depression, the corrosive effects of a chronic psychiatric illness, or a cry for help. Still, NIM positive profiles should not just be accepted and steps should be taken to explore the possibility of malingering or secondary gain. These steps include a review of the reasons for the patient's admission, consideration of the patient's current life circumstances, and assessment of possible motives for or gains from remaining in the hospital. The PAI Malingering Index (MAL) and Rogers Discriminant Function (RDF; Rogers et al., 1996) can also be highly useful in evaluating potential malingering, particularly given their lesser relations to psychopathology but similarly strong sensitivities to dissimulation. Baity et al. (2007) showed that the RDF incremented NIM in detecting efforts to fake bad in a sample from our unit. As with PIM, elevations to NIM accompanied by elevations on MAL or RDF should trigger a careful review of the patient's current presentation and recent history to further assess the possibility of willful distortion. In addition, it can also be useful to make use of the PAI NIM-predicted method in the PAI software (Morey, 1999). The NIM-predicted method can aid the examiner in identifying scales that may have been more greatly influenced by a negative response style and can be helpful in identifying respondents trying to feign specific disorders (see Hopwood, Morey, Rogers, & Sewell, 2007).

DIAGNOSIS

Following review of the validity scales, clinical scale profile interpretation begins. Several strategies have been outlined for this process (see Chapter 12; Morey & Hopwood, 2007). In our setting, we interpret the PAI hierarchically, starting with the mean clinical elevation index (MCE), which provides an excellent measure of global distress. We next proceed to evaluate four clinically relevant scale clusters. The SOM, DEP, ANX, and ARD scales provide a good indication of distress and internalizing psychopathology. The MAN, SCZ, and PAR scales are more associated with severe conditions including disorganized behavior, psychotic processes, or distorted thinking (although for these scales in particular, subscale interpretation is *highly important*). PAR, BOR, and ANT may be indicative of PD presentation during hospitalization (even if the patient seems unlikely to have a PD diagnosis at baseline). Finally, elevations to DRG and ALC indicate that substance abuse is an important consideration in the clinical picture.

Profile evaluation using these four rationally identified clusters allows for a quick assessment of clinical complexity. When patients have elevations on scales *across clusters* it suggests a more complex clinical condition as compared with a pattern of elevations that is limited to scales within a single cluster. Profiles that involve scale elevations that are limited to a single cluster are generally straightforward (even if multiple scales within the cluster are elevated). Elevations limited to the distress cluster suggest that clarifying the presenting complaint and identifying target symptoms to be focused on is the next step in the assessment process. Elevations limited to the PD cluster suggest there will be a strong need for therapeutic interventions and patient management on the unit, and suggest that it will be very important to involve outpatient clinicians in framing the goals of hospitalization. Elevations limited to the substance abuse cluster indicate that a thorough evaluation of recent substance use and determination of the risk for withdrawal is in order and, in many cases, consultation with an expert in substance treatment will be helpful in determining treatment recommendations.

Elevations of scales *across clusters* suggest a more complex clinical scenario with multiple co-occurring problems. For example, elevations in the distress cluster and the psychotic cluster may suggest that a patient is experiencing a psychotic depression, anxiety/depression to the point that thinking and concentration are greatly compromised, medical problems that are negatively affecting cognition, or may be suggestive of a history consistent with a bipolar disorder (rather than a unipolar depression). Elevations of the PD cluster in conjunction with either the distress or severe clusters often indicate a complicated treatment course and suggest that in addition to identifying target symptoms to focus on during the hospitalization, the patient is likely to require more attention from staff and individualized therapy as part of treatment. Elevations on the substance abuse cluster in conjunction with elevations on any of the other clusters increases the probability that substance use may be triggered by other forms of distress or that substance use may be exacerbating distress associated with other conditions, contributing to mood instability and medical problems.

Examination of specific PAI scale and subscale scores can help to clarify target symptoms that will become the focus of the hospitalization (see case example 1). As stated previously, psychiatric inpatients tend to be more complex diagnostically and often meet criteria for multiple disorders (Miller, Dasher, Collins, Griffiths, & Brown, 2001). However, given the goals of inpatient treatment, interventions tend to focus on those aspects of the presentation that are causing the most acute distress. Thus, while multiple scale elevations are common in inpatient settings, treatment often focuses primarily on the one or two areas that appear most related to the patient's current difficulties. Scores on PAI clinical scales exceeding the

Skyline (2 *sd* above the *clinical norms;* Morey, 1991) can be particularly useful for identifying such problem areas. The data presented in Table 3.1 can assist in providing specific information about elevations relative to other inpatients. Scores above these cutoffs often represent an excellent starting point for discussions with inpatient staff and the patient.

Thought disorder is a common diagnostic consideration among inpatients. The majority of patients hospitalized for a psychotic condition do not require elaborate assessment, as signs and symptoms of psychosis are evident (e.g., auditory hallucinations, delusions, frank disorganization). However, some patients present with "soft-signs" of psychosis (e.g., odd presentation, social difficulty, problems with social communication) that require further clarification. In addition, some patients referred for assessment for other reasons sometimes elevate SCZ. In many of these cases, further assessment of thought quality is required. This typically involves a neuro-cognitive screening (Blais & Baity, 2005) and the use of performance-based tests like the Rorschach (Exner & Erdberg, 2005).

The self-report assessment of psychosis is challenging and elevations on the PAI SCZ scale may have one of several meanings. Here a review of the SCZ subscales and even item endorsement is critical. Schizophrenia-Psychotic Experiences (SCZ-P) is composed of items assessing frank psychotic symptoms, and elevations of SCZ-P provide a good indication of current psychosis. In fact, we routinely follow up SCZ-P scores at T > 65 with the Rorschach given its strong association to psychosis. We also consider the Paranoia Persecution (PAR-P) subscale to be strongly related to psychosis and to require additional follow-up when elevated. In contrast, there are a number of reasons, aside from psychosis, that inpatients will elevate measures of Social Detachment (SCZ-S) and Thought Disorder (SCZ-T). SCZ-T taps confusion, poor concentration, and inefficient thinking. Patients with severe depression, anxiety, or neurocognitive disorders such as ADHD often experience significant disruptions in their ability to concentrate and organize their thoughts, leading to elevations on SCZ-T. Likewise, SCZ-S taps social indifference, isolation, and withdrawal. Chronic or persistent mental illness in the absence of psychosis often results in significant social poverty. SCZ elevations resulting solely from elevations in SCZ-S or SCZ-T should be further clarified. In many cases, elevations in these scales will be the result of factors other than psychosis. Nonetheless, if diagnostic clarification cannot be made based upon the available clinical data, further assessment, possibly including a Rorschach or other performance based instruments, may be needed to rule out or rule in a psychotic process.

Risk Assessment

Referrals for assessing a patient's risk for self-harm and suicide are among the most common in inpatient settings, and the majority of inpatients have some risk for either suicide or other self-harm behavior. As can be seen in Table 3.1, the average score for Suicidal Ideation (SUI) is near the clinical range in our sample. In considering a patient's level of risk for self-harm it is important to assess both the immediacy and nature of the risk. Immediacy refers to a patient's risk for engaging in self-harm immediately while on the unit. Patients with high distress (MCE), few resources or supports (Non-Support [NON]), cognitive limitations or distorted thought (SCZ-T), and overt plans or thoughts about suicide (SUI) are at immediate risk. The nature of the patients' risk refers to how aware the patients are that they are at risk, as well as the frequency and intensity of their thoughts regarding self-harm. Some patients are more explicitly suicidal (i.e., having frequent thoughts about suicide and considering it as an option) while others are more implicitly at risk (i.e., prone toward impulsive acts or sudden self-harmful or risky behaviors). Assessing these risk factors early in an admission is critical for inpatient care.

In evaluating the immediacy and nature of a patient's risk, we first consider a patient's score on SUI. SUI is composed of items that tap a wide range of issues related to suicide including past behaviors, current thoughts about death, and specific current consideration of suicide at this time. In the case of a SUI elevation, we encourage clinicians to conduct an item-by-item assessment of responses to SUI items. Item 340 is particularly important, as it refers directly to patients' immediate consideration of suicide and should always be evaluated at the item-level regardless of SUI scores. We often find that openly discussing patients' scores on SUI helps to clarify the immediacy of the risk and often evolves into a conversation on the factors that contribute to the patients' suicidal feelings and safety. SUI scores >85T begin to suggest a level of preoccupation with suicide and are associated with more immediate risk. Such patients require close staff observation and specific safety plans (Morey, 1996).

In addition to SUI, the PAI includes the Suicide Potential Index (SPI). The SPI focuses on factors from prior research (e.g., Bongar, 1991) that increase risk for acting on suicidal impulses. Of note, it *does not* include items directly tapping suicidal behavior or intent. Instead, it taps a wide range of traits and factors associated with elevated risk such as acute interpersonal problems, hopelessness, and poor impulse control. A simplified way of considering the two scales is that SUI taps into explicit thoughts and intentions related to suicide and SPI taps personality and situational risk factors associated with acting on suicidal impulses. These indicators are incrementally predictive of suicidal behavior among inpatients (Hopwood, Baker, & Morey, 2007), suggesting their conjunctive use. Elevations in both SUI and SPI indicate a situation where the patient is both preoccupied with thoughts of death or suicide and has multiple risk factors associated with impulsive self-harming actions. Typically, these patients are at the highest risk level and precautions are taken to ensure their safety on the unit (e.g., 10-minute checks, placed in the ICU, increased staff contact, restrictions on items the patient can have).

Significant elevations on SUI without elevations for SPI are common and indicate that the patient is acutely aware of being suicidal or having thoughts about suicide, while not possessing traits or factors that may place them at long-term risk. This pattern of results *does not mean that the patient is not at heightened risk at the time of the evaluation*. Clinicians are often able to engage such patients directly regarding their suicidal ideation. In fact, patients with elevations on SUI without elevations on the SPI are often experiencing severe distress from their baseline that has resulted in an acute episode of suicidal ideation. These episodes should always be treated as quite important and clinical interventions should focus on reducing risk and immediate distress. Significant elevations of SPI without elevations in SUI can indicate that the patient is at risk for impulsive self-harming behavior despite a lack of acute suicidal ideation. Clinicians often have to skillfully engage with such patients in identifying triggers that activate sudden distress or situational elements that contribute to episodes of risky or self-harming behaviors.

While SUI and SPI scores represent the logical starting points for the assessment of risk for self-harm, information from the scales that compose the SPI can clarify potentially relevant risk factors. For example, when SPI or SUI elevations are accompanied by significant scale elevations for clinical syndromes associated with poor impulse control and difficulty anticipating consequences, the immediacy of the risk is heightened (e.g., Mania [MAN], Borderline Features [BOR]). Similarly, elevations in subscales associated with difficulty thinking clearly (e.g., Depression-Cognitive [DEP-C], Anxiety-Cognitive [ANX-C], SCZ-T) can reflect a limited capacity for problem solving that can increase risk. This is particularly true in the context of poor performance on tests of cognitive function. Patients with elevations on BOR can be at most risk for self-harming behaviors on the unit in situations where they are extremely angry or upset with staff, particularly if the elevation is driven by the Borderline Features-Self-Harm (BOR-S) subscale. Such patients may also utilize self-harming behaviors as a form of interpersonal manipulation. In all cases, when suicide risk is being gauged, it is important to share hypotheses generated from the assessment with inpatient staff and individually with the patient to determine how best to understand and act on the information.

Because patients at risk for violence may pose a danger to other patients on the unit and to staff, this represents another critical assessment domain in inpatient psychiatry. Though aggressive and violent patients are less common on medical-psychiatric inpatient units (as compared with other types of inpatient units), the assessment of such risk is still important. The PAI contains an Aggression scale (AGG) and Violence Potential Index (VPI) to aid in the assessment of potential violence. AGG is composed of items tapping the ease with which an individual becomes angry, difficulties in expressing anger, tendency to express anger verbally, and history of physical violence. Elevations of AGG >70T indicate an individual who is quick to experience anger and likely to express anger or hostility in poorly controlled ways.

When patients elevate AGG into the clinical range, the AGG subscales should be considered to better determine the manner in which aggression is typically expressed (Morey, 1996). AGG is composed of three separate subscales designed to tap Aggressive Attitude (AGG-A), Verbal Aggression (AGG-V), and Physical Aggression (AGG-P). The latter scale is particularly important as it assesses a patient's history for being physically aggressive as an adult (Hopwood, Baker, & Morey, 2007). Collateral information regarding a patient's history of violence as well as information regarding his or her legal history should always be collected for patients that elevate AGG-P. Further, elevations in AGG-P accompanied by elevations on ANT are particularly dangerous, as this pattern tends to suggest a propensity for being violent in conjunction with little care or regard for others. Such patients may be particularly dangerous to other patients as well as staff. Higher scores on AGG-P in conjunction with higher scores on Dominance (DOM) may suggest that patients are more willing to use violence or intimidation to get what they want from others. These patients can be particularly dangerous to staff when in situations where staff refuses to comply with their wishes. Elevations in AGG-P in conjunction with elevations to scales associated with problems with impulsiveness (MAN; BOR) or rapid shifts in mood (Borderline Features-Affect Instability [BOR-A]) can suggest patients who may become violent quite suddenly. Elevations to AGG-P in conjunction with problems thinking clearly (e.g., SCZ-T, poor cognitive test results) can indicate a patient who may have trouble inhibiting violent behavior when upset or frustrated. Such elevations are also notable, as difficulties in thinking may result in an increased number of situations that are likely to be experienced as frustrating by the patient.

Elevations to AGG-V are associated with a willingness to express anger verbally. Patients that score particularly high on this scale are prone to get into verbal conflicts with other patients and with staff. When elevations of AGG-V are accompanied by elevations on VPI or AGG-P, there is increased risk that verbal altercations will become violent. In addition, patients who score high on AGG-V may sometimes interact with other patients in a manner that provokes a violent encounter. As stated previously, elevations to VPI, AGG, AGG-V, or AGG-P should always trigger the clinician to seek further information pertaining to the patient's history of violence, legal history, and history on past units.

The VPI was developed to assist AGG in indicating violence potential based on factors historically associated with violence assessments, such as hostility, suspiciousness, social isolation, and agitation (McNiel & Binder, 1994; Shaffer, Waters, & Adams, 1994). Similar to the relationship of SPI to SUI, the VPI is calculated independent of AGG to so that it may complement AGG scores in the assessment of violence. VPI scores > 70T suggest that a patient is at risk for aggression while scores > 84T suggest that the likelihood for violent behavior should be closely examined. This is particularly true if elevations on the VPI are accompanied by elevations in AGG.

Treatment Planning

While a complete review of the use of the PAI in planning treatments is impossible within the scope of one chapter (see Morey, 1996; Morey & Hopwood, 2007), we will highlight some interpretive considerations that we regard as essential for inpatient assessment. For example, group treatments are often an important element of an inpatient stay. Groups on inpatient units vary with regard to their degree of structure and the extent of required patient participation. Many inpatient units will utilize multiple types of groups that range from highly structured to unstructured approaches. On our unit we have four general types of groups (presented here from the most structured to the least): activity based, psycho-educational (low patient involvement), psycho-educational (high patient involvement), and process groups. Not all patients are appropriate or will benefit from all types of groups, though we often find that as patients' distress level decreases they are better able to engage in a range of different groups.

The PAI contains a number of scales related to interpersonal functioning that, in combination with distress scales, can be useful in determining what patients are appropriate for what groups. Patients experiencing distress in realms that will likely limit their ability to interact with others or follow instructions (e.g., SCZ; MAN; PAR) are typically restricted to activity based groups. Patients who score low on both DOM and Warmth (WRM) and high on scales of social isolation (SCZ-S;

NON; Anxiety Related Disorders-Phobias [ARD-P]) are often better suited to more structured groups and groups that require minimal participation. Patients who score very high on DOM may not always be appropriate for process groups, particularly if such elevations are accompanied by elevations in PAR, BOR, Borderline Features-Negative Relationships (BOR-N), ANT, AGG, or Treatment Rejection (RXR). Patients who score from 45T to 65T for DOM and Warmth (WRM) and have low scores on RXR are typically easily integrated into process groups and psycho-educational groups requiring high levels of patient participation.

Integration with social networks outside of the hospital is another important element of inpatient care and disposition. These matters are usually facilitated by social work staff. Although most patients will require the assistance of a social worker while on the unit, there are some PAI profile patterns that are particularly indicative of the need for social work intervention early in the hospitalization. For example, high scores on the Stress (STR) scale suggest an unstable external environment and in many cases may indicate significant life changes, disruptions in social networks, problematic occupational functioning, or loss of social support. The latter is especially likely when STR elevations are accompanied by elevations on either NON or BOR-N. In such cases, a family meeting or couples session may be in order to provide information to the family or spouse and to discuss the patient's current situation and need for support. Patients who are very low on DOM or very socially withdrawn (SCZ-S or low WRM) may need additional assistance from staff to aid them in communicating meaningfully with those they are close to.

The extent to which patients can engage openly and honestly with staff is an important prognostic indicator that can be indicated by the PAI. As stated previously, in considering PAI responses it is useful to consider self-report test results as a form of structured communication between patient and staff. At times, patients' responses may be markedly different from their presentation or clinical history. While this may indicate intentional distortion (discussed previously), it can also represent a genuine lack of insight. Developing treatment alliances with such patients is difficult. There is strong evidence that alliance between treatment team and patient is an important variable in effective inpatient treatment (Blais, 2004).

It can also be difficult to establish an alliance with some patients due to their disinterest in treatment or beliefs that treatment will not benefit them. Elevations on RXR and the PAI Treatment Process Index (TPI) are excellent starting points for identifying patients who may have a difficulty establishing an alliance. As can be seen in Table 3.1, the mean score for RXR is a 38T, and scores > 50T, the community average, are uncommon, suggesting that the majority of the patients appreciate their need for support and treatment. When patients score significantly higher than expected on RXR, efforts to increase insight and treatment motivation are paramount. Unfortunately, although low scores on RXR suggest that patients are aware of their need for treatment at this time, they do not necessarily indicate that the course of treatment will be smooth. We have found elevations on the TPI to be a good assessment of a potentially difficult treatment process.

In considering therapeutic alliance, we tend to conceptualize high scores on RXR as patients expressing explicit desires *not* to be in treatment, explicit beliefs that they do not require support, or explicit beliefs that their difficulties relate more strongly to others or their situation than factors that they, themselves, can or should change. Surprisingly, it is often easy to work with patients scoring moderately high on RXR because both the clinician and the patient are aware of how the patient feels about treatment. In fact, we typically find that it is most difficult for staff to form alliances with patients scoring low on RXR (i.e., expressing an explicit desire for treatment), but high on TPI. First, this pattern suggests a great deal of clinical severity, since RXR is strongly negatively correlated with the clinical scales and the TPI is strongly positively related with these scales. In addition, such patients may be particularly at risk for pseudo-compliance, help-rejecting behaviors, and in some cases a tendency to believe that staff members are not helping them enough.

Patients scoring high on PAR or low on WRM may also have a difficult time establishing a treatment alliance due to difficulties with trust and fears that the unit staff do not have their best interests at heart. Profiles in which elevations on PAR are complemented by elevations on RXR typically reflect these difficulties. In contrast, elevations on PAR accompanied by low scores for RXR are complicated cases. In such cases, explicitly discussing the patients' suspicion and lack of trust, as well as past events that have contributed to their sense that they cannot trust others or that others will harm them, can often help avoid an interpersonal treatment crisis.

Communication of Results

PAI results are communicated in four related ways. First, immediately following the scoring of the PAI, a single sheet is placed in the patient's chart that indicates if the PAI was completed in a valid manner (if invalid, the reason the profile was deemed invalid is indicated), and provides t-score results for the PAI clinical scales as well as for SUI and AGG. A closing statement indicates that a formal report will follow. This one-sheet results form is intended to rapidly document the PAI results.

The examiner then verbally reviews the results with the patient's treatment team, particularly including the psychiatric resident and attending psychiatrist making the referral. Data are discussed in light of the patient's presentation on the unit, history, and current complaints. Initial data pertaining to referral questions are also discussed. To maximize the impact of the assessment it is also best if the examiner meets individually with the patient to review the results verbally. Again, we strongly advocate a collaborative approach in which the PAI results are discussed in hypothetical terms and the patient and the examiner work to better understand how they relate to the patient's current situation and current hospitalization. Such conversations can be particularly useful for better understanding data for scales that tap constructs in a more general manner. The SOM-Health Concerns, ARD-Traumatic Stress, and ARD-Phobias subscales are all examples of such scales and examiner inquiry with the patient is essential for optimal interpretation of elevations on these scales.

After discussion with the treatment team and review with the patient, a report integrating data from a cognitive screening and the PAI (as well as other tests as indicated) is generated. Inpatient reports are limited in scope and tend to be no longer than two pages. A brief history describing the patient's reason for admission, recent difficulties, demographic data, key historical data (e.g., suicide attempts, past hospitalizations), and the reason for referral is reviewed. PAI results are organized in the order of validity data, referral question and risk issues, psychiatric distress and diagnostic hypotheses, self-image, interpersonal style, and treatment considerations. The first paragraph reviews the PAI validity scales and indices and indicates whether the profile is likely to be valid, invalid, or should be interpreted with specific cautions in mind. The next paragraph begins with a general profile assessment indicating distress level, and when appropriate, the risk for multiple diagnoses or self- or other-harm. Regarding risks for harm, elevations in SUI, SPI, AGG, or VPI are always discussed *early in the report* to ensure that treatment providers are aware of these data and consider all additional data in light of these findings. Next, data pertaining to the referral question are reviewed. Typically, referral questions are related to specific areas of psychiatric difficulty, diagnostic questions, or the potential role of problematic personality features. It is then easy to transition to a more general review of implications arising from the PAI clinical scales and subscales. Typically, clinical scales are reported in order of the internalizing distress scales (SOM, ANX, ARD, DEP), the severe distress scales (MAN, SCZ, PAR), and the PD cluster scales (ANT, BOR). The next paragraph reviews data pertaining to the patient's self-image, interpersonal style, access to social support, and level of stress. Finally, in this section, treatment considerations are discussed using data from RXR, TPI, and the PAI clinical scales (e.g., BOR, ANT, DRG, ALC). When appropriate, data pertaining to risk is discussed in greater detail in this section. A brief summary of the results is discussed, focusing on the referral question, level of risk, and then data pertaining to the patient's treatment on the unit.

Recommendations in the report are always made using all available sources of data, including the PAI. Recommendations are presented regarding immediate treatment issues (e.g., the need for 10-minute checks, considerations for treatment options, themes for psychotherapy), disposition considerations (e.g., the need for partial hospitalization post-hospitalization, potential benefits of substance abuse treatment), and recommendations for treatment beyond the unit (e.g., group therapy, suggestions of adjunctive treatments).

CLINICAL EXAMPLES

In an effort to illustrate some of the suggestions described above, we have included two case examples of patients who completed the PAI as part of their treatment on the inpatient unit.

Patient 1

The first patient was a 60-year-old divorced female with more than 20 years of education who was admitted for depression with suicidal ideation in the context of medical hypertension, diabetes, recent cardiac issues, and worsening depression. She produced a valid PAI with the following clinically significant *t*-scores: NIM 66, PIM 36, SOM 74, ANX 71, ARD 66, DEP 93, SCZ 63, BOR 63, SUI 91, STR 77, NON 75, RXR 31, DOM 47, and WRM 46. All other scores were between a T of 55 and 40. Her profile indicated significant elevations on the internalizing distress scales, as well as a marked elevation on SUI. She was placed in the unit's ICU on suicide precautions. Further clinical inquiry focused on her high level of depression revealed that she had become increasingly anxious regarding her medical condition. Specifically, she was worried that she would be unable to engage in her typical daily life activities (she had recently decided to stop working at a quite stressful job as a result of her cardiac health). Given that her work represented an important part of her life, she was also experiencing acute negative changes in her self-image associated with role loss and her inability to work. This had led her to become increasingly anxious about her future and she feared that others would view her as weak. Though she had tended to be socially active in the past, she had recently become socially withdrawn. She attributed this in part to her concern that others wouldn't want to hear about her medical issues and concerns and that she would become a burden to others.

Despite the severity of her symptoms and level of suicidal ideation, her profile contained clinical elevations in only one cluster suggesting a rather straightforward and focused hospitalization. Treatment goals focused on reducing her level of depression, improving associated conditions (she was experiencing major disruptions to her sleep and energy level), improving her self-image, and increasing her access to support. After a consult for ECT, the treatment team decided to start her on antidepressant medication and to provide her with individual psychotherapy. Data from the PAI were used to inform therapy and suggested that her negative self-image was one factor strongly contributing to her depression. As such, therapeutic interventions focused on increasing her activity level (which could be assessed by MAN-A), reconnecting her with social support (assessed by NON and WRM), and actively attempting to improve her immediate self-image (as assessed by MAN-G). In addition, she also attended process groups and psycho-educational groups focused on depression to give her opportunities to discuss her situation with peers. With the patient's consent, friends and family were also involved in her treatment. A family meeting clarified the ways in which her social support network was available for support and reminded her of the many ways she had helped others who were close to her in the past. Finally, she had a consult from cardiology to help clarify her expectations regarding her cardiac condition and potential treatment options. She was hospitalized for a total of 8 days and at the time of discharge was substantially improved. She was discharged to a 2-week day-treatment program to continue to provide her with support and monitor her symptom recovery, and followed up with individual psychotherapy with a Behavioral Medicine program.

Patient 2

The second patient was a 62-year-old single male with multiple prior hospitalizations and a long history of paranoid schizophrenia with fixed delusions about the FBI and beliefs that his mailperson was a demon. He was living independently, with a high level of social support that included visiting nurses and daily interactions with a case manager, and had not been hospitalized for more than 15 years. At baseline, he tended to be inactive and socially isolated, but managed daily tasks (e.g., hygiene, making his own meals, cleaning). He was referred to the inpatient unit by his case manager in the context of failing to thrive at home.

The initial clinical evaluation suggested that he was highly focused on his belief that the mailperson was a demon. However, he did not appear overly agitated, his thinking was largely logical (aside from his delusions), and his behavior was not disorganized. He was noted to possess severely blunted affect, made minimal eye contact, and produced very little spontaneous speech. He answered questions, but rarely elaborated. There were no indications of medication non-compliance prior to admission. Unit staff questioned him closely about his bizarre beliefs and delusions and he answered in an open and straightforward manner. He appeared to be aware that others found these beliefs odd, but showed minimal insight into the possibility that these beliefs were delusional. A brief cognitive screening did not suggest gross cognitive dysfunction. He produced a valid PAI with clinical elevations for SCZ and DEP, and mild elevations for PAR. All three Depression subscales were above a 70T. Active and pervasive thought disorder seemed unlikely, as SCZ-P and PAR-P were not elevated. Elevations on SCZ-T and SCZ-S were mild and marked, respectively, suggesting some confusion and disconnection from others. Follow-up clinical interviews with the patient were consistent with his PAI profile in indicating that he was experiencing frequent feelings of sadness, anhedonia, disinterest in the things that previously interested him (e.g., television, board games), and diminished energy. In discussing these results with his outpatient case manager the treatment team learned that the case manager had become concerned, not due to his delusions (in fact, according to the case manager the patient had maintained these delusions for over 20 years, but had never acted on them) but rather due to the patient's slow decline in self-care over a roughly 4-month period. Together, these data suggested that major depression, rather than his delusions, was likely the primary cause of these self-care problems. As a result, the treatment focus shifted from his psychotic symptoms (which did not appear to be different from what they were at baseline) to his level of depression.

The patient was started on antidepressant medication, received psychotherapy primarily focusing on behavioral activation techniques designed to increase pleasurable activities, and attended group treatment. Given his high level of social isolation and low scores on both WRM and DOM, he primarily attended the highly structured groups. As would be expected, given significant elevations on two of the PAI clusters, he had a longer than average hospitalization of 14 days. At discharge, he continued to report his delusional beliefs in the same tone as he had prior, continued to make minimal eye contact, and continued to evidence a generally limited range of affective display. Nonetheless, he was more active on the unit; he left his room frequently to watch TV and was more verbally interactive with inpatient staff and his outpatient case manager. He also reported that he felt better. He was discharged to a day-treatment program for continued monitoring of his depressive symptoms and to foster his overall level of activity. Of note, at no point was there a change in the patient's belief system regarding the FBI or the mailperson. This is a good example of how the scale independence and resulting discriminant validity of the PAI can be useful for identifying co-morbid conditions that may be more likely to account for a patient's acute change in functioning or distress level despite the fact that they may not be the patient's primary diagnosis.

CONCLUSIONS

In this chapter we have attempted to discuss a number of ways in which the PAI can be used in an inpatient setting. We view self-report tests, such as the PAI, as a means of structured communication between patient and staff. As with all aspects of inpatient assessments, data from the PAI must be integrated with other sources of clinical information and interpretive hypotheses. In addition, we strongly recommend that results from the PAI be shared with the patient in a collaborative manner that allows both the patient and staff to develop hypotheses regarding the patient's current situation, flesh these hypotheses out using more granular data taken from the patient's life and experience, and develop goals for the hospitalization together. Results from the PAI can often aid clinicians in identifying factors that are contributing to the patient's current decline from baseline functioning and in many cases can aid in the assessment of other important factors such as suicide risk, danger risk, case complexity, and substance abuse. As the PAI becomes increasingly utilized in inpatient settings, we anticipate that clinical observations, such as the ones presented in this chapter, will be further refined through empirical research.

REFERENCES

Baity, M., Siefert, C. J., Chambers, A., & Blais, M. A. (2007). Deceptiveness on the PAI: A study of naïve faking with psychiatric inpatients. *Journal of Personality Assessment, 88,* 16–24.

Blais, M. A. (2004). Development of an inpatient treatment alliance scale. *Journal of Nervous and Mental Disease, 192,* 487–493.

Blais, M. A., & Baity, M. R. (2005). A comparison of mental status examinations in an inpatient psychiatric sample. *Assessment 12,* 455–461.

Bongar, B. (1991). *The suicidal patient: Clinical and legal standards of care.* Washington, D.C.: American Psychological Association.

Boone, D. (1998). Internal consistency reliability of the Personality Assessment Inventory with psychiatric inpatients. *Journal of Clinical Psychology, 54,* 839–843.

Braxton, L. E., Calhoun, P. S., Williams, J. E., & Boggs, C. D. (2007). Validity rates of the Personality Assessment Inventory and the Minnesota Multiphasic Personality Inventory-2 in a VA medical center setting. *Journal of Personality Assessment, 88,* 5–15.

Edens, J. F., & Ruiz, M. A. (2008). Identification of mental disorders in an in-patient prison psychiatric unit: Examining the criterion-related validity of the Personality Assessment Inventory. *Psychological Services, 5,* 108–117.

Eisen, S. V., Dickey, B., & Sederer, L. I. (2000). A self-report symptom and problem rating scale to increase inpatients' involvement in treatment. *Psychiatric Services, 51,* 349–353.

Exner, J. E., Jr., & Erdberg, P. (2005). *The Rorschach: A comprehensive system. Vol.2: Advanced Interpretation* (3rd ed.). New York: Wiley.

Finn, S. E. (2007). *In our client's shoes: Theory and techniques of therapeutic assessment.* Mahwah, NJ: Erlbaum.

Giorgia, T. A., Wood, J., Demidenko, N., & Hany, B. (2002). Using the PAI with an eating disordered population: Scale characteristics, factor structure and differences among diagnostic groups. *Journal of Personality Assessment, 79,* 337–356.

Hopwood, C. H., Baker, K. L., & Morey, L. C. (2008). Extra test validity of selected Personality Assessment Inventory scales and indicators in an inpatient substance abuse setting. *Journal of Personality Assessment, 90,* 574–577.

Hopwood, C. J., Morey, L. C., Rogers, R., & Sewell, K. (2007). Malingering on the Personality Assessment Inventory: Identification of specific feigned disorders. *Journal of Personality Assessment, 88,* 43–48.

Hudson, C. G. (2001). Changing patterns of acute psychiatric hospitalization under a public managed care program. *Journal of Sociology and Social Welfare, 28,* 141–176.

Lave, J. R., (2003). Developing a Medicare prospective payment system for inpatient psychiatric care. *Health Affairs, 22,* 97–109.

LePage, J. P., & Mogge, N. L. (2001). Validity rates of the MMPI-2 and PAI in a rural inpatient psychiatric facility. *Assessment, 8,* 67–74.

Marlowe, D. B. & Wetzler, S. (1994). Contributions of discriminant analysis to differential diagnosis by self-report. *Journal of Personality Assessment, 62,* 320–331.

McNiel, D. E., & Binder, R. L. (1994). The relationship between acute psychiatric symptoms, diagnosis, and short-term risk of violence. *Hospital and Community Psychiatry, 45,* 133–137.

Miller, W. R., & Rollnick, S. (2002). *Motivational interviewing: Preparing people to change addictive behaviors* (2nd ed.). New York: Guilford.

Miller, P. R., Dasher, R., Collins, R., Griffiths, P., & Brown, F. (2001). Inpatient diagnostic assessments: 1. Accuracy of structured vs. unstructured interviews. *Psychiatry Research, 105,* 255–264.

Morey, L. C. (1991). The *Personality Assessment Inventory: Professional Manual.* Odessa, FL: Psychological Assessment Resources.

Morey, L. C. (1996). *An interpretive guide to the Personality Assessment Inventory.* Odessa, FL: Psychological Assessment Resources.

Morey, L. C. (1999). *PAI interpretive explorer module manual.* Odessa, FL: Psychological Assessment Resources.

Morey, L. C. (2003). *Essentials of PAI assessment.* Hoboken, NJ: Wiley.

Morey, L. C. (2007). *Personality Assessment Inventory: Professional Manual (2nd ed.).* Odessa, FL: Psychological Assessment Resources.

Morey, L. C., & Henry, W. (1994). Personality Assessment Inventory. In M. E. Mariush (Ed.), *The use of psychological testing for treatment planning and outcome assessment* (pp. 185–216). Hillsdale, NJ: Lawrence Erlbaum.

Morey, L. C., & Hopwood, C. J. (2007). Casebook for the Personality Assessment Inventory: A structural summary approach. Lutz, FL: Psychological Assessment Resources.

Riley, W. T., & Treiber, F. A. (1989). The validity of multidimensional self-report anger and hostility measures. *Journal of Clinical Psychology, 45,* 397–404.

Rogers, R., Sewell, K. W., Morey, L. C., & Ustad, K. L. (1996). Detection of feigned mental disorders on the Personality Assessment Inventory: A discriminant analysis. *Journal of Personality Assessment, 67,* 629–690.

Schinka, J. A. (1995). PAI profiles in alcohol-dependent patients. *Journal of Personality Assessment, 65,* 35–51.

Shaffer, C. E., Waters, W. F., & Adams, S. G. (1994). Dangerousness: Assessing the risk of violent behavior. *Journal of Consulting and Clinical Psychology, 62,* 1064–1068.

Siefert, C. J., Kehl-Fie, K., Blais, M. A., & Chriki, L. (2007). Detecting back irrelevant responding on the Personality Assessment Inventory in a psychiatric inpatient unit. *Psychological Assessment, 19*, 469–473.

Siefert, C. J., Sinclair, S. J., Kehl-Fie, K., A., & Blais, M. A. (in press). An item-level psychometric analysis of the Personality Assessment Inventory clinical scales in a psychiatric inpatient unit. *Assessment.*

Silk, K. R., Eisner, W., Allport, C., & DeMars, C. (1994). Focused time-limited inpatient treatment of borderline personality disorder. *Journal of Personality Disorders, 8,* 268–278.

Sinclair, S. J., Siefert, C. J., Shorey, H., Antonius, D., Shiva, A., Kehl-Fie, K., & Blais, M. A. (in press). A Psychometric Evaluation of the Personality Assessment Inventory—Short Form (PAI-SF) Clinical Scales in an Inpatient Psychiatric Sample. *Psychiatry Research.*

4

Assessment of Adolescents Using the PAI-A

RADHIKA KRISHNAMURTHY

A dolescent psychopathology and emotional and behavioral adjustment are issues of considerable concern within the broader landscape of mental health care in the United States. While the traditional view of adolescence as a period of storm and stress has been debated and reconceptualized in recent decades, there is general acceptance that adolescence is marked by greater emotional difficulty, mood disruptions, and risk-taking behaviors—including substance abuse—than in other developmental periods (Arnett, 1999). Reports indicate that a substantial number of youths are identified as maladjusted and referred to mental health services in a variety of inpatient, outpatient, and residential settings as well as in educational and juvenile correctional settings. For example, The U.S. Department of Health and Human Services' 1999 report indicated that approximately 20% of all children and adolescents are diagnosed with a psychiatric disorder and 10% were found to have an emotional disturbance producing functional impairment (USDHHS, 1999). A more recent report released by the Substance Abuse and Mental Health Services Administration's (SAMHSA) Office of Applied Studies indicates that approximately 4.5 to 6.3 million youths in the United States experience serious emotional disturbances (SAMHSA, 2009). Mental health professionals have the dual challenges of providing effective treatment and doing so in a time-efficient manner, per the demands of treatment efficacy and efficiency in the current mental health care scenario. In this regard, comprehensive personality assessment is an essential tool for accurate diagnosis, problem description, and identification of client strengths and limitations.

Personality assessment of adolescents can be undertaken using self-report personality measures, as adolescents generally have the requisite developmental capacities to provide information on their subjective states and life experiences. Most currently available measures take the form of relatively short rating scales or checklists; examples include the Youth Self-Report/11–18 within the Achenbach

System of Empirically Based Assessment (Achenbach & Rescorla, 2001) and the family of Beck Youth Inventories for Children and Adolescents, 2nd ed. (Beck, Beck, Jolly, & Steer, 2005). Several of these measures are intended for evaluating youths spanning the preadolescent-to-adolescent age range and are therefore not specific to adolescent evaluation. There are relatively fewer broad-band personality assessment measures for adolescents, as gauged from published surveys (e.g., Archer & Newsom, 2000; Archer, Maruish, Imhof, & Piotrowski, 1991; Cashel, 2002) and test publisher catalogs; the best-known and most widely used ones are the Minnesota Multiphasic Personality Inventory-Adolescent (MMPI-A; Butcher et al., 1992), the Millon Clinical Multiaxial Inventory (MACI; Millon, Millon, & Davis, 1993), the Personality Inventory for Youth (PIY; Lachar & Gruber, 1995), and the Adolescent Psychopathology Scale (APS; Reynolds, 1998). The Personality Assessment Inventory-Adolescent (PAI-A; Morey, 2007) is a significant addition to this set of measures that reflects recent advances in test-construction methods and measurement of unique areas of functioning relative to existing measures.

PAI-A DEVELOPMENT AND DESCRIPTION

The PAI-A was developed as an extension of the adult version, the Personality Assessment Inventory (PAI; Morey, 1991) with the goal of retaining the basic structure of the original test while modifying items to make them suitable for assessing adolescents in clinical settings. The original test's development followed a sequential construct validation approach involving theoretical, empirical, and statistical procedures in selecting and developing items and scales, evaluating their psychometric adequacy, and establishing relevant scale correlates. PAI-A development began with an examination of PAI items to determine their applicability to adolescents. This was followed by various steps including rewording a limited number of items, developing a representative clinical adolescent sample for testing the 344-item experimental form, and eliminating 80 items subsequent to statistical evaluations to achieve a shorter final version without compromising internal consistency. The PAI-A was standardized on a national representative sample of 707 adolescents ages 12–18, stratified according to the 2003 U.S. Census for the demographic variables of age, gender, and ethnicity. In addition, a clinical sample of 1,160 adolescents was obtained from 78 clinical sites to serve as a reference point in clinical interpretation. Details of the test development and standardization are described in Morey (2007).

The PAI-A is a 264-item self-report measure intended for adolescents in the 12–18 age range. PAI-A items are written at the 4th-grade reading level and are answered on a 4-point scale ranging from "not at all true" and "slightly true" to "mainly true" and "very true," thus permitting a dimensional assessment of symptoms and experiences. The test manual indicates the test-taking time to be within 45 minutes. Test materials include an item booklet and use of either a hand-score (Form HS-A) or scan-score (Form SS-A) answer sheet for test administration, profile forms, and a critical item form. Computerized scoring and interpretation options are also available from the test publisher, Psychological Assessment Resources, Inc.

PAI-A test items reflect clinical constructs that are considered important for diagnosis of disorders. However, PAI-A scales are not intended to correspond directly to *Diagnostic and Statistical Manual of Mental Disorders*, 4th ed. (DSM-IV; American Psychiatric Association, 1994) categories. The test contains 22 nonoverlapping scales that are organized into 4 Validity scales, 11 Clinical scales, 5 Treatment Consideration scales, and 2 Interpersonal scales, supplemented with a set of 31 subscales reflecting specific clinical- and treatment-related content areas. Although some of the item content of this adolescent version differs from that of the original PAI, the scale and subscale names from the PAI were retained in the PAI-A to achieve overlap between the two versions and promote ease of interpretation. Subsequent analyses demonstrated the two versions to have comparable inter-item correlations, and validity studies showed compatibility between their measured constructs (Morey, 2007). PAI-A scale raw scores are converted to *T* scores that have a mean of 50 and SD of 10.

Validity Scales

The PAI-A incorporates a set of validity scales to determine whether the obtained profiles are suitable for interpretation. Among the four validity scales, Inconsistency (ICN) and Infrequency (INF) are designed to detect inconsistent and careless or random responding, whereas Negative Impression (NIM) and Positive Impression (PIM) enable detection of motivated response distortions in the direction of over-reporting or under-reporting personal flaws and problems.

Clinical Scales

Measurement of the major symptoms and problems encountered in clinical settings is achieved with the 11 clinical scales and their subscales, shown in Table 4.1. The clinical scales cover a range of internalizing symptoms experienced as anxiety, depression, and somatic concerns, problems involving significant disturbances in thinking and behavior, and substance abuse problems. Unique to the PAI-A is the assessment of borderline features with their attendant fluctuations in anger and other mood states, interpersonal relationships, and impulsivity, which are generally not covered in adolescent measures.

Treatment Consideration Scales

The PAI-A is particularly responsive to clinical assessment needs by its inclusion of scales focused on problem areas that present risk of harm to self or others, involves states of crisis, and interfere with treatment progress. Table 4.2 presents these scales.

Interpersonal Scales

The two bipolar scales of Dominance (DOM) and Warmth (WRM) extend the clinical assessment by assessing domains that relate to interpersonal assertion versus passivity and degree of engagement with others. Given the centrality of peer relationships in adolescents' growing sense of self and progression toward mature reciprocal relationships, these are useful areas to assess for determining the adolescent's interpersonal adjustment.

TABLE 4.1 PAI-A Clinical Scales and Subscales

Scale	Subscale
Somatic Complaints (SOM)	Conversion (SOM-C)
	Somatization (SOM-S)
	Health Concerns (SOM-H)
Anxiety (ANX)	Cognitive (ANX-C)
	Affective (ANX-A)
	Physiological (ANX-P)
Anxiety-Related Disorders (ARD)	Obsessive-Compulsive (ARD-O)
	Phobias (ARD-P)
	Traumatic Stress (ARD-T)
Depression (DEP)	Cognitive (DEP-C)
	Affective (DEP-A)
	Physiological (DEP-P)
Mania (MAN)	Activity Level (MAN-A)
	Grandiosity (MAN-G)
	Irritability (MAN-I)
Paranoia (PAR)	Hypervigilance (PAR-H)
	Persecution (PAR-P)
	Resentment (PAR-R)
Schizophrenia (SCZ)	Psychotic Experiences (SCZ-P)
	Social Detachment (SCZ-S)
	Thought Disorder (SCZ-T)
Borderline Features (BOR)	Affective Instability (BOR-A)
	Identity Problems (BOR-I)
	Negative Relationships (BOR-N)
	Self-Harm (BOR-S)
Antisocial Features (ANT)	Antisocial Behaviors (ANT-A)
	Egocentricity (ANT-E)
	Stimulus-Seeking (ANT-S)
Alcohol Problems (ALC)	
Drug Problems (DRG)	

Critical Items

The 17 critical items of the PAI-A are grouped into the 7 categories of Delusions and Hallucinations, Potential for Self-Harm, Potential for Aggression, Substance Abuse, Traumatic Stressors, Potential Malingering/Negative Distortion, and Unreliability, with each containing 2–3 items. These serve to alert the clinician about specific areas that may require follow-up or immediate intervention, particularly if they are endorsed at a high level of intensity (i.e., as "mainly true").

INTERPRETATION

PAI-A interpretation begins with an assessment of profile validity. If the profile is deemed appropriate for interpretation, the test interpreter proceeds to examine the

TABLE 4.2   PAI-A Treatment Consideration
Scales and Subscales

Scale	Subscale
Aggression (AGG)	Aggressive Attitude (AGG-A)
	Verbal Aggression (AGG-V)
	Physical Aggression (AGG-P)
Suicidal Ideation (SUI)	
Stress (STR)	
Nonsupport (NON)	
Treatment Rejection (RXR)	

full-scale and subscale profiles and generating interpretations. In general, T scores <
60 (i.e., within one standard deviation from the mean) are considered average. T scores
$\geq$ 60, reflecting endorsement of the measured construct to a greater degree than is
the norm for adolescents, are considered clinically significant and $T \geq 70$ represents a
striking elevation. Morey (2007) also provides specific cutting scores for identifying
moderate, high, and marked elevations that vary from scale to scale, reflecting the
fact that the clinical significance of a given T-score level differs across scales depending on the distribution of scores in a clinical population. For example, a marked elevation is identified as $T \geq 77$ on the ARD scale, $T \geq 76$ on PAR, and $T \geq 84$ on DEP.

The following case illustration is used to demonstrate PAI-A interpretation in
the course of describing the interpretive process.

"Rob" is a 14-year-old, 8th-grade Caucasian boy who was brought to an outpatient psychological services clinic by his grandmother, who is his legal
custodian, after he had expressed suicidal intentions. His biological father is
unknown to him. Rob lived with his mother in a series of rented apartments
and trailers until the age of 12, when she turned him over to his grandparents' care and left the state to pursue a new life with a man who had lived
with her and Rob for a year. Reports suggest that this man had physically mal-
treated Rob but no charges were filed. Rob began to have behavioral problems
in school in the 8th grade, with numerous suspensions for getting in physical
fights and a near-expulsion for expressing his intention to bring a gun to school,
which also resulted in a 3-day placement in a psychiatric facility. At home, he
is increasingly defiant toward his grandparents, who currently feel incapable
of managing him. They have grounded him indefinitely, which he ignores, and
feel unable to take any other actions. The current referral was precipitated by
Rob's placing a phone call to his mother and telling her he was holding a knife
and planning to cut his wrists. Rob's PAI-A profiles are shown in Figure 4.1
and Figure 4.2. The current evaluation also included a brief intelligence measure that indicated average intelligence.

Interpretation of Profile Validity

As with all self-report measures, PAI-A profile validity is compromised when a large
number of test items are left unanswered or if multiple responses are provided for

Full Scale Profile

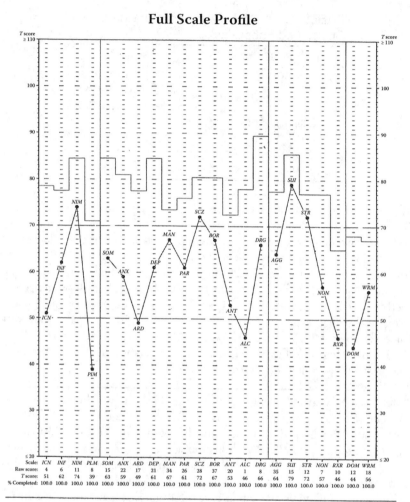

Plotted T scores are based upon a census matched standardization sample of 707 community adolescents 12 to 18 years of age.
■ indicates that the score is more than two standard deviations above the mean for a sample of 1,160 clinical patients.
◆ indicates that the scale has 20% or more missing items.

Figure 4.1   PAI-A Full Scale Profile. Reproduced by special permission of the publisher, Psychological Assessment Resources, Inc., Lutz, Florida from the Personality Assessment-Adolescent Version Software Portfolio (PAI-ASP) by Leslie C. Morey, Ph.D. and PAR Staff, Copyright 1990, 1991, 1993, 1995, 1998, 2000, 2005, 2007 by PAR, Inc.

an item. Morey (2007) suggests that at least 95% of PAI-A items should be answered to obtain valid results, thus requiring that fewer than 14 items are omitted. Rob's profile has no omissions, indicated in the Figure 4.1 profile as a 100% completion rate for all scales, raising no problems in this initial step of validity assessment.

A second issue concerns inconsistency of responding, which can occur when an adolescent is unmotivated to concentrate and give his or her best effort, resulting in careless responding or failing to follow test instructions, or when the adolescent is confused or has reading difficulty. The examiner can take a number of actions to avert such causes of profile invalidity. An important first step is to establish rapport

Subscale Profile

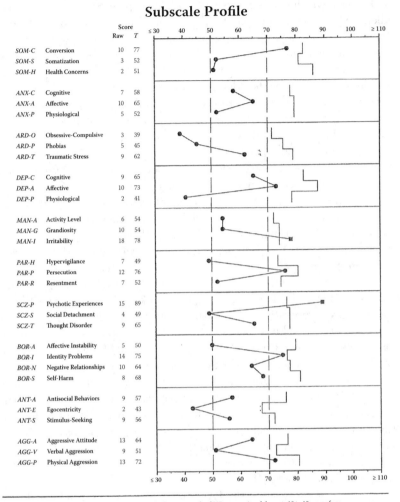

Scale		Raw	T
SOM-C	Conversion	10	77
SOM-S	Somatization	3	52
SOM-H	Health Concerns	2	51
ANX-C	Cognitive	7	58
ANX-A	Affective	10	65
ANX-P	Physiological	5	52
ARD-O	Obsessive-Compulsive	3	39
ARD-P	Phobias	5	45
ARD-T	Traumatic Stress	9	62
DEP-C	Cognitive	9	65
DEP-A	Affective	10	73
DEP-P	Physiological	2	41
MAN-A	Activity Level	6	54
MAN-G	Grandiosity	10	54
MAN-I	Irritability	18	78
PAR-H	Hypervigilance	7	49
PAR-P	Persecution	12	76
PAR-R	Resentment	7	52
SCZ-P	Psychotic Experiences	15	89
SCZ-S	Social Detachment	4	49
SCZ-T	Thought Disorder	9	65
BOR-A	Affective Instability	5	50
BOR-I	Identity Problems	14	75
BOR-N	Negative Relationships	10	64
BOR-S	Self-Harm	8	68
ANT-A	Antisocial Behaviors	9	57
ANT-E	Egocentricity	2	43
ANT-S	Stimulus-Seeking	9	56
AGG-A	Aggressive Attitude	13	64
AGG-V	Verbal Aggression	9	51
AGG-P	Physical Aggression	13	72

Plotted *T* scores are based upon a census matched standardization sample of 707 community adolescents 12 to 18 years of age.
■ indicates that the score is more than two standard deviations above the mean for a sample of 1,160 clinical patients.
◆ indicates that the scale has 20% or more missing items.

Figure 4.2   PAI-A Subscale Profile. Reproduced by special permission of the publisher, Psychological Assessment Resources, Inc., Lutz, Florida from the Personality Assessment-Adolescent Version Software Portfolio (PAI-ASP) by Leslie C. Morey, Ph.D. and PAR Staff, Copyright 1990, 1991, 1993, 1995, 1998, 2000, 2005, 2007 by PAR, Inc..

with the adolescent, clearly explain the purpose of the evaluation, and solicit his or her active participation in the process. Rapport building with adolescents requires bearing in mind that they are typically brought to the evaluation by an adult rather than seeking it on their own and recognizing any attendant feelings of powerlessness, resentment, or confusion. Furthermore, because minors cannot be assured full confidentiality, the examiner would need to inform them upfront that the results would be discussed with their legal guardians. The examiner should also be attuned to the fact that adolescents may view a paper-and-pencil measure as a school-like test, which may activate concerns about "poor performance" (Smith & Handler, 2007). Overall, an honest, empathic, and non-authoritarian stance is a key ingredient of developing a working alliance and obtaining a productive testing session. Additionally, use of a therapeutic assessment method (Finn, 1996b) goes a long way in ensuring motivated participation in the testing process as it conveys interest in and respect for the adolescent's personal goals and establishes a non-coercive tone. An illustration of this approach with adolescents is presented in Archer and Krishnamurthy (2002). In addressing other potential sources of inconsistent responding, a mental status examination may be used to rule out confusional states and a reading subtest from an achievement test could be administrated if the adolescent is suspected to have below 4th-grade reading level or significant difficulties with reading comprehension, or if he or she has been diagnosed with a reading disorder. Alternatively, when reading difficulties are suspected to be mild at most, the examiner can instruct the adolescent to read and respond to the first few items out loud to ensure that he or she comprehends the material.

In evaluating Rob, the purpose of the testing was explained as a means to get his own perspective on what troubles him so that the understanding is not based solely on reports from parental figures and teachers, and to get a sense of his ways of thinking, feeling, and acting that work or do not work well for him. The examiner's collaborative endeavor in obtaining specific questions from Rob for the assessment to address resulted in two initial responses that he presented as statements: "I guess my grandparents want to get rid of me too, they're all fed up" and "I get crazy mad." With the examiner's assistance, the first statement was phrased as two inquiries, "Am I too difficult to handle?" and "Am I capable of being loved?" whereas the second statement was framed as, "Why do I get so upset and angry and how do I deal with it?" Rob had no reported reading difficulties, no special-education placement, his school grades were largely Bs and Cs, and he was therefore considered capable of taking the PAI-A. As an additional check, he was asked to read the test instructions aloud and demonstrated no difficulty with reading and comprehending them.

Inconsistent responding on the PAI-A is detected with the ICN scale that is organized as 10 item pairs. Items within each pair contain related content and are therefore expected to be answered in a consistent direction. T scores < 69 reflect consistent responding, T scores in the 69–77 range reflect moderate inconsistency warranting caution in proceeding with profile interpretation, and the results are best treated as invalid when T scores are ≥ 78 (Morey, 2007). Rob's ICN score of 51 indicates there are no problems of inconsistent responding.

The seven-item INF scale is used to identify atypical responding arising from the endorsement of items that were endorsed at a very low frequency by both clinical and nonclinical samples. The PAI-A manual (Morey, 2007) indicates a mean raw score of 3.23 (SD = 2.29) for the community sample, roughly corresponding to a T score of 50. For the PAI-A clinical reference sample, the mean INF raw score was 4.17 (SD = 2.80; Morey, 2007). T scores in the 66–78 range reflect idiosyncratic responses, and ≥ 79 are likely to indicate invalid results. For Rob, the INF T score of 62 is within the acceptable range and permits progression to examining issues of response style.

Another potential source of profile distortion comes from conscious efforts to present oneself as disturbed by over-reporting psychopathology or as well adjusted by underreporting psychopathology. The PAI-A NIM scale identifies response style efforts to present an overly unfavorable impression. Over-reporting problems may occur in scenarios where the adolescent fails to take the test seriously and decides to exaggerate as a joke, or when he or she is highly distressed, overwhelmed, and "crying for help." Consideration should also be given to any secondary gains that may be derived from malingering disorder (e.g., removal from a conflicted home situation). NIM T scores in the 77–84 range warrant caution and indicate marked distortion to an invalidating degree when ≥ 85. The PIM scale identifies an overly favorable self-presentation that may be motivated by concerns about being judged or by characteristic self-defensiveness. PIM T scores in the 65–71 range warrant caution, whereas scores ≥ 72 suggest the interpretation should be discontinued. Rob's NIM T score of 74, while greater than 2 standard deviations from the mean, is within the acceptable range for profile validity determination; the examiner should make a note, however, of his leaning in the direction of overstating personal problems and take it into consideration when examining profile elevations. His low PIM T score of 39 indicates no problem of exaggerated positive self-presentation. Overall, his test results are relatively free from distorting influences and are suitable for clinical interpretation.

Clinical Interpretation

PAI-A clinical, treatment consideration, and interpersonal scale T scores center around a mean score of 50 as reported by Morey (2007) for the PAI-A community standardization sample, and confirmed in data provided by Fernando and Krishnamurthy (2006) and Krishnamurthy, McCollough, and Goodwin (2006) for college freshman and high school samples, respectively. As might be expected, T scores are higher for adolescents evaluated in clinical or forensic settings. For example, Sears and Krishnamurthy (2001) reported that the five most elevated scales (T ≥ 60) in their sample of adolescent boys and girls obtained from outpatient and residential treatment centers were DRG, DEP, SOM, SUI, and BOR, respectively. Bloomfield and Krishnamurthy (2002) found several elevations for an adolescent male sample in residential substance abuse treatment. The five most elevated (T ≥ 60) clinical scales, excluding ALC and DRG, that were extreme elevations at T > 80, were PAR, ANT, SOM, SCZ, and MAN, respectively. Among the treatment consideration scales, STR was most elevated, followed by SUI and NON. Cashel, Schember, Goodman, and Reed (2006) reported the highest mean clinical scale elevation for their sample of incarcerated adolescent girls as DRG followed by ARD, with AGG as the highest scale among the treatment consideration scales. Table 4.3 and Table 4.4 present reference data from these three samples to facilitate clinical interpretation. Comparison of the sets of scores suggests differences based on gender and setting, in terms of notably higher scores for boys in the Bloomfield and Krishnamurthy (2002) treatment sample than for the girls in the Cashel et al. (2006) correctional sample. The mixed gender treatment sample from Sears and Krishnamurthy generally shows mean scores that lie in between the other two sets of scores. Interpretation is also facilitated by the fact that, similar

TABLE 4.3 PAI-A Scale Means and Standard Deviations From Clinical and Correctional Samples

	Clinical		Correctional
PAI-A Scale	Sears & Krishnamurthy (2001)[a]	Bloomfield & Krishnamurthy (2002)[b]	Cashel et al. (2006)[c]
Somatic Complaints (SOM)	62.90 (16.11)	67.14 (17.71)	56.27 (14.53)
Anxiety (ANX)	59.65 (12.37)	61.76 (10.44)	53.70 (12.09)
Anxiety-Related Disorders (ARD)	59.88 (11.09)	64.68 (11.79)	59.53 (12.40)
Depression (DEP)	63.25 (13.31)	63.52 (10.60)	56.72 (14.14)
Mania (MAN)	60.05 (11.54)	66.74 (11.90)	51.03 (10.81)
Paranoia (PAR)	60.57 (9.53)	69.96 (9.13)	54.75 (11.11)
Schizophrenia (SCZ)	60.38 (13.00)	66.58 (12.46)	53.17 (14.46)
Borderline Features (BOR)	61.56 (10.24)	64.04 (9.38)	57.63 (12.34)
Antisocial Features (ANT)	57.93 (8.97)	68.98 (9.65)	53.10 (9.73)
Alcohol Problems (ALC)	57.89 (17.32)	85.66 (20.33)	51.09 (13.61)
Drug Problems (DRG)	65.22 (16.35)	93.96 (20.89)	68.89 (19.77)
Aggression (AGG)	60.80 (9.24)	59.88 (7.10)	57.53 (11.49)
Suicidal Ideation (SUI)	61.44 (15.07)	61.66 (17.73)	53.19 (13.25)
Stress (STR)	57.02 (12.19)	65.92 (11.00)	50.72 (10.03)
Nonsupport (NON)	56.96 (11.11)	61.06 (11.13)	50.51 (11.31)
Treatment Rejection (RXR)	37.11 (10.60)	48.30 (8.69)	41.96 (10.83)

[a] N = 47, mixed sample of adolescent boys and girls from outpatient and residential treatment programs.
[b] N = 50, adolescent boys, residential substance abuse treatment program.
[c] N = 108, adolescent girls, maximum security correctional facility.

to the method used in the original PAI, Morey (2007) has provided a "skyline" on the PAI-A full scale and subscale profile sheets denoting the level of 2 SDs above the mean for the representative clinical sample. This enables comparison of the particular adolescent's scores to those of a clinical sample and serves to alert the test interpreter to areas of heightened clinical importance, that is, those where the scores equal or exceed the skyline.

Following the convention in adolescent assessment of categorizing adolescents' psychological disturbances as primarily internalizing or externalizing in nature, the test interpreter may choose to examine PAI-A scales in meaningful groupings: (a) a primarily internalizing grouping involving somatoform (SOM), anxious/tense (ANX), fearful (ARD), or dysphoric/hopeless (DEP) manifestations. The treatment consideration scales of SUI and STR may also be inspected within this grouping, and critical item sets related to Potential for Self-Harm and Traumatic Stressors should be examined. (b) A primarily externalizing grouping manifested as overactive, impulsive and irritable (MAN), conduct disordered and interpersonally exploitative (ANT), or as having alcohol- and drug-related problems (ALC, DRG), supplemented with examination of the AGG treatment consideration scale. Critical item sets related to Potential for Aggression and Substance Abuse would also be relevant in this grouping. (c) A primarily thought-disordered grouping manifested as suspicious/paranoid (PAR) or confused/psychotic (SCZ) symptoms,

TABLE 4.4   PAI-A Subscale Means and Standard Deviations From Clinical and Correctional Samples

PAI-A Subscale	Clinical		Correctional
	Sears & Krishnamurthy (2001)[a]	Bloomfield & Krishnamurthy (2002)[b]	Cashel et al. (2006)[c]
Conversion (SOM-C)	61.47 (14.22)	59.08 (14.63)	53.25 (13.05)
Somatization (SOM-S)	58.23 (13.88)	66.64 (15.80)	55.69 (13.99)
Health Concerns (SOM-H)	62.81 (17.00)	66.76 (17.70)	56.01 (15.27)
Cognitive (ANX-C)	59.19 (13.03)	62.16 (11.52)	51.99 (11.96)
Affective (ANX-A)	57.64 (11.81	59.42 (10.26)	50.85 (10.21)
Physiological (ANX-P)	60.28 (13.37)	58.92 (12.18)	57.40 (13.98)
Obsessive-Compulsive (ARD-O)	54.54 (9.98)	59.98 (9.26)	52.72 (8.71)
Phobias (ARD-P)	55.96 (11.82)	55.02 (11.91)	57.59 (13.79)
Traumatic Stress (ARD-T)	59.43 (12.27)	63.34 (12.00)	58.88 (14.33)
Cognitive (DEP-C)	59.47 (13.79)	61.94 (13.30)	54.58 (13.35)
Affective (DEP-A)	62.02 (13.27)	66.20 (10.35)	57.20 (14.21)
Physiological (DEP-P)	60.31 (15.11)	57.08 (10.44)	55.08 (12.43)
Activity Level (MAN-A)	56.70 (12.52)	64.74 (10.85)	46.75 (10.38)
Grandiosity (MAN-G)	55.67 (12.09)	61.10 (11.97)	52.55 (11.03)
Irritability (MAN-I)	58.62 (11.36)	62.78 (10.69)	51.70 (11.66)
Hypervigilance (PAR-H)	54.00 (9.85)	64.28 (9.62)	53.96 (10.34)
Persecution (PAR-P)	65.14 (10.76)	68.86 (11.40)	54.26 (12.69)
Resentment (PAR-R)	56.00 (10.74)	63.64 (11.37)	52.46 (12.57)
Psychotic Experiences (SCZ-P)	57.59 (12.33)	60.52 (13.39)	47.06 (13.13)
Social Detachment (SCZ-S)	58.44 (12.92)	63.36 (11.95)	55.45 (11.65)
Thought Disorder (SCZ-T)	56.79 (13.69)	62.84 (13.02)	52.44 (13.61)
Affective Instability (BOR-A)	61.89 (12.08)	61.88 (10.79)	55.25 (12.17)
Identity Problems (BOR-I)	58.31 (10.95)	57.14 (10.17)	54.65 (11.39)
Negative Relationships (BOR-N)	58.93 (10.15)	62.50 (8.14)	57.55 (10.31)
Self-Harm (BOR-S)	59.17 (13.34)	65.44 (11.72)	54.93 (13.10)
Antisocial Behaviors (ANT-A)	61.19 (8.46)	72.26 (8.33)	58.50 (8.14)
Egocentricity (ANT-E)	53.87 (9.96)	62.62 (12.17)	50.72 (11.79)
Stimulus-Seeking (ANT-S)	53.27 (10.39)	62.58 (11.94)	46.96 (11.60)
Aggressive Attitude (AGG-A)	59.56 (9.97)	57.40 (8.49)	56.92 (11.70)
Verbal Aggression (AGG-V)	55.20 (7.62)	55.96 (7.37)	53.75 (10.61)
Physical Aggression (AGG-P)	63.05 (10.85)	62.74 (9.71)	58.81 (12.48)

[a] N = 47, mixed sample of adolescent boys and girls from outpatient and residential treatment programs.
[b] N = 50, adolescent boys, residential substance abuse treatment program.
[c] N = 108, adolescent girls, maximum security correctional facility.

with supplemental perusal of responses to critical items related to Delusions and Hallucinations. (d) A mixed disturbance grouping involving disruptions in affect, behavior, self-image, and interpersonal relationships (BOR); the NON treatment consideration scale may further identify loss of social supports associated with this disturbance. Within each grouping, individual scale interpretation is aided by examining subscale scores and patterns to determine the specific content areas contributing to the scale elevation; these areas are emphasized in the scale interpretation. The interpersonal scales of DOM and WRM have potential relevance for all clusters. For example, low DOM co-occurring with elevated internalizing scales may compound the adolescent's discomfort, and high DOM co-occurring with elevated externalizing scales may produce heightened interpersonal acting out. Low WRM accompanying elevated thought-disordered scales provides support for the existence of negative symptoms, and high WRM with a high BOR score may reflect the adolescent's intense need for social acceptance.

Alternative organizations of the PAI-A clinical and treatment consideration scales for the purpose of interpretation may be guided by findings from factor analytic studies and cluster analyses data. For example, Morey (2007) reported a robust first factor involving marked distress found for both the community and clinical samples and defined by high positive loadings on DEP, SOM, ANX, ARD, SCZ, BOR, and NIM. Among three additional factors found were an egocentric/interpersonally exploitative factor defined by high positive loadings on MAN, ANT, AGG, and DOM, a substance involvement/abuse factor defined by high positive loadings on DRG and ALC, and an interpersonal detachment/alienation factor defined by high positive loadings on NON and high negative loadings on WRM. Morey's (2007) cluster analysis conducted on the PAI-A reference clinical sample yielded 10 clusters, and their modal profiles are provided in the test manual alongside a description of their core characteristics, permitting a configural interpretation approach.

In the current PAI-A case example, Rob's clinical scale profile is multiply elevated with the highest elevation on SCZ ($T = 72$), followed by MAN and BOR (both at $T = 67$), DRG ($T = 66$), SOM ($T = 63$), DEP and PAR (both at $T = 61$). Among the treatment consideration scales, a very high score on SUI ($T = 79$) is of great concern (albeit likely heightened to some degree by his NIM score) and is followed by STR ($T = 72$) and AGG ($T = 64$). This profile defies a straightforward categorization in terms of a primary internalizing, externalizing, or thought-disordered pattern, given its numerous and varied elevations. However, it has some of the characteristics of the distress-related first factor except for lacking prominent anxiety components. Among the clusters described by Morey (2007), Rob's profile has a moderate fit with a Cluster 2 profile, which is characterized by elevations on AGG, MAN, and BOR, and with the Cluster 3 profile, which is marked by numerous scale elevations at $T > 60$ and a relatively prominent NIM. Cluster 2 describes the adolescent as having deficiencies in impulse control, emotional regulation, and frustration tolerance, and as prone to becoming angry and potentially aggressive when frustrated. He or she is prone to be very reactive to circumstances, particularly those involving interpersonal relationships. Cluster 3 describes the adolescent as being in acute distress, with a broad range of internalizing features including depression, anxiety, somatic complaints, and suicidal ideation. Episodes of poorly controlled behaviors are likely for these teenagers when internalizing mechanisms falter. Together, these descriptions fit the initial impression of a mixed internalizing/externalizing picture for Rob.

Although the configural interpretation provides a good entry into the interpretive process, the test interpreter should not lose sight of the order of scale elevations. For Rob, the highest clinical scale is SCZ. At his score level, difficulties in thinking, concentration, and decision making are very likely; his score is not at the level where an active psychotic episode or schizophrenic symptoms are indicated. The most prominent of his subscale scores, SCZ-P, is at a T score of 89, but SCZ-T is only moderately elevated at $T = 65$. These scores describe the probability of unusual perceptions, sensations, and ideas, magical thinking, confusion, and poor concentration. Rob's critical item endorsements in the Delusions and Hallucinations category indicate hearing voices and feeling he is the target of a conspiracy. Given his recent family life context of his mother's sudden departure from his life, the recent negative attention in school, and the PAI-A configural findings of emotional distress and reactivity, this set of scores and item responses may be conceptualized in terms of his feeling like an anomaly and having cognitive disruptions accompanying his emotional and behavioral difficulties. The role of possible drug use, which Rob may be engaging in to self-medicate against troubling thoughts and feelings, should also be considered in this regard. In the absence of other evidence of psychotic processes, the test interpreter may also hypothesize that his hearing voices might be a mechanism to combat loneliness; however, further investigation into the nature of these experiences is warranted. Rob's MAN score, supported by a clinical elevation on MAN-I, describes him as restless, impulsive, and impatient with others to a degree that strains relationships. MAN-I is at an extreme score that surpasses the clinical skyline, suggesting extensive difficulty in managing frustration. Rob's BOR scale elevation reflects an adolescent who is moody, sensitive, and fundamentally uncertain about his life goals, and who feels angry and suspicious of caretakers while being simultaneously needy and anxious. The primary subscale elevation of BOR-I reflects pronounced identity diffusion beyond what may be expected developmentally for his age, with a poorly integrated conception of self and others. Secondary elevations on BOR-N and BOR-S lend further support to the presence of ambivalence, resentment, feelings of betrayal, and impulsivity in areas with high potential for adverse effects and interference with social and school functioning. Rob's SOM score with prominent SOM-C suggests that at least some of his emotional distress is manifested somatically and is experienced as producing functional impairment. However, a more direct experience of unhappiness is not fully averted, and his unhappiness is likely to be accompanied by subjective feelings of sadness, loss of interest and pleasure in activities, and thoughts of worthlessness, hopelessness, and personal failure (DEP-A and DEP-C). Rob's PAR score also shows him to be cautious and sensitive in interpersonal relationships, with a particular inclination to feel he is treated unfairly (PAR-P). On a positive note, Rob's PAI-A profile reflects the absence of significant problems related to anxiety or antisocial/criminal patterns. However, his mood lability, irritability, and potential for aggressive behavior can place him at increased situational risk of incurring social or legal consequences for his actions, especially if his drug use is problematic.

Consistent with the Cluster 3 pattern of acute distress, Rob's treatment consideration scales of SUI and STR are notably elevated at T scores of 79 and 72, respectively. As noted earlier, these scores are likely to have been elevated to some degree by his moderately high NIM score. Nonetheless, they may be seen as explicit communications of needing help and require an immediate response. While the SUI score level, together with a review of critical items in the area of Potential for Self-Harm, do not necessarily point to imminent suicidal action, they do suggest that Rob strongly feels unsupported, has recurrent thoughts of suicide, feels disinterested in living, and has at some time thought of ways to end his life and even engaged in self-harming actions when upset. On the other hand, the average NON score may reflect a glimmer of recognition of having his grandparents' support, although his distressed feelings may override it. The STR score underscores a sense of powerlessness and turmoil. Complicating this picture is the elevation on AGG and subscales AGG-P and AGG-A, respectively, reflecting his tendency to be easily provoked and angered and to resort to violent actions in response. Among the interpersonal scales, the moderately low DOM score suggests that Rob is not skilled in asserting himself, whereas the moderately high WRM score suggests he wants to be liked by others. Piecing it together with the findings from SUI, STR, and AGG, we get the picture of a teenager who is unable to express his needs effectively or in a manner that is "heard" by the adults in his life and reacts with anger, self-annihilating impulses, and intermittent forceful actions toward others.

The overall clinical picture in this case is that of a teenager with broad-ranging and significant disturbance in emotional, cognitive, interpersonal, and behavioral functioning, with acute intensification subsequent to events in his life over the last couple of years. We see the impact of his experience of abandonment by his mother in terms of his agitation, confusion, misery, self-questioning of personal worth, and reactive acting out as an inept way of claiming attention to his presence and defending against negative feelings. While anxiety is not experienced symptomatically, his distress related to feelings of abandonment, his *fear* of being cast aside again, and his sense of inevitability is conveyed in his remark about his grandparents wanting to get rid of him *too* and *all* being fed up with him. It is no wonder that he rages against others and thinks of taking preemptive action against himself, nor that he desperately tries to manipulate his mother into demonstrating her concern for him. In the midst of this tempest and with the negative attention he has brought on himself in the school environment, it is quite remarkable that Rob has been able to maintain acceptable grades; this might be an area to capitalize on in building a sense of personal worth and identity.

The PAI-A profile is particularly useful in highlighting Rob's crisis state and risks to self or others in concert with fluctuations in his moods, cognitions, and frustration level that warrant swift treatment intervention. Also useful is the comprehensive personality description that reveals, among other things, his core ambivalence about others and uncertainty about himself that impede development of a realistic and positive identity, and his overall volatility that interferes with social adaptation. The PAI-A interpretation also suggests that Rob's acting out patterns are reactive in nature rather than representative of an emerging antisocial direction.

Diagnosis

Because the PAI-A was developed as a clinical instrument for assessing personality and psychopathology, using the PAI-A in clinical assessment provides the kinds of information that facilitate diagnosis. The assessor should note that scale elevations do not simplistically indicate the diagnosis implied by the scale name, particularly as the profile may contain multiple elevations. Rather, he or she should examine the collective findings from the PAI-A assessment in the context of the adolescent's history and presenting problems and consider the base rates of different psychiatric disorders in adolescence in formulating the diagnosis. The diagnostic process is aided by the provision of DSM-IV diagnostic possibilities in the Clinical Interpretive Report developed by Morey and Psychological Assessment Resources, Inc. staff, available through purchase of the Personality Assessment Inventory™-Adolescent Software Portfolio (PAI®-A SP, 2007). Use of this interpretive report generated the following possibilities based on Rob's profile: Axis I—Adjustment Disorder with Mixed Anxiety and Depressed Mood, R/O Dysthymic Disorder, Intermittent Explosive Disorder, Other (or Unknown) Substance Abuse, and Schizophrenia, Paranoid Type.

In Rob's case, in ruling out the diagnosis of schizophrenia at the current time while being alert to monitoring for a possible emerging psychosis, one would consider the relative rareness of developing schizophrenia at his age, the absence of supporting data from his history and background, and the fact that his SCZ and PAR scores may have alternative explanations. Intermittent Explosive Disorder can also be ruled out, as Rob's actions largely have the quality of oppositional and conduct disturbances and because his angry outbursts appear related to depressive features. His degree of substance use is unknown, but does not appear to reach diagnostic criteria when critical items related to substance abuse are examined.

Also to be noted in the course of diagnostic determination is Morey's (2007) report of a strong representation of adolescents diagnosed with Attention Deficit Hyperactivity Disorder (which does not appear to be the case for Rob in light of his academic performance and absence of reported hyperactivity) and those with a history of assaultive behavior in Cluster 3, and of Major Depression in Cluster 4. Taking into account all these considerations, the most suitable diagnosis for Rob appears to be Adjustment Disorder with Mixed Disturbance of Emotions and Conduct, given the reactive nature of his problem behaviors and manifestation in both mood and behavioral difficulties, and there is a strong possibility of Dysthymic Disorder in light of his life events and likely longevity of mood disturbance. The computer-generated report also suggests an R/O of Personality Disorder NOS with borderline, schizotypal, and paranoid features on Axis II. This is probably best deferred until Rob's acute distress abates sufficiently to allow a clearer personality profile to emerge.

Treatment Planning

In clinical settings, the typical application of personality test findings is to guide diagnosis and treatment planning. Specifically, testing is done based on the expectation that the clinician would come to a deeper understanding of the individual and his or her difficulties than the impressions gained in the initial interview and would be able to tailor the interventions to the specific personality and psychopathological profile of the individual, thus optimizing treatment effectiveness. The PAI-A is well suited for giving direction to treatment goals and plans, with useful guidelines provided in the test manual. For example, high scores on ANX, ARD, and DEP suggest the presence of constricted lives and impairments in daily functioning that should be the focus of treatment, whereas the impulsivity and acting out potential associated with MAN, BOR, ANT, and AGG suggests the need for behavioral containment. A high SCZ score, when reflecting a psychotic process, warrants consideration of adjunctive psychopharmacological treatment. Elevations in ALC and DRG point to the need for specific substance abuse treatment, and a variety of scale elevations associated with heightened vulnerability and self-harm risk (e.g., SUI, STR) indicate the need for immediate crisis intervention actions including determination of the need for hospitalization.

The PAI-A RXR scale is a direct indicator of motivation for treatment with high scores reflecting poor motivation. Morey (2007) cautions, however, that the RXR score should not be construed as an indicator of treatment *prognosis,* because motivation alone does not ensure successful treatment, and that the score should be interpreted in the context of the need for treatment reflected by the entire PAI-A profile. Response to treatment is also guided by other scale descriptors. For example, a high SOM score would suggest resistance to psychological explanations and interventions and an elevated PAR score suggests distrust of authority figures. On the other hand, a moderately elevated WRM score suggests a degree of trust and engagement with others that would be conducive to the treatment process.

An important issue to consider in treating adolescents concerns the need for family therapy as, from legal and developmental standpoints, adolescents are not autonomous in making decisions about their lives and need the involvement and support of their parents or guardians. Family therapy is particularly indicated when the teenager's PAI-A responses suggest the absence of supportive bonds with family and peers (NON) or interpersonal detachment (e.g., SCZ-S), or when the adolescent feels immobilized by the magnitude of his or her difficulties.

Treatment planning in the case of Rob is guided by (a) the need for crisis intervention based on multiple indications of significant emotional distress and risk/vulnerability from the PAI-A and reports of his actions that precipitated the referral for evaluation; (b) the need for behavioral management based on multiple indications from the PAI-A of low frustration tolerance and angry volatility and his presenting problems of acting out in school and in the home; (c) evidence of Rob's interpersonal discomfort, sensitivity, and distrust on one hand and identity diffusion on the other hand, revealing his deep-seated uncertainty about self and others; (d) recognition of the limits to the availability and ability of adult caretakers in his life. The most immediate action to be considered is that of removing Rob for a short time from his home and placing him in a residential setting until he stabilizes, which also affords his grandparents a respite and opportunity to regroup. Rob would likely benefit from an individual supportive therapy approach that prioritizes building a strong alliance that he learns to trust over time. Individual psychotherapy should be directed toward addressing Rob's core concern of being unwanted and helping him to carve out a positive role for himself in his world that builds on his personal assets. The use of home-based interventions administered by an applied behavioral analyst would provide the support that Rob's grandparents need around parenting and limit setting. With the relief from such backup, Rob's grandparents can be taught to convey their steadfast support for him and assurance that they will not abandon him, particularly as the degree to which his mother will be available for him is unknown.

Risk Assessment

Compared with adults, adolescents experiencing emotional and behavioral disturbances have some unique risk factors that are grounded in their developmental context. For example, adolescence is characterized by heightened self-focus and self-consciousness and increased conflicts with parental figures in the course of individuation (Archer, 2005); for disturbed adolescents, these may amplify into strong self-criticism and a sense of estrangement from others. Of particular note are findings indicating that rates of depression and suicide attempts increase during adolescence, with higher attempt rates for girls and higher fatality rates for boys (Archer, 2005). Adolescents are also prone to engage in increased risk-taking behavior that may involve alcohol and drug use and risky sexual behaviors (Scott & Grisso, 1998), and certain disorders such as anorexia nervosa and bulimia that pose health risks typically have their onset in adolescence (Stice & Bulik, 2008). In treatment settings, adolescent aggression and self-injurious behaviors constitute prominent risks requiring prompt intervention (see Davis, 2000; D'Onofrio, 2007). Given the complexities of detecting disorders in adolescents, including difficulties in distinguishing between normative experiences and disorder, rates of comorbidity, and likelihood of impulsivity, personality assessment represents an important means of accurate diagnosis and detection of risk (Crespi & Politikos, 2008).

As noted earlier, the PAI-A contains several scales that are particularly well suited to assessing risk. Among the set of PAI-A scales pertinent to this issue, the treatment consideration scales of AGG and SUI are specifically developed for assessing the potential for harm to others and self. The AGG scale measures attitudes and behaviors related to anger, hostility, and aggression, with marked elevations indicating an increased likelihood of explosiveness. Morey (2007) suggested that adolescents scoring a low AGG-V combined with a high AGG-P may explode with little prior warning, and reported AGG-P to be most correlated with measures of dyscontrol and conduct problems. The SUI scale contains items related to thoughts of death and suicide and feelings of hopelessness. Elevations at $T \geq 60$ provide a risk alert that warrants further evaluation and scores at $T \geq 86$ particularly require immediate intervention. Morey (2007) reported SUI scores to be strongly related to measures of depression and suicide. In addition to these specific scales, the astute clinician would also consider the frequency, pattern, and elevation of other PAI-A scales in determining the intensity of risk. For example, a high SUI score combined with multiple elevations on scales such as ANX, DEP, BOR, and DRG presents heightened concern about self-harm. The BOR-S subscale, which reflects the tendency for impulsive and self-destructive behavior, should also be examined.

An elevated AGG score combined with elevations on scales such as MAN, PAR, and ANT magnify the risk of harm to others.

Rob's profile indicators related to risk were discussed earlier in the interpretive process but are considered more fully here. His SUI score of 79 and the BOR-S score of 68, along with the pattern of elevations on DEP and its subscales constitute a significant warning for the potential for suicide. Among the critical items in the category of Potential for Self-Harm, he endorsed items related to hurting himself when upset and having no interest in life as "mainly true" and acknowledged having made plans to kill himself as "slightly true." We also see in Rob's profile an AGG score of 64 with its highest subscale score on AGG-P and scores > 60 on MAN and PAR, which collectively indicate heightened proneness to displays of angry acting out and violence. Among the Potential for Aggression critical items, he endorsed as "very true" that he is sometimes very violent and reported at the "slightly true" level that people are afraid of his temper. It should be noted that these indications of risk to self and others do not cancel each other but serve as distinct indicators of *both* types of risk. Compounding these risks is the evidence of marked stress (STR = 72), reflecting his acute crisis state. These PAI-A findings should clearly be taken as a cry for help.

Indications for Additional Measures

As a self-report measure, the PAI-A offers a means for adolescents to reveal their difficulties and proclivities by endorsing items that fit their personal experiences, which worked well in the case of Rob and provided comprehensive information about his functioning. This is particularly useful for teenagers who have a limited understanding of their struggles or are unable to express them in their own words. The test items therefore serve as the medium for communication. However, when the adolescent is defensive or "closed" in his or her communication, or when factors such as a self-favorable or self-condemning bent operate to limit the interpretive yield, PAI-A findings are ideally supplemented with a performance-based measure such as the Rorschach (Exner & Weiner, 1994). Assessments using both self-report and performance-based measures often provide incremental information that refines the interpretation. For example, a PAI-A profile marked by a moderately elevated NIM and multiple clinical elevations reveals the poor self-concept and range of disturbance experienced by the teenager but may convey relatively little about his or her strengths. In this scenario, the Rorschach might reveal that the teenager has a reserve of internal psychological resources to draw upon for coping, or has adaptive interpersonal capacities that could be utilized to obtain support. Interpretations based on combined PAI-A and Rorschach findings may be guided by the scenarios discussed by Finn (1996a) in relation to integrating the MMPI-2 and Rorschach. In Rob's case, supplementing the PAI-A assessment with the Rorschach would be useful for the aforementioned reasons and may also provide a useful "second opinion" about the status of thought disturbance.

Another useful alternative for adolescents who are verbally expressive is to supplement PAI-A assessment with a sentence completion method such as the Rotter Incomplete Sentences Blank (Rotter, Lah, & Rafferty, 1992), which enables them to go beyond the experiences represented in PAI-A items, or to use a storytelling method such as the Thematic Apperception Test (Murray, 1943). PAI-A assessment may also be supplemented with behavioral checklists when behavioral problems in school and at home are at the center of the reasons for referral; this may also serve as a means to obtain collateral information from parents or guardians and teachers. Finally, one should note the high incidence of Attention Deficit Hyperactivity Disorder and learning disabilities in clinical settings and include relevant intellectual, achievement, and neuropsychological measures so that PAI-A results are appropriately embedded in the context of these conditions.

Communication of Findings

PAI-A results are most useful when, in addition to the findings' being actively applied in the diagnostic and treatment process, they are communicated effectively to the relevant parties involved in the particular case. One method of communicating findings is through generating a psychological assessment report. Assessment reports are typically geared toward a professional audience and may therefore contain professional or technical terms that may be unfamiliar to laypersons but should nonetheless be clear and meaningful. Within the test results and interpretation section of a report, an effective way to organize and convey PAI-A findings is to develop explicit themes and to arrange these themes and their descriptions in the order of significance for the individual case. The report writer should reconcile apparent contradictions in the findings and provide a coherent narrative that creates an idiographic portrait placed within an appropriate life context.

The assessing psychologist also provides oral feedback to the client per the requirements of the ethical and professional standards of psychologists and in keeping with best practices of the profession. In the case of adolescents, the assessor should decide in advance if he or she would be delivering the feedback to the teenager *and* his or her family, and should convey this to the client before the assessment begins. Feedback that is delivered using a therapeutic assessment method, and that is directed toward addressing the client's personal questions, has been demonstrated to reduce symptoms, create feelings of being affirmed, and generate hope (Finn, 1996b). In the case of Rob, the feedback would best be delivered in a session attended by him and his grandparents so that he feels their supportive presence. In the feedback process, the examiner may wish to rearrange the questions Rob framed for the assessment in order to first address those that are likely to be less anxiety-producing or threatening to him. Thus, the examiner would address his third question about why he gets upset and angry and how he can deal with it by describing his emotional distress and interpersonal doubts with an empathic tone, and communicating with confidence that there are methods to calm oneself and feel more self-confident that Rob can learn from his therapist. Next, the examiner could address Rob's question about whether he is too difficult to handle (with the undercurrent of anxiety about being abandoned) by speaking candidly about how his behaviors, while understandable in context, are creating problems for him and his grandparents, but once again offering the assurance that it could be managed with some creative solutions to help them as a family. Rob's grandparents could be enlisted in helping the examiner to address his third question about whether Rob is capable of being loved by communicating their caring and investment in his well being. Therapeutic feedback of this kind sets the tone and direction for discussing treatment plans and proceeding to providing the interventions needed to help the adolescent. The assessor could also plan to communicate the findings in written form (i.e., as a simply worded letter), which has been found to usefully solidify the oral feedback for adult clients (Lance & Krishnamurthy, 2003); it can also serve as a reference point at later stages in the treatment.

ADVANTAGES AND DISADVANTAGES OF THE PAI-A

The PAI-A is a highly useful addition to the relatively limited array of broad-band, adolescent self-report personality inventories. It represents an excellent compromise between the length of the existing adolescent personality inventories and the considerably shorter behavioral checklists that typically focus on a narrower range of disturbance. PAI-A items are easy to read and understand, making minimal demands on reading ability and reading comprehension, and the test can be completed within the 50–60-minute time frame of a typical clinical session. The PAI-A also has the benefit of a literature base built on the PAI adult form that attests to the construct validity of the measure.

PAI-A development was initiated after careful determination of the applicability of PAI scale constructs in adolescent assessment, and the test development strategy of combining rational, empirical, and statistical methods yields an optimal balance of psychometric adequacy and meaningfulness of the measure in clinical assessment. The inclusion of validity scales to detect random and biased responding is an important asset of this measure, rendering it appropriate for use in forensic evaluations. The selection and organization of PAI-A scales to measure clinical disorders, interpersonal styles, and treatment-relevant issues cover the most salient issues arising in clinical settings, and the provision of subscales and critical items aids in deriving accurate interpretations. PAI-A findings are useful in developing treatment plans tailored to the specific problems experienced by the adolescent.

At the current time, the greatest disadvantage of the PAI-A is the scarcity of independent research offering further support for its psychometric adequacy and applications in different settings and treatment populations, an issue that is to be expected in light of the short length of time since its release. However, the rate of research publications on the PAI bodes well for PAI-A research activity. PAI-A research should prioritize evaluating score patterns of adolescents from ethnic minority groups, given the relatively small numbers of African American, Hispanic, Asian American, and other minorities represented in the PAI-A community standardization sample, and evaluating the diagnostic efficiency of the PAI-A in diverse samples to enhance its clinical applications.

REFERENCES

Achenbach, T. M., & Rescorla, L. A. (2001). *Manual for ASEBA School-Age Forms, & Profiles*. Burlington, VT: University of Vermont Research Center for Children, Youth, & Families.

American Psychiatric Association (1994). *Diagnostic and statistical manual of mental disorders* (4th ed.). Washington, DC: Author.

Archer, R. P. (2005). *MMPI-A: Assessing adolescent psychopathology* (3rd ed.). Mahwah, NJ: Lawrence Erlbaum.

Archer, R. P., Maruish, M., Imhof, E. A., & Piotrowski, C. (1991). Psychological test usage with adolescent clients: 1990 survey findings. *Professional Psychology: Research and Practice, 22*, 247–252.

Archer, R. P., & Newsom, C. R. (2000). Psychological test usage with adolescent clients: Survey update. *Assessment, 7*, 227–235.

Archer, R. P., & Krishnamurthy, R. (2002). *Essentials of MMPI-A assessment*. New York: Wiley.

Arnett, J. J. (1999). Adolescent storm and stress, reconsidered. *American Psychologist, 54*, 317–326.

Beck, J. S., Beck, A. T., Jolly, J. B., & Steer, R. A. (2005). *Beck Youth Inventories for Children and Adolescents manual* (2nd ed.). San Antonio, TX: Harcourt Assessment.

Bloomfield, K. J., & Krishnamurthy, R. (2002, March). *MMPI-A and PAI-A substance abuse scales among adolescent substance abusers*. Paper presented at the 48th Southeastern Psychological Association conference, Orlando, FL.

Butcher, J. N., Williams, C. L., Graham, J. R., Archer, R. P., Tellegen, A., Ben-Porath, Y. S., & Kaemmer, B. (1992). *MMPI-A (Minnesota Multiphasic Personality Inventory—Adolescent): Manual for administration, scoring, and interpretation*. Minneapolis: University of Minnesota Press.

Cashel, M. L. (2002). Child and adolescent psychological assessment: Current clinical practices and the impact of managed care. *Professional Psychology: Research and Practice, 33*, 446–453.

Cashel. M. L., Schember, J., Goodman, C., & Reed, P. (2006, March). *Concurrent and predictive validity of the PAI-A for incarcerated female adolescents: Strategies for risk assessment*. In R. Krishnamurthy, (Chair), *PAI-A*. Paper presented at the annual meeting of the Society for Personality Assessment, San Diego, CA.

Crespi, T. D., & Politikos, N. N. (2008). Personality assessment with adolescents: Challenges and guidelines. *Adolescence, 43*, 593–606.

D'Onofrio, A. A. (2007). *Adolescent self-injury: A comprehensive guide for counselors and healthcare professionals*. New York: Springer.

Davis, D. L. (2000). *The aggressive adolescent: Clinical and forensic issues*. New York: Haworth Press.

Exner, J. E., Jr., & Weiner, I. B. (1994). *The Rorschach: A comprehensive system. Vol. 3: Assessment of children and adolescents* (2nd ed.). New York: Wiley.

Fernando, S. C., & Krishnamurthy, R. (2006, March). *MPD correlates of the PAI-A in a college freshman sample*. In R. Krishnamurthy, (Chair), *PAI-A*. Paper presented at the annual meeting of the Society for Personality Assessment, San Diego, CA.

Finn, S. E. (1996a). Assessment feedback integrating MMPI-2 and Rorschach findings. *Journal of Personality Assessment, 67*, 543–557.

Finn, S. E. (1996b). *Manual for using the MMPI-2 as a therapeutic intervention*. Minneapolis: University of Minnesota Press.

Krishnamurthy, R., McCollough, M. L., & Goodwin, K. J. (2006, March). *MMPI-A correlates of the PAI-A in a high school sample*. In R. Krishnamurthy (Chair), *PAI-A*. Paper presented at the annual meeting of the Society for Personality Assessment, San Diego, CA.

Lachar, D., & Gruber, C. P. (1995). *Personality Inventory for Youth manual: Technical guide*. Los Angeles: Western Psychological Services.

Lance, B. R., & Krishnamurthy, R. (2003, March). *A comparison of three modes of MMPI-2 test feedback*. Paper presented at the annual meeting of the Society for Personality Assessment, San Francisco, CA.

Millon, T., Millon, C., & Davis, R. (1993). *Millon Adolescent Clinical Inventory (MACI) manual*. Minneapolis: NCS Assessments.

Morey, L. C. (1991). *Personality Assessment Inventory professional manual*. Odessa, FL: Psychological Assessment Resources.

Morey, L. C. (2007). *Personality Assessment Inventory-Adolescent professional manual*. Lutz, FL: Psychological Assessment Resources.

Morey, L. C., and PAR staff (2007). *Personality Assessment Inventory-Adolescent Software Portfolio*. Lutz, FL: Psychological Assessment Resources.

Murray, H. A. (1943). *Thematic apperception test manual*. Cambridge, MA: Harvard University Press.

Reynolds, W. M. (1998). *Adolescent Psychopathology Scale: Psychometric and technical manual*. Lutz, FL: Psychological Assessment Resources.

Rotter, J. B., Lah, M. I., & Lafferty, J. E. (1992). *Rotter incomplete sentences blank manual* (2nd ed.). San Antonio: Psychological Corporation.

Scott, E. S., & Grisso, T. (1998). The evolution of adolescence: A developmental perspective on juvenile justice reform. *The Journal of Criminal Law and Criminology, 88*, 137–189.

Sears, K. D., & Krishnamurthy, R. (2001, March). *Personality and behavioral correlates of the Devereux Scales of Mental Disorders*. Poster presented at the 47th Southeastern Psychological Association.

Smith, S. R., & Handler, L. (2007). The clinical practice of child and adolescent assessment. In Steven R. Smith and Leonard Handler (Eds.), *The clinical assessment of children and adolescents: A practitioner's handbook* (pp. 1–15). Mahwah, NJ: Erlbaum.

Stice, E., & Bulik, C. M. (2008). Eating Disorders. In T. P. Beauchaine and S. P. Hinshaw (Eds.), *Child and adolescent psychopathology* (pp. 643–669). New York: Wiley.

Substance Abuse and Mental Health Services Administration, Office of Applied Studies. (February 19, 2009). *The NSDUH Report: Adolescent Mental Health: Service Settings and Reasons for Receiving Care*. Rockville, MD.

U.S. Department of Health and Human Services (DHHS) (1999). *Mental health: A report of the surgeon general*. Public release. Rockville, MD: U.S. Department of Health and Human Services.

5

The Clinical Applications of the PAI in Substance Abuse Settings

ALI KHADIVI and ANDREAS EVDOKAS

An estimated 14 to 18 million Americans meet the American Psychiatric Association's *Diagnostic and Statistical Manual of Mental Disorders* (4th ed., 1994) criteria for alcohol abuse or dependence (NIAA, 2004). In addition, there is a high rate of co-morbidity between substance abuse and mental illness (Greenfield & Hennessy, 2004). As a result, the assessment of substance use is essential in any clinical context (Adesso, Cisler, Larus, & Hayes, 2004). The use of patient self-reports in the assessment of substance abuse is supported by the literature (Babor, Brown, & Del Boca, 1990). That is, directly asking patients about their substance use is likely to provide more reliable information than indirect methods of questioning. However, in some settings and contexts, substance-abusing individuals might have incentives not to accurately report the extent and negative impact of their use. As a result, the use of multiscale inventories that can examine response style in the assessment of substance abuse is recommended (Butcher, Dahlstrom, Graham, Tellegen, & Kaemmer, 1989). The objective of this chapter is to critically discuss the clinical application of the Personality Assessment Inventory (PAI; Morey, 1991) in substance abuse settings and to provide base rate data on PAI validity scales for two different types of substance abusing populations and settings.

PROFILE VALIDITY

When assessing substance abusers with the PAI it is important to consider the potential effects of intoxication and withdrawal on profile validity. Although the use of psychological assessment during intoxication and withdrawal is not recommended, this is not always avoidable. At times, patients without observable evidence of withdrawal or intoxication may still experience residual drug effects that are not easily detected during the interview. For example, the withdrawal symptoms of

77

cocaine and amphetamine may be confused with symptoms of clinical depression (Galanter & Kleber, 2004). Finally, substance abusers are often not forthcoming as to the timing or extent of their most recent drug use. These effects may impact their test-taking ability and can potentially lead to item omission and inconsistent or random responding on the PAI.

Inconsistent responding is best detected with elevations in the Inconsistency (ICN) scale. If both the ICN and Infrequency (INF) scales are elevated above the threshold of profile validity, random responding is suggested (Morey, 1991, 2003). Psychologists must be able to determine the causes of an inconsistent or random response set. If reading ability, language problems, and motivational factors can be ruled out, then attention difficulties may be considered as a contributing factor, and such difficulties may be the effects of substance abuse or co-occurring psychiatric conditions.

The PAI also has indicators to assess inconsistent or random responding that can occur midway through the test. Morey and Hopwood (2004) use PAI full- and short-form discrepancies on the Alcohol Problems (ALC) and Suicidal Ideation (SUI) scales to assess back random responding. This method of detecting back random responding was validated in an acute inpatient sample with multiple co-morbidity including substance abuse (Seifert, Kehl-Fie, Blais, & Chriki, 2007). Alternatively, Edens and Ruiz (2005) divide INF items into Front (INF-F) and Back (INF-B) and examine the discrepancy of responding between the two scales to assess partial random responding in a prison population.

Another potential indicator of intoxication and withdrawal symptoms on the PAI is elevation on the Negative Impression Management (NIM) scale. This scale tends to be elevated in substance abusers entering treatment (Altermann et al., 1995; Boyle & Lennon, 1994). It has been suggested that this elevation may also be related to intoxication or detoxification (Morey, 2003). In particular, the elevation of NIM in conjunction with elevations on Conversion (SOM-C), Physiological Anxiety (ANX-P,) Physiological Depression (DEP-P), and Thought Disorder (SCZ-T) subscales may reflect someone who is experiencing detoxification or withdrawal effects such as tremors, anxiety, insomnia, and diminished attention.

Substance abusers may have an incentive to underreport the extent of substance abuse and its related negative effects. Underreporting can occur in the service of deceiving oneself or deceiving others (Morey, 2003). Substance abusers who are engaged in self-deception generally deny or minimize the extent of their abuse. They may also be motivated to underreport in an attempt to conceal the extent of their substance abuse from others. Typically, this occurs in forensic contexts, such as in custody or pre-employment evaluations or in criminal justice system evaluations to determine mandatory substance abuse treatment. The PAI Positive Impression Scale (PIM) has been shown to be sensitive in assessing both self and other deception (Morey, 2007). Fals-Stewart (1996) examined the usefulness of PIM in combination with Drug Problems (DRG) and ALC scales in identifying positive dissimulation in three samples: A forensic substance abuser group that had a positive drug screen but incentive to dissimulate, a substance abusing group instructed to fake good, and a substance abusing group with no incentive to underreport. The study demonstrated that a PIM cut score > 56T had 88% sensitivity, 81% specificity, and a hit rate of 84% for detecting fakers. In a cross-validation study the PIM hit rate dropped to 68% (Fals-Stewart & Lucente, 1997). Application of this cutoff score in the PAI normative sample resulted in a sensitivity of 82% and specificity of 70% (Morey, 1996, 2007).

The Defensiveness Index (DEF; Morey, 1996) consists of a configuration of PAI scales that correlate only modestly with the PIM scale. A score of 6 or above reflects high probability of a more overt attempt at defensiveness (Morey, 1996, 2007). Although the utility of this indicator in a substance abuse setting has not been investigated, DEF scores > 6 are not common in a substance abusing population (Khadivi & Evdokas, 2004). Cashel, Rogers, Sewell, and Martin-Cannici (1995) found a moderate effect size for the DEF in detecting faking good in a prison population. However, the cutoff score of 6 or more produced significantly lower sensitivity. Since diagnosis of substance abuse is relatively common in correctional settings (Edens, Cruise, & Buffington-Vollum, 2001) the findings of Cashel, et al. (1995) might have relevance for substance abuse patients. However, the cutoff may need to be adjusted for different populations (Morey, 2007). Khadivi & Evdokas (2000) reported mean DEF scores of 1.32 (SD = 1.44) in an inpatient alcohol group that was similar to the PAI clinical sample mean (M = 1.66, SD = 1.42).

The Cashel Discriminant Function (CDF) is a product of a study conducted by Cashel et al. (1995) to assess defensive and honest responding in college students and prison inmates. In that study, the derived discriminant function outperformed PIM and DEF in detecting positive dissimulation. Since CDF does not meaningfully correlate with PIM, DEF, or the average clinical scale elevation, high scores (160 or above) on the CDF suggest an overt attempt to fake good or to present oneself in a different light (Morey, 2003). However, there are currently no normative data on the CDF in the substance abusing patients.

The PAI's ALC and DRG scales are more or less face valid and thus are susceptible to under-reporting among motivated respondents (Fals-Stewart, 1996). Several investigators (Edens, Hart, Johnson, Johnson, & Olver, 2000; Morey, 1996) have developed indirect measures of positive dissimulation using scales that are conceptually related to substance abuse. Morey has developed the Estimated ALC T score and Estimated DRG T score equations that utilize five PAI subscales (Borderline Self-Harm [BOR-S], Antisocial Stimulus-Seeking [ANT-S], Antisocial Behavior [ANT-A], Antisocial Egocentricity [ANT-E], and Physical Aggression [AGG-P]) that have moderate correlations with the ALC and DRG scales. The observed scores on ALC and DRG scales are then compared with the estimated scores. If the estimated score exceeds the observed score by more than 9T, then under-reporting is suggested (Morey, 1996, 2003). Edens and Ruiz (2005) developed the Addictive Characteristic Scale (ACS), which uses a similar strategy, but utilizes scales that measure less antisocial features. This scale uses raw scores of BOR-S, Borderline Affective Instability (BOR-A), and ANT-E. They applied the Estimated DRG T score and ACS to a sample of 57 inmates, of whom 46% had a diagnosis of substance use. The results showed that both of these indirect measures of substance abuse performed poorly. Furthermore, both estimated DRG T score and ACS were susceptible to PAI response style. These findings are consistent with the literature that suggests indirect assessment of substance abuse is not as effective as direct inquiry (Bernadt, Mumford, Taylor, Smith, & Murray, 1982; Skinner, Holt, Sheu, & Israel, 1986).

Negative dissimulation (over-reporting) on the ALC and DRG scales can also occur. It is possible that a person currently in the midst of, or subsequent to, a major substance abuse episode may over-report the extent of abuse to make sure that he or she will receive the treatment needed. It is also possible that individuals in recovery who have recently relapsed may be more likely to endorse items on the ALC, DRG, or other related scales because their perception of their problem is a particularly negative one. They are especially likely to endorse those items that assess current problems with drugs and alcohol. As discussed above, NIM was developed to assess negative dissimulation. However, although NIM is strongly sensitive to over negative dissimulation (Morey, 2007), NIM is not considered a pure malingering scale, as more disturbed patients and patients with certain forms of psychopathology often produce high elevations on NIM (Morey, 2003). Several studies show that NIM tends to be elevated in substance abusing populations in a variety of treatment settings, including methadone maintenance (Alterman et al., 1995; Khadivi & Evdokas, 2004b), inpatient alcohol treatment (Boyle & Lennon, 1994; Khadivi & Evdokas, 2000), and inpatient prison psychiatric units (Edens & Ruiz, 2005). These results suggest that Morey's recommended cutoff scores of NIM (> 92T) might exclude too many profiles. Instead, when the PAI profile demonstrates a high elevation on NIM, the clinician needs to first consider the possible impact of substance intoxication or withdrawal. If that is ruled out, the context of the examination needs to be explored. The previously reviewed research suggests that when patients are entering a treatment setting they may over-report their difficulties. One possible interpretation of high NIM elevation is a "cry for help." In some contexts, very high NIM in conjunction with high Malingering Index (MAL) and Rogers Discriminant Function (RDF) indicators may suggest malingering (Morey, 1996), such as when patients may be motivated to obtain certain financial benefit or more desirable housing arrangements.

BASE RATE AND NORMATIVE DATA FOR PAI VALIDITY INDICATORS AMONG SUBSTANCE ABUSERS

In this section we present base rates at recommended cut scores and descriptive normative data for two samples of inner city substance abusing populations. In the first sample, 261 patients with a diagnosis of opioid dependence receiving methadone maintenance treatment were included. A total of 123 patients were prison referred (PR=123) and 138 patients were non-prison referred (NPR=138). The patients consisted of consecutive, non-overlapping, and non-mandated admissions from August 1995 to January 1997. The PAI was given as part of the initial psychiatric assessment during the first two weeks of admission to the program. Patients who appeared intoxicated, as assessed by clinic staff, were excluded. All patients were asked to read and answer the first two items in order to ensure comprehension. The sample was already receiving methadone maintenance treatment at the time of the PAI administration. The demographics of the two groups were not significantly different. The PR group was mostly male (69.9%), had an average age of

36 (SD = 6.8), a mean of 10.9 (SD = 2.1) years of education, and was predominantly minority individuals with 62.6% being Latino and 33% African American. The NPR group was also mostly male (58.7%), had an average age of 39.2 (SD = 7.7), with a mean of 11.8 (SD = 3.5) years of education, and was predominantly minority individuals with 60.16% being Latino and 33.3% African American.

In the second sample, 100 inpatient alcohol subjects (IA) were randomly selected from a pool of 164 consecutive admissions to an inpatient alcohol and drug rehabilitation program. All patients had a primary diagnosis of alcohol dependence based on an independent psychiatric examination. As part of the requirement for admission to the rehabilitation unit, all subjects completed 3 to 5 days inpatient detoxification. None of the subjects was mandated for treatment, and all completed the PAI within 2 weeks of their admission to the unit. All patients completed the English version of the PAI and were again asked to read and answer the first two items. The IA sample had an average age of 38 years (SD = 7.7), were mostly male (60%), and were predominantly minority individuals with 58% being African American and 42% Latino. Table 5.1 shows the percentages of the two samples scoring above the recommended cutoff scores for the PAI validity scales. Since cutoff scores change across settings and with new research, we also provided the means and standard deviations of PAI indicators for both samples (see Table 5.2).

Inconsistent responding as measured by ICN is common in all three samples of substance abusing individuals. Nearly 17% of the methadone maintenance sample and 13% of the inpatient alcohol dependence sample produced invalid PAI profiles due to inconsistent responding. The fact that IA patients had already detoxified from substances prior to the PAI administration suggests that detoxification or withdrawal symptoms did not play a primary role. Instead, it is likely that reading ability or language problems may have been larger contributing factors. The ICN scale has more double-negative worded items than any other scale and, as a result, the misreading of words such as "not" or "no" in the items can occur (Morey, 2007).

Using recommended INF cutoff scores, 29% of the PR sample and 18.1% of the NPR sample produced invalid profiles. In contrast, only 8% of IA patients produced an invalid protocol. A closer examination of the content of INF items revealed that many of the methadone maintenance patients disproportionately

TABLE 5.1   Percentage of Patients Scoring Above Recommended Cutoffs for PAI Validity Indicators

PAI Indicators	PR	NPR	IA
INC ≥ 73T	17%	16.6%	13%
INF ≥ 75T	29%	18.1%	8%
INC ≥ 73T & INF ≥ 75T	10.5%	6.5%	2%
PIM ≥ 57T	17.8%	22.4%	5%
DEF ≥ 6	0.8%	0.7%	1%
NIM ≥ 92T	7.3%	6.5%	22%
MAL ≥ 3	7.3%	10.8%	17%

Note: PR: Prison referred, NP: Non-prison referred, IA: Inpatient alcohol sample, INC: Inconsistency scale, INF: Infrequency scale, NIM: Negative Impression Management scale, PIM: Positive Impression Management scale, MAL: Malingering Index, DEF: Defensive Index.

TABLE 5.2   PAI Validity Indicator Means and Standard
Deviations for Three Substance Abusing Samples

	PR		NPR		IA	
	M	SD	M	SD	M	SD
INC	60.19	12.64	59.28	15.87	59.17	9.81
INF	61.77	16.51	58.36	17.09	56.0	11.64
PIM	43.46	14.16	42.23	16.96	36.81	12.16
DEI	2.15	1.44	2.27	1.45	1.32	1.44
NIM	59.63	18.84	56.55	21.93	73.55	21.93
MAL	0.80	1.02	1.05	1.12	3.47	5.94

Note: PR: Prison referred, NP: Non-prison referred, IA: Inpatient alcohol sample,
INC: Inconsistency scale, INF: Infrequency scale, NIM: Negative
Impression Management scale, PIM: Positive Impression Management
scale, MAL: Malingering Index, DEF: Defensive Index.

endorsed two items in the scored direction ("Sometimes I get ads in the mail that
I don't really want" and "Most people look forward to a trip the dentist"). This suggests that these two items may be experienced and interpreted differently in economically disadvantaged, minority, substance abusing populations. For example,
many patients, especially those recently released from prison, may have unstable
or nonexistent mailing addresses and, therefore, do not receive ads in the mail.
Also, it is possible that individuals who feel under-served may in fact look forward
to seeing a dentist. This may suggest that when INF is elevated, an examination of
selected items might be helpful. In examining the base rate of random responding
according to a combined indicator rule (INC > 73t and INF > 75t) only 2% of IA
patients produced random profiles. This may reflect the fact that these patients
were motivated to be in treatment and had completed a detoxification period. In
contrast, 17% of the methadone maintenance patients show random responding
according to this rule.

With regard to the NIM scale, fewer than 10% of methadone maintenance
patients scored above the cutoff scores of 92T, while 22% of IA patients scored
above this cutoff. This finding supports the idea that the NIM scale can be elevated at the time of entry to some substance abuse treatment settings. However,
since the IA sample had more patients scoring above the NIM cutoff score, it also
suggests that NIM elevation may be more a function of negative evaluation of one's
substance abuse and its negative effects, rather than reflecting the impact of detoxification or withdrawal (all IA patients had completed detoxification treatment prior
to completing the PAI). In other words, patients who decide to enter a 21-day inpatient rehabilitation program may have multiple problems, are distressed, and have
a particularly negative view of their current situation. Also, 17% of the IA sample
scored two standard deviations above the mean on the Malingering Index (MAL),
suggesting some overt attempts to present a less favorable view of themselves.

Examination of positive dissimulation shows that the IA sample is less likely
to be defensive, with 5% of patients scoring above the PIM cutoff of > 56T and
only 1% scoring at or above a DEF score of 6. Since the sample included all
voluntarily admitted patients who have recognized a need for intense inpatient

treatment, an overly positive presentation is less likely to occur. In contrast, a high percentage of methadone maintenance patients show evidence of positive dissimulation, with 17.8% of PR patients and 22.4% of NPR patients scoring above 56T on PIM, and fewer than 1% of both groups scoring at, or above 6 on the DEF. This may suggest that, despite voluntarily entering an outpatient treatment setting, a higher percentage of methadone maintenance patients have more limited insight than those who enter more intensive inpatient settings. The fact that fewer than 1% of methadone maintenance patients score at or above 6 on DEF suggests that self-deception is more likely to be a factor in their positive dissimulation than other deception. That is, the methadone patients in this sample did not appear to be deliberately trying to minimize their substance use.

DIAGNOSIS

The PAI scales, in conjunction with other methods, can be useful in establishing a diagnosis (Morey, 2003). The first task in assessing substance users is to examine the presence and extent of drug or alcohol use. The PAI has two scales that directly inquire about alcohol and drug problems. Each scale consists of 12 items. The items assess both current and past substance use. The rationale for including items in the past tense is that the diagnosis of substance abuse is based, in part, on a history of use (Morey, 1996, 2003). Although none of the PAI substance use items include criteria for duration of use, endorsement of past-tense items can still result in moderate elevations on ALC or DRG for patients who are in recovery (Morey, 2003). The PAI substance abuse scale items focus more on direct use of drugs, negative consequences of drug and alcohol use, loss of control over substance use, and use of drugs and alcohol as a way of coping (Morey, 1996, 2007). No items on the PAI directly ask about symptoms of withdrawal, intoxication, or psychological or physiological tolerance. However, in the DSM-IV-TR, the presence of tolerance or withdrawal symptoms is no longer required to make a diagnosis of substance dependence. Instead, the criteria for the diagnosis of substance dependence focus more on recurrent and compulsive use.

It has consistently been shown that the DRG and ALC scales have the highest elevations of all other PAI scales in multiple substance abuse treatment settings (Morey, 2007). Alterman et al. (1995) found that methadone maintenance outpatients had the highest elevation on the DRG scale with a mean score of 84T. Khadivi & Evdokas (2004b) found a similar profile in a methadone maintenance inner city sample with a mean score of 73T. Ortiz Pedraza (2003) applied the PAI to an inpatient sample of cocaine abusers and obtained a mean DRG scale score of 86T (SD = 9.5). Parker, Daleiden, and Simpson (1999) showed that the ALC and DRG scales had the highest elevation in an alcohol- and drug-abusing sample. Boyle and Lennon (1994) studied a sample of patients undergoing inpatient alcohol treatment and obtained a mean ALC scale of 88T that was significantly higher than a non-substance-using comparison group. Alterman et al. (1995) and Parker et al. (1999) examined the relationship of the DRG scale to the Addiction Severity Scale (ASI; McLellan et al., 1992) and found moderate correlations between the two instruments. Kellogg et al. (2002) studied 100 substance abusers and 100 non-abusers and obtained a significantly high correlation of .81 between the ASI and the DRG scale and noted that, as elevations increase on the DRG scale, so does involvement with drug use and related negative consequences.

PAI scales can also contribute to the assessment of co-occurring psychiatric conditions in substance using individuals, as discussed in several other chapters of this volume and other sources. In general, in the absence of profile validity concerns, any elevation in clinical scales accompanied with high scores on ALC and DRG scales may suggest the presence of a co-occurring psychiatric condition (Morey, 2003). In our experience, this may also reflect a substance-induced psychiatric condition. However, some substance using patients endorse PAI clinical items based solely on their past experiences when under the influence of drugs or alcohol, even if at the time of testing they are abstinent. As a result, it is difficult to distinguish the PAI of a substance-induced condition from the profile of a substance-using individual with psychiatric co-morbidity. In such cases a clinical interview should be used to help clarify the differential diagnosis.

TREATMENT PLANNING

The PAI clinical and treatment consideration scales can assess and provide useful case-specific information that can be the focus of intervention. The PAI profile may identify specific symptoms and personality traits that can be seen from a vantage point of treatment. For example, impulsivity, as indicated by elevations on the BOR-S, BOR-A, and ANT-S subscales can be seen as a potential target for intervention, as well as a factor that may complicate the course of treatment.

In a substance abusing population, the first task is to determine the need for detoxification. High elevations on the ALC or DRG scale accompanied by prominent elevations on NIM, Somatization (SOM), Anxiety (ANX), or Physiological Depression (DEP-P) may suggest a need for more intense treatment. The second task is to determine whether the patient is in need of inpatient drug or alcohol rehabilitation. In practice, patients with active substance abuse who repeatedly fail outpatient treatment may be good candidates for inpatient treatment programs. Also, PAI profiles that show very elevated scores in DRG or ALC coupled with elevated scores on environmental Stress (STR) and Nonsupport (NON) might suggest patients in the midst of an active substance abuse episode, in which they feel out of control and perceive themselves as living in a stressful and chaotic environment with limited support. These are the individuals who might describe their situation as having "hit rock-bottom," and who might be particularly receptive to inpatient treatment. In fact, when entering treatment, substance abusers often talk about life stress and significant problems with social supports. In a sample of methadone maintenance patients (Alterman et al., 1995), the mean scaled scores for the STR and NON scales were significantly greater than the PAI's normative sample. Also, opioid abusers who were released from prison to an inner city methadone maintenance program scored significantly higher on the NON scale than non-prison referred methadone maintenance patients (Khadivi & Evdokas, 2004a). Schinka (1995a), using cluster analysis, identified seven PAI profile types in alcohol dependent patients. Four out of seven cluster profiles had clinically significant elevations on STR or NON scales. Given that stressful and unstable social environments may act as triggers for relapse and perpetuated substance use, this pattern of elevations (high STR and NON) may suggest a need for direct environmental interventions such as supportive housing or placement in a structured substance abuse treatment setting. High elevations on the NON scale may also suggest the need for family interventions, referral to Alcohol or Narcotics Anonymous support groups or other self help programs, and a sponsor for daily contact (Morey, 2003).

Substance abusing individuals entering treatment may have varying levels of motivation for treatment and may be at different stages of readiness for change (Prochaska, DiClemente, & Norcross, 1992). The PAI's Treatment Rejection Scale (RXR) can assess the degree of motivation for change. Morey (2003) reports that RXR elevations (i.e., above 53T) are uncommon in clinical settings. The RXR scale is reverse scored, so low scores (40T or below) are suggestive of motivation to make changes in one's life. The mean score for RXR in Morey's (1996) alcohol and drug abuse samples was below 40T. Other studies with alcohol dependence (Schinka, 1995b) and methadone maintenance patients (Alterman et al., 1995) showed similar mean elevations on the RXR scale. However, the level of motivation for treatment among substance abusing patients varies depending on the context and setting. The elevation on the RXR can be helpful in selecting a treatment intervention. For example, there is evidence to suggest that Motivational Interviewing (MI; Miller, 1996), which utilizes a non-confrontational and empathic strategy to enhance motivation, may be more effective with ambivalently motivated patients than more confrontational interventions. Further, Miller, Benefield, and Tonigan (1993) found that MI is more effective on hostile, ambivalently motivated patients than 12 step or cognitive behavioral interventions. Therefore, a high score (low motivation) on RXR in a substance abusing person may suggest that MI might be more helpful as an intervention. Conversely, a very low score (below 20T) may be indicative of a person who might be experiencing acute distress or may be suggestive of an overly needy person with a possible personality disorder (Morey, 2003). In such cases, it is essential to first rule out any acute distress that the person might be experiencing.

Morey (1996) developed the Treatment Process Index (TPI), which consists of variables that are conceptually related to treatment outcome and processes. In the absence of elevated NIM, high scores on the TPI may suggest difficulty or complications in the course of treatment. Although research on the TPI has generally been limited with substance abusers, Hopwood, Baker, and Morey (2008) found that the indicator significantly predicted dropout in an inpatient substance abuse facility.

RISK ASSESSMENT

Substance abuse disorders and substance intoxication, even in the absence of a formal diagnosis, are associated with both suicide and violence (Monahan et al., 2001; Simon, 2002). Alcohol and drugs can cause disinhibition and therefore increase the risk of self- and other-directed violence. In addition, individuals with significant substance abuse can experience multiple losses and stressors which, in turn, can lead to feelings of anger or hopelessness. The current perspective on risk assessment shifts the focus away from prediction to treatment and management of risk (Simon, 2002). The PAI should never be used as the only method to make risk assessment decisions (Morey, 2003). However, the PAI can supplement other methods of assessment and can contribute to the evaluation of risk in substance abuse treatment settings in a number of ways. First, the PAI has a number of scales that directly inquire about risk, such as the Suicidal Ideation (SUI) and AGG-P scales. Since some of the items measure active violence ("Sometimes I am very violent") and suicidal ideation ("I am considering suicide"), elevation on these scales in the context of substance abuse signals the need for further assessment. Second, the PAI's clinical scales provide case-specific symptoms and personality traits that might have implications for risk management. For example, a PAI profile of a substance using patient with elevations on SUI, BOR-S, and ANT-S suggests different risk factors and intervention strategies than the PAI profile of a person with no evidence of impulsivity but with profoundly negative affect and high elevations in the Affective Depression (DEP-A), Affective Anxiety (ANX-A), and SUI scales.

Finally, the PAI Suicide Potential Index (SPI; Morey, 1996) and Violence Potential Index (VPI; Morey, 1996), which consist of constellations of conceptually relevant variables for self- and other-directed violence, can be used to assess the clinical and environmental context for level of risk (Morey, 1996, 2003). In a recent study, Hopwood, Baker, & Morey (2008) showed that the SPI and SUI were elevated in substance abusing patient with reported history of suicide attempts. The Aggression (AGG) full scale and its three subscales significantly differentiated patients with criminal history of assault from the control. The Antisocial (ANT) full scale predicted unit rule fraction. This study illustrates the external correlates and potential usefulness of the PAI scales and indicators in suicide and risk assessment. Using the PAI's normative and clinical samples, Morey (1996) provided cutoff scores for SPI and VPI corresponding to different levels of risk. Although validation work in different substance abuse treatment settings has been limited thus far, the VPI and SPI can be used to identify potential risk factors that can be assessed further for targeted treatment.

INDICATIONS FOR ADDITIONAL MEASURES

In some clinical contexts, the main purpose of assessment is to arrive at an accurate DSM-IV-TR diagnosis of substance use. For this purpose, the Structured Clinical Interview for DSM-IV AXIS I Disorders (SCID; First, Spitzer, Gibbon, & Williams, 1996) can provide such a diagnosis of substance abuse or dependence. Selective modules of the SCID can also be used to assess substance-induced conditions or to clarify the presence of psychiatric co-morbidities that may have been identified in the PAI profile. When under time constraints, the Substance Dependence Severity Scale (SDSS; Miele et al., 2000), which is an interview-based measure, can be used to arrive at a diagnosis of substance abuse or dependence.

Individuals with substance abuse problems often experience significant psychosocial, legal, or medical difficulties. The PAI profiles of substance abusing patients can also identity problem areas in multiple domains including family/support system (NON), legal (ANT-A), health (SOM-H), interpersonal (BOR-N, SZC-S), and environmental stress (STR) that may require further assessment. To further assess problems in these areas, the ASI, a semi-structured interview, can be utilized. The ASI assesses the severity of unmet needs for treatment in six areas including, medical, employment, legal, family/social, psychiatric, and substance use. The ASI takes into account the subjective experience of the patient's difficulties but at the same time allows the interviewer to arrive at the assessment of treatment needs that might be different from the patient's (McLellan et al., 1992). However, since the ASI and other interview-based measures can be vulnerable to faking good (Rogers, 1997), it is best administered when the PAI profile suggests no positive dissimulation, and the ALC or DRG scales are elevated (Parker et al., 1999). Alterman et al. (1996) have shown that individuals who had invalid PAI profiles due to elevated NIM also exaggerated their difficulties during the course of an interview with the ASI. In cases where the PAI profile is suggestive of dissimulation, collateral information and drug toxicology are needed to clarify the extent of substance use problems (Fals-Stewart, 1996; Morey, 2007). Collateral information can be obtained using Form 90-Collateral self-report (Miller, 1996), which can also be administered as an interview.

ADVANTAGES AND DISADVANTAGES OF THE PAI

The PAI has many advantages over other self-report measures in substance abuse assessment. It has a relatively low reading-level requirement, brief administration time, excellent psychometric properties, and scales that measure constructs in the current nosology (Edens & Ruiz, 2005; Morey & Hopwood, 2006). Furthermore, the PAI has scales that are conceptually relevant to the assessment of substance abuse including separate ALC and DRG scales, scales such as STR, NON, and ANT-A that measure the negative consequences of substance use, and clinical scales to measure trauma and mood symptoms that have implications for initiation or exacerbation of substance use (Glutting, 1996; Greenfield & Hennessy, 2004). Given the fact that all substance abuse measures, including interview based ones, are susceptible to faking (Rogers, 1997), the PAI's validity scales can be used to assess response styles that, in themselves, can provide clinically useful information. This increases its utility across different types of substance use evaluations.

A limitation of the use of the PAI in substance abuse settings has to do with the fact that, with the exception of three studies (Fals-Stewart, 1996; Fals-Stewart & Lucente, 1997; Hopwood, Baker, & Morey, 2008), most of the PAI research in this area has been done with patients who were self-referred or self-identified as substance users. Therefore, to enhance utility and increase confidence in generalizability, cutoff scores for the validity scales need to be studied further in different substance use samples. The PAI has a number of indicators including TPI, SPI, and VPI that are shown to have clinical value in inpatient substance abuse settings (Hopwood, Baker, & Morey, 2008), but they have not been validated with other substance abusing populations. Finally, the PAI does not have items or scales to measure other types of addictive behaviors such as gambling, sex addiction, and binge eating that are often associated with substance use.

COMMUNICATION OF FINDINGS

In practice, clinicians have used the findings from brief alcohol and drug screening self-report measures as a tool to enhance motivation for treatment, validate an individual's experience of substance abuse problems, and help clients see the impact of their substance abuse on their functioning (Adesso et al., 2004). Similarly, the PAI can also be a useful tool for communicating findings to both the patient and the referring clinician. The communication of PAI results is facilitated by items that have content validity and non-overlapping scales. Generally speaking, the scale names correspond to what they measure and PAI results directly indicate what the client has communicated (Morey, 2003; Morey & Hopwood, 2006). In addition, many of the clinical and treatment scales are conceptually relevant for substance abusing patients.

Psychological testing feedback using a collaborative model as an intervention has become a new paradigm in personality assessment (Finn, 1996, 2007). There is empirical evidence suggesting that using this model to give assessment feedback produces therapeutic effects in non-substance abusing college students (Finn & Tonsager, 1992; Newman & Greenway, 1997). Some research suggests that this model can be employed with the PAI. Ackerman, Hilsenroth, Baity, and Blagys (2000) used Finn's model (1996) to demonstrate that non-substance abusing patients who participated in a PAI collaborative assessment feedback session at the initial session of their therapy were more likely to continue therapy than patients who participated in a more traditional, information-gathering type of psychological assessment.

In unpublished studies, Kirby (2004) and Kirby, Khadivi, Wong, & Scarvalone (2004) applied Finn's therapeutic assessment model to substance dependence patients attending 21-day inpatient alcohol and drug rehabilitation. The sample was primarily non-white and economically disadvantaged. The patients were randomly assigned to three groups: the first group received collaborative therapeutic PAI feedback, the second received one therapy session but no PAI feedback, and the third group served as a control group that received neither feedback nor psychotherapy but were permitted to talk about their concerns regarding substance abuse with the examiner. The three groups were not significantly different from each other on demographics or on any baseline symptom ratings. The results indicated that both the PAI therapeutic feedback group and the group that received one psychotherapy session showed significant symptom reduction and demonstrated an increase in self-esteem compared with the control group. The study showed that the PAI therapeutic feedback was as effective as one session of therapy in substance abusing settings. While these findings have not been replicated, the study suggests that in addition to being a useful diagnostic instrument, PAI feedback to patients might also be useful as an intervention in substance abusing populations.

CONCLUSION

This chapter critically discusses the clinical application of the Personality Assessment Inventory (PAI; Morey, 1991) in substance abuse settings. Additionally, the chapter provides base rate and normative data on PAI validity scales for two different types of substance abusing populations and settings. The PAI's ability to assess response style is valuable for assessing substance-abusing individuals who might have incentives to inaccurately report the extent and impact of their use. Furthermore, the PAI has clinical scales that are conceptually relevant to the assessment of substance abuse and the co-morbidities that are often seen in addiction disorders. The PAI can augment treatment planning and provide useful information in suicide or violence risk assessment. Future research should continue to explore the application of the PAI with mandated and other substance abusing patients. Additionally, the use of the PAI feedback as a therapeutic intervention with substance abusing populations needs further development.

REFERENCES

Ackerman, S. J., Hilsenroth, M. J., Baity, M. R., & Blagys, M. D. (2000). Interaction of therapeutic process and alliance during psychological assessment. *Journal of Personality Assessment, 75,* 82–109.

Adesso, V. J., Cisler, R. A., Larus, B. J., & Hayes, B. B. (2004). Substance abuse. In M. Hersen (Ed.), *Psychological assessment in clinical practice: A pragmatic guide* (pp. 147–173). New York: Brunner-Routledge.

Alterman, A. I., Zaballero, A. R., Lin, M. M., Siddiqui, N., Brown, L. S., Jr., Rutherford, M. J. et al. (1995). Personality Assessment Inventory (PAI) scores of lower-socioeconomic African American and Latino methadone maintenance patients. *Assessment, 2,* 91–100.

American Psychiatric Association. (1994). *Diagnostic and statistical manual of mental disorders* (4th ed.). Washington, DC: Author.

Babor, T. F., Brown, J., & Del Boca, F. K. (1990). Validity of self reports on addictive behaviors. Fact or fiction? *Behavioral Assessment, 12(1),* 5–31.

Bernadt, M. W., Mumford, J., Taylor, C., Smith, B., & Murray, R. M. (1982). Comparison of questionnaire and laboratory tests in the detection of excessive drinking and alcoholism. *Lancet, 319,* 325–328.

Boyle, G. J., & Lennon, T. (1994). Examination of the reliability and validity of the Personality Assessment Inventory. *Journal of Psychopathology and Behavioral Assessment, 16,* 173–187.

Butcher, J. N., Dahlstrom, W. G., Graham, J.R., Tellegen, A., & Kaemmer, B. (1989). *Minnesota Multiphasic Personality Inventory-2: Manual for administration and scoring.* Minneapolis: University of Minnesota Press.

Cashel, M. L., Rogers, R., Sewell, K., & Martin-Cannici, C. (1995). The Personality Assessment Inventory (PAI) and the detection of defensiveness. *Assessment, 2,* 333–342.

Edens, J. F., Cruise, K. R., & Buffington-Vollum, J. K. (2001). Forensic and correctional applications of the Personality Assessment Inventory. *Behavioral Sciences and the Law, 19,* 519–543.

Edens, J. F., Hart, S. D., Johnson, D. W., Johnson, J. K., & Olver, M. E. (2000). Use of the Personality Assessment Inventory to assess psychopathy in offender populations. *Psychological Assessment, 12,* 132–139.

Edens, J. F., & Ruiz, M. A. (2005). PAI Interpretive Report for Correctional Settings(PAI-CS). Odessa, FL: Psychological Assessment Resources.

Fals-Stewart, W. (1996). The ability of individuals with psychoactive substance use disorders to escape detection by the Personality Assessment Inventory. *Psychological Assessment, 8,* 60–68.

Fals-Stewart, W., & Lucente, S. (1997). Identifying positive dissimulation by substance-abusing individuals on the Personality Assessment Inventory: A cross-validation study. *Journal of Personality Assessment, 68,* 455–469.

Finn, S. E. (1996). Assessment feedback integrating MMPI-2 and Rorschach findings. *Journal of Personality Assessment, 67,* 543–557.

Finn, S. E. (2007). *In our clients' shoes: Theory and techniques of therapeutic assessment.* Mahwah, NJ: Erlbaum.

Finn, S. E., & Tonsager, M. E. (1992). Therapeutic effects of providing MMPI-2 test feedback to college students awaiting therapy. *Psychological Assessment, 4,* 278–287.

First, M. B., Spitzer, R. L., Gibbon, M., & Williams, J. B. W. (1996). *Structured Clinical Interview for DSM-IV Axis I Disorders, Clinician Version (SCID-CV).* Washington, DC: American Psychiatric Press.

Galanter, M., & H. D. Kleber (Eds.), (2004). *Textbook of substance abuse treatment,* 3rd ed. (pp. 101–119). Washington, DC: American Psychiatric Publishing.

Glutting, J. H. (1996). Childhood abuse, family history, and the development of antisocial personality disorder and alcoholism (Doctoral dissertation, Vanderbilt University, 1996). *Dissertation Abstracts International, 56,* 7045.

Greenfield, S. F., & Hennessy, G. (2004). Assessment of the patient. In: M. Galanter, & H.D. Kleber (Eds.), *Textbook of substance abuse treatment,* 3rd ed. (pp. 101–119). Washington, DC: American Psychiatric Publishing.

Hopwood, C. J., Baker, K. L., & Morey, L. C. (2008). Extra-test validity of Personality Assessment Inventory scales and indicators in an inpatient substance abuse setting. *Journal of Personality Assessment, 90(6),* 571–577.

Hopwood, C. J., Baker, K. L., & Morey, L. C. (2008). Personality and drugs of choice. *Personality and Individual Differences, 44(6),* 1413–1421.

Kellogg, S. H., Ho, A., Bell, K., Schluger, R. P., McHugh, P. F., McClary, K. A., et al. (2002). The Personality Assessment Inventory Drug Problems Scale: A validity analysis. *Journal of Personality Assessment, 79,* 73–84.

Khadivi, A., & Evdokas, A. (2004a, March). *Base rate of the PAI validity indices in economically disadvantaged minority psychiatric patients.* Paper presented at the meeting of the Society for Personality Assessment, Miami, FL.

Khadivi, A., & Evdokas, A. (2004b, March). *The PAI characteristics of substance abusing inmates who are referred to outpatient methadone maintenance treatment program.* Paper presented at the meeting of the Society for Personality Assessment, Miami, FL.

Kirby, A. (2004). Therapeutic value of providing PAI feedback to patients in a hospital alcohol/substance program Dissertation Abstract International, 65, (1B), 442. (UMI N0. AA1318782).

Kirby, A., Khadivi, A., Wong, P., & Scarvalone, P. (2004, March). *Therapeutic effects of providing PAI feedback to an inner-city substance abusing inpatient population.* Paper presented at the meeting of the Society for Personality Assessment, Miami, FL.

McLellan, A. T., Kushner, H., Metzger, D., Peters, R., Smith, I., & Grisson, G. (1992). The fifth edition of the Addiction Severity Index. *Journal of Substance Abuse Treatment, 9,* 199–213.

Miele, G. M., Carpenter, K. M., Cockerham, M.S., Trautman, K. D., Blaine, J., & Hasin, D.S. (2000). Substance Dependence Severity Scale (SDSS): Reliability and validity of a clinician-administered interview for DSM-IV substance use and disorders. *Drug and Alcohol Dependence, 59,* 63–75.

Miller, W. R. (1996). Form 90: A structured assessment interview for drinking and related behaviors. In M.E. Mattson (Ed.), NIAAA Project MATCH Monograph Series (Vol. 5). Bethesda, MD: U.S. Department of Health and Human Services, National Institutes of Health.

Miller, W. R., Benefield, R. G., & Tonigan, J.S. (1993). Enhancing motivation for change in problem drinking: A controlled comparison of two therapist styles. *Journal of Consulting and Clinical Psychology, 61,* 455–461.

Monahan, J., Steadman, H., Silver, E., Appelbaum, S., Robbins, P., Mulvey, E., et al. (2001). *Rethinking risk assessment: The MacArthur study of mental disorder and violence.* New York: Oxford University Press.

Morey, L. C. (1991). *The Personality Assessment Inventory professional manual.* Odessa, FL: Psychological Assessment Resources.

Morey, L.C. (1996). An interpretive guide to Personality Assessment Inventry. Odessa, FL: Psychological Assessment Resources.

Morey, L. C. (2003). *Essentials of PAI assessment.* Hoboken, NJ: Wiley.

Morey, L. C. (2007). *Personality Assessment Inventory professional manual* (2nd ed.). Lutz, FL: Psychological Assessment Resources.

Morey, L. C., & Hopwood, C. J. (2004). Efficiency of a strategy for detecting back random responding on the Personality Assessment Inventory. *Psychological Assessment, 16,* 197–200.

Morey, L. C., & Hopwood, C. J. (2006). The Personality Assessment Inventory. In R. P. Archer (Ed.), *Forensic uses of clinical assessment instruments* (pp. 89–120). Mahwah, NJ: Erlbaum.

Morey, L. C., Lowmaster, S. E., & Hopwood, C. J. (under review). Manual-assisted cognitive therapy with a therapeutic assessment augmentation for borderline personality disorder.

National Institute on Alcohol Abuse and Alcoholism (2004). Ninth special report to the U.S. Congress on alcohol and health. Bethesda, MD: U.S. Department of Health and Human Services, and Public Health Services, National Institutes of Health.

Newman, M. L., & Greenway, P. (1997). Therapeutic effects of providing MMPI-2 test feedback to clients at a university counseling service: A collaborative approach. *Psychological Assessment, 9,* 122–131.

Ortiz Pedraza, F. A. (2003). Depressive symptomatology associated with crack cocaine use: Neuropsychological considerations (Doctoral dissertation, Carlos Albizu University, 2003). *Dissertation Abstracts International, 64,* 2398.

Parker, J. D., Daleiden, E. L., & Simpson, C. A. (1999). Personality Assessment Inventory substance-use scales: Convergent and discriminant relations with the Addiction Severity Index in a residential chemical dependence treatment setting. *Psychological Assessment, 11,* 507–513.

Prochaska, J. O., DiClemente, C. C., & Norcross, J. C. (1992). In search of how people change: Applications to addictive behaviors. *American Psychologist, 47(9),* 1102–1114.

Rogers, R. (Ed.). (1997). *Clinical assessment of malingering and deception* (2nd edition). New York: Guilford Press.

Schinka, J. A. (1995a). PAI profiles in alcohol-dependent patients. *Journal of Personality Assessment, 65,* 35–51.

Schinka, J. A. (1995b). Personality Assessment Inventory scale characteristics and factor structure in the assessment of alcohol dependency. *Journal of Personality Assessment, 64* 101–111.

Siefert, C. J., Kehl-Fie, K., Blais, M. A., & Chriki, L. (2007). Detecting back irrelevant responding on the Personality Assessment Inventory in a psychiatric inpatient setting. *Psychological Assessment, 19,* 469–473.

Simon, R. I. (2002). Suicide risk assessment: What is the standard of care? *Journal of American Academy Psychiatry Law, 30,* 340–344.

Skinner, H. A., Holt, S., Sheu, W. J., & Israel, Y. (1986). Clinical versus laboratory detection of alcohol abuse: The Alcohol Clinical Index. *British Medical Journal, 292,* 1703–1708.

6

Use of the PAI in Assessment of Posttraumatic Stress Disorder Among Help-Seeking Veterans

PATRICK S. CALHOUN, CLAIRE F. COLLIE,
CAROLINA P. CLANCY, LORETTA E. BRAXTON, and
JEAN C. BECKHAM

*P*osttraumatic stress disorder (PTSD) is common in the general population with estimates ranging from 7% to 9% (Kessler et al., 1995; Breslau et al., 1998) and is even more prevalent among patients presenting to primary care settings, where rates range from 12% to 25% (Stein et al., 2000; Magruder et al., 2005). PTSD is particularly common among those exposed to war, among whom lifetime prevalence rates are as high as 20% to 30% (Kulka et al., 1990; Hoge et al., 2004). Given both its high prevalence and the existence of safe and effective treatments for PTSD (Foa et al., 1991; Resick and Schnicke, 1992; Davidson et al., 2001), there is widespread agreement that screening for PTSD is warranted (VA/DoD Clinical Practice Guideline Working Group, Veterans Health Administration, Department of Veterans Affairs and Health Affairs and Department of Defense, 2004; Eisenman et al., 2006). Clinical practice guidelines developed jointly between the Department of Veterans Affairs (VA) and the Department of Defense (DoD) recommend PTSD screening for all veterans (VA/DoD Clinical Practice Guideline Working Group, Veterans Health Administration, Department of Veterans Affairs and Health Affairs and Department of Defense, 2004).

One primary function of many psychologists working in specialized PTSD clinics is the accurate assessment of PTSD, which can be complicated in VA and other settings by issues of secondary gain. Financial compensation in the form of a service-connected disability rating may be a strong incentive to engage in symptom exaggeration or malingering (Hyer, Fallon, Harrison, & Boudewyns, 1987; Jordan, Nunley, & Cook 1992; Smith & Frueh, 1996).

Experts have recommended that optimal assessment of PTSD include measurement of traumatic events, multiple measures of PTSD, broad-based symptom and personality measurement, and the use of structured diagnostic interviews (Calhoun, Earnst, Tucker, Kirby, & Beckham, 2000; Keane, Wolfe, & Taylor, 1987; Sutker, Uddo-Crane, & Allain, 1991). In this context, we find the Personality Assessment Inventory (PAI; Morey, 1991) is particularly useful. Several recent studies involving veterans, college students, and community volunteers have supported the use of the PAI in PTSD assessment and in the assessment of behavioral disturbance associated with PTSD such as anger and aggression (Calhoun et al., in press; Drury et al., 2009; Cherepon & Prinzhorn, 1994; Crawford, Calhoun, Braxton, & Beckham, 2007; McDevitt-Murphy, Weathers, Adkins, & Daniels, 2005; Mozley, Miller, Weathers, Beckham, & Feldman, 2005).

In this chapter we discuss the use of the PAI in the assessment of PTSD in the context of an outpatient specialty PTSD clinic in a VA medical center. In our PTSD evaluations, we routinely use the PAI in combination with a state-of-the-art structured diagnostic interview for PTSD, measurement of combat and noncombat traumatic experiences, and available medical and military records. Our evaluations are typically completed in 2–3 visits that include (1) an introduction to the evaluation process and discussion of informed consent including limitations of confidentiality; (2) administration of the PAI and other self-report instruments assessing trauma exposure, PTSD symptoms, and other relevant measures (e.g., smoking, alcohol and drug use); (3) administration of the Clinician Administered PTSD Scale (CAPS; Blake et al., 1995), a structured diagnostic interview that corresponds to DSM-IV PTSD criteria; and (4) feedback and treatment planning. Based on the CAPS, the base rate of PTSD in our evaluation clinic is 90%. In this context, we find the PAI can provide valuable information in helping to confirm diagnostic formulations, formulate risk assessments, help with treatment planning, and guide the use of additional measures.

We have evaluated more than 3,400 veterans for PTSD and almost 900 have been evaluated using the PAI. Almost all (97%) of those evaluated are male. In this chapter, we provide normative data from male veterans (N = 849) evaluated between 1999 and 2008 who were included in a deidentified archival dataset that was approved for research by the local Institutional Review Board. Sixty-three percent of the sample were veterans of the Vietnam War, 15% were veterans of the wars in Afghanistan or Iraq, 10% were Gulf War Veterans, 3% were Korean War or World War II veterans, and the remainder served in eras between these wars. The mean age of the sample was 50.3 (s.d. = 11.2; range 21–86). Fifty-five percent of the sample was African American, 41% Caucasian, with other races making up the remaining 4% of cases. Fifty-seven percent were currently married, 22% divorced, 8% separated, 2% widowed, and 12% never married. Eight percent had less than a high-school education, 46% completed only high school, 25% had 1–2 years of college, and 15% had 2 or more years of college. The mean Hollingshead Index for the sample was 57.1 (SD = 11.3), which falls in the lower middle class category of socioeconomic status.

The majority of veterans evaluated had either filed a claim with the VA for a service-connected disability related to PTSD (42%) or reported that they planned to apply for VA service-connection (47%). Three percent of the sample was already service-connected for other psychiatric conditions and 45% were service-connected for nonpsychiatric medical conditions.

PROFILE VALIDITY

Extremely high scores on either Inconsistency (ICN) or Infrequency (INF) suggest that the respondent did not attend appropriately to PAI item content and test results are best presumed to be invalid (Morey, 2007). Approximately 9% (72 of 849) of help-seeking veterans in our clinic produce profiles considered to be invalid on the basis of inconsistent responding following Morey's (2007) recommended cutting score (i.e., ICN > 73T). An additional 37 cases (4%) are deemed invalid due to elevations on the INF scale (> 75T). We find that the majority of invalid profiles in our clinic can be attributed to elevations on ICN and INF. When provided feedback on distorted results as assessed with the ICN or INF scales, patients often admit to us that they were careless, confused, or in some cases had difficulty reading (e.g., "I forgot my glasses today"). Further, some admit they answered randomly after becoming bored with the evaluation procedures.

Perhaps the most difficult interpretive dilemma in the use of the PAI or other self-report measure of psychopathology in the assessment of PTSD is the determination of profile validity in relation to effortful negative distortion. The accuracy of self-reported information in the context of PTSD evaluation has long been a concern. While the perspective of the clinician working in a specialty PTSD treatment setting is far different from a forensic psychologist (Melton, 1997) or even the examiner who is charged with evaluating PTSD as part of a formal VA compensation and pension examination, it is important to determine whether PAI results provide an accurate reflection of the respondent's experiences.

The majority of veterans evaluated in specialty PTSD clinic settings are likely to seek VA compensation for PTSD. Disability compensation often depends on obtaining a PTSD diagnosis. Some authors have suggested that veterans view PTSD as the most compensable disorder, which has led some with other legitimate mental health claims to present with symptoms of severe PTSD (Frueh, Gold, & deArellano, 1997). While there is no evidence that compensation-seeking status has an impact on PAI profile presentation (as no studies have examined this question), there is some evidence that disability status may impact presentation on similar self-report measures including the MMPI-2 (Frueh et al., 2003).

We provide preliminary data relevant to this issue. Table 6.1 provides mean scores on the four primary PAI validity scales that assess Inconsistency (ICN), Infrequency (INF), Negative Impression Management (NIM), and Positive Impression Management (PIM) as a function of compensation-seeking status. Results show no differences on ICN, INF, or PIM. Unadjusted results suggested that compensation-seeking veterans had higher scores on the NIM scale; however, after accounting for PTSD symptom severity (CAPS total score) and era of military service there was not a significant effect of compensation-seeking status. There were no effects of compensation seeking in unadjusted or adjusted analyses when examining the Malingering Index (MAL) or the Rogers Discriminant Function (RDF; Rogers, Sewell, Morey, & Ustad, 1996). Thus, it appears in our data that

TABLE 6.1 Unadjusted and Adjusted Mean Scores on Primary Validity Indices

Validity Scales	Compensation Seeking (N = 680)			Non-Compensation Seeking (N = 78)		
	Mean	SD	Adjusted Mean	Mean	SD	Adjusted Mean
Inconsistency (INC)	57.9	10.2	57.6	56.7	11.1	55.9
Infrequency (INF)	53.3	11.3	53.1	52.7	10.9	52.9
Negative Impression (NIM)	73.7	20.4	71.6	66.7	18.9	68.3
Positive Impression (PIM)	39.8	11.7	40.3	40.8	12.5	39.4
Malingering Index	1.5	1.3	1.4	1.3	1.2	1.4
Rogers Discriminant Function (Raw)	–0.41	1.30	–0.49	–0.52	1.31	–0.45

Note: Adjusted mean = mean after accounting for PTSD symptom severity (CAPS total scores) and era of military service.

compensation seeking has little impact on validity scale scores. Given the small number of veterans who reported they did not plan to file a claim for PTSD, however, it is unclear whether these results will generalize to other VA settings.

The DSM-IV guidelines for PTSD assessment caution clinicians to rule out malingering in situations in which financial remuneration or benefit eligibility play a role. Although we routinely inform our patients that our evaluation is for clinical purposes and is not a part of the VA compensation and pension process, there is always a possibility that patients may distort their presentation in hopes of bolstering a disability claim. Although we suggest that the PAI may provide some benefit in the assessment of feigned response styles, it cannot be stressed enough that this measure should not be used alone in making this determination (Morey, 2007). The literature examining malingering and PTSD is complex and remains controversial (see e.g., Frueh et al., 2007; Marx et al., 2008). While a review of this literature is beyond the scope of this chapter, there are some important issues to consider (for reviews see Guriel & Fremouw, 2003; Hall & Hall, 2007; Taylor, Frueh, & Asmundson, 2007). Currently, there are no reliable estimates for the base rates of malingering in VA settings. While some argue that symptom exaggeration is common, occurring in 20%–50% of PTSD cases in VA (Frueh, Hamner, Cahill, Gold, & Hamlin, 2000; Freeman, Powell, & Kimbrell, 2008), the evidence is extremely limited and there is no consensus in the field. In a 2005 report, the VA inspector general reported that only 13 of 2,100 (0.6%) disability cases subjected to a detailed review were found to be potentially fraudulent, suggesting that the rate of pure malingering among those who are actually awarded PTSD disability compensation may be relatively low. The positive and negative predictive power of any test will vary as a function of the prevalence in the setting in which it is applied (Streiner, 2003; Meehl & Rosen, 1955). Thus, the absence of good base rate information makes it difficult, if not impossible, to calibrate cutting scores on screening or diagnostic tests to assess malingering. Currently, there is *no* method or instrument that is recognized as the best tool to detect malingering of PTSD (Guriel & Fremouw, 2003). This includes scores on the PAI or other self-report measures of psychopathology. A growing literature has examined the utility of PAI validity scales to distinguish individuals feigning PTSD from others. While validity scales have been shown to be effective in discriminating between controls and persons instructed to malinger PTSD (Calhoun et al., 2000; Guriel-Tennant & Fremouw, 2006; Liljequist, Kinder, & Schinka, 1998), they tend to misclassify true patients as malingerers (Calhoun et al., 2000; Eakin, Weathers, Benson, Anderson, & Funderburk, 2006; Guriel-Tennant & Fremouw; 2006). This is due to the fact that true cases produce profiles that appear negatively distorted (Calhoun et al., 2000). In fact, elevations on NIM are common among veterans seeking help for PTSD (Calhoun et al., 2000; Mozley et al., 2005). Table 6.2 displays the mean validity scores of patients with and without PTSD who had a valid profile based on ICN (> 73T) and INF (> 75T). As can be seen, the mean NIM score of patients diagnosed with PTSD is almost 74T, which falls in the "moderately" elevated range (i.e., 73T to 84T).

One must use other data (i.e., clinical interview, behavioral observations, history, medical and military records, and informant reports if available) to help determine whether NIM elevations are due to extreme distress associated with PTSD and co-morbid psychopathology or effortful exaggeration. In the absence of other data, it is impossible to determine to what extent these elevations reflect patients' accurate negative evaluation of themselves or some deliberate distortion of the clinical picture. When faced with high scores on NIM (> 92T) the clinician should cautiously view any interpretive hypotheses generated by the profile as suspect. In our clinic, we rarely provide any written interpretation of clinical scales when NIM is above 110T, as scores greater than this are often an indication of intentional negative distortion (Morey, 2007). After eliminating profiles due to ICN and INF, we exclude about 4% (34 additional cases) of profiles due to NIM scores greater than 110T. Given our clinical setting, elevations on PIM are rare and only 1 of the 849 profiles had a t-score greater than 68T on PIM.

In total, as many as 17% (144 of 849) of patients produce profiles that are best considered invalid after considering ICN, INF, and NIM (> 110T). While this is a significant number, we have found that the proportion of valid profiles is higher among VA inpatients and outpatients when they are administered the PAI rather than MMPI-2 (Braxton, Calhoun, Williams, & Boggs, 2007). After eliminating cases as described above, we find scores of 5 or greater on the MAL index occur in only 4 cases (< .01%) although as many as 15% (106 of 705) have scores of 3 or

TABLE 6.2   Average Validity Scores of PTSD and Non-PTSD Patients

Validity Scales	PTSD (N = 669)			Non-PTSD (N = 71)		
	Mean	SD	Median	Mean	SD	Median
Inconsistency (ICN)	55.5	8.5	55	54.9	8.5	55
Infrequency (INF)	51.0	8.8	51	50.5	7.4	51
Negative Impression (NIM)	73.5	20.4	70	60.0	14.9	55
Positive Impression (PIM)	38.6	11.4	38	45.8	12.3	50
Malingering Index	1.6	1.3	1	0.9	1.2	1
Rogers Discriminant Function (Raw)	–0.51	1.27	–0.52	–0.95	1.0	–0.98

Note: Profiles considered invalid due to ICN or INF were excluded.

greater on the MAL index. Seventy patients (10%) have RDF scores greater than 70*T* with as many as 30% above 59*T*. While we suggest those in a clinical setting be particularly cautious of interpreting elevated PAI negative response distortion indices as clear evidence of malingering, elevated scores can be used as one of many pieces of evidence to suspect that an individual is attempting to portray himself negatively.

PTSD DIAGNOSIS

An increasing number of studies provide evidence for the use of the PAI in the diagnosis of PTSD (Calhoun et al., 2000; Calhoun et al., in press; Cherepon & Prinzhorn, 1994; Drury et al., 2009; Holmes, Williams, & Haines, 2001; McDevitt-Murphy et al., 2005, 2007; Mozley et al., 2005). These studies include examinations of veterans, college students, and adult community volunteers. Studies (Cherepon & Prinzhorn, 1994; McDevitt-Murphy et al., 2005; Mozley et al., 2005) have examined PAI profiles of patients with PTSD as well as scale differences between persons with and without PTSD.

Studies examining differences between those with and without PTSD typically find that the largest effect between groups is found on the PAI Traumatic Stress subscale (ARD-T) (Cherepon & Prinzhorn, 1994; McDevitt-Murphy et al., 2005). McDevitt-Murphy et al. (2005) investigated the ability of ARD-T to differentiate between women with and without PTSD. They reported that a cutting score of 71*T* on ARD-T resulted in a sensitivity of 0.79, specificity of 0.88, with an overall efficiency of 0.85. Note, however, that while the existing literature indicates that ARD-T may be a useful tool for the identification of PTSD, Morey (1996) has cautioned against relying on this scale in isolation, as it was not intended to reflect the entire spectrum of PTSD symptomatology.

To aid clinicians in making accurate diagnoses, Morey (1991; see also Morey, 1996 for a discussion) developed a series of diagnostic rules that are incorporated into the PAI interpretive software program. Among these rules, the PTSD LOGIT function is an empirically derived actuarial formula for the assessment of PTSD including information from several PAI subscales including ARD-T. Although little research has examined the LOGIT function, current evidence suggests it can effectively discriminate between those with and without PTSD (Calhoun et al., 2000; Calhoun et al., in press). Using signal detection analysis (Hanley & McNeil, 1983), we found that the LOGIT function had an 86% probability of correctly classifying PTSD in a recent study of female community volunteers (Calhoun et al., in press). The cutting score built into the program, however, appears less sensitive to milder cases of PTSD as found in our sample of women (sensitivity = 0.39) than it was in a sample of combat veterans with PTSD (sensitivity = 0.83; Calhoun et al., 2000). We suggest that clinicians must exercise caution and avoid the dangers of overvaluing an interpretive report that may utilize cutting scores that are inappropriate for the target population. More research is needed to examine the PTSD LOGIT function.

Given that the base rate of PTSD is 90% in our clinic, we don't rely on the PAI to rule out PTSD. In general, tests are best used to rule in, but not rule out a condition when the prevalence of disorder is high (Streiner, 2003). For example, if we were to apply a cutting score ARD-T (> 70T) which was thought to have a sensitivity of 0.79 and a specificity of 0.88, we would end up with a negative predictive value of only 0.32. This means that 68% of negative test results would be false negatives.

As discussed by Morey (1996), a number of PAI scales and subscales tap symptoms and features of PTSD. Trauma exposure will lead to increased ARD-T elevations. DSM-IV PTSD Cluster B (re-experiencing symptoms) including flashbacks and unwanted memories may lead to moderate SCZ-P elevations. Nightmares and associated sleep disturbances can lead to elevations on the physiological symptoms of the Depression subscale (DEP-P). Physiological reactivity to trauma cues leads to elevations on ANX-P. PTSD Cluster-C symptoms (avoidance and numbing) may lead to DEP-A elevations (diminished interest in once-significant activities), low scores on WRM and elevations on SCZ-S (social detachment). Individuals with PTSD often turn to drugs and alcohol as an avoidance strategy and elevations on these PAI scales are not uncommon. PTSD Cluster D (hyperarousal symptoms) are reflected by elevations on PAR-H (hypervigilance), MAN-I (irritability), SCZ-T (problems with concentration), and elevations on Aggression. Associated features of PTSD including strong feelings of guilt are often reflected on elevations on DEP-C.

There is converging evidence related to the shape of a typical PTSD profile (Cherepon & Prinzhorn, 1994; Holmes et al., 2001; McDevitt-Murphy et al., 2005; Morey, 1996; Mozley et al., 2005). In an earlier report of data collected in our clinic we found the same elevations as Holmes and colleagues (2001) even though samples were from quite different populations. These elevations include the Somatic Complaints (SOM), Anxiety (ANX), Anxiety-Related Disorders (ARD), Depression (DEP), and Schizophrenia (SCZ) clinical scales.

The mean profile of veterans (N = 635 after excluding profiles based on ICN > 73T, INF > 75T, NIM > 110T, PIM > 68T) in our clinic diagnosed with PTSD is displayed in Figure 6.1. Mean combat exposure and PTSD symptom severity for these veterans is displayed in Table 6.3. Scores on the Combat Exposure Scale

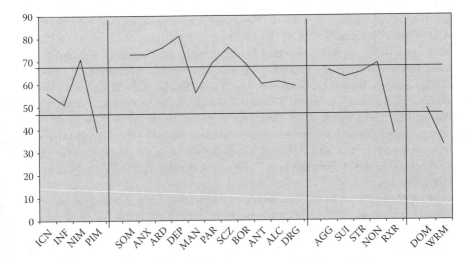

Figure 6.1   Mean PAI profile of veterans with PTSD (N = 635).

TABLE 6.3   Mean Combat-Exposure and PTSD Measures

| | | | PAI Measure | |
Scale	Mean	SD	ARD	ARD-T
CES	20.8	11.0	.07	.15°°
MISSISSIPPI	118.0	18.5	.60°°	.64°°
DTS	98.1	24.7	.55°°	.55°°
CAPS Severity	80.2	20.2	.43°°	.46°°

Note: °p<.05; °°p<.01°°p<.001; CES = Combat Exposure Scale; MISSISSIPPI = Mississippi Scale for Combat-Related PTSD; DTS = Davidson Trauma Scale; CAPS = Clinician Administered PTSD Scale.

(CES; Keane et al., 1989) suggest that on average, our sample reported moderate combat exposure. The Anxiety-Related Disorder full scale and ARD-T were strongly correlated with PTSD symptoms but were less strongly correlated with combat exposure.

Means and standard deviations for all PAI scales and subscales are shown by selected military era in Table 6.4 and Table 6.5. Given the relatively large sample sizes, there are a number of statistically significant differences on PAI subscales between eras although most are not clinically meaningful. A review of Tables 6.4 and 6.5 does indicate a number of clinically significant differences (i.e., differences of 5 or more points) as a function of military era on some PAI scales. It appears that veterans of WWII/Korean War tended to produce a profile that is somewhat less hostile, aggressive, suspicious, and socially isolated than veterans of other eras. For example, mean scores of WWII/Korean War veterans were 5 or more points lower on PAR, SCZ, ANT, and Agression (AGG) scales, and were 5 or more points higher on WRM than most other eras.

Despite some mean differences as described above, the shape of the PAI profile is remarkably consistent across eras. Consistent with Morey's (1991) original work examining profiles of PTSD subjects in the PAI normative sample, there are marked elevations of ARD-T. Eighty-percent of profiles had elevations on ARD-T over 70T and 60% had elevations of 80T or more. Veterans with PTSD have been shown to have increased health complaints, diagnosed medical problems, medical service use, and mortality (Beckham et al., 1998, 2003; Boscarino, 2006, Calhoun, Bosworth, Grambow, Dudley, & Beckham, 2002; Calhoun, Wiley, Dennis, & Beckham, in press). Concern over physical functioning is common in our setting, where we often see elevations of above 70T on the SOM scale (60% of cases). Consistent with previous work, the average profile of the current sample of help-seeking veterans with PTSD also includes elevations above 70T on the ANX (57% of cases), ARD (66% of cases), DEP (77% of cases), and SCZ (60% of cases) clinical scales.

Few studies examining PAI profile configuration have assessed or reported rates of additional psychiatric co-morbidity (Drury et al., 2009). We find rates of depression as high as 63% in our clinic and previously reported that veterans in our clinic who had a co-morbid diagnosis of major depressive disorder scored significantly higher on DEP, ANX, SOM, Suicide Ideation (SUI), and Stress (STR) scales and lower on the Warmth (WRM) scale than those with PTSD alone (Mozley et

TABLE 6.4   Mean PAI Scale Elevations Among Veterans with PTSD by Military Era

Scale	WWII/Korea N = 28 Mean	SD	Vietnam N = 424 Mean	SD	Gulf War N = 59 Mean	SD	OEF/OIF N = 95 Mean	SD
ICN	57.9	8.1	56.2	8.1	53.7	7.8	52.6	9.9
INF	50.3	5.6	50.9	8.2	51.8	8.8	50.5	11.7
NIM	68.2	15.9	71.6	16.2	73.2	18.5	64.0	17.5
PIM	42.7	10.1	39.5	11.3	37.6	10.5	39.5	10.7
SOM	76.7	13.2	81.2	13.5	81.8	15.2	76.7	15.8
ANX	74.8	15.0	73.1	12.5	75.6	14.1	68.7	15.4
ARD	74.4	13.9	76.2	11.7	76.7	13.4	71.0	14.9
DEP	76.7	13.2	81.2	13.5	81.8	15.2	76.7	15.8
MAN	53.4	8.9	55.0	10.4	60.6	10.9	56.4	11.4
PAR	61.3	12.5	68.7	13.6	71.0	16.6	67.4	15.3
SCZ	68.4	13.2	76.2	14.9	76.4	17.2	71.7	16.6
BOR	64.6	10.3	69.1	11.0	70.9	11.4	67.2	13.0
ANT	53.2	10.1	59.7	11.0	59.0	11.6	60.3	12.6
ALC	59.1	15.7	62.2	17.5	59.8	16.3	54.0	15.8
DRG	58.5	8.7	61.4	14.2	56.3	10.6	51.7	13.4
AGG	60.0	14.0	69.0	13.3	69.0	13.3	65.5	16.0
SUI	58.0	14.4	64.5	18.2	62.6	18.4	57.0	18.6
STR	61.6	13.2	64.8	13.0	66.6	13.1	62.1	14.5
NON	63.5	13.2	69.0	13.3	69.0	13.3	65.5	16.0
RXR	39.9	9.1	38.0	9.8	36.5	9.0	38.5	10.2
DOM	48.8	8.0	48.1	10.6	52.8	11.9	50.8	11.8
WRM	39.7	11.0	33.2	11.6	34.8	14.8	33.4	13.6

al., 2005). Influences of other Axis I disorders on clinical profiles, however, were not addressed. In a recent study of female community volunteers, we examined the impact of one or more Axis I conditions on PAI profile configuration. Not surprisingly, higher co-morbidity rates were associated with higher mean profile elevations and broader range of endorsed symptoms. The group with the highest rate of co-morbidity produced profiles most similar to previously published reports of patients with PTSD. Thus, the literature examining PAI profile configuration is likely more reflective of PTSD with high rates of co-morbidity found in clinical settings rather than a single diagnosis of "pure" PTSD.

TREATMENT PLANNING

To date, no studies have specifically evaluated PAI indicators of treatment motivation and predictors of treatment process among veterans with PTSD. While we view working with veterans with PTSD as an honor and privilege, these veterans often display characteristics such as high hostility, impulsivity, and aggression

TABLE 6.5   Mean PAI Subscales Among PTSD Veterans by War Era

Scale	WWII/Korea N = 28 Mean	SD	Vietnam N = 424 Mean	SD	Gulf War N = 59 Mean	SD	OEF/OIF N = 95 Mean	SD
SOM-C	76.3	20.3	76.3	16.7	78.1	19.4	64.0	15.1
SOM-S	69.2	12.0	69.5	12.2	75.0	12.4	66.1	11.5
SOM-H	71.3	12.4	69.2	12.3	70.8	12.8	60.4	12.9
ANX-C	69.4	13.0	67.4	11.8	70.2	13.0	64.7	14.7
ANX-A	72.2	15.1	71.6	12.0	72.9	14.2	69.3	12.2
ANX-P	76.3	15.3	74.3	14.0	76.9	14.8	69.5	12.6
ARD-O	58.7	11.8	59.1	10.8	61.6	12.6	58.8	11.0
ARD-P	62.3	9.6	62.5	11.5	61.1	13.9	57.9	12.6
ARD-T	80.3	15.8	83.3	12.9	83.6	13.4	79.0	14.6
DEP-C	68.6	14.5	73.9	15.7	73.0	16.6	70.7	16.3
DEP-A	73.4	14.5	78.6	14.2	80.1	15.8	75.0	14.2
DEP-P	74.6	7.6	75.9	9.4	75.6	14.2	73.9	10.1
MAN-A	50.9	7.9	54.3	10.6	57.5	10.6	56.9	9.7
MAN-G	47.5	8.4	46.1	10.3	50.8	13.0	48.7	11.4
MAN-I	59.4	12.8	61.8	12.1	66.8	12.7	62.0	12.0
PAR-H	58.8	11.8	66.7	12.3	69.3	15.1	68.3	14.5
PAR-P	57.8	13.1	64.7	15.4	66.5	17.5	62.9	15.2
PAR-R	61.6	10.2	66.0	11.8	67.2	14.4	64.9	12.6
SCZ-P	52.7	12.4	59.4	15.5	59.3	16.6	54.7	13.4
SCZ-S	66.0	14.0	74.8	13.7	74.1	15.5	72.2	14.7
SCZ-T	70.3	12.5	72.6	14.4	74.0	16.1	72.8	14.7
BOR-A	67.5	11.8	70.1	11.7	73.1	12.1	69.0	12.0
BOR-I	63.1	10.3	65.4	10.6	67.3	10.7	64.8	12.5
BOR-N	62.9	12.1	67.1	11.1	67.9	12.3	65.7	11.6
BOR-S	50.8	9.0	56.9	12.3	56.8	14.1	56.4	13.9
ANT-A	54.9	10.8	60.2	10.3	57.8	12.0	59.0	11.5
ANT-E	50.8	9.6	56.4	12.5	54.6	11.0	54.4	12.8
ANT-S	51.3	8.7	56.6	11.5	59.4	13.3	63.9	13.4
AGG-A	61.3	13.3	64.0	12.2	65.9	11.0	63.1	13.4
AGG-V	52.5	11.1	57.0	11.0	59.6	12.2	58.9	13.4
AGG-P	62.1	16.2	69.6	16.1	74.1	17.4	68.8	17.2

that make treatment challenging. The PAI Treatment Process Index (TPI), which is an operationalization of 12 factors thought to be important predictors of treatment process and outcome, may be beneficial for making predictions about how challenging the therapeutic process with a particular patient may be. The TPI is scored by counting the number of positive items. Morey (1996) notes that TPI

TABLE 6.6   Treatment Process Factors Among Veterans With PTSD

Characteristic	PAI Problem Indicators	Frequency in Sample
1. Friendliness	PAR-R > 70T AGG-A > 70T WRM < 30T	62%
2. Likability	BOR > 70T ANT > 70T	48%
3. Motivation	RXR > 60T PIM > 60T	5%
4. Psychological-minded	BOR-S > 70T ANT-E > 70T SOM > 70T ANT-A > 70T	67%
5. Conscience factors	ANT-E > 70T	13%
6. Self-discipline	BOR > 70T ANT > 70T ALC > 70T DRG > 70T NIM > 70T	67%
7. Impulse control	BOR-S > 70T AGG > 70T ANT-A > 70T ANT-S > 70T	47%
8. Defensive style	BOR > 70T ANT > 70T ALC > 70T DRG > 70T	59%
9. Internalization	PAR > 70T	43%
10. Empathy	MAN-G > 70T DOM > 70T ANT-E > 70T	16%
11. Parental Factors	ARD-T > 70T NON> 70T	86%
12. Social supports	NON > 70T STR > 70T	57%
Total Score M		5.7
Total Score SD		3.2

scores below 4 suggest that an individual has numerous personal assets that may assist the treatment process. Scores of 7–10 suggest, however, that there are a variety of obstacles to a smooth treatment process and therapy is likely to be difficult. With scores in this range, problems tend to be more refractory and chronic. Marked elevations (> 10) represent individuals who are likely among the most challenging of any patients to treat (Morey, 1996). Table 6.6 displays the frequency of each predictor of treatment amenability from the TPI in our sample. The mean TPI among our patients is almost 6. In our clinic, 37% of patients have TPI elevations of 7 or above and as many as 8% have scores of 11 or greater.

RISK ASSESSMENT

The PAI may be useful for identifying issues associated with potential for suicide and violence. The SUI measures thoughts about suicide and scores from 60T–69T are typical among clinical respondents (Morey, 1996). In our clinic, the mean score of PTSD patients on SUI is 63T, which reflects periodic thoughts of self harm. Morey (1996) suggests that scores from 70–80T reflect recurrent thoughts related to suicide and should be considered a warning sign of the potential for suicide, and scores between 85T and 99T are typical of individuals who have been placed on suicide precautions. Scores above 100T suggest the respondent is preoccupied with death and may have completed many steps toward suicide and should be a significant warning sign of the potential for suicide. In our setting, we find that as many as 30% of veterans with PTSD have SUI scores above 70T, including 9% who score between 85 and 99T, and as many as 6% who score above 100T.

The Suicide Potential Index (SPI) contains 20 risk factors for completed suicide that can be assessed with the PAI. While little research has examined the SPI among patients with PTSD, initial support for its validity has been demonstrated in the PAI normative sample (Morey, 1996). Raw scores at or above 13 and 18 are suggestive of moderate and marked numbers of suicide risk factors. Scores in this range merit further evaluation of suicide risk. There is some indication, however, that SPI scores are correlated with measures of response distortion and overall degree of psychopathology represented by the profile (Morey, 1996). In our setting, the mean score on the SPI is 12.6 (SD = 4.4). While 48% of profiles have SPI scores at or above 13, only 5% of scores suggest marked numbers of risk factors (i.e., SPI > 18).

The PAI may also be helpful in assessing risk for violence. There is a large literature documenting that, in addition to reporting a history of arrest (Calhoun, Malesky, Bosworth, & Beckham, 2004), veterans with PTSD experience more problematic anger and exhibit more violent or aggressive behavior than veterans without PTSD (Beckham, Feldman, Kirby, Hertzberg, & Moore, 1997; Begic, & Jokic-Begic, 2001; Freeman & Roca, 2001; McFall, Fontana, Raskind, & Rosenheck, 1999; McFall, Wright, Donovan, & Raskind, 1999). Anger and aggression negatively impact family members of veterans with PTSD (Calhoun, Beckham, & Bosworth, 2002) and both patients and family members cite irritability and explosive anger as a primary reason for seeking mental-health treatment (Blum, Kelley, Meyer, Carlson, & Hodson, 1984; Calhoun et al., 2002). Thus, the assessment of a patient's problems with aggression and violence is an important treatment consideration for help-seeking veterans with PTSD.

The PAI Aggression full and subscales, as well as the Violence Potential Index (VPI) identify problematic aggression and risk for violent behavior. The AGG full-scale score provides an assessment of behavioral and attitudinal factors associated with aggression, anger, and hostility intended to reflect Riley and Treiber's (1989) three-factor model of aggression (Morey, 1996). The AGG subscales include Aggressive Attitude (AGG-A), i.e., general emotions and attitudes facilitative of aggressive behavior; Verbal Aggression (AGG-V), i.e., a readiness to exhibit anger verbally; and Physical Aggression (AGG-P), which taps past and present attitudes regarding physically aggressive behavior (Morey, 1996). The VPI is a "constellation" of risk factors for violence composed of 20 features of the PAI profile that are consistent with existing evidence on the prediction of dangerousness (Morey, 1996). The VPI taps a variety of psychological problems such as anger directed outward, history of antisocial behavior, impulsivity, and disinhibition due to substance abuse, and was designed to supplement the AGG scales in assessing dangerousness. VPI raw scores above 9 and 17 are indicative of moderate and marked risk of violent behavior, and samples with a history of violence obtained mean scores above 6 in preliminary studies (Morey, 1991).

High scores on the AGG scales are common among combat veterans with PTSD. As displayed in Figure 6.1, the mean score on AGG is 66T, with mean subscale scores of 64, 57, and 70 on AGG-A, AGG-V, and AGG-P respectively. We previously evaluated the validity of the PAI AGG scales and VPI in male combat veterans in our clinic (Crawford et al., 2007). In addition to high scores on AGG scales, results showed that the mean VPI score of PTSD veterans (M = 7.2; SD = 4.1) was greater than those obtained in samples with a documented history of violence such as individuals convicted of assault or rape (Morey, 1996). High VPI scores may be in part related to the high correlation between the VPI and measures of psychiatric symptom severity or response distortion (Morey, 1996), which, as discussed previously, is common in this sample.

Overall, results provided strong evidence of the incremental validity of the AGG composite scale and suggest that the PAI may provide a very useful indicator of problematic aggression in combat veterans with PTSD (Crawford et al., 2007). Specifically, we found that the AGG was a significant predictor of patients' self-reported violence history (scores on the Violence subscale of the Conflict Tactics Scale; Straus, 1989) even after accounting for their recent history of violence (i.e., "Have you had difficulty controlling violent behavior in the past 30 days?"), PTSD symptom severity, and demographic variables. The AGG composite scale also explained more variance in interpersonal violence scores than MMPI–2 scales associated with aggression or externalization of anger as well as other PAI scales measuring traits that may be related to aggression (e.g., ANT). The VPI, however, failed to explain any variance in violence scores after accounting for AGG (Crawford et al., 2007).

INDICATIONS FOR ADDITIONAL MEASURES

As noted, we use the PAI in context of an assessment battery that includes multiple measures of traumatic events, PTSD symptoms, and a clinical structured interview for PTSD. As the PAI does not contain an assessment of all 17 DSM-IV symptoms of PTSD it is not adequate as a measure of PTSD symptom severity. Brief PTSD specific scales such as the Davidson Trauma Scale (DTS; Davidson et al., 1997) or the PTSD Checklist (PCL; Weathers, Litz, Herman, Huska, & Keane, 1993; Blanchard, Jones-Alexander, Buckley, & Forneris, 1996) provide a measure of self-reported PTSD symptom severity that is more readily administered repeatedly to track treatment gains. Similarly, while the PAI ARD-T subscale provides a measure of exposure to traumatic events, it is not sufficient as a measurement of traumatic events for a formal PTSD evaluation. We utilize both the Combat Exposure Scale (Keane et al., 1989) and the Traumatic Life Event Questionnaire

(Kubany et al., 2000, 2004), which provide a measure of combat exposure as well as exposure to a variety of childhood and adult traumatic events. As discussed previously, the assessment of PTSD is complicated by issues of secondary gain. High elevations on NIM, MAL, or RDF call for the collection of additional data including a review of clinical interviews, behavioral observations, history, medical and military records, and informant reports to help rule out malingering. Currently, there is no widespread agreement on the best method to assess malingering. While there is a need for more research in this area, clinical interviews such as the Structured Interview of Reported Symptoms (SIRS; Rogers, 1992) may have value in assessing for malingering in PTSD although it is not perfect in discriminating between feigned PTSD and psychiatric disorders (Rogers, Kropp, Bagby, & Dickens, 1992). Given that concentration difficulties are a common feature of PTSD, neuropsychological tests of malingering can be used in the assessment of malingered PTSD. We now administer the Test of Memory Malingering (TOMM; Tombaugh, 1996; 1997) when other evidence including PAI scales raise the possibility of exaggerated or malingered symptoms.

SUMMARY AND ADVANTAGES AND DISADVANTAGES OF THE PAI

While the MMPI-2 remains the most commonly used psychological test in a variety of environments (Boccaccini & Brodsky, 1999; Piotrowski, 1992, 1999), the PAI is rapidly gaining in popularity (Piotrowski, 2000). Veterans Affairs administrative data suggest that an increasing number of clinical psychologists within the VA Healthcare system are relying on the PAI to assist them in obtaining valid, clinically relevant information on a patient's attitudes, traits, and psychopathology, while usage of the MMPI-2 has been on the decline (Crawford et al., 2007). In our view, the PAI has several advantages over the MMPI-2, including a lower reading level, shorter length, and non-overlapping clinical scales. In general, administration of the PAI results in a larger number of profiles that are considered to be valid and interpretable within a VA setting (Braxton et al., 2007). Further, there is some evidence that the PAI has better discriminant validity for assessing PTSD than the MMPI-2 (McDevitt-Murphy et al., 2007). On the other hand, the MMPI-2 may be better at detecting feigned PTSD than the PAI (Eakin et al., 2006). More research on the application of the PAI Aggression, SPI, and TPI among PTSD patients will increase the utility of the PAI in this setting.

REFERENCES

American Psychiatric Association. (1994). *Diagnostic and statistical manual of mental disorders (4th ed.)*. Washington, DC: Author.

Beckham, J. C., Moore, S. D., Feldman, M. E., Hertzberg, M. A., Kirby, A. C., & Fairbank, J. A. (1998). Health status, somatization, and severity of posttraumatic stress disorder in Vietnam combat veterans with posttraumatic stress disorder. *American Journal of Psychiatry, 155*, 1565–1569.

Beckham, J. C., Taft, C. T., Vrana, S. R., Feldman, M. E., Barefoot, J. C., Moore, S. D., Mozley, S.L., Butterfield, M.I., & Calhoun, P.S. (2003). Ambulatory monitoring and physical health report in Vietnam veterans with and without chronic posttraumatic stress disorder. *Journal of Traumatic Stress, 16,* 329–335.

Beckham, J. C., Feldman, M. E., Kirby, A. C., Hertzberg, M. A., & Moore, S. D. (1997). Interpersonal violence and its correlates in Vietnam veterans with chronic posttraumatic stress disorder. *Journal of Clinical Psychology, 53,* 859–869.

Begic, D., & Jokic-Begic, N. (2001). Aggressive behavior in combat veterans with posttraumatic stress disorder. *Military Medicine, 166,* 671–676.

Blake, D. D., Weathers, F. W., Nagy, L. M., Kaloupek, D. G., Gusman, F. D., Charney, D. S., et al. (1995). The development of a clinician-administered posttraumatic stress disorder scale. *Journal of Traumatic Stress, 8,* 75–80.

Blanchard, E. B., Jones-Alexander, J., Buckley, T. C., & Forneris, C. A. (1996). Psychometric properties of the PTSD Checklist (PCL). *Behaviour Research and Therapy, 34*(8), 669–673.

Blum, M. D., Kelley, E. M., Meyer, K., Carlson, C. R., & Hodson, L. (1984). An assessment of the treatment needs of Viet Nam-era veterans. *Hospital and Community Psychiatry, 35,* 691–696.

Boccaccini, M. T., & Brodsky, S. L. (1999). Diagnostic test usage by forensic psychologists in emotional injury cases. *Professional Psychology Research, & Practice, 30*(3), 253–259.

Boscarino, J. A. (2006). External-cause mortality after psychologic trauma: The effects of stress exposure and predisposition. *Comprehensive Psychiatry, 47*(6), 503–514.

Braxton, L.E., Calhoun, P.S., Williams, J.E., & Boggs, C.D. (2007). Validity Rates of the Personality Assessment Inventory and the Minnesota Multiphasic Inventory-2 in a VA Medical Center Setting. *Journal of Personality Assessment, 88,* 5–15.

Breslau, N., Davis, G., Andreski, P., Federman, B., Anthony, J. C., & Dohrenwend, B. P. (1998). Epidemiological findings on posttraumatic stress disorder and co-morbid disorders in the general population. In *Adversity, stress, and psychopathology.* (pp. 319–330). New York: Oxford University Press.

Butcher, J. N., Dahlstrom, W. G., Graham, J. R., Tellegen, A., & Kaemmer, B. (1989). *MMPI–2: Minnesota Multiphasic Personality Inventory–2: Manual for administration and scoring.* Minneapolis: University of Minnesota Press.

Calhoun, P. S., Beckham, J. C., Feldman, M. E., Barefoot, J. C., Haney, T., & Bosworth, H. B. (2002). Partners' ratings of combat veterans' anger. *Journal of Traumatic Stress, 15,* 133–136.

Calhoun, P. S., Boggs, C., Crawford, E., & Beckham, J. C. (in press). Utility of the Personality Assessment Inventory LOGIT Function for PTSD in the Assessment of Posttraumatic Stress Disorder. *Journal of Personality Assessment.*

Calhoun, P.S., Beckham, J.C., & Bosworth, H.B. (2002). Caregiver burden and psychological distress in partners of veterans with chronic posttraumatic stress disorder. *The Journal of Traumatic Stress, 15,* 205–212.

Calhoun, P. S., Bosworth, H. B., Grambow, S. C., Dudley, T. K., & Beckham, J. C. (2002). Medical service utilization by veterans seeking help for posttraumatic stress disorder. *American Journal of Psychiatry, 159,* 2081–2086.

Calhoun, P. S., Earnst, K. S., Tucker, D. D., Kirby, A. C., & Beckham, J. C. (2000). Feigning combat-related posttraumatic stress disorder on the personality assessment inventory. *Journal of Personality Assessment, 75*(2), 338–350.

Calhoun, P. S., Wiley, M., Dennis, M. F., & Beckham, J. C. (in press). Self-reported health and physician diagnosed illnesses in women with posttraumatic stress disorder and major depressive disorder. *Journal of Traumatic Stress.*

Calhoun, P. S., Malesky, A. L., Jr., Bosworth, H. B., & Beckham, J. C. (2004). Severity of posttraumatic stress disorder and involvement with the criminal justice system. *Journal of Trauma Practice, 3,* 1–16.

Cherepon, J. A., & Prinzhorn, B. (1994). Personality Assessment Inventory (PAI) profiles of adult female abuse survivors. *Assessment, 1,* 393–399.

Clancy, C. P., Graybeal, A., Tompson, W. P., Badgett, K. S., Feldman, M. E., Calhoun, P. S., Erkanli, A., Hertzberg, M. A., & Beckham, J. C. (2006). Lifetime trauma exposure in veterans with military-related posttraumatic stress disorder: Association with current symptomatology. *Journal of Clinical Psychiatry, 67,* 1346–1353.

Crawford, E. F., Calhoun, P. S., Braxton, L., & Beckham, J. C. (2007). Validity of the Personality Assessment Inventory aggression scales and Violence Potential Index in veterans with PTSD. *Journal of Personality Assessment, 88,* 91–99.

Davidson, J. R. T., Book, S. W., Colket, J. T., Tupler, L. A., Roth, S., David, D., Hertzberg, M., et al. (1997). Assessment of a new self-rating scale for posttraumatic stress disorder: The Davidson Trauma Scale. *Psychological Medicine, 27,* 153–160.

Davidson, J. R. T., Rothbaum, B. O., van der Kolk, B. A., Sikes, C. R., & Farfel, G. M. (2001). Multicenter, double-blind comparison of sertraline and placebo in the treatment of posttraumatic stress disorder. *Archives of General Psychiatry, 58,* 485–492.

Davidson, J. R. T., Tharwani, H. M., & Connor, K. M. (2002). Davidson Trauma Scale (DTS): Normative scores in the general population and effect sizes in placebo-controlled SSRI trials. *Depression and Anxiety, 15,* 75–78.

Department of Veterans Affairs Office of Inspector General. Review of State Variances in Disability Compensation Payments (#05–00765–137). (2005). Washington, DC: Department of Veterans Affairs Office of Inspector General.

Drury, P., Calhoun, P.S., Boggs, C., Araujo, G., Yeatts, B., Dennis, M. F., & Beckham, J. C. (2009). Influences of comorbid disorders on personality assessment inventory profiles in women with posttraumatic stress disorder. *Journal of Psychopathology and Behavioral Assessment, 31;* 119–128.

Eakin, D. E., Weathers, F.W., Benson, T.B., Anderson, C.F., & Funderburk, B. (2006). Detection of feigned posttraumatic stress disorder: A comparison of the MMPI-2 and PAI. *Journal of Psychopathology and Behavioral Assessment, 28,* 145–155.

Eisenman, D., Weine, S, Green, B., de Jong, J., Rayburn, N., Ventevogel P, Keller, A., & Agani, F. (2006). The ISTSS/Rand guidelines on mental health training for primary healthcare providers for trauma-exposed populations in conflict-affected countries. *Journal of Traumatic Stress, 19,* 5–17.

First, M. B., Spitzer, R. L., Miriam, G., & Williams, J. B. W. (2002). Structured Clinical Interview for DSM-IV-TR Axis I Disorders, Research Version, Patient Edition With Psychotic Screen (SCID-I/P W/ PSY SCREEN). New York: Biometrics Research, New York State Psychiatric Institute.

Foa, E. B., Rothbaum, B. O., Riggs, D. S., & Murdock, T. B. (1991). Treatment of posttraumatic stress disorder in rape victims: A comparison between cognitive-behavioral procedures and counseling. *Journal of Consulting and Clinical Psychology, 59,* 715–723.

Freeman, T. W., & Roca, V. (2001). Gun use, attitudes toward violence, and aggression among combat veterans with chronic posttraumatic stress disorder. *Journal of Nervous and Mental Disease, 189,* 317–320.

Freeman, T., Powell, M., & Kimbrell, T. (2008). Measuring symptom exaggeration in veterans with chronic posttraumatic stress disorder. *Psychiatry Research, 158,* 374–380.

Frueh, B. C., Gold, P. B., & deArellano, M. A. (1997). Symptom overreporting in combat veterans evaluated for PTSD: Differentiation on the basis of compensation-seeking status. *Journal of Personality Assessment, 68,* 369–384.

Frueh, B. C., Elhai, J. D., Gold, P. B., Monnier, J., Magruder, K. M., Keane, T. M., et al. (2003). Disability compensation seeking among veterans evaluated for posttraumatic stress disorder. *Psychiatric Services, 54,* 84–91.

Frueh, B. C., Grubaugh, A. L., Elhai, J. D., & Buckley, T. C. (2007). U.S. Department of Veterans Affairs disability policies for posttraumatic stress disorder: Administrative trends and implications for treatment, rehabilitation, and research. *American Journal of Public Health, 97,* 2143–2145.

Frueh, B. C., Hamner, M. B., Cahill, S. P., Gold, P. B., & Hamlin, K. L. (2000). Apparent symptom overreporting in combat veterans evaluated for PTSD. *Clinical Psychology Review, 20,* 853–885.

Guriel, J., & Fremouw, W. (2003). Assessing malingered posttraumatic stress disorder: A critical review. *Clinical Psychology Review, 23,* 881–904.

Hall, R. C. W., & Hall, R. C. W. (2007). Detection of malingered PTSD: An overview of clinical, psychometric, and physiological assessment: Where do we stand? *Journal of Forensic Science, 52,* 717–725.

Hanley, J. A., & McNeil, B. J. (1983). A method for comparing the areas under receiver operating characteristic curves derived from the same cases. *Radiology, 148,* 839–843.

Hoge, C. W., Castro, C. A., Messer, S. C., McGurk, D., Cotting, D. I., & Koffman, R. L. (2004). Combat duty in Iraq and Afghanistan, mental health problems, and barriers to care. *New England Journal of Medicine, 351,* 13–22.

Hollingshead, A. B., & Redlich, R. L. (1958). *Social class and mental illness.* New York: John Wiley.

Holmes, G. E., Williams, C. L., & Haines, J. (2001). Motor vehicle accident trauma exposure: Personality profiles associated with posttraumatic diagnoses. *Anxiety, Stress, & Coping: An International Journal, 14*(3), 301–313.

Hyer, L., Boudewyns, P. A., Harrison, W. R., O'Leary, W. C., Bruno, R. D., Saucer, R. T., & Winsch, D. L. (1988). Vietnam veterans: Overreporting versus acceptable reporting of symptoms. *Journal of Personality Assessment, 52,* 475–486.

Hyer, L. F., Fallon, J. H., Harrison, W. R., & Boudewyns, P. A. (1987). MMPI Overreporting by Vietnam combat veterans. *Journal of Clinical Psychology, 43,* 79–83.

Jordan, R. G., Nunley, T. V., & Cook, R. R. (1992). Symptom exaggeration in PTSD inpatient population: Response set or claim for compensation. *Journal of Traumatic Stress, 4,* 633–642.

Keane, T. M., Fairbank, J. A., Caddell, J. M., Zimering, R. T., Taylor, K. L., & Mora, C. A. (1989). Clinical evaluation of a measure to assess combat exposure. *Psychological Assessment, 1,* 53–55.

Keane, T. M., Caddell, J. M., & Taylor, K. L. (1988). Mississippi Scale for Combat-Related Posttraumatic Stress Disorder: Three studies in reliability and validity. *Journal of Consulting and Clinical Psychology, 56,* 85–90.

Keane, T. M., Wolfe, J., & Taylor, K. L. (1987). Post-traumatic stress disorder: Evidence of diagnostic validity and methods of psychological assessment. *Journal of Clinical Psychology, 43,* 32–43.

Kessler, R. C., Sonnega, A., Bromet, E., & Hughes, M. (1995). Posttraumatic stress disorder in the National Comorbidity Survey. *Archives of General Psychiatry, 52,* 1048–1060.

Kubany, E. S. (2004). Traumatic Life Events Questionnaire and PTSD Screening and Diagnostic Scale. Los Angeles, CA: Western Psychological Services.

Kubany, E. S., Leisen, M. B., Kaplan, A. S., Watson, S. B., Haynes, S. N., Owens, J. A., & Burns, K. (2000). Development and preliminary validation of a brief broad-spectrum measure of trauma exposure: The Traumatic Life Events Questionnaire. *Psychological Assessment, 12,* 210–224.

Kubany, E. S., Haynes, S. N., Leisen, M. B., Owens, J. A., Kaplan, A. S., Watson, S. B., et al. (2000). Development and preliminary validation of a brief broad-spectrum measure of trauma exposure: The Traumatic Life Events Questionnaire. *Psychological Assessment, 12,* 210–224.

Kulka, R. A., Schlenger, W., Fairbank, J. A., Hough, R. L., Jordan, B. K., Marmar, C. R., & Weiss, D.S. (1990). *Trauma and the Vietnam War generation: Report of findings from the National Vietnam Veterans Readjustment Study.* New York: Brunner-Mazel.

Lees-Haley, P. R., (1989). Malingering post-traumatic stress disorder on the MMPI. *Forensic Reports, 2*, 89–91.

Liljequist, L., Kinder, B. N., & Schinka, J. A. (1998). An investigation of malingering posttraumatic stress disorder on the Personality Assessment Inventory. *Journal of Personality Assessment, 71*, 322–336.

Lund, M., Foy, D., Sipprelle, C., & Strachan, A. (1984). The Combat Exposure Scale: A systematic assessment of trauma in the Vietnam War. *Journal of Clinical Psychology, 40*, 1323–1328.

Magruder, K. M., Frueh, B. C., Knapp, R. G., Davis, L., Hamner, M. B., Martin, R. H., et al. (2005). Prevalence of posttraumatic stress disorder in Veterans Affairs primary care clinics. *General Hospital Psychiatry, 27*, 167–179.

Marx, B. P., Miller, M. W., Sloan, D. M., Litz, B. T., Kaloupek, D. G., & Keane, T. M. (2008). Military related PTSD, current disability policies, and malingering. *American Journal of Public Health, 98*, 773.

McDevitt-Murphy, M. E., Weathers, F. W., Adkins, J. W., & Daniels, J. B. (2005). Use of the Personality Assessment Inventory in assessment of posttraumatic stress disorder in women. *Journal of Psychopathology and Behavioral Assessment, 27*, 57–65.

McDevitt-Murphy, M. E., Weathers, F. W., Flood, A. M., Eakin, D. E., & Benson, T. A. (2007). The utility of the PAI and the MMPI-2 for discriminating PTSD, depression, and social phobia in trauma-exposed college students. *Assessment, 14*, 181–195.

Mcfall, M., Fontana, A., Raskind, M., & Rosenheck, R. (1999). Analysis of violent behavior in Vietnam combat veteran psychiatric inpatients with posttraumatic stress disorder. *Journal of Traumatic Stress, 12*, 501–517.

Mcfall, M. E., Wright, P. W., Donovan, D. M., & Raskind, M. (1999). Multidimensional assessment of anger in Vietnam veterans with posttraumatic stress disorder. *Comprehensive Psychiatry, 40*, 216–220.

Meehl, P. E., & Rosen, A. (1955). Antecedent probability and the efficiency of psychometric signs, patterns, or cutting scores. *Psychological Bulletin, 3*, 195–216.

Melton, G. (1997). Psychological evaluations for the courts: A handbook for mental health professionals and lawyers (2nd ed.). New York: The Guilford Press.

Morey, L. C. (1991). *The Personality Assessment Inventory professional manual.* Odessa, FL: Psychological Assessment Resources.

Morey, L. C. (2007). *Personality Assessment Inventory professional manual* (2nd ed.). Lutz, FL: Psychological Assessment Resources.

Morey, L. C. (1996). *An interpretive guide to the Personality Assessment Inventory (PAI).* Odessa, FL: Psychological Assessment Resources.

Morey, L. C. (1998). *PAI SP PAI Software Portfolio, Windows Version 2, Manual,* Odessa, FL: Psychological Assessment Resources.

Mozley, S. L., Miller, M. W., Weathers, F. W., Beckham, J. C., & Feldman, M. E. (2005). Personality assessment inventory (PAI) profiles of male veterans with combat-related posttraumatic stress disorder. *Journal of Psychopathology and Behavioral Assessment, 27*(3), 179–189.

Novaco, R. W., & Chemtob, C. M. (2002). Anger and combat-related posttraumatic stress disorder. *Journal of Traumatic Stress, 15*, 123–132.

Orr, S. P., Claiborn, J. M., Altman, B., Forgue, D. F., de Jong, J. B., Pitman, R. K., & Harz, L. R. (1990). Psychometric profile of posttraumatic stress disorder, anxious, and healthy Vietnam veterans: Correlations with psychophysiologic responses. *Journal of Consulting and Clinical Psychology, 58*, 329–335.

Piotrowski, C. (1999a). Assessment practices in the era of managed care: Current status and future directions. *Journal of Clinical Psychology, 55*, 787–796.

Piotrowski, C. (1999b). Use of tests and measures in marital and family research. *Psychological Reports, 84*, 1251–1252.

Piotrowski, C. (2000). How popular is the Personality Assessment Inventory in practice and training? *Psychological Reports, 86*, 65–66.

Resick, P. A., & Schnicke, M. K. (1992). Cognitive processing therapy for sexual assault victims. *Journal of Consulting and Clinical Psychology, 60*, 748–756.

Riley, W. T., & Treiber, F. A. (1989). The validity of multidimensional self-report anger and hostility measures. *Journal of Clinical Psychology, 45*, 397–404.

Rogers, R. (1992). Structured Interview of Reported Symptoms. Odessa, FL: Psychological Assessment Resources.

Rogers, R., Kropp, P. R., Bagby, R. M., & Dickens, S. E. (1992). Faking specific disorders: a study of the Structured Interview of Reported Symptoms (SIRS). *Journal of Clinical Psychology, 48*, 643–648.

Rogers, R., Ornduff, S. R., & Sewell, K. W. (1993). Feigning specific disorders: A study of the Personality Assessment Inventory (PAI). *Journal of Personality Assessment, 60*, 554–560.

Rogers, R., Sewell, K. W., Morey, L. C., & Ustad, K. L. (1996). Detection of feigned mental disorders on the Personality Assessment Inventory: A discriminant analysis. *Journal of Personality Assessment, 67*, 629–640.

Smith, D. W. & Frueh, B. C. (1996). Compensation seeking, comorbidity, and apparent exaggeration of PTSD symptoms among Vietnam combat veterans. *Psychological Assessment, 8*, 3–6.

Stein, M. B., McQuaid, J. R., Pedrelli, P., Lenox, R., & McCahill, M. E. (2000). Posttraumatic stress disorder in the primary care medical setting. *General Hospital Psychiatry, 22*, 261–269.

Streiner, D. L. (2003). Diagnosing tests: Using and misusing diagnostic and screening tests. *Journal of Personality Assessment, 81*, 209–219.

Sutker, P. B., Uddo-Crane, M., & Allain, A.N. (1991). Clinical and research assessment of posttraumatic stress disorder: A conceptual overview. *Psychological Assessment: A Journal of Consulting and Clinical Psychology, 3*, 520–530.

Tombaugh, T. N. (1996). Test of Memory Malingering (TOMM). New York: Multi-Health Systems, Inc.

Tombaugh, T. N. (1997). The Test of Memory Malingering (TOMM): Normative data from cognitively intact and cognitively impaired individuals. *Psychological Assessment, 9*, 260–268.

Taylor, S., Frueh, B. C., & Asmundson, G. J. G. (2007). Detection and management of malingering in people presenting for treatment of posttraumatic stress disorder: Methods, obstacles, and recommendations. *Journal of Anxiety Disorders, 21*, 22–41.

VA/DoD Clinical Practice Guideline Working Group, Veterans Health Administration, Department of Veterans Affairs and Health Affairs, Department of Defense. (2004). Management of post-traumatic stress (No. Office of Quality and Performance publication 10Q-CPG/PTSD-04). Washington, D.C.: Author.

Weathers, F., Litz, B., Herman, D., Huska, J., & Keane, T. (October 1993). The PTSD Checklist (PCL): Reliability, Validity, and Diagnostic Utility. Paper presented at the Annual Convention of the International Society for Traumatic Stress Studies, San Antonio, TX.

7

Clinical Applications of the PAI in Criminal Justice Settings

MARK A. RUIZ and EZRA OCHSHORN

INTRODUCTION

The United States has the highest incarceration rate in the world (Walmsley, 2007; Warren, 2008) and it is estimated that 1 of every 37 adults are current or former inmates (Bonczar, 2003). Many more individuals have had some involvement with the criminal justice system. In 2007, over 14 million people were arrested and approximately 24% of these arrests were for violent crimes (U.S. Department of Justice, Federal Bureau of Investigation, 2008). High rates of mental health and substance use disorders are often found in individuals involved in the criminal justice system and these disorders are thought to contribute to re-offending (James & Glaze, 2006; National Gains Center, 2004; Sacks & Pearson, 2003). There is increasing recognition of the need to provide effective treatment interventions to address these disorders (Ditton, 1999). Interventions have been developed for community settings and correctional facilities in order to address mental health and addictive problems of offenders. Community efforts include drug and mental health programs that, in many jurisdictions, are monitored by specialized drug and mental health courts (Peters & Osher, 2004; Steadman, Davidson, & Brown, 2001). Many individuals who in the past would have faced criminal sanctions are often diverted to these mandated treatments (Marlowe & Kirby, 1999; Redlich, Steadman, Monahan, Robbins, & Petrila, 2006). Correctional programs typically focus on rehabilitation and community re-entry planning in addition to the psychiatric problems that inmates present with (Osher, Steadman, & Barr, 2002; Peters & Bekman, 2007). Preliminary studies suggest that these treatments can decrease re-offending and violence (Belenko, 1998; McNiel & Binder, 2007; Spohn, Piper, Martin, & Frenzel, 2001).

The delivery of effective treatment within criminal justice settings relies upon accurate individual assessment. The Personality Assessment Inventory (PAI) is one instrument that may be particularly useful for this task. Early research supported the PAI's use in forensic and correctional settings given the instrument's breadth of content, psychometric properties, and empirical support (Douglas, Hart, & Kropp, 2001; Edens, Cruise, & Buffington-Vollum, 2001; Morey & Quigley, 2002). More recent work has provided increased evidence of the instrument's reliability, validity, and clinical utility (Morey, 2007; Morey & Hopwood, 2006, 2007). Particularly relevant to criminal justice applications, a large multi-site normative sample of correctional inmates has been collected and an adolescent version of the instrument (PAI-A) has been published (Edens & Ruiz, 2005; Morey, 2008). Collectively, these developments have improved the clinical utility and admissibility of the PAI within criminal justice settings (Archer, Buffington-Vollum, Stredny, & Handel, 2006; Mullen & Edens, 2008).

In this chapter we review research regarding the clinical application of the PAI with individuals within the criminal justice system. We discuss findings in light of observations we have made while using the PAI in criminal-forensic evaluations and in research conducted within correctional settings. This review highlights legal, correctional, and community-control factors that impact the clinical interpretation of the instrument when used with defendants and offenders.

PROFILE VALIDITY

Two factors heighten the importance of profile validity in criminal justice settings. First, the criminal justice process is adversarial. Law enforcement officers focus on maintaining public safety, prosecuting attorneys work to ensure that offenders are held accountable for their criminal behavior, and correctional or probation officers aim to monitor individuals placed under their supervision. Meanwhile, defendants and their legal representation seek to avoid responsibility for criminal behavior or, if found guilty, try to minimize punishment. In addition, family members and co-defendants may have a stake in the outcome of any case. The adversarial nature of criminal proceedings provides strong incentive for individuals to manage their clinical presentation for ulterior gain (Rogers, 2008). The presence of severe mental health impairment may allow individuals to avoid prosecution, receive a mitigated sentence, or be transferred to relatively safe and comfortable treatment facilities. Evaluators working in criminal justice settings will likely encounter individuals motivated to manipulate the assessment in some manner.

A second factor that heightens the importance of profile validity is the high rate of antisocial and psychopathic personality disorders found within forensic and correctional settings (Hare, 1993; Widiger et al., 1996). Such individuals tend to be uncooperative, misleading, and deceitful and they are likely to malinger within the criminal or legal context (American Psychiatric Association, 2000). Absent these severe personality disorders, offenders may nonetheless have criminogenic tendencies that manifest in irresponsibility, disregard for authority, pro-criminal thinking, and entitlement (Walters, 2007a). These characteristics can complicate evaluations that rely on forthright and cooperative participation. Misinformation, inaccurate recall of personal experiences, or the use of response styles by individuals with the noted personality disorders or criminogenic tendencies can impact assessment results. The validity of information obtained during any evaluation must be scrutinized with caution.

Random or Idiosyncratic Responding

Evaluation of random or idiosyncratic response styles through the use of the PAI's Infrequency (INF) and Inconsistency (ICN) scales is a first step in assessing profile validity. Our experience suggests approximately 3–5% of individuals in criminal justice settings exhibit clinically significant INF or ICN elevations (Edens & Ruiz, 2005; Ruiz, Poythress, Lilienfeld, & Douglas, 2008). We have found that this rate drops when examinees are prescreened for reading impairments, intellectual limitations, or English language difficulties. Usually, these issues are noticeable during initial contacts with the individual or from the use of brief reading screening instruments. Alternative options that can be considered in these situations include the use of the Spanish-language or audio versions of the PAI.

It is also helpful to ask examinees if they are willing to participate in the evaluation. Although informed consent is typically required for any assessment, many offenders do not perceive that they have a choice in participating. Furthermore, many clinicians assume that an offender's passive cooperation is an indication of his or her intention to provide maximum effort on the task. Rather than becoming openly defiant, offenders can resist participation through more subtle means (e.g., random responding) that affect testing results. In cases where individuals exhibit some hesitancy about completing the instrument, we typically stop the evaluation and ask them to reconsider participating at a later date. This is not always feasible, but clinicians will benefit from offering alternatives when cooperation is limited. Identifying individuals with low motivation, language difficulties, or intellectual impairments typically reduces the number of invalid protocols. Individuals with these characteristics who are not identified in prescreening, however, are likely to produce significant INF or ICN elevations (Morey, 1991).

Although the INF and ICN scales effectively identify completely random profiles, identification efficiency drops in cases of partial random responding (Clark, Gironda, & Young, 2003). Partially random profiles, seen when an individual responds randomly (or irrelevantly) to the second half of the inventory, are common in correctional settings. Many offenders lack the patience or attentional capacity for completing the instrument, even when they initially agree to cooperate with the assessment. A promising approach for identifying partially random profiles is to calculate and compare short-form t-scores (from the first 160 items) and long-form t-scores for the Suicidal Ideation (SUI), Alcohol Problems (ALC), and Drug Problems (DRG) scales. Differences equal to or greater than $5T$ on any two of these scales have been found to identify partial random responding in clinical and community settings (Morey & Hopwood, 2004; Siefert, Kehl-Fie, Blais, & Chriki, 2007). Another approach is through the use of the experimental INF-Back scale (INF-B), which comprises INF items from the second half of the PAI. INF-B scores can be compared with the INF scale from items from the first half of the instrument (INF-F; Edens & Ruiz, 2005). Large INF-B/INF-F differences suggest partial idiosyncratic responding, though no research has demonstrated the validity of this approach.

Defensive Responding

Defensive response styles are common among individuals entering the criminal justice system. We encounter this issue especially with those undergoing pre-adjudicative assessments for possible diversion. These offenders are frequently concerned that the admission of severe problems will increase treatment length or result in additional charges, drug testing, or restricted housing during incarceration. They tend to admit to some problems that are already documented, but will categorically deny other problems associated with criminal or violent behavior. This pattern of partial honesty can complicate the assessment process.

The PAI can be used to detect defensiveness. PAI indicators of defensiveness, such as Positive Impression Management (PIM), the Defensiveness Index (DEF), and the Cashel Discriminant Function index (CDF), are valid indicators of defensive responding (Morey, 2007; Sellbom & Bagby, 2008). For example, PIM correlates with the Minnesota Multiphasic Personality Inventory-2 (Butcher, Dahlstrom, Graham, Tellegen, & Kaemer, 1989) K and L validity scales and moderates the relationship between Antisocial Features (ANT) scores and disciplinary infractions in offenders (Carr, Moretti, & Cue, 2005; Edens & Ruiz, 2006). Although these results are encouraging, PIM can have significant error rates, which may increase when respondents are coached on the presence and nature of the validity scales (Baer & Wetter, 1997; Fals-Stewart, 1996). The additional defensiveness indexes, DEF and CDF, can be used to supplement the interpretation of PIM scores. CDF scores are not associated with PIM and they can provide an indication, when elevated, that the respondent might be attempting to "fake good." Although DEF is correlated with PIM ($r = .56$), primarily because PIM scores contribute to this index, these indicators have some different relationships with the clinical scales (Morey, 2006); the magnitude of the relationships between DEF and some externalizing scales (e.g., ANT, ALC, and Aggression [AGG]) is much lower than what is seen with PIM.

Collateral information can further clarify the issue of defensiveness in many cases. Information from criminal records, arrest reports, or other sources, all of which are readily available in most criminal justice contexts, can provide data that can be compared with PAI results to identify discrepancies. For example, individuals arrested for drug possession or driving under the influence often have a substance use disorder; suppressions on ALC and DRG in individuals with this type of criminal history should raise suspicions of defensiveness. Similar comparisons can be made for individuals with extensive histories of violent behavior because these individuals are likely to have elevated scores on the ANT, AGG, and the Violence Potential Index (VPI). Evaluators can also review item responses in relation to documented clinical history. Edens and Ruiz (2005) discussed the use of this strategy in the development of the Inconsistency-Corrections Index (ICI). The ICI contains two items that ask about historical events almost always experienced by individuals within correctional settings (e.g., trouble with the law; past illegal behavior). These events are usually well documented in most cases. Offenders who deny past illegal behavior *and* trouble with the law are possibly distorting their responses. The PAI-sensitive items are another source of information that may be useful. Comparing the documented case history to item endorsements can provide additional information that is helpful for evaluating defensiveness.

Malingering

Malingering is fairly common in criminal justice evaluations. Many defendants realize that feigning a mental disorder may help them avoid prosecution or receive a reduced sentence. The Negative Impression Management (NIM), Malingering Index (MAL), and Rogers Discriminant Function (RDF) indicators have been validated for identifying feigned mental illness (Blanchard, McGrath, Pogge, & Khadivi, 2003; Rogers, Sewell, Morey, & Ustad, 1996; Sellbom & Bagby, 2008). Morey (2007) noted, however, that coaching may help individuals to successfully malinger, particularly when they feign less severe mental health disorders. Although there are frequent instances of PAI profiles that are invalid due to prominent negative distortion, a more common situation is to encounter individuals who exhibit a "mixed" profile containing an exaggeration on scales measuring mood, psychotic, and anxiety disorders but suppressions on scales assessing aggression, substance abuse, and antisocial tendencies.

The use of NIM-predicted profiles is particularly helpful for evaluating the impact of response exaggeration (Morey & Hopwood, 2007). The adjusted NIM-predicted profiles are compared with the observed profiles and this provides critical data on the nature and degree of response distortion (Hopwood, Morey, Rogers, & Sewell, 2007). The party who requested the psychological evaluation typically needs some type of information, regardless of the profile's validity. Thus, the use of NIM-predicted profiles can help the clinician describe the pattern of negative response distortion in a manner that is clinically informative. This approach is useful when the offender uses a mixed response style as the NIM-predicted profiles can help identify the location of distortion.

DIAGNOSIS AND TREATMENT PLANNING

Diagnosis

Treatment received within the criminal justice system may help offenders address problems that contribute to criminal behavior, thereby reducing re-offending and re-incarceration (Steadman et al., 2001). Accurate diagnosis is the foundation for treatment planning. Preliminary work has identified numerous scale and subscale configurations that are likely to be important (Morey 1991, 1996, 2007). Individual PAI scales have been validated for identifying personality disorders (Edens, Hart, Johnson, Johnson, & Olver, 2000; Trull, 1995; Trull, Useada, Conforti, & Doan, 1997), depressive disorders (Edens & Ruiz, 2008), traumatic stress disorders (Mozley, Miller, Weathers, Beckham, & Feldman, 2005), and substance use disorders (Parker, Daleiden, & Simpson, 1999; Ruiz, Dickinson, & Pincus, 2002). Despite these encouraging results, few individual offender profiles exhibit straightforward scale or subscale elevations that reliably identify *DSM-IV* diagnoses (American Psychiatric Association, 2000). Most profiles that we encounter in criminal justice settings reflect complex clinical presentations. This complexity often stems from the interacting effects of diagnostic comorbidity, co-occurring substance abuse, and situational factors (e.g., sentencing, incarceration). Additionally, medical conditions that occur at high rates within offenders can impact psychological functioning. Many offenders have been exposed to infectious diseases (HIV/AIDS, hepatitis B/C) that can complicate the clinical presentation (Beck & Maruschak, 2004; Maruschak, 2005).

Taking all these factors into account, we typically use a configural approach for interpreting PAI results. This approach incorporates both elevations and suppressions of the scale scores in order to understand the most salient areas of impairment (Morey & Hopwood, 2007). We have observed three recurring configurations of impairment. The first configuration is paranoia. These tendencies manifest in elevated Resentment (PAR-R), Hostility (PAR-H), Social Isolation (SCZ-S), and Aggressive Attitudes (AGG-A) scores, in conjunction with a suppressed Warmth (WRM) score (see Morey, 2006). A number of factors contribute to the increased levels of paranoia in criminal justice settings. The adversarial nature of these settings often exacerbates paranoid tendencies in many offenders, who are typically suspicious that information gathered during an evaluation will be used against them. Additionally, there are many offenders who, because of their actions prior to or during incarceration, have violent conflicts with others; other people may actually be "out to get" them. These circumstances increase the threat of physical or sexual attacks during incarceration, which adds to the sense of vulnerability, suspicion, and fear.

Generalized distress is a second type of profile configuration frequently found in offenders. We have typically observed this when the individual is awaiting adjudication or sentencing. The uncertainty and duration of pre-adjudication proceedings is highly stressful given the potential for a loss of freedom, heavy fines, or (in capital cases) possible death. Occupational, financial, and social support resources are highly disrupted for those who are incarcerated during the pre-adjudication period (Toch, 1992). As noted earlier, many correctional facilities pose ongoing threats of physical and sexual assault and exposure to infectious disease. These stressors frequently exacerbate preexisting psychological impairments. We often find PAI profiles with high (> 60T) Mean Clinical Elevation (MCE) scores and significant elevations on two or more clinical scales. Additional elevations are observed on the Stress (STR) and Nonsupport (NON) scales. Thus, it is helpful to consider the acute situational factors that affect the PAI performance in these circumstances.

A third common profile configuration we find is one reflecting co-occurring substance use and mental health disorder. Co-occurring disorders present unique challenges for the assessment and treatment of offenders (Center for Substance Abuse Treatment, 2005; Epstein, Barker, Vorburger, & Murtha, 2004; Sacks, Melnick, & Grella, 2008). Prolonged drug or alcohol use can damage the neurological substrates that regulate emotional, cognitive, and motivational functioning (Kalivas & Volkow, 2005; Volkow & Fowler, 2000; Volkow, Fowler, & Wang, 2003). Many individuals we evaluate exhibit elevations on the PAI substance use scales (ALC, DRG) along with elevations on personality, mood, and anxiety disorder scales. Active or recent substance use frequently contributes to these elevations. Marked improvement in mental health functioning is commonly seen in drug-involved offenders after 30–60 days of abstinence. While the forced abstinence due incarceration can improve functioning for some, those who used substances as a primary coping mechanism can experience a worsening of symptoms. Interestingly, these three configurations noted here have some similarity to dimensions of pathology that have been identified in PAI factor analytical studies (see Hoelzle & Meyer, 2009).

Treatment Planning

The value of assessment for treatment planning is widely recognized (Ben-Porath, 1997; Morey, 1996; Morey & Hopwood, 2007), yet this task presents unique challenges in criminal justice settings. Compliance is a significant issue for many jail diversion or conditional release programs. When treatment is provided in lieu of incarceration or criminal charges, an individual's compliance and progress are typically monitored closely by criminal justice professionals (Peters & Osher, 2004). Failure to attend sessions or evidence of drug relapse (e.g., positive drug screens) may result in criminal sanctions (Marlowe & Kirby, 1999). The PAI's Treatment Process Index (TPI) is helpful for identifying treatment noncompliance. The TPI measures personality and lifestyle characteristics that are common in criminal justice populations and often interfere with treatment (see Chapter 1). Studies conducted with patients receiving outpatient therapy, court-referred residential substance use treatment, or chronic pain treatment have found that high TPI scores are associated with treatment noncompliance and dropout (Hopwood, Ambwani, & Morey, 2007; Hopwood, Creech, Clark, Meagher, & Morey, 2008; Hopwood, Baker, & Morey, 2008).

The Treatment Rejection (RXR) scale, a measure of an individual's motivation for treatment, is another indicator that can help identify potential problems with treatment compliance. Two studies, one conducted with sex offenders and one with general offenders, found small to medium associations between RXR and treatment compliance or staff ratings of treatment success (Caperton, Edens, & Johnson, 2004; Edens & Ruiz, 2005). It is important to note, however, that these studies were conducted with male offenders and it is unclear whether similar findings would emerge with female offenders. RXR scores also moderate the relationship between treatment compliance and dropout in some studies (Hopwood, Creech, et al., 2008; Hopwood, Baker, et al., 2008). The RXR is included in the TPI and this may confound interpretations in some cases.

Treatment plans for offenders must consider the risk to self or others. Many individuals evaluated in criminal justice settings have documented histories of violence; the extent of that violence and their risk for future violence will impact placement and management options. Many courts will not place dangerous individuals in community-based treatment settings. Clinicians are frequently asked to evaluate the individual's propensity for violence or re-offending in order to inform decision-makers about possible risks involved with certain decisions (e.g., outpatient placement). The PAI Interpretive Report for Correctional Settings (PAI-CS; Edens & Ruiz, 2005) presents results that may be informative for these purposes. The Risk Circumplex presents an individual's scores on ANT and MCE (see Figure 7.1) so clinicians can consider the interaction of both domains. ANT

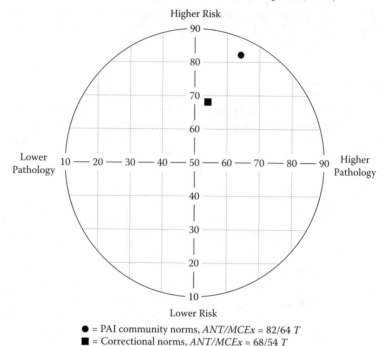

Institutional Risk Circumplex
Vertical Axis: Antisocial Features (*ANT*)
Horizontal Axis: Mean Clinical Elevation Excluding *ANT* (*MCEx*)

● = PAI community norms, *ANT/MCEx* = 82/64 *T*
■ = Correctional norms, *ANT/MCEx* = 68/54 *T*

Figure 7.1   PAI Risk Circumplex from the PAI Interpretive Report for Correctional Settings. Reproduced by special permission of Psychological Assessment Resources, Inc., Lutz, Florida. Leslie C. Morey, Ph.D. and PAR Staff, Copyright by PAR, Inc.

provides a measure of the tendency to act out and MCE assesses generalized mental health impairment. Individuals with high risk and impairment levels, often referred to as disturbed violent offenders (Toch & Adams, 1994), are most likely to pose challenges to management and safety. Although significant mental health impairment requires treatment, those with concomitant risk for violence or re-offending are less likely to benefit from traditional interventions. They may also engage in disruptive behaviors, such as staff assaults or escape attempts, while in treatment. The Risk Circumplex provides a global summary of the interactions of these dimensions and can inform treatment planning. However, an individual's elevation on ANT or AGG in the absence of severe mental health impairment may still reflect an elevated risk for certain misconduct (e.g., Walters, 2007b).

The Risk Circumplex presented in Figure 7.1 was taken from a PAI-CS report and is typical of profiles we encounter in our evaluations. The data illustrate that this individual falls within the Higher Risk/Higher Pathology quadrant of the circumplex due to his high level of antisocial features in conjunction with his above average generalized distress (MCE). Both the community norms and the correctional norms are plotted and both place this individual within this quadrant. His risk level is consistently elevated when using these two normative reference points.

RISK ASSESSMENT

Risk is a general term that refers to the likelihood an individual will engage in certain unwanted behaviors. Risk is affected by contextual and individual factors. Assessments of risk are guided by multiple contextual factors, including the behavior in question (violence, sexual re-offending) and the timeframe for prediction (Fabian, 2008; Monahan & Steadman, 1996). Another contextual factor is the characteristic of the potential target; predictions are moderated by whether the target is another offender or treatment provider (McDermott, Edens, Quanbeck, Busse, & Scott, 2008). Additional contextual factors become relevant when evaluating individuals within the criminal justice system. Correctional inmates are prone to a variety of high-risk behaviors unique to these settings given the lack of privacy, decreased autonomy, and increased stress they encounter.

Validated conceptualizations of risk typically organize the individual difference factors that contribute to risk into static (history of violence, age of first offense) or dynamic (current substance use, negative attitudes, impulsivity) categories (Douglas & Skeem, 2005; Webster, Douglas, Eaves, & Hart, 1997). Though the distinction between the contextual and individual factors presented here is blurred in some cases, any risk assessment needs to consider all relevant factors.

The PAI provides useful information for identifying individual risk factors that contribute to overall risk levels. Relatively strong empirical support exists for using the ANT and AGG scales to assess risk potential. ANT scores are predictive of institutional misconduct and violence with both male and female inmates (Edens & Ruiz, 2005; Skopp, Edens, & Ruiz, 2007; Walters, 2007b; Walters, Duncan, & Geyer, 2003). ANT exhibits small-to-moderate associations with general and violent recidivism among offenders within 1 to 3 years of release into the community (Salekin, 2008; Salekin, Rogers, Ustad, & Sewell, 1998). ANT scores have also been associated with measurements of psychopathy and Antisocial Personality Disorder (Edens et al., 2000; Edens, Poythress, & Watkins, 2001; Salekin, Rogers, & Sewell, 1997). Finally, significant correlations have been reported between ANT and criminal-thinking styles such as entitlement, power orientation, and aggressive attitude (Walters & Geyer, 2005).

Although AGG has received less attention than ANT for risk assessment, AGG scores are associated with institutional misconduct and a history of criminal offending (Edens & Ruiz, 2005; Skopp et al., 2007; Walters, 2007b). AGG is associated with interview and self-report measures of psychopathy, hostility, and pathological anger expression (Morey, 2007). However, the incremental validity of AGG beyond ANT is unclear. Some research suggests that AGG provides little information beyond ANT, while other studies suggest differently (see Walters, 2007b). One possible explanation for these disparate findings is that the particular risk behavior dictates which scale is most predictive. AGG may be more important for violence and aggression prediction, whereas ANT may cover a broader range of risk behaviors (Hopwood, Baker, et al., 2008).

The PAI can provide further information relevant to static individual risk factors. With respect to static factors, the PAI evaluates personality and dispositional variables important for risk assessment. Personality dysfunction reflected in elevated Borderline Features (BOR) scores can provide predictive information regarding hostility, impulsivity, and emotional instability. Although BOR measures characterologically based problems, it is important to note that these symptoms often fluctuate over time and their designation as "static" variables may be questionable (Lenzenweger, Johnson, & Willet, 2004). The Paranoia scale (PAR) is also useful for assessing hostility, though it is not clear whether these scores are reflective of personality disorder. BOR and PAR can be used to qualify the potential impact of contextual factors such as the individual's likely adjustment to overcrowded correctional facilities or unsupervised community placement. When integrated with information from criminal records, clinical interviews, and collateral sources, elevations on these PAI scales provide criminal justice personnel with contextualized assessments that can inform public safety and facility management decisions.

The PAI also measures dynamic individual risk factors. Elevated levels of current distress, generalized impairment, or social isolation—assessed with the Stress (STR), MCE, and Non-support (NON) scales, respectively—can lead to increased susceptibility for high-risk behavior. We have observed instances of self-mutilation, rule infractions, or staff assaults when offenders are under extreme stress during their early adjustment to confinement. Conversely, risk upon community re-entry may be mitigated if stress and social isolation are addressed with treatment. An individual's involvement with substances is another dynamic factor. Individuals with current or prior substance abuse, as evidenced by elevations on the PAI substance abuse scales (ALC, DRG) may require additional interventions to prevent relapse. Use of the PAI to identify such dynamic variables has benefits for risk management as these factors are usually the most responsive to intervention (Douglas & Skeem, 2005).

INDICATIONS FOR ADDITIONAL MEASURES

A psychological evaluation should never rely solely on the PAI. Rather, information from multiple sources should contextualize assessment findings. In addition to clinical interviews, we routinely integrate information from three sources when interpreting PAI data. The first source is the individual's criminal record. These records provide information regarding the nature, extent, and onset of offending; such input is critical for gauging risk level and functional capacity. Unfortunately, criminal records include only offenses that were detected, documented, and successfully prosecuted. Documented offenses may be limited to a certain jurisdictions; county records do not always match National Crime Information Center (NCIC) records and many clinicians do not have ready access to national data bases. Furthermore, criminal records typically do not describe the nature of the offense and the documented charge may differ from what actually occurred due to plea bargaining or other adjudicative compromises. Despite such limitations, these records are vital for assessing future potential for re-offending and violence

(Gendreau, Goggin, & Law, 1997) because many offenders are unwilling to provide accurate information about their prior offenses. Relying solely on self-reported information, whether gathered through the PAI or clinical interview, can leave the clinician with an incomplete assessment.

Routine screening of reading ability is another valuable source of information. The average PAI item is written at a 4th-grade reading level (Morey, 2007). However, some scales or items may require a 5th- or 6th-grade reading level (Schinka & Borum, 1993) and this can create problems for certain offenders. Many individuals within criminal justice settings have reading comprehension difficulties due to a lack of education, limited English proficiency, or cognitive impairment secondary to head injury or prolonged substance dependence. These offenders often produce PAI profiles with an excessive number of missing items or significant elevations on ICN and INF. We have observed that such individuals are frequently unable to complete the PAI in 90 minutes even when clinicians are available to provide clarifications of item content. Thus, it is important to screen for gross reading difficulties before deciding to administer the PAI. Clinically, we have found that questioning offenders about their level of completed education and history of reading difficulties can identify many individuals who will have problems with the instrument. Alternatively, it is sometimes appropriate to obtain a more formal evaluation of reading ability through the use of an instrument such as the North American Adult Reading Test (NAART; Uttl, 2002). The NAART is a screening instrument for reading difficulties that can be administered in a relatively brief timeframe. The instrument can estimate intelligence, which may be equally informative for evaluating an individual's ability to complete the PAI (see Johnstone, Callahan, Kapila, & Bouman, 1996).

In addition to evaluation of criminal records and reading ability, elevations on certain PAI scales or specific referrals for risk assessments warrant further assessment. For example, significant elevations on indictors of violence or offending risk (ANT, AGG, PAR, and VPI) often require further evaluation of risk potential. While PAI data is valid for predicting certain risk behaviors, no structured procedure exists for integrating these data with other information. The use of structured procedures for organizing assessment data is increasingly employed in forensic risk assessments (Fabian, 2008). Evidence-based violence assessment instruments, such as the HCR-20, provide detailed guidelines for integrating multiple information sources to determine risk potential (Webster et al., 1997). Additionally, this procedure allows clinicians to develop a contextualized understanding of factors that may aggravate or mitigate risk. This is useful when an individual presents with interacting risk factors that heighten the potential for acting out in certain circumstances. PAI data can be integrated into existing schemes because such data provide measurements for many of the constructs used within these schemes (substance use, impulsivity, hostility, paranoia). However, we recommend that clinicians rely on validated risk-assessment instruments whenever questions arise about an individual's potential for violence or re-offending.

ADVANTAGES AND DISADVANTAGES OF THE PAI

Advantages

When used with criminal justice populations, two advantages of the PAI are the breadth of clinical information provided and the availability of multiple norms. The PAI captures a broad range of clinical information that includes internalizing and externalizing problems (Ruiz & Edens, 2008). This comprehensive assessment of mental health disorder is useful when dealing with the complex presentations that are often encountered in criminal justice settings. Multiple dimensions can be integrated to obtain a detailed assessment of an individual. For example, Figure 7.2 presents the Co-occurring Disorders Circumplex model included in the PAI-CS (Edens & Ruiz, 2005). This circumplex is based on the quadrant model of co-occurring disorders that is frequently used to understand drug-involved patients (Center for Substance Abuse Treatment, 2005; Minkoff, 2001). Information provided by the PAI is used to plot an individual's location within the circumplex model

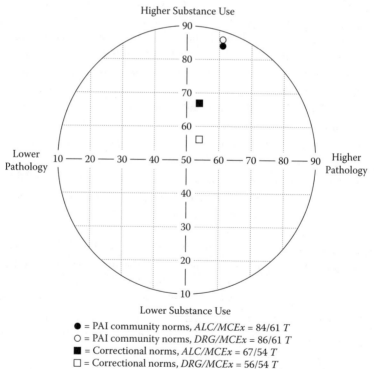

Figure 7.2   Co-occurring Disorders Circumplex from the PAI Interpretive Report for Correctional Settings (PAI-CS). Reproduced by special permission of Psychological Assessment Resources, Inc., Lutz, Florida. Leslie C. Morey, Ph.D. and PAR Staff, Copyright by PAR, Inc.

and can inform treatment decisions. For example, an individual with high levels of substance and mental health impairment likely requires integrated treatment that addresses both problems. Individuals with significant mental health impairment but mild substance impairment may not require integrated treatment, unless their substance use impedes treatment compliance. The Co-occurring Disorders Circumplex, like the Risk Circumplex discussed earlier, effectively alerts clinicians to potential interactions between two areas of impairment.

Another advantage of the PAI is the availability of multiple norms. Large and representative normative samples have been collected from community-dwelling adults, inpatients and outpatients in clinical settings, and incarcerated offenders (Edens & Ruiz, 2005; Morey, 1991, 2007). Most published PAI validation findings, especially those related to scale cut-scores, have used *t*-scores based on the community sample; this sample should be the primary reference point for interpretive hypotheses (Morey, 1996). However, interpretations based on the community norms can be supplemented with information derived from comparisons with the clinical and correctional norms. Figure 7.3 presents a Full Scale profile, generated from the PAI-CS, for an incarcerated individual. The profile presents PAI *t*-scores based on both the community and correctional samples. The clinical skyline, the score that is two standard deviations above the mean in the PAI clinical normative sample, is also presented. Scores evaluated in relation to these different reference points provide useful information for clinicians. Not surprisingly, PAI *t*-scores derived from the community norms are typically elevated for many externalizing scales (BOR, ANT, ALC, DRG, and AGG) among those entering the criminal justice system. These scale elevations may not be useful for making placement or management decisions given the high base rate of externalizing problems in these settings. Therefore, interpretation may benefit from comparing the scores with the average offender. Although most individuals entering correctional institutions will exhibit similar elevations when compared with people from the community, offenders with impairments greater than the average offender probably warrant the most concern. Another example can be seen in evaluations used to refer offenders to residential mental health treatment. With treatment resources limited, placements may be reserved for those whose profiles are elevated in relation to the clinical normative sample. The clinical skyline may play an important role in this interpretive process.

The profile in Figure 7.3 presents numerous areas where the different normative samples can help qualify PAI scores. For example, the community norms suggest that this individual's substance abuse (ALC, DRG) and character issues (ANT, BOR) are severe. The correctional norms suggest that these problems, while still above average, are much less pronounced when compared with the average offender. The interpretive significance of these findings will be guided by the referral question and the nature of the setting, but the use of multiple reference points can enhance the understanding of any case.

Disadvantages

Most PAI clinical scales contain theoretically relevant subscales. The Depression scale, for example, contains subscales assessing affective, cognitive, and behavioral

PAI Full Scale Profile

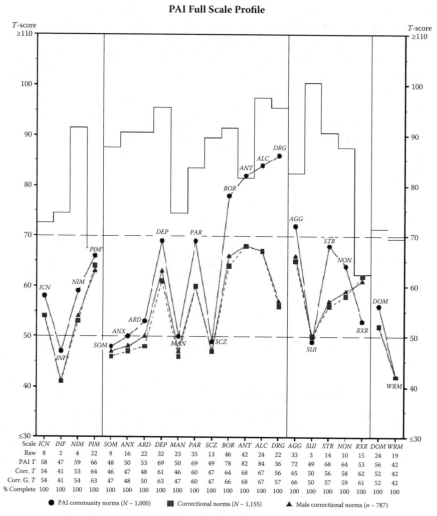

Scale	ICN	INF	NIM	PIM	SOM	ANX	ARD	DEP	MAN	PAR	SCZ	BOR	ANT	ALC	DRG	AGG	SUI	STR	NON	RXR	DOM	WRM
Raw	8	2	4	22	9	16	22	32	23	35	13	46	42	24	22	33	3	14	10	15	24	19
PAI T	58	47	59	66	48	50	53	69	50	69	49	78	82	84	36	72	49	68	64	53	56	42
Corr. T	54	41	53	64	46	47	48	61	46	60	47	64	68	67	56	65	50	56	58	62	52	42
Corr. G. T	54	41	54	63	47	48	50	63	47	60	47	66	68	67	57	66	50	57	59	61	52	42
% Complete	100	100	100	100	100	100	100	100	100	100	100	100	100	100	100	100	100	100	100	100	100	100

● PAI community norms (*N* – 1,000)   ■ Correctional norms (*N* – 1,155)   ▲ Male correctional norms (*n* – 787)

Note. "Corr. *T*" refers to Correctional *T*-score and "Corr. G. *T*" refers to gender-based Correctional *T*-score.
Skyline represents scores that are two standard deviations above the mean for a sample of 1,246 clinical patients.

Figure 7.3   Sample PAI Full Scale Profile from the PAI Interpretive Report for Correctional Settings (PAI-CS). Reproduced by special permission of Psychological Assessment Resources, Inc., Lutz, Florida. Leslie C. Morey, Ph.D. and PAR Staff, Copyright by PAR, Inc.

aspects of depressive disorders. Subscale configurations can suggest important diagnostic and treatment considerations. One disadvantage, however, is that subscales are not available for the substance use (ALC, DRG) or Traumatic Stress (ARD-T) scales. Post-traumatic Stress Disorder (PTSD) and substance use disorders often have complex and multifaceted presentations (American Psychiatric Association, 2000), yet the PAI provides only limited, one-dimensional assessments for these impairments. This is problematic because criminal justice evaluations typically require detailed information about these conditions. For instance, the presence of dissociative symptoms, sometimes a component of PTSD, may significantly impact the adjudication process if used as an exculpatory or mitigating factor (Melton, Petrila, Poythress, & Slobogin, 2007). Substance use histories are likewise varied and complex. An individual exhibiting severe withdrawal symptoms secondary to longstanding substance dependence may require specialized placements that can address any medical complications that may arise. Alternatively, a substance user without these symptoms may not require intensive services. Overall, ALC or DRG elevations can help determine the general severity of substance use disorder (Morey, 1996), but detailed assessment of the course, nature, and responsiveness to treatment of these problems is ultimately required for diagnosis and treatment planning. The development of abuse and dependence subscales for the ALC and DRG scales would be an improvement for PAI.

A second disadvantage is the instrument's ambiguous time frame for questions asking about past experiences. The PAI requires a respondent to evaluate his or her functioning without reference to specific time periods. While many PAI items contain language differentiating current and past behavior, these distinctions are often missed by respondents. Moreover, items referring to past behavior often do not clarify whether the respondent should report recent past behavior (last month) or remote past behavior (lifetime). This ambiguity creates problems because many offenders have understandable concerns about admitting criminal behavior, substance use, or violence. Offenders in correctional settings or on probation may be reluctant to report past substance use, fearing that the admission might be misinterpreted as admitting current use. Other individuals believe that their responses will result in additional criminal charges or that the information will be used against them during current or future legal proceedings. In our research studies, participants frequently annotate PAI responses to clarify that their answers do not contradict information provided elsewhere (e.g., under oath, during statements to law enforcement). Clinicians may elect to notate when specific events occurred in order to prevent confusion when interpreting the PAI. However, this is not always feasible in group administration settings.

It is not clear how to address this problem given the need for standardized administration instructions. One approach may be to obtain assurances from law enforcement, correctional, or court personnel that the PAI results will not be used for legal or investigative purposes. These assurances are difficult to obtain because psychological evaluations conducted within criminal justice contexts do not have the same confidentiality protections as those conducted in health care settings (Petrila, 2007). Additionally, many offenders are unlikely to be persuaded by a clinician's verbal assurances that law enforcement or other entities agreed to this arrangement. This underscores the importance of interpreting the PAI within the context of a comprehensive psychological evaluation that allows someone to clarify the details surrounding past behaviors.

COMMUNICATION OF FINDINGS

Throughout the criminal justice system there is an inherent struggle between protecting civil liberties and maintaining public safety. The balancing of these two goals presents unique challenges when communicating findings. Most criminal justice professionals are not mental health clinicians and they typically lack training in interpreting psychological reports. These personnel nonetheless have a stake in the conclusions and recommendations provided by the clinician. Indeed, non-clinical professionals are often the decision-makers on issues of adjudication, correctional placement, and community monitoring. As with any psychological evaluation, clinicians must adhere to basic ethical standards and guidelines (American Psychological Association, 2002). This means providing comprehensive findings that incorporate data from multiple sources in a useful manner. While the PAI provides a broad array of data, interpretive statements should consider clinical and criminal histories. Elevated scores on the ANT and AGG scales, for instance, would carry different weight for someone convicted of aggravated sexual assault in contrast to someone without a history of violence. Some may regard the utilization of historical information as introducing extraneous information into the actuarial process of score interpretation. However, historical data, particularly past criminal behavior, is a valid predictor of future offending and is essential for criminal justice evaluations (Gendreau et al., 1997). Failure to incorporate historical information lessens the validity of any evaluation.

In addition to being comprehensive, communicated findings must be relevant and practical. Conclusions and recommendations should be geared toward the criminal justice professionals who are not likely to have specialized training in mental health assessment. Reports that contain technical jargon or speculative clinical inferences are of little use for most purposes. Clinical findings should clearly address environmental factors and should provide realistic recommendations. For example, recommendations for incarcerated offenders need to consider security concerns of the correctional officers and logistical constraints with the setting (e.g., housing, transportation) that can impede treatment access. In our experience, criminal justice professionals are interested in speculative clinical inferences provided they are labeled as such and have some factual basis. Melton and colleagues (2007) noted the potential for problems when reports contain excessive information, opinions beyond the scope of the referral question, or language that is unnecessarily confusing (e.g., preoedipalization of current conflicts) or prejudicial (e.g., drug addict). These recommendations are useful guidelines when communicating findings. Additionally, we typically remove statistical and scoring data from reports that are used for criminal justice purposes. For example, we never include the Circumplex or profile graphs within reports that go to non-mental-health professionals.

A final concern for the communication of findings is the use of computer-generated interpretive reports. Different computer-generated interpretive reports are available for the PAI (Edens & Ruiz, 2005; Morey, Goldin, & Rodriguez, 2000). These reports provide score profiles and basic interpretive hypotheses that can be easily integrated into existing word processing files. Operating with limited resources and personnel, it is understandable that the criminal justice system seeks procedures that increase efficiency. However, the information provided by computer-generated interpretive reports was never intended to replace a formal clinical evaluation; clinical decisions should not be based solely on computer-generated interpretive statements. We have encountered a handful of instances when non-mental-health professionals were interested in using these reports but lacked an understanding of their limitations.

CONCLUSION

The high rate of mental health and substance use disorders found among offenders, along with increased interest in providing treatment within criminal justice settings, heightens the need for evidence-based assessment methods. Although many instruments are available, the PAI is particularly well-suited for criminal justice populations. The instrument has strong, well-replicated psychometric properties and a growing body of research demonstrates its validity for evaluating many of the issues important for forensic and correctional evaluations. Researchers should continue to expand our knowledge of the instrument's functioning in order to better understand its strengths and limitations (Grisso & Vincent, 2005).

Author Note: Mark Ruiz is an author of the PAI Interpretive Report for Correctional Settings (PAI-CS) published by Psychological Assessment Resources, Inc. However, he has no ongoing financial interest in this product.

REFERENCES

American Psychiatric Association. (2000). *Diagnostic and statistical manual of mental disorders* (4th ed., text revision). Washington, D.C.: Author.

American Psychological Association. (2002). Ethical principles of psychologists and code of conduct. *American Psychologist, 57,* 1060–1073.

Archer, R. P., Buffington-Vollum, K. K., Stredny, R. V., & Handel, R. W. (2006). A survey of psychological test use patterns among forensic psychologists. *Journal of Personality Assessment, 87,* 85–95.

Baer, R. A., & Wetter, M. W. (1997). Effects of information about validity scales on underreporting of symptoms on the Personality Assessment Inventory. *Journal of Personality Assessment, 68,* 402–413.

Beck, A. J., & Maruschak, L. M. (2004). Hepatitis testing and treatment in state prisons. *Bureau of Justice Statistics Special Report.* Washington, DC: U.S. Department of Justice-Office of Justice Programs.

Belenko, S. (1998). Research on drug courts: A critical review. *National Drug Court Institute Review, 1,* 1–42.

Ben-Porath, Y. S. (1997). Use of personality assessment instruments in empirically guided treatment planning. *Psychological Assessment, 9,* 361–367.

Blanchard, D. D., McGrath, R. E., Pogge, D. L., & Khadivi, A. (2003). A comparison of the PAI and MMPI-2 as predictors of faking bad in college students. *Journal of Personality Assessment, 80,* 197–205.

Bonczar, T. P. (2003). Prevalence of imprisonment in the U.S. Population, 1974–2001. *Bureau of Justice Statistics Special Report.* Washington, DC: U.S. Department of Justice.

Butcher, J. N., Dahlstrom, W. G., Graham, J. R., Tellegen, A., & Kaemer, B. (1989). *The Minnesota Multiphasic Personality Inventory-2: Manual for administration and scoring.* Minneapolis: University of Minnesota Press.

Caperton, J. D., Edens, J. F., & Johnson, J. (2004). Predicting sex offender institutional adjustment and treatment compliance using the Personality Assessment Inventory. *Psychological Assessment, 16,* 187–191.

Carr, G. D., Moretti, M. M., & Cue, B. J. H. (2005). Evaluating parenting capacity: Validity problems with the MMPI-2, PAI, and CAPI, and ratings of child adjustment. *Professional Psychology: Research and Practice, 36,* 188–196.

Center for Substance Abuse Treatment. (2005). *Substance Abuse Treatment for Persons with Co-Occurring Disorders. Treatment Improvement Protocol (TIP) 42.* S. Sacks, Chair & R. Reis, Co-Chair, Consensus Panel. DHHS Pub. No. (SMA) TBD. Rockville, MD: Substance Abuse and Mental Health Services Administration.

Clark, M. E., Gironda, R. J., & Young, R. W. (2003). Detection of back random responding: Effectiveness of MMPI-2 and Personality Assessment Inventory Validity Indices. *Psychological Assessment, 15,* 223–234.

Ditton, P. M. (1999). *Mental health and treatment of inmates and probationers.* Washington, D.C.: U.S. Department of Justice, Office of Justice Programs, Bureau of Justice Statistics.

Douglas, K. S., Hart, S. D., & Kropp, P. R. (2001). Validity of the Personality Assessment Inventory for forensic assessments. *International Journal of Offender Therapy & Comparative Criminology, 45,* 183–197.

Douglas, K. S., & Skeem, J. L. (2005). Violence risk assessment: Getting specific about being dynamic. *Psychology, Public Policy, and Law, 11,* 347–383.

Edens, J. F., Cruise, K. R., & Buffington-Vollum, J. K. (2001). Forensic and correctional applications of the Personality Assessment Inventory. *Behavioral Sciences and the Law, 19,* 519–543.

Edens, J. F., Hart, S. D., Johnson, D. W., Johnson, J. K., & Olver, M. E. (2000). Use of the Personality Assessment Inventory to assess psychopathy in offender populations. *Psychological Assessment, 12,* 132–139.

Edens, J. F., Poythress, N. G., & Watkins, M. M. (2001). Further validation of the Psychopathic Personality Inventory among offenders: Personality and behavioral correlates. *Journal of Personality Disorders, 15,* 403–415.

Edens, J. F., & Ruiz, M. A. (2005). *PAI Interpretive Report for Correctional Settings (PAI-CS) Professional Manual.* Lutz, Florida: Psychological Assessment Resources.

Edens, J. F., & Ruiz, M. A. (2006). On the validity of validity scales: The importance of defensive responding in the prediction of institutional misconduct. *Psychological Assessment, 18,* 220–224.

Edens, J. F., & Ruiz, M. A. (2008). Identification of mental disorders in an inpatient psychiatric unit: Examining the criterion-related validity of the Personality Assessment Inventory. *Psychological Services, 5,* 108–117.

Epstein, J., Barker, P., Vorburger, M., & Murtha, C. (2004). *Serious mental illness and its co-occurrence with substance use disorders, 2002.* Rockville, MD: Substance Abuse and Mental Health Services Administration, Office of Applied Studies.

Fabian, J. M. (2008). Current standards and practices in violence risk assessment at a maximum security forensic hospital following a high profile sexual homicide. *Aggression and Violent Behavior, 13,* 337–345.

Fals-Stewart, W. (1996). The ability of individuals with psychoactive substance use disorders to escape detection by the Personality Assessment Inventory. *Psychological Assessment, 8,* 60–68.

Gendreau, P., Goggin, C., & Law, M. A. (1997). Predicting prison misconducts. *Criminal Justice and Behavior, 24,* 414–432.

Grisso, T., & Vincent, G. M. (2005). The empirical limits of forensic mental health assessment. *Law and Human Behavior, 29,* 1–5.

Hare, R. D. (1993). *Without conscience: The disturbing world of the psychopaths among us.* New York: Guilford.

Hoelzle, J. B., & Meyer, G. J. (2009). The invariant component structure of the Personality Assessment Inventory (PAI) full scales. *Journal of Personality Assessment, 91,* 1–12.

Hopwood, C. J., Ambwani, S., & Morey, L. C. (2007). Predicting non-mutual therapy termination with the Personality Assessment Inventory. *Psychotherapy Research, 17,* 706–712.

Hopwood, C. J., Morey, L. C., Rogers, R., & Sewell, K. (2007). Malingering on the Personality Assessment Inventory: Identification of specific feigned disorders. *Journal of Personality Assessment, 88,* 43–48.

Hopwood, C. J., Creech, S. K., Clark, T. S., Meagher, M. W., & Morey, L. C. (2008). Predicting the completion of an integrative and intensive outpatient chronic pain treatment with the Personality Assessment Inventory. *Journal of Personality Assessment, 90,* 76–80.

Hopwood, C. J., Baker, K. L., & Morey, L. C. (2008). Extra-test validity of selected Personality Assessment Inventory scales and indicators in an inpatient substance abuse setting. *Journal of Personality Assessment, 90,* 574–577.

James, D. J., & Glaze, L. E. (2006). *Bureau of Justice Statistics Special Report: Mental Health Problems of Prison and Jail Inmates.* Washington, D.C.: U.S. Department of Justice.

Johnstone, B., Callahan, C. D., Kapila, C. J., & Bouman, D. E. (1996). The comparability of the WRAT-R reading test and NAART as estimates of premorbid intelligence in neurologically impaired patients. *Archives of Clinical Neuropsychology, 11,* 513–519.

Kalivas, P. W., & Volkow, N. D. (2005). The neural basis of addiction: A pathology of motivation and choice. *American Journal of Psychiatry, 162,* 1403–1413.

Lenzenweger, M. F., Johnson, M. D., & Willet, J. B. (2004). Individual growth curve analysis illuminates stability and change in personality disorder features: The longitudinal study of personality disorders. *Archives of General Psychiatry, 61,* 1015–1024.

Marlowe, D. B., & Kirby, K. C. (1999). Effective use of sanctions in drug courts: Lessons from behavioral research. *National Drug Court Institute Review, 2,* 1–31.

Maruschak, L. M. (2005). HIV in prisons, 2003. *Bureau of Justice Statistics Bulletin.* Washington, DC: U.S. Department of Justice, Office of Justice Programs.

McDermott, B. E., Edens, J. F., Quanbeck, C. D., Busse, D., & Scott, C. L. (2008). Examining the role of static and dynamic risk factors in the prediction of inpatient violence: Variable and person-focused analyses. *Law and Human Behavior, 32,* 325–338.

McNiel, D. E., & Binder, R. L. (2007). Effectiveness of a mental health court in reducing criminal recidivism and violence. *American Journal of Psychiatry, 164,* 1395–1403.

Melton, G. B., Petrila, J., Poythress, N. G., & Slobogin, C. (2007). *Psychological evaluations for the courts: A handbook for mental health professionals and lawyers* (3rd ed.). New York: Guildford Press.

Minkoff, K. (2001). Developing standards of care for individuals with co-occurring psychiatric and substance use disorders. *Psychiatric Services, 52,* 597–599.

Monahan, J., & Steadman, H. J. (1996). Violent storms and violent people: How meteorology can inform risk communication in mental health law. *American Psychologist, 51,* 931–938.

Morey, L. C. (1991). *Personality Assessment Inventory professional manual.* Odessa, Florida: Psychological Assessment Resources.

Morey, L. C. (1996). *An interpretive guide to the Personality Assessment Inventory.* Odessa, Florida: Psychological Assessment Resources.

Morey, L. C. (2007). *Personality Assessment Inventory professional manual* (2nd ed.). Lutz, FL: Psychological Assessment Resources.

Morey, L. C. (2008). *Personality Assessment Inventory adolescent version professional manual.* Lutz, FL: Psychological Assessment Resources.

Morey, L. C., Goldin, J. N., & Rodriguez, M. S. (2000). *PAI software portfolio windows version 2 manual.* Lutz, Florida: Psychological Assessment Resources, Inc.

Morey, L. C., & Hopwood, C. J. (2004). Efficacy of a strategy for detecting back random responding on the Personality Assessment Inventory. *Psychological Assessment, 16,* 197–200.

Morey, L. C., & Hopwood, C. J. (2006). The Personality Assessment Inventory. In R. Archer (Ed.). *Forensic use of clinical assessment instruments* (pp. 89–120). New York: Routledge.

Morey, L. C., & Hopwood, C. J. (2007). *Casebook for the Personality Assessment Inventory: A structural summary approach.* Lutz, FL: Psychological Assessment Resources.

Morey, L. C., & Quigley, B. D. (2002). The use of the Personality Assessment Inventory (PAI) in assessing offenders. *International Journal of Offender Therapy & Comparative Criminology, 46,* 333–349.

Mozley, S. L., Miller, M. W., Weathers, F. W., Beckham, J. C., & Feldman, M. E. (2005). Personality Assessment Inventory (PAI) profiles of male veterans with combat-related postraumatic stress disorder. *Journal of Psychopathology and Behavioral Assessment, 27,* 179–189.

Mullen, K. L., & Edens, J. F. (2008). A case law survey of the Personality Assessment Inventory: Examining its role in civil and criminal trials. *Journal of Personality Assessment, 90,* 300–303.

National GAINS Center. (2004). *The prevalence of co-occurring mental illness and substance use disorders in jails. Fact Sheet Series.* Delmar, NY: The National GAINS Center.

Osher, F., Steadman, H. J., & Barr, H. (2002). *A best practice approach to community reentry from jails for inmates with co-occurring disorders: The APIC model.* Delmar, NY: The National GAINS Center.

Parker, J. D., Daleiden, E. L., & Simpson, C. A. (1999). Personality Assessment Inventory Substance-Use Scales: Convergent and discriminant relations with the Addiction Severity index in a residential chemical dependence treatment setting. *Psychological Assessment, 11,* 507–513.

Peters, R. H., & Bekman, N. M. (2007). Treatment and reentry approaches for offenders with co-occurring disorders. In R. B. Greifinger, J. Bick, & J. Goldenson (Eds.), *Public health behind bars: From prisons to communities* (pps. 368–384). New York: Springer Publishers.

Peters, R. H., & Osher, F. C. (2004). *Co-occurring disorders and specialty courts.* Washington, D.C: Substance Abuse and Mental Health Services Administration.

Petrila, J. (2007). *Dispelling myths about information sharing between the mental health and criminal justice systems.* Delmar, NY: National GAINS Center.

Redlich, A., Steadman, H., Monahan, J., Robbins, P., & Petrila, J. (2006). Patterns of practice in mental health courts: A national survey. *Law and Human Behavior, 30,* 347–362.

Rogers, R. (2008). An introduction to response styles. In Richard Rogers (Ed.). *Clinical assessment of malingering and deception* (3rd ed.) (pp. 1–13). New York: Guilford Press.

Rogers, R., Sewell, K. W., Morey, L. C., & Ustad, K. L. (1996). Detection of feigned mental disorders on the Personality Assessment Inventory: A discriminant analysis. *Journal of Personality Assessment, 67,* 629–640.

Ruiz, M. A., & Edens, J. F. (2008). Recovery and replication of internalizing and externalizing dimensions within the Personality Assessment Inventory. *Journal of Personality Assessment, 90,* 585–592.

Ruiz, M. A., Dickinson, K. A., & Pincus, A. L. (2002). The concurrent validity of the Personality Assessment Inventory Alcohol Problems scale (ALC) in a college student sample. *Assessment, 9,* 261–270.

Ruiz, M. A., Poythress, N. G., Lilienfeld, S. O., & Douglas, K. S. (2008). Factor structure and correlates of the Dissociative Experiences Scale in a large offender sample. *Assessment, 15,* 511–521.

Sacks, S., Melnick, G., & Grella, C. E. (2008). Synthesis of studies of co-occurring disorder(s) in criminal justice and a research agenda. *Behavioral Sciences and the Law, 26,* 475–486.

Sacks, S., & Pearson, F. S. (2003). Co-occurring substance use and mental disorders in offenders: Approaches, findings, and recommendations. *Federal Probation, 67,* 32–39.

Salekin, R. T. (2008). Psychopathy and recidivism from mid-adolescence to young adulthood: Cumulating legal problems and limiting life opportunities. *Journal of Abnormal Psychology, 117,* 386–395.

Salekin, R. T., Rogers, R., & Sewell, K. W. (1997). Construct validity of psychopathy in a female offender sample: A multitrait-multimethod evaluation. *Journal of Abnormal Psychology, 106,* 576–585.

Salekin, R. T., Rogers, R., Ustad, K. L., & Sewell, K. W. (1998). Psychopathy and recidivism among female inmates. *Law and Human Behavior, 22,* 109–128.

Schinka, J. A., & Borum, R. (1993). Readability of adult psychopathology inventories. *Psychological Assessment, 5,* 384–386.

Sellbom, M., & Bagby, R. M. (2008). Response styles on multiscale inventories. In R. Rogers (Ed.). *Clinical assessment of malingering and deception* (3rd ed.) (pp. 182–206). New York: Guilford Press.

Siefert, C. J., Kehl-Fie, K., Blais, M. A., & Chriki, L. (2007). Detecting back irrelevant responding on the Personality Assessment Inventory in a psychiatric inpatient setting. *Psychological Assessment, 19,* 469–473.

Skopp, N. A., Edens, J. F., & Ruiz, M. A. (2007). Risk factors for institutional misconduct among incarcerated women: An examination of the criterion-related validity of the Personality Assessment Inventory. *Journal of Personality Assessment, 88,* 106–117.

Spohn, C., Piper, R. K., Martin, T., & Frenzel, E. D. (2001). Drug courts and recidivism: The results of an evaluation using two comparison groups and multiple indicators of recidivism. *Journal of Drug Issues, 31,* 149–176.

Steadman, H. J., Davidson, S., & Brown, C. (2001). Mental health courts: Their promise and unanswered questions. *Psychiatric Services, 54,* 257–258.

Toch, H. (1992). *Living in Prison: The ecology of survival.* Washington, D.C.: American Psychiatric Association.

Toch, H., & Adams, K. (1994). *The disturbed violent offender* (Revised edition). Washington, DC: American Psychological Association.

Trull, T. J. (1995). Borderline personality disorder features in nonclinical young adults: I. Identification and validation. *Psychological Assessment, 7,* 33–44.

Trull, T. J., Useada, D., Conforti, K., & Doan, B. (1997). Borderline personality disorder features in nonclinical young adults: 2. Two-year outcome. *Journal of Abnormal Psychology, 106,* 307–314.

U.S. Department of Justice-Federal Bureau of Investigation. (2008). *Crime in the United States, 2007.* Washington, D.C.: U.S. Department of Justice.

Uttl, B. (2002). North American Adult Reading Test: Age norms, reliability, and validity. *Journal of Clinical and Experimental Neuropsychology, 24,* 1123–1137.

Volkow, N. D., & Fowler, J. S. (2000). Addiction, a disease of compulsion and drive: Involvement of the orbitofrontal cortex. *Cererbral Cortex, 10,* 318–325.

Volkow, N. D., Fowler, J. S., & Wang, G. (2003). The addicted human brain: Insights from imaging studies. *Medical Imaging, 111,* 1444–1451.

Walmsley, R. (2007). *World prison population list: Seventh edition.* London, England: International Centre for Prison Studies.

Walters, G. D. (2007a). The latent structure of the criminal lifestyle: A taxometric analysis of the Lifestyle Criminality Screening Form and the Psychological Inventory of Criminal Thinking Styles. *Criminal Justice and Behavior, 34,* 1623–1637.

Walters, G. D. (2007b). Predicting institutional adjustment with the Lifestyle Criminality Screening Form and the Antisocial Features and Aggression scales of the PAI. *Journal of Personality Assessment, 88,* 99–105.

Walters, G. D., Duncan, S. A., & Geyer, M. D. (2003). Predicting disciplinary adjustment in inmates undergoing forensic evaluation: A direct comparison of the PCL-R and the PAI. *Journal of Forensic Psychiatry & Psychology, 14,* 382–393.

Walters, G. D., & Geyer, M. D. (2005). Construct validity of the Psychological Inventory of Criminal Thinking Styles in relationship to the PAI, disciplinary adjustment, and program completion. *Journal of Personality Assessment, 84,* 252–260.

Warren, J. (2008). *One in 100: Behind bars in America 2008.* Public Safety Performance Project. Washington, DC: PEW Center of the States.

Webster, C. D., Douglas, K. S., Eaves, D., & Hart, S. D. (1997). *HCR-20: Assessing risk for violence (version 2).* Vancouver, BC: Mental Health, Law, and Policy Institute at Simon Fraser University.

Widiger, T. A., Cadoret, R., Hare, R., Robins, L., Rutherford, M., Zanarini, M. et al., (1996). DSM-IV Antisocial Personality Disorder field trial. *Journal of Abnormal Psychology, 105,* 3–16.

8

Cross-Cultural Applications of the PAI

AMOR A. CORREA and RICHARD ROGERS

AN OVERVIEW ON PSYCHOLOGICAL ASSESSMENTS AND MINORITIES

*E*thical guidelines from the American Psychological Association require that psychologists working with ethnically, linguistically, and culturally diverse populations should recognize these characteristics as important factors affecting a person's experiences, attitudes, and psychological presentation (Bersoff, 2004). Differences between the test scores of individuals from a minority group and those from the dominant culture become problematic when they lead to inaccurate predictions or diagnoses for minority individuals (Graham, 1990). Thus, mental health professionals should consider the validity of information derived from assessment measures while always keeping in mind the cultural character-istics of the person being assessed and how such attributes likely affect his or her responses. In this manner, professionals working in the mental health field can refine their clinical interpretations of standardized measures in order to make more accurate assessments of individuals from a diverse cultural background and create treatment recommendations that are best suited for such patients (Dana, 2005).

Psychologists and other mental health practitioners are generally aware that standardized assessment measures were developed for the evaluation of persons proficient in English and sharing the mainstream culture. More recently, norma-tive studies have begun to include census-matched standardization samples that provide proportional representation of minority groups. While such inclusions are valuable, they represent only the first of many steps in validating psychological measures for three related but distinct constructs: culture, ethnicity, and diverse linguistic backgrounds. Therefore, assessments with ethnic minority populations must be conducted with the knowledge that most standard assessment instruments were not constructed or validated with these populations in mind. Interpretation of test results based solely on mainstream-based guidelines and cut-scores contained in the test manuals can lead to biased results and incorrect classification of individuals from different cultural groups. Assessment bias can be minimized when clinicians are well informed about the populations they are testing, recognize limitations of their measures, and use cultural measures to aid in their interpretation of assessment results (Dana, 2005). This chapter focuses on the use of the Personality Assessment Inventory (PAI; Morey, 1991, 2003) with ethnic minority populations and Spanish-speaking populations, based on current research.

INTERPRETATION OF PROFILE VALIDITY

An important issue in the validity of any assessment measure used with ethnic minority populations is consideration of the etic and emic qualities of the test (Dana, 1993, 2005). Etic measures are those with "universal" applications, whose constructs are equally applicable to individuals of all different groups. It is expected that an individual's assessment results on an etic measure can be interpreted based on the same set of norms, regardless of the individual's membership in any particular cultural group. Emic measures, on the other hand, are culture-specific; their clinical applications can be specific to populations based on age, gender, ethnicity, or any other grouping classification. It is understood that emic measures are appropriate only for use with the groups for whom they were designed.

Researchers (Berry, 1969, 1988; Berry, Kin, Power, Young, & Bujaki, 1989; Dana, 2005) have observed for some time that most standardized assessment measures are normed on samples comprising mainly European Americans. Based on current clinical practices, they fall into the category of imposed etic tests. This is to say, interpretive norms were developed mostly on individuals of European American heritage without further testing on other cultures, and remain valid for only the European American culture. The recent practice of adding proportionate but comparatively small samples of minority populations to test norms improves their representativeness. However, it is not a substitute for minority group validation studies to establish culturally relevant cut scores and interpretation guidelines. Without such work, test developers appear to imply that European American-based cut scores are universally valid and generalize to all cultures. This omission in test development effectively forces minority individuals into the same interpretative categories as European Americans, thereby creating a substantial possibility for misdiagnosis and misinterpretation of test results (Dana, 1993; Todd, 2005).

CLINICAL INTERPRETATION AND DIAGNOSIS

As in most assessment measures, there remains a dearth of available PAI research for its clinical use with most minority populations. Because of this lack, it is difficult to estimate the extent to which minority individuals are affected by the "imposed etic" interpretative practices. It is also difficult for clinicians to know which caveats to provide while interpreting assessment data and making treatment recommendations. An in-depth discussion of the PAI's construction, as well as available research, is included below to help clinicians understand important areas to be considered when using the PAI for patients of diverse ethnic backgrounds.

Morey (1991) was appropriately concerned that PAI items would be potentially biased with respect to culture, gender, and other demographic features. He assembled a panel with 12 of the 14 members representing African Americans, Hispanic Americans, and European Americans. Composed of psychologists, clergy, and community members, the panel identified some items intended to measure psychopathology, which were "normative in a particular subculture" (Morey, 2007, p. 120). In addition, a few items deemed potentially offensive were deleted or revised. As acknowledged by Morey, the panel review was the first important step in addressing cultural issues.

The normative samples included in the PAI manual create some limitations in interpreting results for members of different cultural groups. Ethnic differences are explored in the test manual for the census-matched standardized sample but were apparently not considered for the representative clinical sample. A second limitation was the collapsing of all minority groups except African Americans into a single "other" group (see Romain, 2000; Todd, 2005). In addition to not allowing specific comparisons for larger minority groups, such as Hispanic Americans, it creates a second, potentially serious problem of masking minority differences—not to mention the fact that this grouping makes the erroneous assumption (intended or not) that all minority groups are alike, except for African Americans. For instance, high scores for Native Americans on a particular scale might be balanced by low scores from another culture; this averaging of high and low scores might lead to an erroneous conclusion regarding the similarity of this scale between European Americans and the other minority samples. Clinical standardization samples, described in the more recent version of the PAI manual (Morey, 2007) are composed of 78.8% European Americans, 12.6% African Americans, and 8.6% "other" minority groups. Published research conducted with clinical samples has not systematically attempted to identify differences in response patterns of ethnic minority populations or special diagnostic considerations. Such information would need to be culturally specific and avoid composite groups.

Hispanic Americans

Before addressing cultural differences specific to the PAI, we review culture-specific response patterns identified in the literature that affect the validity of psychological assessments in general. In a classic study, Molina and Franco (1986) found significant differences in self-disclosure based on ethnicity and gender. Overall, Mexican Americans tended to self-disclose less than their European American counterparts. Moreover, Mexican American men self-disclosed even less than Mexican American women. It is imperative that clinicians are aware of cultural response patterns. If individuals from a different cultural background, such as Latino, appear to respond in a guarded or defensive manner during assessment, this can have a significant impact on the validity of their clinical profiles and the subsequent accuracy of their diagnoses (Helms, 1992). Research conducted with Hispanic individuals and the Minnesota Multiphasic Personality Inventory (MMPI) suggests results similar to Molina and Franco are found on multiscale inventories.

In an early review by Campos (1989), several studies consistently found significant "L" scale elevations among Hispanic Americans when compared with European Americans. Similar results have been found for Hispanic American women on the MMPI-2 (Callahan, 1998). The most logical conclusion is that Hispanic Americans, consistent with their culture, are reluctant to disclose their psychological issues in the formal context of an evaluation. This reticence to express feelings can best be described as a desire for privacy and selectivity regarding with whom personal problems can be shared, rather than as a defensive response style—the common interpretation used for European Americans.

Rogers and his colleagues (Fantoni-Salvador & Rogers, 1997; Rogers, Flores, Ustad, & Sewell, 1995) conducted several studies on the clinical usefulness of the Spanish-language PAI. Rogers et al. (1995) conducted the first validation study on mostly first- and second-generation Mexican Americans involved in mental health services. The internal consistencies for clinical and treatment scales were generally lower than found in the representative clinical sample and other non-Hispanic studies (see Morey, 2007) Interestingly, the PAI clinical scales had lower alphas for Spanish ($M = .68$) than English ($M = .76$) versions. However, the findings were (1) very positive for the Spanish test-retest reliability with monolingual clients (Mclinical $r = .78$) and (2) moderately good between English and Spanish administrations for bilingual clients (Mclinical $r = .71$). These findings suggest the Spanish version of the PAI yields consistent results when administered multiple times to the same person and moderately consistent results when administered in both English and Spanish to a bilingual individual.

Fantoni-Salvador and Rogers (1997) conducted a more elaborate study of the Spanish PAI and Spanish MMPI-2 using a Spanish version of the Diagnostic Interview Schedule (DIS; Robins, Helzer, Croughan, & Ratcliff, 1981) as an independent criterion. Good convergent validity was found for the PAI with DIS symptoms of major depression (DEP $r = .59$), schizophrenia (SCZ $r = .57$), and alcohol dependence (ALC $r = .80$). Anxiety disorders were more modest but still represented the highest correlation (ANX $r = .39$). These results compared very favorably with the Spanish MMPI-2 using the same sample and diagnostic criteria.

Most psychological research with Hispanic Americans has failed to take into account important within-minority differences (Puente, 1990). Fantoni-Salvador and Rogers (1997) compared results for Puerto Ricans, Mexican Americans, and Latin Americans. Using DIS symptoms as covariates, they found no significant between group differences or even noteworthy trends for the PAI ($Fs < 1.00$; ps = ns). While preliminary, these findings have important implications for the PAI usefulness with different Hispanic populations, as they begin to explore whether cultural differences occur in response styles of individuals from different countries of origin.

One omission from the Fantoni-Salvador and Rogers (1997) study was an examination of PAI validity indicators that could address the previously described issue regarding a reticence of Hispanic Americans to disclose as much as European Americans. A study conducted by Hopwood, Flato, Ambwani, Garland, & Morey (2009) looked closely at the PAI and socially desirable response styles in Hispanic Americans. Using undergraduate students, Hispanic American participants attained higher scores than European Americans on all socially desirable response measures used in the study, with statistically significant differences for the following: PAI Defensiveness Indicator (PAI DEF), PAI Cashel Discriminant Function (PAI CDF), and the Marlowe-Crowne Social Desirability Scale (MC). However, these differences produced only modest effect sizes, (ds = .28, .37, and .38, respectively). Predictably, the study found significant cultural differences, with Hispanic Americans identifying much more with Latino culture (d = 1.59) and less with mainstream American culture (d = .50) than European Americans. Because the samples did not differ significantly in overall clinical severity between Hispanic and European American groups, one hypothesis is that differences found in response style are influenced by cultural factors. Obviously, this hypothesis should be carefully evaluated with clinical samples before drawing any firm conclusions.

Regarding response style issues, a dissertation by Romain (2000) found that more than 40% of the PAI protocols from Hispanic Americans were considered "invalid" based on the standard cut scores outlined in the PAI manual (Morey, 1991), as compared with 20% of the European American profiles. Unfortunately, she did not provide specific data about response styles so it is unclear what proportion was potentially defensive, feigned, or highly inconsistent. Some of these differences for Hispanic Americans may be attributable to acculturation: 45% of the monolingual versus 37% of the bilingual individuals had invalid profiles. Although Hispanic Americans had higher "Positive Impression Management (PIM)" scores than European Americans (Cohen's d = .60), both groups evidenced very little withholding or defensiveness, with mean PIM scores of 45.32 and 38.06 respectively (see Table 8.1). Romain's data also suggest Hispanic Americans are scoring in a non-normative or atypical manner on items unrelated to psychopathology (i.e., INF scale). While INF elevations may reflect carelessness, confusion, or reading difficulties, psychologists may wish to consider issues of reading comprehension and acculturation before entertaining other alternatives. Given its large effect size (d = 1.00), the INF scale may indicate a culturally specific response pattern beyond differences in reading abilities. As summarized in Table 8.1, differences in treatment scales raise the possibility that Hispanic Americans are potentially reluctant to disclose treatment issues related to suicidal potential and support from others, although these effect sizes are small (ds of .43 and .42). The alternative is that these issues are less salient to Hispanic American clients.

TABLE 8.1   Medium- and Large-Effect Sizes for PAI Scales Between European American and Hispanic American Outpatients

	European American M	Hispanic American M	d
Infrequency (INF)	49.68	58.00	*1.00*
Positive Impression (PIM)	38.06	45.32	.60
Suicidal Ideation (SUI)	67.72	59.34	.43
Nonsupport (NON)	68.68	62.70	.42
Treatment Rejection (RXR)	33.40	40.79	.69

Note: Effect sizes were calculated from Romain (2000, p. 55, Table 5); Medium effect sizes (.50 to .80) are shown in bold; Large effect sizes (.81 and above) are shown in bold italics.

Reproduced by special permission of Psychological Assessment Resources, Inc., Lutz, Florida. Leslie C. Morey, Ph.D. and PAR Staff, Copyright by PAR, Inc.

African Americans

Other than data from the PAI's general normative sample published by Morey (2007), we found no published clinical data on African American response patterns specific to the PAI. However, it is widely acknowledged that African Americans tend to score higher than European Americans on measures of social aggression and psychotic symptoms even when studies control for age, gender, and level of education (Cuellar & Paniagua, 2000; Dana 1993, 2000). Researchers believe that these results are closely tied with cultural identity and beliefs, and are not necessarily indicative of psychopathology. Culture-related stressors, such as racism and adjustment to mainstream European American culture, play an important role in the types of distress African Americans tend to report. Guarding against prejudice and residual anger toward racial tensions can manifest itself as aggression, hypervigilance, or paranoia on multi-scale inventories (Marcella & Yamada, 2000; Ewart & Suchday, 2002).

A dissertation by Todd (2005) explored cultural response patterns on the PAI in a sample of African American college students. He discovered significant differences between African Americans and European Americans on the Paranoia (PAR) scale, PAR-H subscale, PAR-P subscale, Stress (STR) scale, and Nonsupport scale (NON). African Americans tended to score higher on each of these scales. Todd attributes these results to minority individuals' reactions to prejudice and continued efforts to guard against future experiences of discrimination from the dominant culture.

Todd's findings regarding the PAR scale are consistent with results found in Morey's (2007, p. 94) Census-Matched Standardization sample. When African Americans and European Americans are compared, we found a medium effect size (Cohen's d = .75) for the PAR scale (see Table 8.2), with African Americans averaging about 7 points higher. Like Todd, this significance is also found for two of the three PAR subscales (PAR-H, d = .87; PAR-P, d = .71).

Regarding the clinical scales, a consistent pattern emerges, with African Americans averaging higher than European Americans across the clinical scales. However, the differences in clinical elevations tend to be slight, typically ranging from 2 to 3 T points. It also remains to be seen whether these relatively minor differences will also hold for clinical populations. Of course, the final test will be to compare elevations for both ethnic groups with relevant external criteria.

Morey (2007, pp. 324–325) provides separate T score conversions for African Americans. Using 70T as a benchmark, the average raw score for African American norms is 35.00 as compared with the standard norms with 31.27. A raw score differential of > 5 was found for 4 of 11 clinical scales: SOM (6), ANX (5), PAR (6), and SCZ (5.5). However, Morey strongly recommends use of the standard norms to "maintain the test's interpretive consistency across demographic groups" (p. 91).

Regarding response styles, a medium effect size (d = .55) is observed in the Negative Impression Management (NIM) scale between these two cultural groups, with African Americans having much more variability in scores (SD = 13.85 vs. 8.84) and averaging 5 points higher. It suggests that substantial numbers of non-clinical African Americans may achieve elevated scores on NIM (e.g., M + 1 SD = 68.40).

TABLE 8.2   Effecst Sizes for PAI Scales Based on Race/Ethnicity for the Census-Matched Standardization Sample

	European American		African American			Other		
	M	SD	M	SD	d	M	SD	d
Inconsistency (ICN)	49.67	9.51	53.74	12.73	.41	50.69	10.67	.11
Infrequency (INF)	49.40	8.99	52.99	13.49	.37	54.91	12.63	**.60**
Negative Impression (NIM)	49.27	8.84	54.55	13.85	**.55**	53.97	14.68	.48
Positive Impression (PIM)	49.97	9.77	50.72	11.60	.08	47.81	10.53	.22
Somatic Complaints (SOM)	49.70	9.71	52.60	11.74	.26	51.34	11.85	.14
Anxiety (ANX)	49.59	9.65	51.87	11.76	.23	54.97	10.41	**.56**
Affective (ANX-A)	49.67	9.75	51.15	11.08	.15	56.22	10.52	**.67**
Anxiety-Related Disorders (ARD)	49.59	9.89	51.99	10.18	.24	53.28	12.44	.37
Depression (DEP)	49.71	9.86	51.20	10.69	.15	52.03	11.56	.23
Mania (MAN)	49.58	9.91	52.44	10.33	.29	51.91	9.98	.24
Paranoia (PAR)	48.93	9.52	56.12	10.30	**.75**	55.94	11.46	**.73**
Hypervigilance (PAR-H)	48.67	9.36	57.03	11.17	**.87**	56.34	10.99	**.81**
Persecution (PAR-P)	48.89	9.24	55.81	12.55	**.71**	54.72	14.11	**.62**
Schizophrenia (SCZ)	49.43	9.53	52.86	11.84	.35	54.66	12.6	**.54**
Psychotic Experiences (SCZ-P)	49.43	9.66	52.39	10.98	.30	55.47	11.96	**.62**
Borderline Features (BOR)	49.55	9.71	52.38	10.97	.29	54.25	11.86	.48
Antisocial Features (ANT)	49.58	9.74	52.50	10.42	.30	52.59	13.31	.30
Alcohol Problems (ALC)	49.72	9.95	50.71	9.97	.10	52.81	13.50	.31
Drug Problems (DRG)	49.62	9.51	53.52	11.77	.40	52.63	12.67	.31
Aggression (AGG)	49.73	10.07	51.05	9.29	.13	53.06	10.15	.33
Suicidal Ideation (SUI)	49.58	9.92	50.65	11.03	.11	52.44	11.41	.29
Stress (STR)	49.73	9.91	51.14	10.82	.14	50.81	9.99	.11
Nonsupport (NON)	49.45	9.75	53.63	10.71	.42	52.41	10.47	.30
Treatment Rejection (RXR)	50.25	9.95	48.68	10.37	.16	48.91	10.43	.13
Dominance (DOM)	49.82	10.05	51.36	9.58	.15	48.94	9.74	.09
Warmth (WRM)	50.11	9.74	49.60	11.52	.05	47.63	10.85	.25

Note: Effect sizes were calculated from Morey (2007, p. 49, Table 4.18); Medium effect sizes (.50 to .80) are shown in bold.

Reproduced by special permission of Psychological Assessment Resources, Inc., Lutz, Florida. Leslie C. Morey, Ph.D. and PAR Staff, Copyright by PAR, Inc.

An important consideration is that NIM for African American students is typically higher than the clinical representative sample (i.e., 2.69 raw or approximately 8 to 10 T points) composed mostly of European Americans. Therefore, clinicians must be very cautious in interpreting the lower range of moderate elevations, which spans 73T to 83T, for African American clients. A study conducted by Calhoun et al. (2000), investigated combat post traumatic stress disorder (PTSD) using under-graduate simulators and genuine inpatients. With the sample composed of 60% African American inpatients, nearly two-thirds (65%) of those with genuine PTSD had elevated scores (NIM cut score > 73T). Moreover, 21.0% had extreme NIM elevations (NIM > 92T). It is unclear whether the sample composition with its majority of African Americans contributed to these high percentages of moderate and extreme NIM elevations. Further studies are needed to evaluate the role of ethnicity with PAI interpretation on NIM among African American patients.

Language

The effects of language are vitally important to take into account when considering the accuracy of the assessment process. The psychometric properties of standardized assessment measures are likely to change when administered to individuals who are culturally different from the normative sample (Marin & Marin, 1991). Furthermore, multilingual individuals who are not tested in their preferred language can suffer a detachment effect (Bamford, 1991); they fail to adequately connect with the assessment questions and be able to fully express their emotional and psychological issues. The detachment effect can result in poor communication about symptoms and less self-disclosure (Dana, 1995); however, it is often remedied when individuals are tested in their preferred language. For example, Guttfreund (1990) shows that bilingual Hispanic American patients who prefer to speak Spanish are more able to effectively express their emotions when tested in that language rather than English. To date, the PAI has been translated and published in Spanish as well as English. For the Spanish PAI, clinicians must take into account a client's language preference prior to beginning the assessment process. In cases where the client is conversant in both languages and expresses only a minor preference, practitioners might choose the English version—given its extensive validation and superior alphas. When a strong preference is expressed for Spanish or English language abilities are limited, the Spanish version would be the most appropriate.

The PAI test manuals (Morey, 1991, 2003) do not describe the translation process for the Spanish version. However, Psychological Assessment Resources, their publisher, has standardized a translation process that includes an independent back-translation and review/approval by the test's author (see http://www3.parinc.com/dynspage.aspx?PageCatgory=Permissions&id=2). This process is an essential step for ensuring linguistic equivalence.

Hambleton (2001) summarized the International Test Commission (ITC) Test Translation and Adaptation Guidelines, which require additional steps when a test is adapted into a new language. As a general principle, test developers and publishers must apply appropriate research methods and statistical techniques to establish the validity of a test in each population for whom the translated version is intended. Test developers should use research results to improve the accuracy of the adaptation process and identify issues that may be problematic with the intended populations. In addition, the validity of any translated version must be determined separately from the validation of the original measure. It should not be assumed that a translated version has acceptable validity simply because it is adequate for the English version (Anastasi, 1988).

The ITC standards are consistent with the *Standards for Educational and Psychological Testing*, coauthored by the American Psychological Association

(AERA, APA, NCME, 1999). These standards require that psychologists and other professionals refrain from using a translated version until the reliability and validity of that new measure has been established. The danger in administering tests that have not been validated is that clinicians interpret the results based on an assumption that the test continues to function in the intended manner (Fantoni-Salvador, 1997).

As previously cited, the Rogers et al. (1995) study established reliability of the Spanish PAI using a sample of Mexican American patients. Measures on internal reliability were adequate for the clinical and treatment scales, whereas the test-retest estimates were moderately good across a median interval of 14 days. The equivalency between the English and Spanish versions of the PAI was examined for a small bilingual sample and produced moderately high correlations. One limitation was found in the stability of clinical elevations; slightly less than half the elevations remained stable for Spanish–Spanish (45.5%) and Spanish–English (48.5%) administrations. However, greater stability should be expected for clinical scores that are greater than or equal to 76T.*

In addition to evaluating the construct validity of the Spanish PAI, Fantoni-Salvador and Rogers (1997) also evaluated clinical elevations for the four primary disorders: major depression, schizophrenia, anxiety disorders, and alcohol dependence as categorical constructs using 70T as the benchmark. Although the sensitivities were generally good (M = .80; range from .69 to .90), the positive predictive powers (PPP) were more variable (M = .59; range from .40 to .82). Therefore, we stress that dimensional use of PAI clinical scales (i.e., using elevations to gauge relative levels of distress related to symptom groups) has better empirical validation than their categorical use (i.e., presence or absence of a disorder), and should be used particularly for the Spanish PAI.

In summary, the two studies by Rogers and his colleagues provide valuable data regarding the PAI Spanish translation. They provide good evidence for the reliability and validity of the PAI clinical scales as dimensional constructs. As categorical constructs, clinical elevations have substantial problems with test-retest reliability (concordance of 48.5%) and establishing the presence of a disorder (M PPP = .59). Therefore, we recommend the interpretation of the Spanish PAI on a dimensional basis.

Romain (2000) compared PAI scales for two separate samples of Hispanic American outpatients: English-speaking and Spanish-speaking. Outpatients receiving the Spanish version averaged 10 points higher than the English version on four clinical scales (see Table 8.3), producing medium effect sizes: SOM (d = .71), ANX (d = .61), ARD (d = .65), and SCZ (d = .70). For the first three scales, these averages were in the clinically interpretable range, with the ANX being particularly elevated (M = 76.18). The Spanish group was also higher on Nonsupport (NON; d = .69) and lower on interpersonal scales—apparently showing less than average Dominance (DOM) and Warmth (WRM); see Table 8.3). These consistent differences could

---

* Using Fantoni-Salvador and Rogers (1997) M rtest-retest = .78 and Morey's (2007) SDs for Other Ethnic groups (M = 12.00), the standard error of measurement for the Spanish translation is 5.63. As a general benchmark, the majority of clinical scale elevations are apt to remain stable at 1 SEM (> 76T).

TABLE 8.3 Effect Sizes for Significant Differences in PAI Scales Based on Language

| | Hispanic American Sample | | |
	English M	Spanish M	d
Somatic Complaints (SOM)	62.56	72.68	**.71**
Anxiety (ANX)	65.88	76.18	**.61**
Anxiety-Related Disorder (ARD)	60.88	71.18	**.65**
Schizophrenia (SCZ)	56.92	69.14	**.70**
Nonsupport (NON)	57.72	67.14	**.69**
Dominance (DOM)	46.64	40.75	**.60**
Warmth (WRM)	46.80	39.21	**.66**

Note: Effect sizes were calculated from Romain (2000, p. 56, Table 5); Medium effect sizes (.50 to .80) are shown in bold.
Reproduced by special permission of Psychological Assessment Resources, Inc., Lutz, Florida. Leslie C. Morey, Ph.D. and PAR Staff, Copyright by PAR, Inc.

be showing limits in translation equivalence or effects of acculturation, the process in which members of one cultural group adopt the beliefs and behaviors of another group. Alternatively, they could be demonstrating true differences in sample characteristics between English-speaking and Spanish-speaking clientele. For instance, a scarcity of Spanish-speaking therapists could lead to triaging, with only the more impaired monolingual clients being referred for services. Romain's study did not control for clinical severity across groups, so it is possible that these differences reflect only the differences within her sample. However, this criticism can be applied to most other cross-cultural studies. For example, the Hopwood et al. (2009) finding of no overall clinical differences suffers from the same criticism.

Other Cultural Groups

Morey (2007) provides composite data on "other" minority groups. As summarized in Table 8.2, this composite group has far more medium effect sizes than found in similar comparisons of African Americans with European Americans. Other minorities have higher clinical scales that European Americans on the following: PAR ($d = .73$), ANX ($d = .56$), and SCZ ($d = .54$), plus nearly a medium effect size for BOR ($d = .48$). Among community participants, some of the item content on these scales may be culturally normative rather than indicative of psychopathology. For instance, the Anxiety-Affective (ANX-A; $d = .67$) and Schizophrenia-Psychotic Experiences (SCZ-P; $d = .62$) may have several culturally normative items. Without item-level analyses, we cannot determine which specific items are affected. As noted in the beginning of this chapter, these comparisons need to be decomposed into specific minority groups before additional analyses are conducted.

INDICATIONS FOR ADDITIONAL MEASURES

PAI assessments, especially with first-, second-, and third-generation immigrants, should go beyond cultural issues per se and consider the level of acculturation for individual examinees. With low levels of acculturation, clients continue to identify with the values of their ethnic group despite frequent interactions with the mainstream culture (Wagner & Gartner, 1997); this identification begins to shift with further acculturation. This process may account for within-group differences in response patterns, personality characteristics, and psychopathology (Okazaki & Sue, 1995). Of particular clinical concern, some clients do not acculturate well and may experience "marginality" with distress and alienation because they lack identification with either culture (Berry, 1989).

Therefore, comprehensive evaluations often benefit from the inclusion of an acculturation measure as part of the assessment process (Dana, 1993; Wagner & Gartner, 1997). For PAI administrations, the use of an acculturation measure will often clarify the certitude of the interpretations, which increase with higher levels of acculturation. They may also assist in refining the clinical interpretations in light of the client's current acculturation. Although many acculturation measures are available, psychologists may wish to consider the Scale of Ethnic Experience (SEE; Malcarne, Chavira, Fernandez, & Liu, 2006), which has been widely adapted to diverse cultures, and the Acculturation Rating Scale for Mexican Americans-II (ARSMA-II; Cuellar, Arnold, & Maldonado, 1995), which has a widely researched and validated Spanish language version.

TREATMENT PLANNING

In light of the PAI research literature, mental health professionals should be more circumspect in rendering interpretations for culturally diverse groups than with mainstream culture. We propose that the following recommendations be considered:

1. Cautionary statements should be included for all PAI interpretations involving clients with low levels of acculturation. As with all multi-scale inventories, PAI profiles have not been extensively researched for clients identifying closely with a minority culture.
2. Based on normative differences, marginal elevations (e.g., 70–75T) may reflect psychopathology or ethnically sensitive content. The PAI's interpretive manual does not specify alternative cut scores or wider confidence intervals for minority individuals. Thus, one option for practicing clinicians making interpretations of marginal elevations of minority clients is to also provide alternative explanations such as the following: "Alternatively, small differences have been observed on this scale between mainstream culture and minorities. This elevation could be due to these cultural differences."
3. For interpretations of depression, anxiety, and stress, mental health professionals should consider whether problems with acculturation are contributing to these dysphoric feelings (Cuellar & Roberts, 1997). Such hypotheses can be very valuable in tailoring clinical interventions to individual needs.

4. For African Americans, higher scores on Paranoia (PAR) scale and two of its subscales (PAR-H and PAR-P) appear to be normative, with 7 to 8 points being expected. Assuming no systematic biases in collecting the census-matched sample, these differences apply across a broad range of African Americans in terms of educational levels and professions. Therefore, mental health professionals do not need to find personal experiences of racial bias and prejudice when interpreting the PAR scale with African Americans.

5. The Spanish language PAI can be used in clinical settings with a moderate level of correspondence between English and Spanish versions for first- and second-generation Hispanic Americans. These findings are bolstered by independent appraisals for common Axis I disorders. However, no research has examined the usefulness of the Spanish PAI for evaluating response styles, such as malingering. Its use for this purpose is not recommended.

6. Treatment reluctance and reticence to disclose mental health problems are common in minority cultures. While some efforts to downplay symptoms and treatment needs will be detected by the PAI PIM and the Treatment Rejection (RXR) scales, clinicians should be alert that significant symptoms may not be disclosed. Use of family members as independent collateral sources may be important in augmenting PAI interpretations.

In closing, psychologists and other mental health professionals practice in culturally diverse settings that require understanding and expertise informed by dissimilar cultural experiences. Even the manifestation of symptoms may be culturally influenced, such as found with the somatic expressions of depression (Wagner & Gartner, 1997). Moreover, cultural stigmas surrounding mental health services must be taken into account when establishing rapport and planning psychological assessments. Measures such as the PAI must be considered within the broader framework of cultural differences and possible stigmas. If minority referrals can genuinely understand its purpose and potential helpfulness, then the PAI can be a powerful assessment tool for identifying psychological problems and treatment needs.

In communicating test results to either patients or other mental health professionals, it is important to clearly convey the limitations of using the PAI with members of minority populations when it is designed for persons with mainstream American values. Second, when patients' values differ substantially because of their cultural identity, this discrepancy may cause the PAI to be misinterpreted with respect to their concerns and possible symptoms. Some concerns may be more affected by external than internal factors. For example, elevations on the Non-Support Scale (NON) might be better explained by discrimination in the workplace, rather than deficits in a person's primary support system. As mentioned earlier, research has established that guarding against prejudice can manifest itself as aggression, hypervigilance, or paranoia on multi-scale inventories (Marcella & Yamada, 2000; Ewart & Suchday, 2002). Each of these explanations and any alternative interpretations should be discussed with patients during feedback to ensure they do not feel misdiagnosed or over-pathologized.

REFERENCES

American Educational Research Association, American Psychological Association, & National Council on Measurement in Education [AERA, APA, NCME] (1999). *Standards for educational and psychological testing*. Washington, DC: Author.

Anastasi, A. (1988). *Psychological testing* (6th ed.). New York: Macmillan.

Bamford, K. W. (1991). Bilingual issues in mental health assessment and treatment. *Hispanic Journal of Behavioral Sciences, 13*, 377–390.

Berry, J. W. (1969). On cross-cultural comparability. *International Journal of Psychology, 4*, 119–128.

Berry, J. W. (1988). Imposed etics-emics-derived etics: The operationalization of a compelling idea. *International Journal of Psychology, 24*, 721–735.

Berry, J. W., Kin, U., Power, S., Young, M., & Bujaki, M. (1989). Acculturation attitudes in plural societies. *Applied Psychology: An International Review, 38*, 185–206.

Bersoff, D. N. (Ed.). (2004). *Ethical conflicts in psychology*. Washington, DC: American Psychological Association.

Calhoun, P. S., Earnst, K. S., Tucker, D. D., Kirby, A. C., & Beckham, J. C., (2000). Feigning combat-related posttraumatic stress disorder on the Personality Assessment Inventory. *Journal of Personality Assessment, 75*, 338–350.

Callahan, W. J. (1998). MMPI-2, symptom reports, and acculturation of White- and Mexican-Americans in psychiatric, college, and community settings. *Dissertation Abstracts International 58(8-B)*, 4439.

Campos, L. P. (1989). Adverse impact, unfairness, and bias in the psychological screening of Hispanic peace officers. *Hispanic Journal of Behavioral Sciences, 11*, 122–135.

Cohen, J. (1988). *Statistical power analysis for the behavioral sciences* (2nd ed.). Hillsdale, NJ: Lawrence Erlbaum Associates.

Cuellar, I., Arnold, B., & Maldonado, R. (1995). Acculturation Rating Scale for Mexican Americans-II: A revision of the original ARSMA Scale. *Hispanic Journal of Behavioral Science, 17*, 275–304.

Cuellar, I., & Paniagua, F. A. (Eds.). (2000). *Handbook of multicultural mental health*. San Diego, CA: Academic Press.

Cuellar, I., & Roberts, R. E. (1997). Relations of depression, acculturation, and socioeconomic status in a Latino sample. *Hispanic Journal of Behavioral Science, 19*, 230–238.

Dana, R. H. (1993). *Multicultural assessment perspectives for professional psychology*. Boston: Allyn & Bacon.

Dana, R. H. (1995). Culturally competent MMPI assessment of Hispanic populations. *Hispanic Journal of Behavioral Sciences, 17*, 305–319.

Dana, R. H. (2000). *Handbook of cross-cultural and multicultural personality assessment*. Mahwah, NJ: Lawrence Erlbaum.

Dana, R. H. (2005). *Multicultural assessment principles, applications, and examples*. Mahwah, New Jersey: Lawrence Erlbaum Associates.

Ewart, C. K., & Suchday, S. (2002). Discovering how urban poverty and violence affect health development and validation of a Neighborhood Stress Index. *Health Psychology, 21(3)*, 254–262.

Fantoni-Salvador, P., & Rogers, R. (1997). Spanish versions of the MMPI-2 and PAI: An investigation of the concurrent validity with Hispanic patients. *Assessment, 4*, 29–39.

Garcia, M., & Marks, G. (1989). Depressive symptomatology among Mexican-American adults: An examination with the CES-D Scale. *Psychiatry Research, 27*, 137–148.

Graham, J. R. (1990). *MMPI-2: Assessing personality and psychopathology* (2nd ed.). New York: Oxford University, Inc.

Guttfreund, D. G. (1990). Effects of language usage on the emotional experience of Spanish-English and English-Spanish bilinguals. *Journal of Consulting and Clinical Psychology, 58*, 604–607.

Hambleton, R. K. (2001). The next generation of the ITC test translation and adaptation guidelines. *European Journal of Psychological Assessment, 17*, 164–172.

Helms, J. E. (1992). Why is there no study of cultural equivalence in standardized cognitive ability testing? In N. R. Goldberger & J. B. Veroff (Eds.), *The cultural and psychology reader* (674 – 719). New York: New York University Press.

Hopwood, C. J., Flato, C., Ambwani, S., Garland, B. H., & Morey, L. C. (2009). A comparison of Latino and Anglo positive responding. *Journal of Clinical Psychology, 65*(7), 769 – 780.

Malcarne, V., Chavira, D., Fernandez, S., & Liu, P. (2006). The Scale of Ethnic Experience: Development and psychometric properties. *Journal of Personality Assessment, 86*(2), 150–161.

Marin, G., & Marin, B. (1991). *Research with Hispanic populations.* Newbury Park: Sage Publications.

Marcella, A. J., & Yamada, A. M. (2000). Culture and mental health: An introduction and overview of foundations, concepts, and issues. In I. Cuellar, & F. A. Paniagua (Eds.), *Handbook of mental health* (pp. 3–24). San Diego, CA: Academic Press.

Molina, R. A., & Franco, J. N. (1986). Effects of administrator and participant sex and ethnicity on self-disclosure. *Journal of Counseling and Development, 65*, 160–162.

Morey, L. C. (1991). *The Personality Assessment Inventory.* Odessa, FL: Psychological Assessment Resources, Inc.

Morey, L. C. (2007). *The Personality Assessment Inventory* (2nd ed). Lutz, FL: Psychological Assessment Resources, Inc.

Okazaki, S., & Sue, S. (1995). Methodological issues in assessment research with ethnic minorities. *Psychological Assessment, 7*, 367–375.

Radloff, L. S. (1977). The CES-D Scale: A self-report depression scale for research in the general population. *Journal of Applied Psychological Measurement, 1*, 385–401.

Robins, L. N., Helzer, J. E., Cottler, L. B., & Goldring, E. (1989). NIMH Diagnostic Interview Schedule, Version III-revised. St. Louis: Washington University School of Medicine.

Rogers, R., Flores, J., Ustad, K., & Sewell, K. W. (1995). Initial validation of the Personality Assessment Inventory—Spanish Version with clients from Mexican-American communities. *Journal of Personality Assessment, 64*, 340–348.

Romain, P. M. (2000). Use of the Personality Assessment Inventory with an ethnically diverse sample of psychiatric outpatients. *Dissertation Abstracts International, 61*(11-B), 6147.

Todd, W. (2005). Race/ethnicity and the Personality Assessment Inventory (PAI): The impact of culture on diagnostic testing in a college counseling center. *Dissertation Abstracts International, 65*(10-B), 5425.

Urdaneta, M. L., Saldana, D. H., & Winkler, A. (1995). Mexican-American perceptions of severe mental illness. *Human Organization, 54*, 70–77.

Wagner, J., & Gartner, C. G. (1997). Highlights of the 1996 Institute on Psychiatric Services. *Psychiatric Services, 48*, 51–55.

9

PAI Assessment in Medical Settings

TIMOTHY S. CLARK, SARAH R. OSLUND, and CHRISTOPHER J. HOPWOOD

G iven the potentially profound influences of psychological variables on the experience, expression, and treatment of medical conditions (Turk & Melzack, 2001), it is critical to efficiently and adequately assess such factors in medical settings. The Personality Assessment Inventory (PAI; Morey, 1991) is commonly used for this purpose. However, although research on the PAI in medical settings has expanded dramatically during the last several years, the overall research base remains relatively limited. Furthermore, most existing research has focused on particular populations such as those with chronic pain, nonepileptic seizures, and head injuries, or specific applications such as the validity of neuropsychological data. As a result, clinical recommendations for using the PAI in such settings must be relatively tentative. The purpose of this chapter is to briefly review published studies and provide suggestions for using the PAI with medical patients based on the literature and the clinical experience of the first author, who has been using the PAI with chronic-pain patients for more than 6 years.

INTERPRETATION OF PROFILE VALIDITY

Test validity and response styles can be critically important in the assessment of medical patients. For instance, some patients with chronic pain describe levels of physical discomfort and concentration difficulties that may interfere with completing a relatively long questionnaire. In addition, there is good reason to believe that response style can affect the expression of pain and treatment outcomes (Burns et al., 2001). As such, it is important to assess these characteristics in medical settings. Although no study has explicitly tested the operating characteristics of PAI validity indicators in medical patients to detect random responding or intentional feigning, previous studies have shown that PAI indicator properties in medical settings are similar to those in other populations (Demakis, Hammond, Knotts, Cooper,

Clement et al., 2007; Karlin, Creech, Grimes, Clark, Meagher et al., 2005; Kurt, Shealy, & Putnam, 2007).

Two studies have investigated the effects of head injury on the PAI. Demakis et al. (2007) obtained PAI profiles from individuals 9 to 12 months following well-documented, moderate to severe traumatic brain injury (TBI). Using conventional validity standards, 83% of obtained profiles were judged valid, similar to validity rates in other settings (Braxton, Calhoun, Williams, & Boggs, 2007). Furthermore, multivariate analyses suggested a factor structure similar to that of multiple other samples (Hoelzle & Meyer, 2009). Overall, this study generally suggests the validity of the PAI even for people with dramatic cognitive insult. Kurtz, Shealy, & Putnam (2007) also found that even severe TBI had limited effects on PAI profile validity scale scores. Thus, even with persons with cognitive impairments, the PAI appears to retain its validity.

The PAI validity indicators may also have some potential to indicate the validity of other measures, although results in this regard are mixed and appear to suggest that this potential is highest for other self-report measures. Hopwood, Creech, Clark, Meagher, & Morey (2008a) showed that including PAI Positive Impression Management (PIM) in the assessment of pain patients with the Multidimensional Pain Inventory (MPI; Kerns, Turk, & Rudy, 1985) improved that measure's validity, consistent with previous research on the role of "repression" in pain samples. However, research testing the ability of PAI validity indicators to detect insufficient effort on neuropsychological testing has been less promising. In one study utilizing a sample of persons applying for psychiatric disability due to occupational stress, the PAI validity scales and indices did not significantly predict which patients would fail cognitive effort measures (Sumanti, Boone, Savodnik, & Gorsuch, 2006). PAI validity scales demonstrated weak relationships with an established measure of effort, the Victoria Symptom Validity Test (VSST, Slick, Hopp, Strauss, & Spellacy, 1996) in another study (Haggerty, Frazier, Busch, & Naugle, 2007), although a significant correlation between Negative Impression Management (NIM) and both accuracy and latency measures on the VSST was observed. In a third investigation, the PAI was ineffective for identifying patients who demonstrated suboptimal effort as measured by the *Word Memory Test* (WMT; Green, Allen, & Astner, 1996) in college students being evaluated for attention deficit hyperactivity and learning disorders (Sullivan, May, & Galbally, 2007). Overall, these data suggest that the PAI validity scales are not sensitive to lack of effort in examinations of neuropsychological functioning.

Practically speaking, the most common validity issues in medical patients involve negative distortion. The configural analysis approach described by Morey & Hopwood (2007) may be helpful in distinguishing patients who may be over-reporting due to unconscious distortion from those who are deliberately attempting to highlight their distress. This distinction is useful in discriminating patients who feel overwhelmed from patients who may have issues of secondary gain.

In summary, validity scales appear robust for their intended applications among medical patients, but are unlikely to be as useful when applied to purposes for which they were not designed. We recommend Morey's (1996, 2003; Morey & Hopwood, 2007) guidelines for interpreting the validity of PAI profiles and patient response sets with medical patients, but also suggest supplementing PAI validity indicators with other measures and desire further research on PAI validity indicators in medical populations.

Diagnosis

Psychological measures such as the PAI can be used for diagnosing psychiatric conditions that may moderate the expression of symptoms, amenability for treatment, or response to treatment. For example, Brednza, Ashton, Windover, and Stillman (2005) reported that headache patients with elevations on Somatic Complaints (SOM) were more likely to be referred to an interdisciplinary program combining psychological and medical interventions, demonstrating the recognition that psychological variables present in the patients' difficulties affect decisions about medical treatment. The performance of the PAI in several medical conditions has been explored.

Nonepileptic Seizures   Although the PAI was not designed to assess issues that are specific to medical settings, some research suggests promise in this regard. One area of particular potential involves differentiating epileptic and nonepileptic seizures (ES, NES, respectively). The contemporary diagnostic standard for this differentiation is long-term video electroencephalography (VEEG). In light of the cost and complexity of this procedure, the utility of other brief and less costly measures, such as the PAI, has been investigated. Recent research shows that patients with NES tend to have higher scores on Depression (DEP), especially the physiological subscale (DEP-P) as well as SOM and the conversion subscale (SOM-C; McDaniel et al., 2007; Pritchard, Wagner, & Topping, 2002; Wagner et al, 2005). In one study, SOM-C alone classified patients (using VEEG as the diagnostic standard) with a sensitivity of 67% and a specificity of 89% (Pritchard et al., 2002). Another study (Wagner, Wymer, Topping, & Pritchard, 2005) found the two groups differed on the SOM-C subscale by more than $10T$ (NES = $77T$, ES = $65T$).

Wagner et al. (2005) created an "NES indicator" score to further improve classification. The authors reasoned that for patients with ES, Health Concerns (SOM-H) would tend to elevate, reflecting the impact of seizures on patients' lives and their concerns about overall health. In contrast, they predicted that SOM-C subscale, with its assessment of dramatic and unlikely physical complaints, would be elevated above that of the SOM-H in NES patients. The indicator score was derived by subtracting the T score of SOM-H from SOM-C. A positive score would suggest the presence of NES while a negative score would suggest ES. The initial investigation (Wagner et al., 2005) found a significant difference between the two groups (NES = 11.7, ES = −5.3), with the indicator demonstrating a sensitivity of 84% and specificity of 73.3% for VEEG-defined NES. A separate research group (McDaniel et al., 2007) replicated this finding by demonstrating positive numbers for the NES group (NES = 6) and negative number for ES group (NES = −7). Furthermore, only a minor attenuation in classification rates (overall hit rate for NES = 68%; for ES = 74%) was observed in this independent follow-up. These data suggest that the PAI, and especially the NES indicator proposed by Wagner et al. (2005), is useful as a screening measure for differentiating NES from ES.

Chronic Pain   The broadest line of PAI research in medical settings has occurred among pain patients. Interest in the psychological assessment of persons with chronic pain has been longstanding (e.g., Hanvik, 1951), and psychometric testing continues to be viewed as useful in light of the complex multidimensional nature of pain. Extensive research has been conducted examining the impact of psychological processes on a person's experience of pain and the expression of this pain using a variety of measures (Gatchel & Turk, 1996; Banks & Kerns, 1996; Turk & Melzack, 2001).

Overall, the PAI bears promise for use in chronic pain assessment. The range of scales speaks to the instrument's potential to evaluate the impact of pain on patients' emotional state and depict the biopsychosocial context in which pain occurs (Turk & Melzack, 2001; Gatchell & Weisberg, 2000). For example, validity scales are useful because patients often have differential levels of focus or preoccupation with their pain and they may also vary in the degree to which they disclose their distress. Clinical scales are critical because of symptomatic overlap between pain and some psychiatric conditions and because pain and psychological disorders can exacerbate one another. Interpersonal related scales on the PAI are helpful because these factors affect use of social support, willingness to express pain behavior, dependency behaviors, and interpersonal conflict. Treatment consideration scales can be helpful in identifying problematic behaviors such as substance abuse, aggression, or suicidal thinking and risks.

In a study of pain patients Karlin et al. (2005) demonstrated that PAI scales have similar internal consistencies and factorial structure in medical and non-medical populations. Notably, Cheng, Frank, and Hopwood in Chapter 11 in this volume, show similar characteristics among MVA claimants, suggesting that this result may generalize to similar samples (e.g., workers' compensation populations) as well. Other research has investigated the criterion-related validity of the PAI in medical settings. Hopwood et al. (2007) correlated the PAI with criterion measures in a pain program. DEP and SOM demonstrated significant correlations with several measures of mental and physical well-being. Interestingly, although SOM was significantly correlated with measures of physical distress and dysfunction, it had somewhat stronger correlations with mental health measures, suggesting that SOM may reflect emotional distress more than physical limitations in this population. In this study, both the PAI and the MPI were generally insensitive to treatment effects. These results highlight the importance of using the PAI and other psychological instruments to augment a comprehensive and multi-method assessment battery in pain and other medical contexts.

Sleep Deprivation   In a small but interesting criterion-validity study, the PAI was sensitive to changes following 56 hours of continuous wakefulness (Kahn-Greene, Killgore, Kamimori, Balkin, & Killgore, 2007). Sleep deprivation resulted in significant increases in SOM (especially SOM-H), Anxiety (ANX; especially physiological anxiety [ANX-P]), DEP (including cognitive [DEP-C] and affective [DEP-A] subscales), and Paranoia (PAR). However, the highest average score on any of these scales was only 55T. This finding suggests that, while sleep deprivation does not necessarily lead to a manifestation of significant clinical issues, it does negatively impact psychological functioning, and the PAI is sensitive to such changes.

Psychiatric Disorders   In addition to using the PAI to indicate medical issues directly, the instrument can also serve the important function of indicating psychiatric conditions that may influence the expression or treatment of medical conditions. In the Karlin et al. (2005) study, most (67%) pain patients had at least one clinical scale elevation > 70T. Of those patients with clinical scale elevations, evaluation of the clinical scales revealed primary difficulties involving somatic concerns and emotional distress. As expected, the highest elevation was found for SOM (M = 72T, SD = 11.6). Similar levels on SOM were obtained in another study of headache patients (Brendza et al., 2005). In the Karlin et al. data, DEP was the only other scale to fall above 60T (T = 66.9, S.D. = 14.5), with the primary subscale elevation being that of physiological symptoms. ANX and Stress (STR) were mildly elevated but below 60T on average. This is consistent with a general characterization of pain patients as being psychologically involved with their medical condition, with concomitant anxiety, stress, and depression. It also highlights the importance of considering the extent to which these and other factors may influence treatment considerations.

Suggestions for PAI Diagnostic Interpretation in Medical Settings
Clinical interpretation of the PAI in medical settings can adopt several approaches. In general, multiple aspects of patient personality and functioning need to be integratively considered in evaluating patients in medical settings (see Blais and Hopwood, Chapter 12, this volume), although specific PAI indicators such as Wagner et al.'s (2005) NES algorithm may be used for more targeted purposes. Morey & Hopwood (2007) provided two case examples of how the PAI structural summary approach can be used in medical patients involving nonepileptic seizures and chronic pain symptoms. Theses cases also represent the broad range of issues that can be evaluated using the PAI in medical settings. Future research efforts with the PAI in medical populations should begin to examine the predictive validity and clinical utility of the additional sources of information from the PAI discussed by Morey and Hopwood. In particular, the Impression Management Configural Analysis appears to hold promise for the evaluation of response styles, the meaning of pain behavior, and the impact of repression and other perceptual factors on somatic complaints.

In addition to viewing the standard profile based on the original normative population, it may also be helpful to compare a patient's performance with data from other patients with a similar diagnosis or problem (e.g., Karlin et al., 2005 for pain patients, Cheng, Frank, and Hopwood, Chapter 11, this volume for MVA claimants). This comparison with the reference profile of patients in order to detect clinically significant variance from the "standard" person with a given medical condition may be useful in two ways.

First, this approach can help quantify and communicate a patient's level of somatic preoccupation or distress. For example, by computing a simple z score with a conversion to a percentile rank, it is possible to compare the patient's scale score with means and standard deviations from the Karlin et al. (2005) sample. It is helpful in communicating with a referral source to state that a patient is reporting higher somatic complaints than 90% of other persons from a broad chronic pain sample. This also limits the potential for the "over-interpretation" of findings (e.g., of a score which is high relative to community norms but typical in pain patients).

Second, it may be important to note scale elevation patterns that are not typical for persons with chronic pain. Minor elevations on such scales are often clinically significant even though they might be unremarkable in a psychiatric setting. For example, a score of 60 on Alcohol Problems (ALC) reflects a score that is 2 standard deviations above the mean at the Baylor Center for Pain Management (i.e., 46.0, S.D. = 7.1; Karlin et al., 2005), and thus is of considerable interest even if it doesn't "stand out" in first looking at the profile. In both of these approaches, some caution must be used to ensure the reference data are appropriate for the patient being evaluated. For instance, it is likely that pain patients seen at a general medical clinic will be different from litigating pain patients in a worker's compensation clinic.

Another approach that can be useful for patient diagnosis involves the computation and interpretation of factor scores, code types, or cluster-based typologies, although it should be noted that this type of interpretation risks losing important information relative to a standard interpretation of PAI scales and indicators. In experiences with chronic pain patients and in initial studies at the Baylor Center for Pain Management (Karlin et al., 2005), the first author of this chapter has found several clinically relevant patterns of the basic scales/patient groupings that may be clinically relevant and should be followed up in future research.

- Unelevated profiles are relatively common and often indicate "adaptive" patients with medical problems but low distress or preoccupations with their symptoms. All things equal, these patients generally have a relatively good prognosis.
- Elevated PIM and Treatment Rejection (RXR) characterize "guarded and defensive" patients who may be difficult to engage because of their unwillingness to fully participate in psychological aspects of treatment.
- Elevated SOM (~ 80T) with no other major scale elevations suggests "emotionally repressed yet somatically preoccupied" patients who are likely to report severe physical symptoms but limited emotional distress. This pattern may suggest a "hysterical" adaptation that could interfere with physical and psychological interventions.
- "Over-utilizers of medical resources" are often characterized by high SOM paired with high Dominance (DOM), a pattern that suggests the need to target this problem behavior directly.
- "Highly distressed" patients are often characterized by elevated NIM and elevations over 70T on SOM, ANX, Anxiety-Related Disorders (ARD), DEP, STR, and Suicidal Ideation (SUI). It is often helpful to employ substantial empathy in order to help these kinds of patients appreciate, despite their pain and distress, the potential for improvement and the necessity for them to play an important role in treatment.
- "Angry and estranged" patients are characterized by elevated PAR, Borderline features (BOR), Aggression (AGG), and Nonsupport (NON). Interpersonal difficulties often must be worked through with these patients in order for other interventions to be effective.
- "Loners" who use pain as a social "excuse" to avoid difficult anxiety-provoking interpersonal situations such as work, are often characterized by elevated SOM and social withdrawal (SCZ-S) but low DOM and Warmth

(WRM). Psychosocial interventions are likely to prove difficult with this group of patients.

RISK ASSESSMENT AND TREATMENT PLANNING

The PAI can also serve an important treatment planning function. Hopwood et al. (2008b) investigated the utility of the PAI to indicate treatment completion vs. discontinuation. In general, this research showed that dropouts had higher clinical scale scores (e.g., ANX d = .45; BOR d = .33) suggestive of greater initial distress. Perhaps more importantly, and replicating studies in outpatient therapy and inpatient substance abuse samples, elevations on both the Mean Clinical Elevation (MCE), an indicator of generalized distress/ pathology, and the Treatment Process Index (TPI), an indicator of low amenability to treatment, demonstrated modest but significant discrimination with dropouts being predicted by both (Cohen's d = .42 and .34 respectively).

Furthermore, and although no main effect was observed for RXR, this scale was found to moderate the predictive validity of MCE. Clinically, results from this study suggested that for patients who are very resistant (very high RXR) or "hyper-motivated" (very low RXR), psychiatric severity as measured by MCE will not distinguish graduates from non-graduates. However, for patients with RXR elevations in the midrange (i.e., those who were appropriately open to treatment), psychiatric severity yields a moderate to large effect size across completers and non-completers. This suggests that a range of factors may influence dropout for individuals who are either not sufficiently motivated (e.g., the difficulties inherent in pain treatment) or who are too motivated (e.g., perception of limited initial returns of treatment), but that psychological concerns and psychiatric disorders can be quite important among individuals with appropriate or moderate levels of motivation.

The PAI may also indicate variables that moderate the effect of pharmacotherapy. Keely, Smith, and Miller (2000) reported on patients who completed the PAI upon being diagnosed with depression. Baseline depression scores were predictably elevated (M = 83T). After initiation of treatment, patients were followed with office visits and telephone calls over a 14-week period. One third of the group terminated treatment prematurely due to side effects. Non-completers demonstrated markedly elevated SOM (M = 81T) relative to completers (M = 65T), suggesting that sensitivity to somatic difficulties may exacerbate problematic side effects.

In another study, Hopwood et al. (2008c) showed that Antisocial Features (ANT) predicted patients who misused medications prescribed for chronic pain. Furthermore, PIM moderated this effect, suggesting that (a) antisocial personality features are associated with potentially unethical misuse of prescribed medication, and that (b) this effect is less likely to be observed in more defensive responders, who are unlikely to admit to either antisocial features or medication non-compliance.

Finally, and despite generally modest PAI predictions of treatment outcome reported by Hopwood et al. (2007) in a pain sample, the PAI may also be useful for indicating certain treatment effects with implications for medical assessment. In one study of participants in breast cancer support groups, membership was associated with lower levels of anxiety, stress, and a feeling of being supported (Stevens & Duttlinger, 1998) as measured by PAI ANX, STR, and NON, respectively. In general, this is consistent with the assumption that the PAI is more likely to be predictive of and sensitive to mental health than medical health changes.

Overall, the PAI appears to hold some promise for identifying patients at risk to drop out of treatment for reasons related to psychiatric distress, motivation, or medication side effects, that PAI indicators can be used as a measure of some outcomes of successful treatment, and that the PAI can be used to predict treatment-interfering behaviors such as medication non-compliance. However, more research is needed to replicate and extend existing results.

INDICATIONS FOR ADDITIONAL MEASURES

The PAI was not designed to assess many of the issues that are typically important in medical settings, most notably including medical diagnoses. As such, the assessment of medical patients will almost always require measures other than or in addition to the PAI. Hopwood et al. (2007) conducted a conjoint factor analysis of the PAI and the MPI, one of the most commonly utilized instruments in chronic pain settings. This analysis identified five orthogonal factors accounting for 59% of the variance in MPI and PAI scales. Pattern coefficients suggested that the two instruments appear to measure different domains. Three of the factors loaded most strongly on the PAI: internalizing (DEP, ANX, BOR), externalizing (Mania [MAN], ANT, AGG, and DOM), and impulsivity (Alcohol Problems [ALC], Drug Problems [DRG], Inconsistency [ICN], and Infrequency [INF]). Despite some overlap, the MPI scales loaded primarily on the other two factors that appeared to involve physical dysfunction and social support (notably, PAI NON loaded heavily on this last factor). These data were interpreted as suggesting that the MPI and PAI could be used conjunctively in describing persons with chronic pain. Further research is needed to inform the composition of optimal psychological assessment batteries across various medical settings.

ADVANTAGES AND DISADVANTAGES OF THE PAI

As highlighted throughout this chapter, the primary disadvantage of the PAI in medical settings involves limitations of research in many areas, although a recent increase in this regard is beginning to correct this problem. For example, there is a broader body of research regarding the MMPI (Hathaway & McKinley, 1943). Furthermore, clinicians may have concerns over the absence of certain well established MMPI scales when using the PAI. For example, although SOM may adequately substitute for MMPI Scale 1, the PAI may not capture phenomena assessed by Scale 3, which assessors in medical settings often find useful. Clinicians may also miss the information provided by some of the new scales and reformulations being developed for the MMPI and its more recent editions, which may provide significant information above that of the basic clinical scales (e.g., Deardorf, 2000). Finally, the MMPI has a longer history of clinical use based on research in answering certain clinical questions. For example, until relevant research is carried out with the PAI, the MMPI would appear to be best suited for pre-surgical psychological screening (Robinson & Riley, 2001).

Although the MMPI may have a richer clinical history in medical settings than the PAI, a number of scholars have noted its limitations in medical populations (Turk & Fernandez, 1995; Vendrig, 2000). In particular, item overlap confounds scale elevations, limits discriminant validity, and complicates interpretation (Kurtz et al., 2007). For example, a large proportion of the items on Scale 1 are also on Scale 3, in part explaining the commonness of a "conversion V" profile and making differentiations based on these scales difficult. In addition, of the 10 basic scales, 8 include items with somatic content. Given this extensive item overlap, clinicians are left to either use a correction factor (e.g., Gass, 1991) or use clinical judgment to try to distinguish the true meaning of the scales.

Unfortunately for clinicians trying to select one of these instruments, few studies have directly compared the MMPI and the PAI in medical populations. In a study discussed previously (Kurtz et al., 2007), the effects of traumatic brain injury on PAI and MMPI profiles were compared across two groups varying in the severity of their head injury. Previous research had shown that MMPI scales tend to have higher elevations in respondents with mild as opposed to severe TBI. In the Kurtz et al. study, the groups did not significantly differ on validity scales for either the PAI or MMPI. As in previous studies, the MMPI was more elevated in the milder group. The PAI revealed a more specific pattern, such that the milder group had higher SOM and DEP scores but the more severe group had higher ANT and ALC scores; the mean PAI clinical scale score was equivalent across groups. Kurtz et al. suggested that this result likely related to the lack of item overlap on the PAI and the resulting increased discriminant validity and interpretive clarity. Furthermore, lower average clinical scale scores on the PAI relative to the MMPI further speak to discriminant validity, given that none of the clinical scales on either instrument assess TBI directly. Notably, a similar effect has been observed in an epilepsy sample (Brewer, Westerveld, Loring, Chelune, & Bozeman, 2002).

It is recommended that future researchers compare the PAI and similar instruments such as the MMPI in the same medical population, so as to inform clinicians regarding the relative efficacy of various available self-report multiscale psychopathology measures. For now, both science and pragmatics may suggest a preference for the PAI relative to similar instruments such as the MMPI. As reviewed in Chapter 1, a primary reason for the PAI's growing popularity may involve general aspects of the instrument's construction. In the experience of the first author, patients find this instrument more "user friendly" than the MMPI because it is briefer, the items seem to be easier to understand, and respondents generally prefer the 4-point response option. These factors probably also contribute to the instrument's tendency for fewer "invalid" profiles than the MMPI (Braxton et al., 2007). At the same time, in the current mental health climate, even an instrument such as the PAI that was designed to balance efficiency with breadth may be too time consuming in many situations. In such cases, the short or screening forms of the PAI may represent appropriate alternatives.

COMMUNICATION OF FINDINGS

Communication With Professionals

In communicating with medical professionals, it is useful to organize results around several core areas reflected in the organization of the test. It is usually appropriate to begin by commenting on the validity scales, which can be framed in terms of the patient's approach to the test. Interpretation in the context of both community and local norms can be helpful. For example, even a modestly elevated PIM score would be atypical in chronic pain patients, and such a score is likely to be clinically revealing and informative to other professionals. It is also useful to develop hypotheses regarding the impact of response sets, as indicated by PAI scales and indicators, on other instruments that do not have validity indicators such as the Multidimensional Pain Inventory or the Beck Depression Inventory.

For medical professionals it can be useful to organize the interpretation of the diagnostic and psychosocial results according to a logical sequence of issues. Although this sequence can be individualized according to the patient and referral questions, health issues are often primary. Diagnostic feedback may begin with a discussion of the level of somatic complaints (SOM, and SOM-S), unusual nature of complaints (SOM-C), and perception of the impact of medical issues (e.g., SOM-H, ANX, DEP, SCZ-S, NON) on overall life quality. Of note, the conversion (SOM-C) subscale must be used with caution, as it may be elevated in patients with true physical pathology, and is probably most informative as an indicator of conversion symptoms when it is elevated even relative to other SOM subscales.

Another logical domain to cover with professionals involves the severity and nature of emotional distress. Again, it is also helpful to provide a context of the expected level of distress in the population using local norms. The breakdown of ANX and DEP subscales can be especially helpful because assessors can comment on discrepancies between physical symptoms that may be directly related to medical diagnoses versus cognitive and affective symptoms, which are more likely to reflect psychiatric disorders or affective consequences of medical disorders. Beyond standard principles of diagnostic interpretation for the PAI, several scales can be particularly helpful in indicating oft-relevant factors such as the impact of emotional distress on cognition (SCZ-T), perceived level of life stress (STR), social resources (NON), or past events impacting functioning (ARD-T).

Personality patterns that could impact adaptation to health problems are often of interest to treatment providers or other referring parties. As elevations on scales such as PAR, ANT, and BOR are relatively unusual in medical populations, additional time exploring their impact on functioning is often warranted. However, as Cheng et al. (Chapter 11) describe, elevations on these scales may reflect conditions other than personality disorders, and should be approached with clinical nuance. Similarly, interpersonal style is likely to impact the patient's behavior with families and health care providers and thus be particularly important for an assessment of factors maintaining distress and treatment predictions. For example, assertiveness (DOM) and interpersonal warmth and need for affiliation (WRM) may lead to high rates of medical care utilization, and individuals with these characteristics are usually very forthcoming regarding their medical and other difficulties.

Conversely, low DOM and WRM may suggest the need for extra effort on the part of professionals to probe and explore more to understand the patient's symptoms and their meaning.

Obviously, any maladaptive issues such as substance abuse (Alcohol and Drug Problems scales) or risk to harm self (Suicidal Ideation scale and Suicide Potential Index) or others (Aggression scale and Violence Potential Index) are very important to other professionals, and if there are concerns in this area, this domain may be among the first discussed in a consultation. Treatment related indicators such as the Treatment Rejection scale and Treatment Process Index often represent a good domain to end a consultation with, given that they can directly inform treatment-related decisions.

Communication With Patients

The PAI development, structure, and scale names are sufficiently clear that the developmental logic and actual profile can be shared with patients, although for some patients a simple summary of the most important findings may be more appropriate. In either case, leaning on the basis of interpretations in the relationship between a respondent's scores and normative data, and in the context of previous validity research can often limit defensiveness in patients or power struggles regarding the meaning of test data. For example, with patients with high SOM scores, it can be helpful to reflect, "Even compared with other persons with chronic pain, it appears that your pain is very distracting to you and concerns you a great deal. It may make it hard to focus on other things. You seem to feel that your pain has taken over your life." In this manner, the test findings can be used to build rapport and avoid creating conflict over the reality of the physical foundation of their complaints. As a general rule, it is likely to be most helpful to provide feedback in a hypothesis-testing manner and to give patients ample opportunity to respond to the test data, explore their meaning, and challenge standard interpretations. Getting patients to collaboratively engage in the assessment process is particularly helpful for helping them make more effective and active use of ongoing treatment. Ultimately, therapeutic use of the feedback can validate patients' concerns and may broaden the discussion beyond their medical problem (which they may experience as out of their control) to their coping, distress, and other relevant issues around which they have more agency and self-efficacy (Finn, 2007).

CONCLUSION

This is an exciting time for research and practice with the PAI in medical settings. In the context of its growing use for the assessment of medical patients, we will close with several recommendations for ongoing research that can inform clinical applications of the instrument. First, investigators are strongly encouraged to provide descriptive summaries of all PAI scales and indicators in their research for the purpose of future quantitative reviews. In terms of areas of need, research should generally seek to answer core questions in light of the overarching biopsychosocial model that links psychological and medical functioning. Specific issues such as repression, somatoform disorders, primary and secondary gain, pain behavior, expressive emotional styles, chronicity, and the influences of social support on medical functioning represent important targets for ongoing study. Research regarding the discrimination of epileptic and nonepileptic seizures with the PAI exemplifies a theory-guided, practical approach to research and represents an excellent model for further investigations in these and other areas. Finally, research should determine the ability of the PAI to address practical clinical concerns such as sensitivity to response sets and probability of treatment response in circumscribed medical populations. In addition, issues specific to such populations, such as the need to detect poor effort on neuropsychological testing, may require derivation of new indicators (e.g., response latencies, time to completion, discriminant functions) given that early research with existing scales has shown limited benefit.

In summary, the PAI is currently a very valuable tool in many medical settings. We hope that, as further research emerges, clinicians will use the PAI to make statements about patients' functioning and predict their response to treatment with even greater confidence.

REFERENCES

Banks, S. M., & Kerns, R. D. (1996). Explaining higher rates of depression in chronic pain: A stress-diasthesis framework. *Psychological Bulletin, 119*, (1), 95–110.

Blais, M. A., & Hopwood, C. J. (in press). Personality focused assessment using the PAI. In M. A. Blais, M. R. Baity, & C. J. Hopwood (Eds.). *Clinical applications of the Personality Assessment Inventory*. New York: Routledge Mental Health.

Braxton, L. E., Calhoun, P. S., Williams, J. R., & Boggs, C. D. (2007). Validity rates of the Personality Assessment Inventory and the Minnesota Multiphasic Personality Inventory-2 in a VA Medical Center setting. *Journal of Personality Assessment. 88*, 5–15.

Brednza, D. E., Ashton, K., Windover, A., & Stillman, M. (2005). Personality Assessment Inventory (PAI) predictors of therapeutic success or failure in chronic headache patients. [Abstract] *Headache, 45*, 779.

Brewer, C., Westerveld, M., Loring, D. W., Chelune, G. J., & Bozeman, E. C. (2002). Assessing psychological function in patients with epilepsy: A comparison of the MMPI–2 and PAI. *Archives of Clinical Neuropsychology, 17*, 739.

Burns, J. W., Kubilus, A., Bruehl, S., & Harden, R. N. (2001). A fourth empirically derived cluster of chronic pain patients based on the Multidimensional Pain Inventory: Evidence for repression within the dysfunctional group. *Journal of Consulting and Clinical Psychology, 69*, 663–673.

Deardorf, W. W. (2000). The MMPI-2 and chronic pain. In R. J. Gatchel, & J. N. Weisberg (Eds.), *Personality characteristics of patients with pain* (pp. 109–125). Washington, D.C.: American Psychological Association.

Demakis, G. J., Hammond, F., Knotts, A., Cooper, D. B., Clement, P., Kennedy, J., & Sawyer, T. (2007). The Personality Assessment Inventory in individuals with traumatic brain injury. *Archives of Clinical Neuropsychology, 22*, 123–130.

Fairbank, J. C. T., Couper, J., Davies, J., & O'Brien, J. P. (1980). The Oswestry Low Back Pain Questionnaire, *Physiotherapy, 66*, 271–273.

Finn, S.E. (2007). *In our clients' shoes: Theory and techniques of therapeutic assessment*. Mahwah, NJ: Lawrence Erlbaum.

Gass, C. S. (1991). MMPI-2 interpretation and closed head injury: A correction factor. *Psychological Assessment, 3*, 27–31.

Gatchel, R. J., & Turk, D. C. (1996). *Biopsychosocial approaches to pain management*. New York: Guilford.

Gatchel, R. J., & Weisberg, J. N. (2000). *Personality characteristics of patients with pain*. Washington, D.C.: American Psychological Association.

Green, P., Allen, L., & Astner, K. (1996). *The Word Memory Test: A manual for the oral and computerized forms*. Durham, NC: CogniSyst, Inc.

Haggerty, K. A., Frazier, T. W., Busch, R. M, & Naugle, R. I. (2007). Relationships among Victoria Symptom Validity Test indices and Personality Assessment Inventory validity scales in a large clinical sample. *The Clinical Neuropsychologist, 21*, 917–928.

Hanvik, L. J. (1951). MMPI profiles in patients with low-back pain. *Journal of Consulting Psychology. 15*, 350–353.

Hathaway, S. R., & McKinley, J. C. (1943). *The Minnesota Multiphasic Personality Inventory*. Minneapolis: University of Minnesota Press.

Hoelzle, J. B., & Meyer, G. J. (2009). The invariant component structure of the Personality Assessment Inventory (PAI) full scales. *Journal of Personality Assessment, 91*, 175–186.

Hopwood, C. J., Creech, S. K., Clark, T. S., Meagher, M. W., & Morey, L. C. (2007). Convergence and predictive validity of the Multidimensional Pain Inventory and the Personality Assessment Inventory among individuals with chronic pain. *Rehabilitation Psychology, 52*, 443–450.

Hopwood, C. J., Creech, S. K., Clark, T. S., Meagher, M. W., & Morey, L. C. (2008a). Optimal Multidimensional Pain Inventory scoring in a chronic pain sample. *Journal of Clinical Psychology in Medical Settings 15*(4), 301–307.

Hopwood, C. J., Creech, S. K., Clark, T. S., Meagher, M. W., & Morey, L. C. (2008b). Predicting completion of an integrative and intensive outpatient chronic pain treatment with the Personality Assessment Inventory. *Journal of Personalty Assessment, 90*, 76–80.

Hopwood, C. J., Creech, S. K., Clark, T. S., Meagher, M. W., & Morey, L. C. (2008c). The prediction of medication misuse among individuals with chronic pain with the Personality Assessment Inventory. *Society for Personality Assessment, New Orleans, LA*.

Kahn-Greene, E. T., Kilgore, D. B, Kamimori, G. H., Balkin, T. J., & Killgore, W. D. S. (2007). The effects of sleep deprivation on symptoms of psychopathology in healthy adults. *Sleep Medicine, 8*, 215–221.

Karlin, B. E., Creech, S. K., Grimes, J. S., Clark, T. S., Meagher, M. W., & Morey, L. C. (2005). The Personality Assessment Inventory with chronic pain patients. *Journal of Clinical Psychology, 61*, 1571–1585.

Keely, R., Smith, M., & Miller, J. (2000). Somataform symptoms and treatment nonadherence in depressed family medicine outpatients. *Archives of Family Medicine, 9*, 46–54.

Kerns, R. D., Turk, D. C., & Rudy, T. E. (1985). The West Haven-Yale Multidimensional Pain Inventory. *Pain, 23*, 345–356.

Kurtz, J. E., Shealy, S. E., & Putnam, S. H. (2007) Another look at paradoxical severity effects in head injury with the Personality Assessment Inventory. *Journal of Personality Assessment, 88*, 66–73.

McDaniel, S. J., Fertig, E., Spann, M., Caontardo, C., & Westerveld, M. (2007). Use of the Personality Assessment Inventory in patients with NES. *Epilepsia, 48*(s6) 216.

Morey, L. C. (1991). *Personality Assessment Inventory professional manual*. Odessa, FL: Psychological Assessment Resources.

Morey, L .C. (2007). *Personality Assessment Inventory professional manual, second edition*. Lutz, FL: Psychological Assessment Resources.

Morey, L. C., & Hopwood, C. J. (2007) *Casebook for the Personality Assessment Inventory (PAI): A structural summary approach.* Lutz, FL: Psychological Assessment Resources.

Pritchard, P. B., Wagner, M. T., & Topping, K. (2002). Prediction of nonepileptic seizures with the Personality Assessment Inventory. *Epilepsia, 43,* 161.

Robinson, M. E., & Riley, J. L. III (2001) Presurgical psychological screening. In D. C. Turk & R. Melzack (Eds). *Handbook of pain assessment, second edition* (pp. 385–399). New York: Guilford Press.

Slick, D. J., Hopp, G., Strauss, E., & Spellacy, F. J. (1996). Victoria Symptom Validity Test: Efficiency for detecting feigned memory impairment and relationship to neuropsychological tests and MMPI-2 validity scales. *Journal of Clinical and Experimental Neuropsychology, 18,* 911–912.

Stevens, M. J., & Duttlinger, J.E. (1998) Correlates of participation in a breast cancer support group. *Journal of Psychosomatic Research, 45,* 263–275.

Sullivan, B. K., May, K., & Galbally, L. (2007). Symptom exaggeration by college adults in attention-deficit hyperactivity disorder and learning disorder assessments. *Applied Neuropsychology, 14,* 189–207.

Sumanti, M., Boone, K. B., Savodnik, I., & Gorsuch, R. (2006). Noncredible psychiatric and cognitive symtoms in a workers' compensation "stress" sample claim. *The Clinical Neuropsychologist, 20,* 754–765.

Turk, D. C., & Fernandez, E. (1995) Personality assessment and the Minnesota Mutliphasic Personality Inventory in chronic pain: Underdeveloped and overexposed. *Pain Forum, 4,* 104–107.

Turk, D. C., & Melzack, R. (2001) *Handbook of pain assessment* (second edition). New York: Guilford.

Vendrig, A. A. (2000). The Minnesota Multiphasic Personality Inventory and chronic pain: A conceptual analysis of a long-standing but complicated relationship. *Clinical Psychology Review, 20,* 533–559.

Wagner, M. T., Wymer, J. H., Topping, K. B., & Pritchard, P. B. (2005). Use of the Personality Assessment Inventory as an efficacious and cost-effective diagnostic tool for non-epileptic seizures. *Epilepsy & Behavior, 7,* 301–304.

Ware, J. E., Snow, K. K., Kosinski, M., & Gandek, B. (1993). *SF-36 health survey manual and interpretation guide.* Boston: New England Medical Center Health Institute.

10

Use of the PAI in Personnel Selection

PETER A. WEISS

*P*sychological assessment for the purposes of determining suitability for employment has become an important part of personnel selection in recent years, particularly for jobs that require considerable responsibility or on-the-job stress. Examples of such occupations include air traffic controller, airline pilot, firefighter, nuclear power plant operator, emergency medical technician (EMT), correctional officer, and police officer (Graham, 2006; Roberts, Thompson, & Johnson, 2004; Weiss, Weiss, & Gacono, 2008). The purpose of this screening is to identify individuals who either exhibit psychopathology that would interfere with job performance, or who possess personality characteristics shown to be associated with poor performance at that particular job (Weiss, Hitchcock, Weiss, Rostow, & Davis, 2008). This type of screening has become especially popular (even mandated in many jurisdictions) for the hiring of law enforcement officers (see for example Super, 2006; Weiss, Weiss, & Gacono, 2008). Personnel selection procedures involving psychological assessment with law enforcement officers have been more extensively researched than for any other occupation. As a result, the guidelines presented in this chapter are drawn largely from procedures typically used by psychologists to select law enforcement officers.

The psychological assessment of job applicants typically occurs near the end of the personnel selection procedure, following interviews and skills assessments. Other procedures specific to jobs that involve considerable responsibility, stress, or personal risk, such as background checks, strength and fitness tests, drug testing, and relevant interviews, may also occur prior to the psychological evaluation. Usually, obviously unfit job applicants are screened out in the early stages of this process and the applicants who are seen by the psychologist are under serious consideration for hire; the Americans With Disabilities Act mandates that psychological evaluations are conducted only after all other employment factors are reviewed (Weiss, Weiss, & Gacono, 2008). When applicants are seen for a psychological evaluation, the psychologist should review the applicant's file prior to the appointment. The evaluation itself then typically consists of an extensive clinical interview, including a mental status examination and an assessment of psychosocial functioning, and the administration of one or more psychological assessment measures (Weiss, Weiss, & Gacono, 2008).

While a wide variety of personality assessment measures have been used for purposes of personnel selection, the Personality Assessment Inventory (PAI; Morey, 2007) has been gaining in popularity for this purpose. Its use in this area has become sufficiently important that a Law Enforcement, Corrections, and Public Safety Selection Report (Roberts, Thompson, & Johnson, 2004) service is currently available from Psychological Assessment Resources for assistance in screening police and corrections officers, firefighters, EMTs, and communications dispatchers. In addition, Super (2006) asserts that 42% of the agencies that participated in his study of police selection procedures were using the PAI as part of their selection process at the time the study was conducted.

The purpose of this chapter is to show how the PAI can be effectively used as a tool in personnel selection. It will discuss the relevant aspects of validity and profile interpretation, and how to make conclusions about employment suitability based on these data. Results of criterion-related validity studies will also be reviewed to show which scales are most effective in making selection decisions and also to demonstrate the empirical basis for its use. Other important clinical issues related to the selection procedure, such as integrating the PAI with other forms of data, will also be discussed.

PROFILE VALIDITY

Establishing profile validity in the personnel screening scenario is similar to other clinical and research settings in which the PAI is used, but with some important differences. This section examines the use of the four PAI validity scales in personnel selection.

Inconsistency and Infrequency

The Inconsistency (ICN) and Infrequency (INF) scales on the PAI are used largely to determine whether the examinee is paying appropriate attention to item content when taking the test. Elevated scores on ICN indicate an individual who has not been answering similar test items in a consistent fashion due to problems with attention, reading comprehension, or carelessness. A T-score of 73 or higher on this scale indicates an invalid protocol that should not be interpreted because the individual was for one of the above reasons not able to attend appropriately to the test items (Morey, 2003, 2007).

The INF scale consists of a series of items that are designed to be answered in a similar fashion by all examinees regardless of their diagnosis or the purpose of the test administration. These statements are nearly always answered in the same way by all examinees because they either indicate unusual personal characteristics or express commonsense attitudes. Typically, individuals who obtain elevated scores on this scale do so because they are responding to the test items in a careless or even random manner. Regardless of the reason, scores of T > 75 mean that the individual did not attend appropriately to test items and the profile should be considered invalid (Morey, 2003, 2007).

For purposes of personnel selection, ICN and INF should be interpreted based on the most recent edition of the PAI manual (Morey, 2007). Profiles with elevated scores on these two scales are invalid and the clinical scales should not be interpreted. Hiring decisions therefore cannot be made on the basis of the clinical scales and other information must form the basis of the conclusion of the psychological evaluation. However, extremely elevated scores on ICN and INF would be unusual in a personnel screening situation because individuals applying for jobs that involve psychological screening, particularly law enforcement positions, tend to be relatively high functioning and report less psychopathology than the general population (Roberts, Thompson, & Johnson, 2004; Weiss, Davis, Rostow, & Kinsman, 2003). Research on elevated ICN and INF profiles may ultimately show that high scores on these scales are suggestive of poor employee performance in one or more occupations due to the inherent lack of attention or other factors indicated by such scores, but until now no systematic explorations of ICN or INF have been performed with a pre-employment sample.

Negative Impression

The Negative Impression (NIM) scale is designed to measure the degree to which an individual is presenting him or herself in a more negative manner than would be expected. Elevations on this scale can be found for a variety of reasons, such as malingering, exaggeration of genuine symptoms, or careless/random responding. Individuals with severe emotional problems can also obtain elevated scores on NIM (Morey, 2007).

It is very unusual to obtain elevated scores on NIM in personnel selection settings (see for example Roberts et al., 2004). Psychologists who are faced with interpreting a profile that has even a slight (approximately T = 73) elevation on NIM in a pre-employment setting should first attempt to find out the reason for the elevation on this scale, as that information will be important in making the final recommendation to the employer. This will sometimes occur as a result of attentional factors, so the scores for ICN and INF should be closely examined and the appropriate conclusion drawn (see previous discussion on ICN and INF). If these scores are in the normal range, elevations on one or more of the clinical scales are likely to be noted as the individual is trying to exaggerate some sort of emotional difficulty. While this is an unusual finding in personnel selection evaluations, conclusions can then be made on the basis of clinical scale scores as the elevation is likely to be related to the individual's psychological functioning. It should be noted, however, that studies by Weiss, Rostow, Davis, & Decoster-Martin (2004) and Weiss, Zehner, Davis, Rostow, & Decoster-Martin (2005) showed that elevated NIM scores are modestly correlated with problem performance as a police officer, including behaviors such as neglect of duty, conduct mistakes, and reprimands by supervisors, so elevated NIM (T > 73) may be sufficient to exclude a job candidate from the applicant pool in law enforcement settings.

Positive Impression

Some attention should be given to interpreting the Positive Impression (PIM) scale in personnel selection evaluations, as considerable research has been conducted on this topic in the last few years. Results of these studies show that PIM is an important variable in predicting future performance for some occupations that typically involve a psychological evaluation as part of the screening process.

An important issue in interpreting PIM with job applicants is that the job applicant scenario appears to "pull" for elevated scores on validity scales related to positive self-presentation (Roberts et al., 2004; Weiss, Weiss, Cain, & Manley, in press). Such applicants will tend to obtain higher scores on measures of defensiveness and positive impression management, such as the PAI PIM scale, and the L and K scales on the MMPI-2, than will individuals given the test for other purposes. This is because the pre-employment situation encourages applicants to present themselves in a positive light to a much greater degree than they would normally. Therefore, higher cutoff scores should be used to determine levels of defensiveness (see for example Weiss et al., in press). Roberts et al. (2004) make the point that elevated scores on PIM (T = 70 in one of the sample cases presented) are within the normal range for law enforcement and public safety applicants. Therefore, the evaluating psychologist should not label a profile as extremely defensive or deceptive unless the PIM score is extraordinarily elevated.

Numerous recommendations exist for eliminating applicants from employment consideration due to elevated L-scale scores when the MMPI-2 is given in personnel selection situations (Weiss et al., 2003; Weiss et al., in press). The L scale has frequently been associated with poor performance at high-risk jobs. However, this is not the case with PIM when the PAI is administered, because research in employment settings suggests that PIM and L measure somewhat different forms of impression management (Weiss, Serafino, & Serafino, 2000). In their factor analytic study of validity indexes used in law enforcement selection, Weiss et al. (2000) identified two main validity factors measured by personality assessment instruments administered to 42 state police officer candidates. These were a Guardedness/Defensiveness factor and a Social Desirability factor. While PIM is strongly related to Social Desirability, or a need to present oneself in a positive light, this study suggests that the MMPI-2 L scale measures a different aspect of impression management, one that is not only related to Social Desirability but also to Guardedness and Defensiveness, which is a more deceptive attitude toward responding.

Confirmation that the L and PIM scales are measuring different personality characteristics in job applicants is confirmed in the study by Weiss et al. (2004) which showed that PIM was in fact positively correlated with good performance as a police officer on some outcome variables. Therefore, the PIM scale on the PAI measures a different, more positive aspect of self-presentation than the L scale (which is associated with a more blatant, "lying" orientation) on the MMPI-2. Therefore, it should not be assumed that a job applicant is lying or being deliberately deceptive on the PAI unless his or her score on PIM is extraordinarily elevated. Unlike with the MMPI-2 L scale, a high score on PIM is not necessarily interpreted as meaning that the individual is a poor candidate for jobs that involve considerable personal risk or responsibility, such as that of police officer.

Supplemental Validity Indicators

The PAI has several supplemental validity indicators that have been developed to help examiners better understand examinee response style. Two of these, the Malingering Index (MAL) and Rogers Discriminant Function (RDF) are designed to assist with detecting fake-bad or malingering profiles and are unlikely to be factors in personnel selection due to the kinds of impression management issues found in personnel selection. However, MAL and RDF have not been investigated with regard to personnel selection settings and this could be of interest to personnel selection researchers wishing to further validate the PAI for this purpose.

The other supplemental validity indicators measure positive impression management and may be of more interest in personnel selection settings because impression management attempts in personnel selection tend to be in the positive direction. The Defensiveness Index (DEF) and Cashel Discriminant Function (CDF) are the two supplemental indices designed to detect fake-good profiles. While the PIM scale seems to measure something different to personnel selection evaluations than the MMPI-2 L scale, these other indices have potential for use in personnel settings because high scores on them may serve to allow examiners to screen out applicants, whereas high PIM is actually predictive of good performance. Although DEF and CDF have not yet been investigated in criterion-related research for personnel selection, prior research on the relationship of these scales to other measures suggests their usefulness. For example, the DEF correlates significantly with the MMPI-2 L Scale (Morey, 2003), which has frequently been used to screen out applicants in law enforcement personnel selection because of the connection between high scores and poor job performance. The CDF may also be important for investigation because the CDF score appears to be relatively independent of actual mental health status (Morey, 2003). It therefore may be the best indicator of the kind of deliberate impression management that is sometimes associated with poor future job performance in some studies. While these supplemental indicators have not yet been validated for use in employment evaluations, they appear to be an exciting avenue for future research in this area.

INTERPRETATION OF CLINICAL/TREATMENT/ INTERPERSONAL SCALES AND RISK ASSESSMENT

Based on the current status of research on the use of the PAI for personnel selection evaluations, the bulk of the risk assessment (in this case the degree of risk involved in hiring the individual for a particular position) is largely based on the results on the clinical scales. For an instrument to be used in effective pre-employment screening, that instrument (in this case, the PAI) must first be validated for that purpose (Weiss et al., 2008). Multiple validation studies have been conducted for the PAI with regard to personnel selection in the last several years, and the present interpretation section focuses on scales of the PAI that have been empirically validated for personnel selection purposes.

Before focusing on specific scales and associated research findings, it should be noted that job applicants, particularly police and public safety candidates who have been studied extensively by psychologists, typically obtain scores on the clinical scales that are lower even than those individuals in the national norming sample. For example, in one recent study of the PAI in law enforcement selection that involved a large sample, applicants obtained PAI clinical scale scores that were, on average, one-half standard deviation lower than the average for a nonclinical population (Weiss et al., 2008), most likely due to a combination of psychological health and the demand characteristics of the pre-employment setting. Therefore, any applicant who obtains scores on the 11 clinical scales of T > 70 should be regarded with serious caution when making a recommendation to an employer, because a score of 70 is considered diagnostic on most scales in clinical settings. In personnel selection, even moderate elevations on clinical scales (T > 60) should be carefully considered. Specific scales on the PAI have been associated with problem performance as a law enforcement officer, and these are discussed below.

Personality Disorder, Alcohol, and Drug Scales

Most of the empirical research that supports the use of the PAI in the personnel selection of law enforcement applicants has been performed on the scales measuring personality disorders and the Alcohol Problems (ALC) and Drug Problems (DRG) scales. The use of the Antisocial (ANT) Scale and its subscales for law enforcement selection has been well researched by William Weiss and colleagues (2004, 2005). In these two studies, Weiss and colleagues assessed the relationship between the ANT subscales and a number of performance criteria provided by the officers' supervisors after a period of 1 year of employment. These two studies showed significant relationships between elevated scores on all three Antisocial subscales (ANT-A/Antisocial Behaviors, ANT-E/Egocentricity, ANT-S/Stimulus Seeking) and problem performance characteristics for law enforcement officers, notably insubordination, excessive citizen complaints, and neglect of duty. In addition, high scores on ANT-E and ANT-S were predictive of other future performance issues, such as conduct mistakes and termination for cause. Further investigation of these scales using a multiple regression format (Weiss et al., 2005) showed that these scales can collectively be used to predict poor performance in law enforcement personnel.

It is clear from these results that the ANT Scale and its subscales are important predictors of future performance in law enforcement officers when used as part of a pre-employment process. This finding makes sense when the nature of the ANT scales is examined—these individuals tend to get themselves into trouble due to antisocial behavior or impulsivity, and would not make good law enforcement officers because they create the kind of difficulties that make bad press for law enforcement agencies. In addition, the lack of empathy seen in individuals with high scores on ANT-E is likely to cause problems for them in policing, which is an interpersonally oriented and frequently help-focused occupation.

Because of the prior research on the PAI and law enforcement, it is recommended that individuals who obtain elevated scores (T > 70) on either the ANT scale or any of its individual subscales be removed from the applicant pool. These individuals appear to be a significant risk for problem performance based on prior research, and represent a liability for law enforcement agencies due to their impulsivity, lack of empathy, and tendency to get into trouble. While published data for other professions does not currently exist in the assessment literature, it appears likely because of the characteristics of high ANT scorers that these are people who would not succeed in any kind of sensitive occupation that involves a psychological evaluation as a condition of hire.

Research also exists connecting the Borderline Scale (BOR) and subscales as well as the DRG with problematic performance as a police officer. Weiss et al. (2008) performed a comprehensive assessment of the predictive power of the BOR Scale and subscales, DRG, and ALC on police performance. This analysis included 632 police officers who had taken the PAI as part of their pre-employment screening; a questionnaire was then completed by each officer's supervisor after the officer had been employed for a period of 1 year. This questionnaire contained 32 items, and was scored by the investigators by giving each officer one "point" for each question answered in the direction of poor performance. Each officer therefore obtained a score ranging from 0 to 32. While the initial regression analyses in that study did not show a relationship with job performance, significant results were obtained when the analyses were performed with the 132 poorest performing officers in the sample (score > 3). Significant correlations with poor performance were found for this subsample of officers with BOR, BOR-N, and DRG. In addition, BOR-N and DRG were found to be significant predictors of performance when used in an exploratory stepwise regression with the N = 123 subsample. Results of this study show that the BOR and DRG Scales may be modestly predictive of who will be a poor law enforcement officer.

Elevations (T > 70) on BOR, BOR-N, or DRG would suggest eliminating that individual from the applicant pool in a law enforcement setting based on currently available research. The previously discussed research findings are not surprising given that individuals with elevated BOR scores tend to be individuals with severe personality disorders (Morey, 2007). The fact that BOR-N and DRG seemed to be the most predictive of this group of scales in the Weiss et al. (2008) study was interesting. Policing is a fundamentally interpersonal occupation and those with high scores on BOR-N most likely lack the interpersonal skills needed to be a successful police officer. Those with more elevated scores on DRG tend to be individuals who are relatively unconcerned with legal violations (due to the illegality of drug use), and for whom violating police department norms and rules is also less of a concern than for most officers. ALC was not a predictor of problem performance in that study, most likely due to the social acceptability of alcohol use, and somewhat elevated scores on this scale are probably less of a concern in a pre-employment setting than are elevations on DRG, even though high scores on ALC (especially those above T > 84) should obviously be considered carefully before making a hiring decision.

Other Validated Scales for Use in Law Enforcement Selection

Research evidence also exists supporting the use of the Obsessive-Compulsive (ARD-O) subscale in the selection of law enforcement officers (Decoster-Martin, Weiss, Davis, & Rostow, 2004). This study showed a small but significant correlation between ARD-O and improved performance as a law enforcement officer. This study noted that law enforcement officers with modest elevations (T = 55 to 65) on ARD-O were less likely to have been involved in on- or off-duty motor vehicle accidents, engaged in undesirable off-duty conduct, or to have been the subject of citizen complaints. However, Descoster-Martin et al. (2004) note that candidates with T > 75 are not likely to make good law enforcement officers because of intrusive thoughts and the belief that their impulses are out of control. Decoster-Martin et al. go on to state that such individuals with T > 75 would be very unusual in a personnel selection sample because they are usually eliminated from the applicant pool very early in the process.

What this means for the psychologist doing personnel selection in the law enforcement arena is that individuals with "high normal" ARD-O scores may be good candidates for law enforcement positions provided the results of their clinical interview, file review, and any other tests administered are satisfactory. However, as Decoster-Martin et al. (2004) state, individuals with extreme scores on ARD-O are probably not satisfactory candidates.

Significant findings also exist for the use of the Aggression (AGG) Scale and its subscales in the pre-employment selection of police officers. Weiss et al. (2004) found relationships between elevated scores on the AGG subscales and a number of negative performance characteristics in their sample of hired police officers who had taken the PAI as part of a pre-employment screening process. High scores on Physical Aggression (AGG-P) were associated with reports of insubordination and excess citizen complaints from police supervisors, as well as the number of times that an officer has discharged his or her weapon in the line of duty (using a firearm multiple times in the line of duty over the course of 1 year is often indicative of performance problems). Scores on Verbal Aggression (AGG-V) were associated with voluntary resignation, while Aggressive Attitude (AGG-A) was associated with officers being more likely to receive suspensions or written reprimands. It is not surprising that the Aggression Scale and its subscales are associated with poor performance as a law enforcement officer as officers must use force at times but use it judiciously. Moreover, AGG-V and AGG-A tap into problematic interpersonal styles, and successful law enforcement officers must possess good interpersonal skills. Officers who exhibit overly aggressive behavior or interpersonal styles are thus more likely to encounter on-the-job trouble. Elevated scores (T > 70) on AGG or any of its subscales would therefore justify removing an officer from the applicant pool prior to hire.

Other Clinical Scales

Virtually no peer-reviewed research exists at present for decision making based on the results of the Depression (DEP), Mania (MAN), Paranoia (PAR), or Schizophrenia (SCZ) scales in personnel selection. This lack of published research stems from the fact that these scales are indicative of serious psychopathology, and individuals with these complaints are, as mentioned earlier, typically eliminated from the applicant pool long before the psychologist becomes involved. Finding an individual with a T score much above the mean in a personnel selection sample would be unusual indeed. This also results in a truncation of range in research samples. A psychologist evaluating an individual who obtains an elevated (T > 70) score on any of the above scales should carefully consider his or her hiring recommendation and also integrate other sources of data to strengthen the case for the decision.

While data showing an association between poor performance and elevations on these scales have not yet been published, such data exist for similar scales on the MMPI-2. Brewster & Stoloff (1999) make a case for eliminating anyone from law enforcement applicant pools who obtains an elevated score on any of the MMPI-2 clinical scales (with the possible exception of scales 5 and 0). Considering the significant correlations between many of the PAI clinical scales and the MMPI-2 clinical scales in law enforcement and public safety personnel selection samples (Roberts, Thompson, & Johnson, 2004), this may be an appropriate recommendation for psychologists using the PAI as well. However, more research with these scales is needed to further validate the PAI for personnel selection.

Other Treatment and Interpersonal Scales

Less research has been conducted on the role of the treatment and interpersonal scales in personnel selection than on other scales on the PAI. While evidence supporting the use of AGG exists, research on the role of the other treatment or interpersonal scales does not exist at present for purposes of personnel selection. Therefore, it may be difficult to make hiring decisions on the basis of these scales, which include Suicidal Ideation (SUI), Stress (STR), Nonsupport (NON), Treatment Rejection (RXR), Dominance (DOM), and Warmth (WRM). These scales would be interesting to investigate in future research, because, with the exception of SUI (which is very unlikely to be elevated in personnel samples, for reasons described previously), these scales tap into dimensions of personality not directly related to psychopathology and that therefore will have less restriction of range in employment settings. These scales may ultimately be quite useful in determining suitability for employment, and researchers are encouraged to investigate them on the PAI.

INDICATIONS FOR ADDITIONAL MEASURES

I do not recommend the use of the PAI as a stand-alone measure in personnel selection. The reasons for this are twofold. First, the recent standard has been to use multiple sources of data in conducting psychological evaluations for employment purposes. Super (2006) in his survey of the practices of psychologists performing pre-employment law enforcement screenings, noted that most psychologists made use of multiple measures. Super states that an effective pre-employment evaluation (in addition to interviews) will include, *at a minimum*, a test of psychopathology, a test of normal personality functioning, and a test of cognitive or problem solving ability. The PAI would conceivably cover the role of the test of psychopathology, with some scales also measuring aspects of normal personality functioning. While the PAI certainly provides a great deal of information, it is important to include other measures to cover the range of areas required for an adequate assessment of the functioning of individuals applying for sensitive occupations.

It is also possible that the evaluating psychologist may wish to give more than one test related to psychopathology, depending on the nature of the evaluation. In evaluations such as those for personnel selection that could potentially result in legal action, more data is generally better, and for this reason administering the PAI along with other self-report tests like the MMPI-2 would certainly not be problematic. In addition, personnel selection evaluations often result in test protocols with validity issues (discussed previously), and giving more than one such test can at times provide one valid test from which conclusions can be drawn when another is not interpretable due to validity scale elevations.

Another reason for using other measures in addition to the PAI is the current emphasis on multimethod assessment in clinical psychology in general, the result of many years of competition between the proponents of various single methods (Erdberg, 2008). Erdberg states that for purposes of psychological assessment, interviews, self-report measures, performance based personality tests (for example, the Rorschach and Thematic Apperception Test), and behavioral measures all provide different types of information. As mentioned earlier, the standard of practice in personnel selection assessment is also moving in the multimethod direction, perhaps because of this overall trend. Roberts et al. (2004) and Super (2006) provide examples of a variety of instruments used together in personnel selection, citing the importance of multiple instruments because they all provide different kinds of information to the evaluating psychologist.

In addition, psychologists are continuing to develop new screening procedures for sensitive occupations as a deeper understanding of the importance of multimethod assessment is reached (Weiss et al., 2008). For example, recent investigations of integrating new tests into personnel selection procedures have involved exploring the utility of the Rorschach Comprehensive System (Weiss et al., 2008; Brewster et al., in press). The importance of validating new measures for personnel screening procedures has continued to receive attention because of occasional instances of well-publicized misconduct by individuals in professions requiring psychological evaluation for hire. However, this continued validation research is done with the assumption that such measures are used within a multimethod context. Therefore, the PAI should be used in conjunction with one or more of the additional measures mentioned above for the most effective personnel selection evaluation.

ADVANTAGES AND DISADVANTAGES OF THE PAI

Advantages Relative to the MMPI-2

The PAI has several characteristics that are advantages for its use in personnel selection. While the two tests clearly complement each other, if only one self-report measure of psychopathology and personality is to be used, the PAI may have some advantages over the MMPI-2 in personnel selection. The PAI is a shorter test, with only 344 items as compared with 567. Although it is shorter, the PAI has still been shown to be a comprehensive self-report test that has predictive power in personnel selection (Roberts et al., 2004; Weiss et al., 2004). The brevity of the test may be important in employment screening environments in which a psychologist is expected to evaluate a large number of applicants in a limited amount of time. The PAI takes less time to complete than the MMPI-2 and is, on the whole, quite cost effective (Morey, 2003), making it an ideal instrument for use in this setting.

Another advantage of the PAI in personnel selection settings is the format of the test. The test items are easy to understand and are written on a fourth-grade level, making them readily accessible to the vast majority of applicants in personnel selection settings. In addition, the test is scored on a 4-point Likert scale format as opposed to the MMPI-2 forced choice (True-False) format, which may allow the psychologist conducting the personnel evaluation to more readily detect milder levels of a construct (Weiss et al., 2004, 2005). In addition, the PAI has several scales, notably those measuring personality disorders, which are relatively unique to self-report personality assessment. These scales measuring personality disorders have been shown to be effective in pre-employment screening, particularly for law enforcement officers. The ability to detect personality disorders in law enforcement candidates and other job applicants may be a key to pre-employment screening, as such individuals are prone to engaging in problem on-the-job behaviors but often lack the obvious psychopathology that would exclude them at an earlier stage of the hiring process (Weiss, 2002; Weiss et al., 2008).

Software and Interpretive Report

Another recent development that makes the PAI advantageous for use in personnel selection is the PAI Law Enforcement, Corrections, and Public Safety Selection Report service, available from Psychological Assessment Resources (Roberts et al., 2004). As mentioned earlier, this is a computerized report service that compares PAI scores for applicants with norms for law enforcement and other occupations (corrections officers, firefighters, EMTs, and communications dispatchers) that frequently involve pre-employment psychological evaluations as part of the hiring process. In addition to making this norm comparison, the program evaluates critical items and makes a statement about the applicant's risk level and suitability for the job being applied for. While, like all computerized interpretation aids, this report service should not operate as a stand-alone, it does provide a valuable and exciting aid to the psychologist who routinely conducts pre-employment evaluations.

Need for Further Validation Research

The chief disadvantage of the PAI in personnel selection is that its validation for this purpose is still incomplete. Criterion-related validity studies published in peer-reviewed journals on using the PAI for personnel selection have appeared only in the last few years, and these studies focus almost exclusively on using the test for selecting law enforcement officers. While the PAI appears to have sufficient validity for selecting law enforcement officers based on the published studies discussed above, much work remains to be done, especially with regard to validating the test for use with other professions. The psychologist using the test for selecting professions not related to law enforcement should tread carefully, as studies related to these professions do not yet exist. Of course, this does not mean that the test cannot be used in these evaluations; on the contrary, it is likely to be highly effective based on the previous results of law enforcement studies. Psychologists interested in using the test with these other professions are encouraged to collect and publish data regarding these applications.

In addition, even though the PAI has been shown to be effective at predicting future performance as a law enforcement officer when administered as part of the hiring process, much research remains to be done in this area as well. While some of the clinical scales have still not been investigated in criterion validity studies (see above), the interpersonal and treatment scales appear to have considerable potential and, with the exception of the Aggression (AGG) scales, have not been systematically investigated at present. Law enforcement researchers are therefore encouraged to attempt to establish the criterion validity of these as yet unexplored scales for purposes of personnel selection in law enforcement.

COMMUNICATION OF FINDINGS

In psychological evaluations for personnel selection, communication of findings is done in a report directly to the hiring agency. These evaluations are done only for sensitive, high-risk occupations such as that of police officer or firefighter, which often involve a government agency. In most cases, the applicant signs a form waiving privilege and confidentiality prior to testing, so that the results of the evaluation can be given directly to the referring agency by the psychologist. Usually, the applicant will not have direct access to the report.

The psychologist can use any report format that is professionally acceptable and with which he or she is comfortable. However, if the evaluation is requested by a government agency, certain aspects of the evaluation may be legally mandated, including report format, and the psychologist should be aware of any laws or regulations required by the jurisdiction or agency for whom he or she is working (Melton, Petrila, Poythress, & Slobogin, 2007). The results of the PAI should be integrated into the report, taking into account other sources of data.

A major difference between this type of report and a traditional psychological assessment report is that the psychologist is asked to make a pass or fail recommendation. In other words, in the report, the psychologist is asked to answer the referral question, "Is this individual suitable for the occupation for which he or she is applying?" In most cases, the psychologist will make a positive recommendation, because most individuals who are not ultimately hired are eliminated from the applicant pool at earlier stages than the psychological evaluation (for reasons elaborated earlier in this chapter). However, if PAI findings reveal that the officer has personality characteristics similar to those of problem officers who have taken the PAI, this should be stated in the report. Ultimately, the psychologist does not have the power to hire or not hire the applicant; that power rests with the referring agency. Such agencies are not required to follow the recommendation of the psychologist, although hiring someone over the objection of the psychologist would be very unusual.

If the applicant is not hired as a result of the psychological evaluation, they sometimes can appeal the finding. Allowances for this appeal process are common, for example, in police officer applicant evaluations, although the exact procedure varies by jurisdiction and occupation. In the case of an appeal, the results of the initial evaluation are usually forwarded to a second psychologist, who conducts an independent evaluation that may involve re-administering the PAI. A full explanation of this process can be found in Khadivi (in press). While infrequent, applicants who fail a second opinion evaluation may at times seek legal action if they think that they have been treated unfairly in the hiring process. This may result in lawsuits against the employer, department, or government agency that requested the original evaluation for hiring purposes. In such circumstances, the PAI data and results may need to be presented in court. The PAI has been demonstrated to meet current standards for admissibility as evidence in court (Morey, Warner, & Hopwood, 2007; Weiner & Greene, 2008). As a well-validated self-report test, the psychologist presenting expert testimony should not have difficulty presenting PAI findings as long as the conclusions can be backed up by empirical research, such as that presented in this chapter (for further discussion of how legal standards apply to psychologically based evidence, see Rostow, Davis, & Levy, 2002).

CONCLUSION

Ultimately, the PAI is an effective instrument for use in psychological evaluations for personnel selection. It has many advantages for this application, and can even be used in conjunction with similar tests such as the MMPI-2 because of the unique information that it adds to the applicant data set. It has already gained wide acceptance for use in this area, and with continued research into its use for personnel selection, the PAI will certainly be viewed as one of the premier instruments for this purpose.

REFERENCES

Brewster, J., & Stoloff, M. L. (1999). Using the good cop/bad cop profile with the MMPI-2. *Journal of Police and Criminal Psychology, 14*(2), 29–34.

Brewster, J., Wickline, P., & Stoloff, M. L. (in press). Using the Rorschach Comprehensive System in police psychology. In P. A. Weiss (Ed.), *Personality assessment in police psychology: A 21st century perspective.* Springfield, IL: Charles C Thomas.

Decoster-Martin, E., Weiss, W. U., Davis, R. D., & Rostow, C. D. (2004). Compulsive traits and police officer performance. *Journal of Police and Criminal Psychology, 19*(2), 64–71.

Erdberg, P. (2008). Multimethod assessment as a forensic standard. In C. B. Gacono and F. B. Evans (Eds.), *The handbook of forensic Rorschach assessment* (pp. 561–566). New York: Routledge.

Graham, J. R. (2006). *MMPI-2: Assessing personality and psychopathology* (4th ed.). New York: Oxford University Press.

Khadivi, A. (in press). Second opinion conditional evaluations of police officer candidates. In P. A. Weiss (Ed.), *Personality assessment in police psychology: A 21st century perspective.* Springfield, IL: Charles C Thomas.

Melton, G. B., Petrila, J., Poythress, N. G., & Slobogin, C. (2007). *Psychological evaluations for the courts.* (3rd ed.). New York: Guilford Press.

Morey, L. C. (2003). *Essentials of PAI assessment.* New York: Wiley.

Morey, L. C. (2007). *Personality Assessment Inventory: Professional manual* (2nd ed.). Lutz, FL: Psychological Assessment Resources.

Morey, L. C., Warner, M. B., & Hopwood, C. J. (2007). Personality Assessment Inventory: Issues in legal and forensic settings. In A. M. Goldstein (Ed.), *Forensic psychology: Emerging topics and expanding roles* (pp. 97–126). Hoboken, NJ: Wiley.

Roberts, M. D., Thompson, J. A., & Johnson, M. (2004). *PAI law enforcement, corrections, and public safety selection report: Manual.* Lutz, FL: Psychological Assessment Resources.

Rostow, C. D., Davis, R. D., & Levy, J. P. (2002). Police psychology: The influence of Daubert and its progeny. *Journal of Police and Criminal Psychology, 17*(2), 1–8.

Super, J. T. (2006). A survey of pre-employment psychological evaluation tests and procedures. *Journal of Police and Criminal Psychology, 21*(2), 83–90.

Weiner, I. B., & Greene, R. L. (2008). *Handbook of personality assessment.* Hoboken, NJ: Wiley.

Weiss, P. A. (2002). Potential uses of the Rorschach in the selection of police officers. *Journal of Police and Criminal Psychology, 17*(2), 63–70.

Weiss, P. A., Hitchcock, J. H., Weiss, W. U., Rostow, C., & Davis, R. (2008). The Personality Assessment Inventory borderline, drug, and alcohol scales as predictors of overall performance in police officers: A series of exploratory analyses. *Policing and Society, 18,* 301–310.

Weiss, P. A., Weiss, W. U., & Gacono, C. B. (2008). The use of the Rorschach in police psychology: Some preliminary thoughts. In C. B. Gacono and F. B Evans, (Eds.), *The handbook of forensic Rorschach assessment* (pp. 527–542). New York: Routledge.

Weiss, W. U., Davis, R., Rostow, C., & Kinsman, S. (2003). The MMPI-2 L scale as a tool in police selection. *Journal of Police and Criminal Psychology, 18*(1), 57–60.

Weiss, W. U., Rostow, C., Davis, R., & Decoster-Martin, E. (2004). The Personality Assessment Inventory as a selection device for law enforcement personnel. *Journal of Police and Criminal Psychology, 19*(2), 23–29.

Weiss, W. U., Serafino, G., & Serafino, A. (2000). A study of the interrelationships of several validity scales used in police selection. *Journal of Police and Criminal Psychology, 15*(1) 41–44.

Weiss, W. U., Weiss, P. A., Cain, S., & Manley, B. (in press). Impression management in police officer candidacy on the MMPI-2. *Journal of Police and Criminal Psychology.*

Weiss, W. U., Zehner, S. N., Davis, R. D., Rostow, C., & Decoster-Martin, E. (2005). Problematic police performance and the Personality Assessment Inventory. *Journal of Police and Criminal Psychology, 20*(1), 16–21.

11

Assessment of Motor Vehicle Accident Claimants With the PAI

MICHAEL K. CHENG, JEREMY B. FRANK,
and CHRISTOPHER J. HOPWOOD

*M*otor vehicle accident (MVA) claimants often present for assessment and treatment with a wide range of complex problems including symptoms related to chronic pain, depression, posttraumatic stress, and adjustment difficulties. Most are involved in the pursuit of accident benefits from their insurer (e.g., psychological or physical treatment, income replacement, assistance with household maintenance, etc.). Many are also pursuing tort claims against other parties (i.e., suing the person who caused the MVA for lost income, funding for future treatment, pain and suffering, etc.). In such complex cases, the assessment of personality and psychopathology is important for determining accurate diagnoses and identifying psychosocial factors including response style, personality variables, coping responses, social supports, and social interactions that are relevant to treatment planning and addressing common referral questions. The Personality Assessment Inventory (PAI; Morey, 1991) is a promising tool for assessing such clients, although little is currently known about the psychometric characteristics of the PAI in MVA settings and there currently exist no standard interpretive recommendations for professionals who use the PAI with MVA claimants.

This chapter has two overarching purposes. First, we present descriptive PAI data for MVA claimants who were seen in a private-practice psychology clinic in Hamilton, Ontario. Our intent is that this will facilitate the interpretive process for researchers and clinicians who work in similar settings by adding population-specific reference data in addition to the community and clinical normative data already available. The second purpose of this chapter is to provide interpretive guidelines for assessment cases in similar contexts. These guidelines will be based on the clinical experiences of the first two authors as well as the descriptive data described presently. The chapter will conclude with a brief clinical case description designed to further explicate our recommendations.

INTERNAL CONSISTENCY, FACTOR STRUCTURE, AND DESCRIPTIVE STATISTICS FOR PAI SCALES AND INDICATORS AMONG MVA CLAIMANTS

Reference data were provided by 1,566 individuals referred to a private-practice psychology clinic in Hamilton, Ontario that specializes in the assessment and treatment of MVA victims. Before describing this sample and PAI data in greater detail, it may be helpful to briefly review the automobile insurance system in the Province of Ontario and the assessment process used in the clinic from which data were gathered. Currently, Ontario has a no-fault insurance system whereby victims of MVAs receive accident benefits (e.g., psychological or physical treatment, income replacement, assistance with household maintenance, etc.) from their own insurer. In addition, there is a tort-based system whereby victims of MVAs can pursue claims (i.e., suing for future income loss, funding for future treatment, pain and suffering, etc.) against the at-fault party. While the data that will be presented are likely to generalize to similar settings, the interpreter should be sensitive to the possibility that norms and other psychometric characteristics could differ depending in part on legal and cultural contexts.

Participants were assessed between 2000 and 2008 and were self-referred or referred by friends, family, or a range of professionals including family physicians, physiotherapists, occupational therapists, and legal representatives. Although nearly all of the individuals assessed at the clinic were involved in an MVA, a small number were referred for non-MVA-related medico-legal assessment regarding future employability and future care needs. A random subsample of 200 names were selected and presented to the clinic director, who determined that 100% of this subsample were involved in MVAs. While we do not believe that all individuals in the full sample were involved in an MVA, this finding clearly indicates that the vast majority of participants were. All individuals involved in an MVA were involved in the pursuit of accident benefits from their insurer and many were also pursuing tort claims against other parties.

As a matter of procedure, the large majority of individuals who request assessment and treatment services at the clinic first undergo a telephone screening to ensure that they are indeed reporting accident-related psychological symptoms. This screening forms the basis of an application to the insurer to request compensation for a psychological assessment. Once an assessment is approved, individuals are asked to complete a battery of psychological tests including the PAI before being interviewed by a clinic psychologist. Although individuals may be asked to complete the PAI at other times in the course of treatment, only pre-treatment PAI administrations are included in this investigation.

Out of the initial participant pool of 1,566 individuals, 47 were excluded because they omitted more than 33 PAI items (Morey, 1991). The mean age of participants was 40.54 years (SD = 12.94). The sample was 61% female and 39% male; 49.5% were married, 8.4% divorced, 25.6% single, 2.3% widowed, and 14.1% identified their marital status as "other." The mean level of participant education was 12.93 years (SD = 2.78, Mdn = 12). Reliable information regarding race, ethnicity, and income was not available.

We investigated the internal consistency, factor structure, and descriptive statistics of PAI scales. Cronbach alpha coefficients and mean inter-item correlations for the PAI scales (Table 11.1) are generally consistent with those from previous reports (e.g., see Morey, 2007) including an analogous chronic pain sample (Karlin, Creech, Grimes, Clark, Meagher, & Morey, 2005) and indicate adequate internal consistency for PAI scales and subscales. Table 11.1 also shows the means and standard deviations for PAI scales and indicators in this sample in the metric of normative community sample *t*-scores. As anticipated, given the nature of this sample, significant average elevations (i.e., > 70T) were observed on the Somatic Complaints (SOM) and Depression (DEP) scales. Other details regarding this averaged profile are described in discussing interpretive strategies for MVA claimants.

A Principal Components Analysis (PCA) with varimax rotation was performed on the 22 PAI scales in accordance with the procedure described by Morey (1991). Scree test suggested the retention of four factors that accounted for 64% of the total variance in PAI scales. Pattern coefficients for these factors are provided in Table 11.2. These coefficients are generally consistent with those identified in previous studies (Morey, 1991; Hoelzle & Meyer, 2008) and particularly consistent with those identified by Karlin et al. (2005) in a chronic pain sample. These components appear to generally reflect affective distress, acting out, social isolation, and carelessness, respectively. Overall, internal consistency, factor structure, and descriptive results speak to the reliability and validity of the PAI in MVA claimants.

Interpretation of Profile Validity

Assessing whether a respondent meets the education or reading abilities required to participate in testing is an important consideration in an MVA claimant assessment setting. Many patients in Ontario are educated in languages other than English and can vary greatly in their degree of acculturation (see Correa & Rogers, Chapter 8). Furthermore, pain is often reported to interfere with reading activities. The Inconsistency (ICN) and Infrequency (INF) scales allow clinicians to empirically assess patients' understanding of item content and the degree to which issues related to carelessness, inattention, reading difficulties, or other factors may affect profile validity. Table 11.1 shows that scores on these scales are similar to those in other clinical (Morey, 2007) and pain (Karlin et al., 2005) samples, suggesting that cutoffs recommended by Morey (2007) are likely to be useful in this setting.

When ICN and INF cutoff scores are approached or exceeded, we recommend querying respondents regarding specific items in order to develop hypotheses about what may have influenced scale level elevations. Even when ICN and INF cutoff scores are not exceeded but these scales are somewhat elevated, interpretation of PAI results based on normative data should proceed cautiously, particularly when significant cultural, educational, or other factors that could influence the integrity of self-report data may be present. Responses that do not appear to fit the clinical presentation (e.g., endorsing marked emotional distress despite the appearance of reasonably good functioning during the interview) should also be queried and the patient's agreement with the clinical picture presented by the PAI should be assessed.

TABLE 11.1   Internal Consistencies and Descriptive Statistics for PAI
Scales and Subscales

PAI Scales	Alpha	Mean Corrected Inter-item r	Mean T-Score	S.D.
INF°	—	—	53.8	9.14
ICN°	—	—	53.1	9.34
NIM	.68	.21	60.8	13.9
PIM	.76	.26	46.9	11.4
MAL°	—	—	55.2	12.7
RDF°	—	—	50.8	10.0
DEF°	—	—	45.9	10.6
CDF°	—	—	51.6	9.6
SOM	.88	.23	70.4	12.6
SOM-C	.74	.26	66.6	14.6
SOM-S	.73	.25	72.5	13.0
SOM-H	.75	.26	64.5	11.9
ANX	.93	.35	65.7	14.1
ANX-C	.85	.41	62.9	13.1
ANX-A	.79	.32	64.3	13.7
ANX-P	.83	.37	65.6	14.9
ARD	.85	.18	63.3	14.4
ARD-O	.63	.17	54.8	11.5
ARD-P	.65	.19	58.9	12.6
ARD-T	.87	.44	64.6	15.5
DEP	.92	.32	74.0	15.2
DEP-C	.83	.38	66.5	15.6
DEP-A	.87	.46	70.9	16.0
DEP-P	.75	.28	72.5	12.0
MAN	.81	.15	49.1	10.1
MAN-A	.51	.12	49.0	10.2
MAN-G	.75	.27	45.5	9.9
MAN-I	.81	.35	53.6	11.9
PAR	.88	.25	54.6	12.4
PAR-H	.75	.27	53.6	12.7
PAR-P	.76	.32	52.5	11.4
PAR-R	.71	.24	55.4	11.9
SCZ	.88	.23	59.9	13.8
SCZ-P	.67	.24	49.7	11.1
SCZ-S	.85	.41	55.9	13.0
SCZ-T	.84	.39	65.9	15.1
BOR	.88	.23	59.4	12.0
BOR-A	.76	.35	60.8	12.2
BOR-I	.74	.32	60.9	12.7
BOR-N	.66	.24	56.7	11.7
BOR-S	.69	.28	50.1	11.0

TABLE 11.1   Internal Consistencies and Descriptive Statistics for PAI Scales and Subscales (Continued)

PAI Scales	Alpha	Mean Corrected Inter-item r	Mean T-Score	S.D.
ANT	.83	.19	48.2	9.8
ANT-A	.75	.29	48.7	10.0
ANT-E	.58	.16	48.4	9.2
ANT-S	.69	.24	48.5	9.9
ALC	.83	.39	48.1	9.5
DRG	.68	.23	51.8	9.7
AGG	.89	.33	52.6	12.4
AGG-A	.83	.44	52.1	12.4
AGG-V	.72	.30	51.1	11.2
AGG-P	.77	.40	53.4	12.5
SUI	.91	.51	55.4	14.7
STR	.79	.32	61.0	12.4
NON	.80	.33	54.5	12.5
RXR	.73	.25	44.8	10.4
DOM	.78	.23	48.3	10.9
WRM	.82	.28	47.8	11.4
TPI	—	—	69.44	13.72
VPI	—	—	68.41	13.19
SPI	—	—	84.65	13.57

Note: For full scale names, see Chapter 1.
* Internal consistencies not computed for non-scale indicators.

MVA claimants do not generally tend to produce elevations on Positive Impression Management (PIM) that exceed commonly recommended cutoffs (i.e., 57T), as evidenced by the average T-score of 47 in this sample. Respondents who produce elevated scores on this scale are typically unaware of their problems or are attempting to portray themselves in a positive light (Morey, 2003). In contrast, it has been our observation that most MVA patients openly admit to experiencing significant problems, are seeking treatment on their own or because of feedback that they have received from others, or are involved in demonstrating accident-related impairments for the purposes of a tort case. Similarly, significant elevations on the Defensiveness Index (DEF) or the Cashel Discriminant Function (CDF) are predictably uncommon.

In contrast, it is not uncommon for us to see moderate elevations on Negative Impression Management (NIM), as evidenced by the average T-score of 61 in this sample. Respondents who produce elevated NIM scores are typically portraying themselves in a more negative light than an objective observer would report. It is important to note that NIM is not a "pure" measure of malingering but rather assesses a negative response style that may be influenced by effortful and non-effortful symptom magnification. Non-effortful symptom magnification can include the perceptual and cognitive distortions characteristic of many psychological disorders that cause respondents to see themselves, others, and the world in a

TABLE 11.2   Pattern Coefficients of PAI Scales Against Varimax Rotated Principal Components

PAI Scale	Component 1	Component 2	Component 3	Component 4
ICN	.142	.011	.008	.798
INF	−.012	.024	.195	.403
NIM	.753	.281	.086	.144
PIM	−.601	−.489	−.178	.169
SOM	.771	−.094	−.115	.132
ANX	.850	.099	.153	.001
ARD	.827	.098	.065	−.035
DEP	.846	−.026	.269	.108
MAN	.411	.661	−.338	−.085
PAR	.518	.493	.368	.083
SCZ	.753	.273	.344	.086
BOR	.718	.505	.259	.065
ANT	.094	.825	.010	.194
ALC	−.001	.576	.110	.314
DRG	.121	.349	−.062	.743
AGG	.312	.740	.087	.040
SUI	.546	.181	.259	.256
STR	.618	.228	.094	.116
NON	.440	.323	.550	.180
RXR	−.715	−.248	−.133	.027
DOM	−.181	.346	−.702	−.055
WRM	−.239	−.254	−.768	−.091
% variance explained	40.70	10.26	7.62	5.53

more negative light than objective observation would endorse (Morey, 2003) and which may be common consequences of MVA (e.g., depression). As such, NIM is sensitive not only to effortful and non-effortful symptom magnification but also to clinical severity. NIM's sensitivity to clinical severity may explain its modest elevation in this sample, which is very close to Morey's (1991) clinical normative sample mean. The mean Malingering Index (MAL) and Rogers Discriminant Function (RDF) scores for this sample are also very similar to Morey's clinical and community sample means.

While NIM tends to correlate significantly with the clinical scales, Morey (2003) suggests that MAL should show more modest correlations and the RDF should be essentially uncorrelated with the clinical scales. NIM and MAL should furthermore show moderate correlations with each other while RDF should show only limited correlations with NIM and with MAL. The pattern of elevations across these indicators as described and correlations of NIM and MAL (r = .61), NIM and the RDF (r = .15), and MAL and the RDF (r = .11) in this sample are consistent with these expectations. Based on this pattern of relationships, Morey has further suggested that a NIM elevation in the absence of MAL or RDF elevations may be best explained as non-effortful negative distortion characteristic of some forms of psychopathology such as depression. In contrast, elevations across NIM, MAL, and the RDF are more likely to be caused by some degree of deliberate negative distortion.

However, the meaning of high RDF scores in the absence of NIM elevations has not been fully explored. Sumanti et al. (2006) opine that NIM and MAL may be measures of global symptom magnification while the RDF may assess subtle and specific symptom magnification. Visual inspection of the clinical scales of those who produced significantly elevated RDF scores in our sample without producing significantly elevated NIM scores support Sumanti, Boone, Savodnik, & Gorsuch's (2006) perspective. This group produced a specific clinical profile very similar to our general sample, including marked (≥ 70T) elevations on SOM and DEP and significant (≥ 60T) elevations on ANX, ARD, SCZ, and BOR. Currently, it is not clear how this subsample differs from the general sample. One hypothesis is that this subsample is engaging in a specific pattern of effortful presentation of symptoms not easily detectable by NIM or MAL but representative of the kinds of concerns that are expectable following an MVA. A second hypothesis is that this subsample differs from our general clinical sample primarily in experiencing increased psychological issues that are important for the calculation of the RDF. We echo Sumanti et al.'s call for further research involving meaning of the RDF, particularly in the absence of NIM elevations.

We have observed that some assessors have regarded multiple clinical scale elevations that exceed PAI profile clinical skyline scores as potentially indicative of over-reporting. The logic of this approach is undergirded by the statistical rarity of these scores, which are achieved by a very small proportion of individuals (i.e., those with scores > 2 S.D. above average in clinical populations). Having two or more clinical scale scores above skyline demarcations should therefore be exceedingly rare. Further research is needed to justify this algorithm and to test its incremental utility beyond well-validated indicators such as NIM, MAL, and the RDF. This is particularly the case for some scales that are commonly elevated in certain populations. For example, when using Morey's (1991) clinical sample data for computing T-scores (which is used to calculate skyline scores) our sample produced scores of 58T for SOM (S.D. = 12.6) and 56T for DEP (S.D. = 15.2). This indicates that the PAI clinical skyline scores may tend to under-represent extremity for these scales among MVA claimants. We therefore recommend caution in interpreting SOM and DEP elevations above skyline scores as over-reporting of symptoms in the absence of other markers of negative dissimulation.

Overall, validity scale scores for this MVA claimant sample are similar to those presented in Morey (2007) and Karlin et al. (2005) and provide good preliminary support for use of established cutoffs and profile interpretation guidelines with an MVA claimant population.

DIAGNOSIS

The mean T-scores and standard deviations for the clinical scales and subscales are described in Table 11.1. Compared with Morey's (1991) community sample means, our sample shows marked elevations (> 70T) on SOM and DEP and significant elevations (60–70T) on Anxiety (ANX), Schizophrenia (SCZ), and Borderline Features (BOR). In some cases, we believe that these elevations reflect genuine problems in the domain of interest assessed by the scale. It is not surprising that individuals who experienced a recent MVA are in pain (SOM), experience dysphoria (DEP) and dysregulated mood (BOR), are tense and worrisome (ANX), and have difficulty concentrating (SCZ). Indeed, some of these scales reflect the phenomenology of the most common psychiatric diagnoses in this sample, which include Major Depressive Disorder, Pain Disorder, Posttraumatic Stress Disorder, Adjustment Disorder, and subclinical NOS codes reflecting these syndromes.

In other cases, however, such elevations may result from symptoms related to pain and injury and are less directly related to the psychiatric construct targeted by the scale. Based on our clinical observations and collateral information, we believe that our patients are more likely to present with problems associated with physical functioning, cognitive problems, depression, and anxiety compared with the general population but are not more likely to be schizophrenic or have borderline personality disorder. Morey (1996) and Morey and Hopwood (2007) describe the use of algorithms for regarding certain subscales as indicative of constructs that are distinct from their parent full scales that can be interpretively useful in such cases. For example, because SCZ-T assesses problems with concentration and attention, elevated scores should be expected from non-schizophrenic groups such as pain patients, who often report difficulties in this area. We note that among the SCZ subscales, Karlin et al.'s (2005) chronic pain sample also produced the highest scores on SCZ-T.

Similarly, elevations on the BOR scale may best be explained by pain and related life disruptions rather than borderline character problems. Three of the BOR subscales assess reasonable consequences of MVA. For instance, Affective Instability (BOR-A; 61T in our sample) assesses changes in mood that can often accompany the onset of pain. Identity Diffusion (BOR-I; 61T) assesses uncertainty about life and difficulty identifying one's purpose, issues that are common in individuals who experience impairments in important areas of functioning such as those related to pain and injury. Negative Relationships (BOR-N; 57T) assesses relational conflicts that often occur in the context of pain, life disruption, and loss. As a group, our patients are not more likely to produce elevations on Self-harm (BOR-S; 50T), which assesses impulsivity, a construct we would not expect to be affected by pain. Karlin et al.'s (2005) chronic pain sample produced a similar pattern of slight elevations in the BOR-A, BOR-I, and BOR-N subscales while also failing to produce higher elevations in BOR-S compared with the community sample. It is further notable that BOR is among the PAI scales most sensitive to clinical change (Hong, 2002), and that recent research questions the longstanding assumption that borderline personality characteristics are more stable than other kinds of psychiatric symptoms (e.g., Zanarini, Frankenburg, Reich, Silk, Hudson & McSweeney, 2007). With these data taken together, it may be reasonable to interpret BOR elevations as indicative of the transient disruption associated with serious MVAs rather than chronic personality disorder. Thus, although personality factors are often very important in understanding MVA patients (either as pre-accident diatheses or post-accident responses) we do not believe these problems are more likely to take the form of borderline personality disorder than in other clinical settings.

Likewise, although it is not uncommon for our patients to report symptoms related to depression and anxiety, we note that elevations on the DEP and ANX scale are sometimes higher than expected based on our clinical impressions. Descriptive data suggest that this discrepancy can best be explained by endorsement of physical symptoms related to pain that inadvertently contribute to elevated physiological subscale scores (DEP-P and ANX-P), which have the highest elevations among ANX and DEP subscales in both our sample and in the Karlin et al. (2005) data.

In sum, we would like to reiterate Morey's (2003) caveat that many PAI scales and subscales assess discriminable, if related, constructs. In the practice of psychiatric diagnosis, different categories can share phenomenology, suggesting the need for dynamic interpretive strategies that include the conjunctive use of PAI subscales (Morey & Hopwood, 2007). Given these and other complexities of psychological assessment and interpretation, we recommend that the PAI should be used only by clinicians and researchers trained in psychometrics and knowledgeable of their patient or research population.

TREATMENT PLANNING AND RISK ASSESSMENT

MVA assessors are often asked to make recommendations regarding the treatment of psychological sequelae of accidents. Several PAI indicators are helpful in this regard. Because of limited research on assessment of psychosocial treatment planning factors among MVA patients, general guidelines such as those described by Kurtz in this volume are recommended. Only one study has addressed the issue of assessment of treatment planning factors in pain sufferers. Hopwood et al. (2008a) tested the validity of the Treatment Process Index (TPI), Treatment Rejection Scale (RXR), and Mean Clinical Elevation (MCE) to predict early termination from a chronic pain treatment. They showed that higher scores on both the TPI and MCE indicators significantly predict early termination. Furthermore, they demonstrated that RXR moderates this effect. In other words, when RXR is high, suggestive of low motivation for treatment, or when RXR is low, suggestive of "hyper-motivation" (e.g., unrealistic expectations) for treatment, TPI and MCE are less predictive of early discontinuation than when RXR suggests appropriate motivation (i.e., is between 40–50T). Other research in outpatient psychotherapy settings suggests a similar effect (Hopwood, Ambwani, & Morey, 2007). Overall, the TPI, MCE, and RXR means in Table 11.1 are similar to those for other clinical samples (Morey, 2007) suggesting that TPI, MCE, and RXR can be used conjunctively to formulate treatment predictions in this population in a manner similar to what has been recommended for other groups. That is, high TPI and MCE scores should be regarded as indicating a risk for early termination, particularly if RXR is between 40 and 50T.

Treatment planning also involves questions regarding appropriate treatment approaches. Morey (1996) has provided detailed guidelines regarding using the PAI for treatment planning that are generally helpful in MVA cases. The use of adjunctive treatments such as physical and occupational therapy are often of particular importance in this setting. Recommendations for these treatments are typically based on an assessment of the degree to which pain or other consequences of

MVA have resulted in diminished functioning. Such an indication can be gleaned from scales that are commonly elevated in this MVA sample, such as SOM, DEP, ANX, and SCZ-T, but the use of additional measures is often needed to inform these kinds of recommendations, as described later.

Risk for harm to self or others is not a common consideration in MVA assessment as indicated by marginal average scores on scales like Aggression (AGG) and Suicidal Ideation (SUI, Table 11.1). Nevertheless, as in any psychological assessment cases, these issues are sufficiently important that they should receive very careful attention any time psychometric indicators suggest elevated risk. Furthermore, many patients in the sample reported on in this chapter have personality characteristics associated with elevated risk for suicidal and violent behavior, as indicated by the Suicide and Violence Potential Indicator means in Table 11.1, suggesting the need for careful attention to such issues in MVA settings. These factors may include confusion (SCZ-T), affective instability (BOR-A), and problems with social supports (STR, NON). Authors in this volume and other interpretive chapters and books (e.g., Morey, 1996) have provided excellent recommendations for how to use these scales and indicators to predict risk for harm to self or others.

INDICATIONS FOR ADDITIONAL MEASURES

The PAI does not have a scale that directly assesses pain (see Kurtz, Chapter 2 and Clark, Oslund, & Hopwood, Chapter 9), which is clearly an important construct in MVA claimants. Items highly correlated with this construct are instead distributed across scales and subscales assessing physiological functioning (e.g., SOM, DEP-P, ANX-P, etc.). We therefore recommend the use of a specific measure of pain that provides information on severity and impairment such as the Multidimensional Pain Inventory (MPI; Kerns, Turk, and Rudy, 1985). For example, Hopwood et al. (2007) compared the PAI and the MPI in a chronic pain population. Overall, they concluded that while some overlap exists, these measures assess unique features of pain and related psychological functioning and can be used together to assess multidimensional aspects of chronic pain. Hopwood et al. (2008b) also showed that supplementing the MPI with validity scales such as PAI's PIM augments its predictive validity, further portending their conjunctive use in a setting where the assessment of pain is important.

We would also recommend a measure of psychiatric symptoms developed in pain samples and designed for use in such settings, such as the Pain Patient Profile (P3; Tollison and Langley, 1995). Measures developed in pain settings for pain practitioners may be particularly effective at discriminating between pain and psychopathology, given their developmental contexts. Finally, structured interviews or performance-based methods that assess malingering or psychiatric diagnoses would likely augment self-report methods.

ADVANTAGES AND DISADVANTAGES OF THE PAI

Many features of the PAI recommend its use with an MVA claimant population, such as the availability of validity indicators, low text complexity, high discriminant validity, and the inclusion of scales assessing a wide range of clinical features relevant to pain, stress, and adjustment. The PAI validity indicators facilitate an assessment of many factors that could interfere with the accurate measurement of clinical and personality features. For instance, MVA claimant patients may have limited education, education in languages other than English, or cognitive or pain symptoms that interfere with their ability to read. Such difficulties can be indicated by elevations on INF or ICN. We would argue that a formal assessment of response style is important in any kind of psychological assessment, but is particularly important in medico-legal contexts including the assessment of an MVA claimant population. PAI NIM, PIM, DEF, MAL, RDF, and CDF appear to be very useful for such assessments.

The PAI's low text complexity and lower reading level relative to similar measures (Schinka & Borum, 1993) accommodates individuals who may have language or reading difficulties and leads to lower risk of invalid profiles compared with other measures with higher text complexity. In psychological assessment, clearer items are generally better (Holden & Fekken, 1990). However, even on the PAI, which is relatively strong in this regard, ambiguous language in some items, particularly those that are reverse-scored, can result in patient frustration and elevated ICN scores even when overall comprehension appears to be good. As discussed, we generally suggest close inspection of item content in cases of elevated ICN scores.

Unlike most other multiscale measures, the PAI was developed with a strong emphasis on discriminant validity. Discriminant validity is critical in the assessment of an MVA claimant population for two reasons. First, in cases where the validity scales and external sources suggest that overt symptom magnification is unlikely, adequate discriminant validity facilitates confidence that scale elevations reflect genuine co-morbidity and are not simply an artifact of high scale intercorrelations. In other measures of personality and psychopathology, problematically high scale intercorrelations due to item overlap or developmental inattention to discriminant validity can complicate interpretation even when the respondent reports symptoms in a straightforward manner. Second, in cases where the validity scales and external sources suggest that there are reasons to suspect symptom magnification, high discriminant validity facilitates the formation of hypotheses regarding which specific disorders may be deliberately presented. For example, Hopwood, Morey et al. (2007) demonstrate the use of a NIM-predicted profile to identify specific areas of symptom magnification that capitalizes on the discriminant validity of the PAI.

An advantage of the PAI relative to briefer, more targeted measures is its inclusion of scales that assess a wide range of clinical factors relevant to MVA claimant patients. In addition to scales assessing specific diagnostic categories including physical complaints (SOM), depression (DEP), and anxiety (ANX), the PAI also assesses important variables such as personality features (BOR and Antisocial Features [ANT]), Alcohol (ALC) and Drug (DRG) problems, Aggression (AGG), Suicidal Ideation (SUI), Stress (STR), environmental Nonsupport (NON), and Treatment Rejection (RXR). The wide range of clinical factors assessed by the PAI assists in developing a richer understanding of patients' lives than would be possible with briefer measures that focus on specific problem areas.

At the same time, this breadth comes at the cost of test length. The length of the PAI limits the practicality of its frequent use in follow-up and progress assessments.

All assessors face the problem of need for breadth vs. need for efficiency, and clinicians must struggle with issues regarding when to use the PAI or briefer measures. Notably, the 22-item Personality Assessment Screener (PAS; Morey, 1997) can be useful when a more limited assessment is indicated.

Perhaps the primary disadvantage of the PAI for this setting involves the limited research on the instrument in MVA claimant samples. We hope that we have begun to address this issue here but note that further work is needed. Specific areas of research needed include the operating characteristics of validity indicators, diagnostic validity of clinical scales, and utility of the PAI for treatment planning among MVA patients.

COMMUNICATION OF FINDINGS

Communication of findings involves sharing test results with the patient, the insurer, and others in a way that will be easily understood. We will describe the general feedback process used in the clinic from which data presented in this chapter were drawn. After a draft of the initial assessment report is completed, patients are invited to return to the clinic for a feedback interview. During this interview, autobiographical data are reviewed for errors, test results are described, and diagnoses and conceptualizations are shared. During this time, patients are offered the opportunity to correct factual errors or amend comments to their report. A proposed treatment plan, including outlines of the expected frequency and length of sessions and total duration of treatment is reviewed. Possible outcomes of submission of the treatment plan, such as insurer approval or denial and alternative courses of action including referral to the public health system are also discussed.

As in many settings, an assessment report may be read by a wide audience with differing motivations and purposes. For example, with MVA claimants, insurers' interests often involve the cost and length of treatment, prognosis for recovery, and concerns about symptom magnification. Patients' legal representatives are often interested in how psychiatric diagnoses impair functioning in a wide range of domains. Family physicians are often concerned with the effects of psychiatric diagnoses on daily functioning and physical health. The aforementioned advantages of the PAI, including validity scales, high discriminant validity, and assessment of a wide range of factors of clinical interest assist the examiner in addressing the concerns of a diverse audience.

CASE STUDY

To highlight some of the interpretive recommendations outlined, we conclude with a brief case presentation. Ms. M is a 37-year old Caucasian woman who was involved in a motor vehicle accident 1.5 years prior to her initial assessment at the clinic. She reported that she was the seat-belted driver and sole occupant of a small-size sedan when her vehicle was struck on the passenger side by an SUV leaving a plaza parking lot. She stated that she anticipated the impact just before the accident and was terrified, and that her neck was turned to the right at the time of the impact and her arms were braced against the steering wheel. Ms. M denied any secondary head impact or loss of consciousness but reported experiencing immediate neck and right arm pain. She stated that she was transported to a hospital by emergency services, examined, provided with pain medication, and referred to her family physician.

Ms. M said that she attended her family physician's office the next day and that her physician ordered further medical investigation and referred her to physiotherapy. She reported starting physiotherapy approximately 2 weeks post-accident, and that she initially attended 5 times per week and was attending 2 times per week at the time of the initial psychological assessment. She stated her opinion that physiotherapy resulted in significant benefit for approximately 1 year after the index accident but was not resulting in further improvement in pain or functioning at the time of the psychological evaluation.

After consenting, Ms. M completed the PAI and other measures, and this assessment was followed by an extensive interview. Regarding social functioning, Ms. M reported a difficult childhood marked by parental abuse and neglect. She stated that she married when she was 20 to a partner who was initially warm and supportive but eventually became distant and abusive. She said that he had engaged in several extramarital affairs and eventually abandoned the marriage 2 years before her accident. Ms. M reported raising their teenage son alone at the time of the evaluation. She expressed longstanding worry regarding harming her son and that this concern may have resulted in permissive parenting including limited expectations regarding completion of household chores.

With regard to educational history and work functioning, Ms. M said that she completed high school and then worked in factory and cleaning positions before marriage. She described work interruption for approximately 4 years related to childbirth and care. She stated that she had been working for approximately 4 years with the same employer cleaning office buildings at night before the index accident, often working 50 hours per week. Ms. M said that she attempted a return to work the week of the index accident but experienced significant pain and difficulties concentrating. She reported that her employer was unwilling to modify her hours or duties so she discontinued working and was unemployed at the time of the evaluation.

Ms. M denied any significant pre-accident medical history. At intake, she reported that she had been prescribed an antidepressant and pain medication by her family physician and also used over-the-counter pain medication on a regular basis. She denied any problems associated with substance use or abuse or significant pre-accident headache or brain trauma history. She reported low mood following her divorce but stated that she did continue with work and social activities with friends prior to her accident.

With regard to psychological functioning, Ms. M reported depressed mood, anhedonia, irritability and anger with her teenage son, active suicidal ideation without intent, significant pain, reductions in occupational and household activities, difficulty achieving and maintaining sleep due to worry and physiological arousal, reduced appetite with associated weight loss, difficulty controlling worry related to poverty, loss of sexual interest, regularly occurring nightmares without clear content, and driving and passenger anxiety. During the initial assessment, her affect appeared depressed and she became tearful easily. She cried while recounting details of the index accident, stating that it had "ruined [her] life." Her behavior suggested moderately severe and unrelenting pain.

With regard to behavioral functioning, Ms. M reported significant impairment including marked decreases in important activities and almost no activities outside of the house. She reported difficulty initiating household and social activities due to low motivation, hopelessness, irritability, and fear of re-injury and criticism from others. She stated poor persistence and rapid discontinuation of all activities with the onset of pain, and reported coping with pain by discontinuing activity, resting, and applying heat. She said that she avoided driving whenever possible and closed her eyes as a car passenger.

Ms. M's scores on the validity scales of the PAI showed no significant elevations on ICN, INF, or PIM but a moderate elevation on NIM (T = 84). Inspection of MAL and RDF scores showed no significant elevations, suggesting that her elevated NIM score was more likely to reflect cognitive distortions related to depression rather than deliberate symptom magnification. Notable elevations on the clinical scales of the PAI included SOM (78T), DEP (90T), Anxiety-Related Disorders (ARD; 73T; driven mostly by Traumatic Stress [ARD-T] and Obsessive-Compulsive [ARD-O] subscales) and moderate elevations on BOR (65T). There were also moderate elevations on STR (65T), NON (62T), and Warmth (WRM, 62T). Her scores on pain-normed diagnostic measures similarly showed elevations on indicators of somatization, anxiety, and depression compared with most pain patients. Her scores on an alternative measure of posttraumatic stress showed mild to moderate re-experiencing symptoms and moderate to severe avoidance and physiological symptoms. Based on these data, the assessor formulated the following diagnostic impressions:

Axis I: Major Depressive Disorder, Moderate to Severe without Psychotic
   Features; Pain Disorder Associated with both Psychological Factors and
   a General Medical Condition, Moderate; and Anxiety Disorder NOS,
   Symptoms of Posttraumatic Stress Disorder, Mild to Moderate
Axis II: Obsessive-Compulsive and Dependent Personality features
Axis III: Reported Neck and Right Arm Pain, Headaches
Axis IV: Unemployed, Divorced, Economic Problems, Difficulties with Son
Axis V: 55 (initial assessment)

The assessor consulted with Ms. M's family physician, who stated low risk of re-injury but high pain sensitivity. The assessor then worked with Ms. M to identify treatment goals and priorities and coordinated the services of a driving rehabilitation service that provided weekly, graded exposure to driving activities while promoting extinction of avoidance-based responding. Based on PAI and other data, the assessor made the following treatment recommendations:

1. *Structured Psychological Treatment for Depression*—Given the severity
   of her depressive symptoms and some indication of obsessive (ARD-O)
   and dependent (NON, WRM, suppressed AGG and DOM) personality
   traits, initial psychological treatment should be structured and focused on
   relating negative mood states to intra-psychic experiences in order to promote a sense of self-control over her mood. Initial psychological treatment
   for depression should include: (a) identification of maladaptive cognitions

related to worthlessness, hopelessness, and helplessness and others' criticism; (b) connection of maladaptive cognitions to negative moods; (c) connection of maladaptive cognitions to learned experiences; and (d) development of a more adaptive cognitive style such as probabilistic and balanced thoughts regarding intrinsic self-worth, others' limitations, and behavioral risks (e.g., of driving).

2. *Structured Psychological Treatment for Pain*—Once Ms. M. has made progress in employing therapeutic techniques to control her mood, cognitive behavioral principles should be extended to address her pain symptoms and related impairments. Cognitive behavioral therapy for pain can include: (1) identification of maladaptive cognitions related to harm, weakness, and endless suffering and maladaptive behaviors including increased tension and guarding; (2) graded exposure in-session and inter-session to pain- and anxiety-eliciting activities; and (3) generation of adaptive cognitions related to safety and adaptive coping behaviors such as relaxation.

3. *Exploration of Interpersonal Issues*—The presence of significant personality and interpersonal factors as indicated by her history as well as the assessment profile (elevations on BOR, NON, STR, WRM, and the TPI) suggest the need to provide extended time to form a productive therapeutic relationship, and that treatment reversals should be expected. Consequently, a lengthier treatment plan is proposed than would be necessary in the absence of significant potential for interpersonal factors to interfere with therapeutic progress. These issues should be closely monitored and discussed early in treatment to normalize them prior to their occurrence and limit the extent to which they interfere with more active treatment ingredients.

4. *Ongoing Physical and Occupational Therapy*—Given ongoing medical problems that interfere with psychological, behavioral, and work functioning, physical and occupational therapies should continue. Further, given the likelihood that psychiatric issues may interfere with these treatments, ongoing communication and collaboration across the medical team is strongly recommended.

CONCLUSIONS

The PAI has significant promise for the psychological evaluation of MVA claimants. More research is needed to understand the psychometric characteristics of the instrument in this setting but data provided in this chapter suggest interpretive strategies similar to those in other clinical, and particularly pain, settings. Given that legal parameters around MVA assessment vary, professionals should attend closely to how their setting differs from the one in which these data were gathered. In addition, assessment should proceed with an explicit awareness regarding the limits of any self-report psychological assessment for this purpose, and in particular the limitations of this instrument. Clinical skill and careful consideration of factors related to MVA, psychological assessment, psychopathology, and cultural and legal contexts are essential ingredients of effective PAI assessment in an MVA claimant population.

ACKNOWLEDGMENTS

We would like to express our thanks to the clinicians and staff at Kaplan and Kaplan Psychologists in Hamilton, Ontario for their support, and our special thanks to Ron Kaplan, Ph.D., Faith Kaplan, Ph.D., Amber Smith-Paterson, Ph.D., Brian Levitt, Psy.D., and Barbara Szechtman, B.A. for their instrumental support, technical assistance, thoughtful suggestions, and encouragement.

REFERENCES

Boone, K. B., Lu, P., Back, C., King, C., Lee, A., Philpott, L., Shemiah, E., & Warner-Chacon, K. (2002). *Archives of Clinical Neuropsychology, 17*, 625–642.

Hawes, S. W., & Boccaccini, M.T. (2009). Detection of overreporting of psychopathology on the Personality Assessment Inventory: A meta-analytic review. *Psychological Assessment, 21*, 112–124.

Hoelzle, J. B. & Meyer, G. J. (2009). The invariant component structure of the Personality Assessment Inventory (PAI) full scales. *Journal of Personality Assessment, 91*, 175–186.

Holden, R. R., & Fekken, G. C. (1990). Structured psychopathological test item characteristics and validity. *Psychological Assessment: A Journal of Consulting and Clinical Psychology, 2*, 35–40.

Hong, P. Y. (2002). Dialectical behavior therapy for borderline personality disorder: A component analysis of DBT Skills Training Group. Doctoral Dissertation, University of Kansas, Lawrence, KS.

Hopwood, C. J., Ambwani, S., & Morey, L. C. (2007). Predicting non-mutual therapy termination with the Personality Assessment Inventory. *Psychotherapy Research. 17*(6), 706–712.

Hopwood, C. J., Creech, S. K., Clark, T. S., Meagher, M. W., & Morey, L.C. (2007). The convergence and predictive validity of the Multidimensional Pain Inventory and the Personality Assessment Inventory among individuals with chronic pain. *Rehabilitation Psychology, 52*, 443, 450.

Hopwood, C. J., Creech, S. K., Clark, T. S., Meagher, M. W., & Morey, L. C. (2008a). Predicting the completion of an integrative and intensive outpatient chronic pain treatment. *Journal of Personality Assessment, 90*(1), 76–80.

Hopwood, C. J., Creech, S. K., Clark, T. S., Meagher, M. W., & Morey, L. C. (2008b). Optimal Multidimensional Pain Inventory scoring in a chronic pain sample. *Journal of Clinical Psychology in Medical Settings 15*(4), 301–307.

Hopwood, C. J., Morey, L. C., Rogers, R., & Sewell, K. (2007). Malingering on the Personality Assessment Inventory: Identification of specific feigned disorders. *Journal of Personality Assessment, 88*, 43–38.

Karlin, B. E., Creech, S. K., Grimes, J. S., Clark, T. S., Meagher, M. W., & Morey, L. C. (2005). The Personality Assessment Inventory with chronic pain patients: Psychometic properties and clinical utility. *Journal of Clinical Psychology, 61*, 1571–1585.

Kerns, R. D., Turk, D. C., & Rudy, T. E. (1985). The West Haven-Yale Multidimensional Pain Inventory (WHYMPI). *Pain, 23*, 345–356.

Kucharski, L. T., Toomey, J. P., Fila, K., & Duncan, S. (2007). Detection of malingering of psychiatric disorder with the Personality Assessment Inventory: An investigation of criminal defendants. *Journal of Personality Assessment, 88*, 25–32.

Morey, L. C. (1991). *Personality Assessment Inventory professional manual.* Odessa, FL: Psychological Assessment Resources.

Morey, L. C. (1996). *An interpretive guide to the Personality Assessment Inventory.* Odessa, FL: Psychological Assessment Resources.

Morey, L. C. (2003). *Essentials of PAI Assessment.* Hoboken, NJ: Wiley.

Morey, L. C. (2007). *Personality assessment screener professional manual.* Odessa, FL: Psychological Assessment Resources.

Morey, L. C. (2007). *Personality Assessment Inventory professional manual, second edition.* Lutz, FL: Psychological Assessment Resources.

Morey, L. C., & Hopwood, C. J. (2007). *Casebook for the Personality Assessment Inventory: A structural summary approach.* Lutz, FL: Psychological Assessment Resources.

Rogers, R., Sewell, K. W., Morey, L. C., & Ustad, K. L. (1996). Detection of feigned mental disorders on the Personality Assessment Inventory: A discriminant analysis. *Journal of Personality Assessment, 67,* 629–640.

Rogers, R., Ornduff, S. R., & Sewell, K. (1993). Feigning specific disorders: A study of the Personality Assessment Inventory (PAI). *Journal of Personality Assessment, 60,* 554–560.

Schinka, J. A., & Borum, R. (1993). Readability of adult psychopathology inventories. *Psychological Assessment, 5,* 384–386.

Sumanti, M., Boone, K. B., Savodnik, I., & Gorsuch, R. (2006). Noncredible psychiatric and cognitive symptoms in a workers' compensation "stress" claim sample. *The Clinical Neuropsychologist, 20,* 754–765.

Tollison, D. C. & Langley, J. C. (1995). *Pain Patient Profile Manual.* Minneapolis: National Computer Services.

Zanarini, M. C., Frankenburg, F. R., Reich, D. B., Silk, K. R., Hudson, J. I., & McSweeney, L. B. (2007). The subsyndromal phenomenology of borderline personality disorder: A 10-year follow-up study. *American Journal of Psychiatry, 164,* 929–935.

12

Personality Focused
Assessment With the PAI

MARK A. BLAIS and CHRISTOPHER J. HOPWOOD

*T*he power of psychological assessment can be fully realized only when we
move beyond the identification of linear score–behavior relationships and
integrate multisource data in a manner that describes, explains, and pre-
dicts complex human behaviors (Handler & Meyer, 1998). Unfortunately, achieving
this degree of proficiency in psychological assessment is challenging and requires
more than experience and technical skill. An explicit knowledge of how personality
works is required to become a truly expert assessment psychologist. In particular,
such an understanding of personality is essential for organizing and systematically
integrating assessment findings (Blais & Smith, 2008; Handler & Meyer, 1998). In
this chapter we present a personality focused approach to psychological assessment
that uses a model of personality organization (PO) to enhance the data interpretation and integration.

Schafer (1954), Lerner (1998), Sugarman (1991) and others have written about
the benefits to be gained by linking assessment data to a comprehensive theory
of personality. According to Sugarman, clinicians are better able to organize and
integrate assessment data, clarify gaps or contradictions that appear in the data,
and achieve greater predictive power when they are guided by a theory of personality. However, there is currently no dominant theory of personality, and most
psychologists are no longer fluent in the comprehensive psychodynamic theory of
mind. The absence of such a theory can greatly handicap efforts to conduct meaningful psychological assessments. Without the aid of a larger organizing perspective, psychological assessments risk being centered on specific tests or psychiatric
disorders and losing sight of the person being evaluated. While such endeavors
may be helpful for answering narrowly specified referral questions, they represent
psychological testing, not psychological assessment (Handler & Meyer, 1998), and
fail to deliver the full benefit of assessment to patients and colleagues. In sum,

having a theory of personality suitable to guide psychological assessment is critical for producing a report that captures the complexity of human beings.

Psychology may lack a grand theory of personality, but recent developments in personology provide a new foundation for conceptualizing how personality works. In particular, Mayer's (1998 & 2005) systems framework helps locate personality in relation to other levels of analysis (e.g., biological or social). It also describes the major subdivisions of personality as well as the organization and dynamics of personality development. Mayer's model is sufficiently generic to bridge findings from subfields of psychology as diverse as social psychology and cognitive neuroscience, and is adaptable to the needs of specific applied domains such as clinical assessment. Guided by Mayer's systems framework, we have been developing a model of PO tailored to the needs of psychological assessment but also capable of incorporating emerging research in other allied fields. Previously, Blais and Smith (2008) articulated the basic structure and properties of the model. In this chapter we present an expanded version of the model and illustrate the value personality focused assessment has for integrating multisource assessment data into a comprehensive description of human behavior.

A MODEL OF PERSONALITY ORGANIZATION

At the center of personality focused assessment is the trans-theoretical model of personality organization. As Figure 12.1 shows, our model of personality identifies five primary structures or subdivisions of personality: (1) self-awareness and regulation, (2) information and knowledge (thinking), (3) emotion processing (feeling), (4) self-image, and (5) representations of others. It also describes the main psychological processes associated with each structure. The model accounts for both implicit and explicit levels of personality functioning and illustrates the dynamic relationships among the systems (and processes) that are required to account for complex behavior. Most important for assessment psychology, the model makes explicit the relationship between multisource assessment data and various personality structures

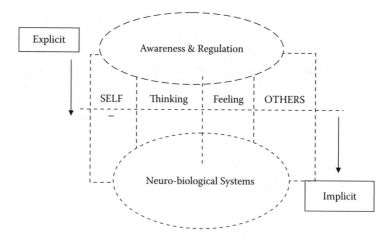

Figure 12.1   Trans-theoretical model of personality organization..

and processes. Also, by clarifying how assessment data relate to the major domains of personality, it facilitates linkages between traditional personality instruments and more basic areas of psychological, cognitive, and neuroscience research.

Personality Organization: The Subsystems

1. *Thinking—The Information and Knowledge System:* Thinking involves the perception of external and internal stimuli and the interpretation of these perceptual experiences. The primary goal of thinking is to generate information and knowledge that help us understand and act effectively in and upon the world. In psychological assessment, we typically measure many components of thinking, including perceptual accuracy, quality of associations (logic and goal directedness of thinking), control (attention and concentration), clarity of thought, problem solving ability, range and depth of knowledge, and prominent thought content. These qualities combine in individually unique ways to provide people with a personalized knowledge and understanding of their world.

2. *Feeling—The Emotion Processing System:* Emotions represent the evaluative component of perceived information and knowledge (Barrett, Mesquita, Ochsner, & Gross, 2007). Emotions further provide rapid, broadband evaluative information about the environment, social, and interpersonal situations while also predisposing us to specific behavioral responses. While feelings (i.e., moods) are experienced consciously, much processing of emotionally relevant information is implicit and precedes conscious cognitive perception (Surakka, Tenhunen-Eskelinen, Hietanen, & Sams, 1998). Psychologically, individuals differ substantially in the degree of importance they place on their feelings, the clarity with which they experience their emotions, and how malleable their emotions are once activated. In addition, emotions can also be experienced along three dimensions: pleasant–unpleasant, activating–depleting, and diffuse–differentiated. Multisource psychological assessment data can help describe the complexity of emotional experiences while also identifying specific mood disorders (e.g., depression and bipolar disorder) and the propensity for mood dysregulation (e.g., neuroticism).

    The thinking and feeling systems are dynamic, and continually interact with each other to shape our understanding and reaction to the world. There is growing evidence from cognitive neuroscience that the processes of thinking and feeling interact and modify each other. For example, the experience of depression alters how the brain processes perceptual information, particularly the extent to which the frontal and limbic systems are activated (Davidson, Pizzagalli, Nitschke, & Putnam, 2002). Furthermore, the activation of higher order (top-down) corticolimbic systems (thinking) is associated with reappraisal and reduction of dysphoric affect (Johnstone, Reekum, Urry, Kalin, & Davidson, 2007). Coping with life challenges requires the smooth interaction of thinking and feeling for generating optimal responses to environmental events. Because individuals differ in the ratio of thinking to feeling that they habitually employ when solving life problems, psychological assessment can help clarify and describe the dynamic interplay between these two major personality systems and their resulting behavioral and psychological consequences.

The personality systems in our model represent hypothetical constructs within the human mind which, through repeatable patterns of interaction, give rise to personality. However, personality as we encounter it in everyday life is a unitary entity that is evident in our behaviors, communications (e.g., verbal and emotional expressions), and life commitments. The external expression of personality provides the means for connecting our inner biological systems with the outer social systems that surround us (Mayer, 2005). Locating personality at the intersection of our biological and social worlds gives us an insight into the primary role of personality: personality developed to efficiently mediate between our internal/evolutionary needs and external social/environmental forces and constraints (Buss, 2001; Freud, 1923). The next two personality systems provide the foundation for effective interpersonal and social interactions.

3. *Self—the Identity System:* The self-system contains our self-beliefs and self-evaluations (Campbell, Assanand, & Paula, 2003). The goal of the self-system is to generate our sense of identity. The self-system provides the answers to such questions as, "Who am I?", "What is my purpose in life?", "How competent am I?", and "How do I feel about myself?" Although assessors typically measure only a few aspects of the self-system, such as self-esteem or stability, other dimensions of the self including the complexity or differentiation of the self-concept, affective tone of self-referents, and degree to which various aspects of the self are experienced as an integrated coherent whole are also critical (Campbell, Trapnell, Heine, Katz, Lavalle, & Lehman, 1996). Assessment of autobiographic narratives and early memories can also be of value in assessing self-image and identity (Ackerman, Fowler, & Clemence, 2008).

4. *Others—The Interpersonal and Relational System:* The ability to accurately interpret the actions and intentions of others and to participate in smooth reciprocal relationships is paramount to human success. The relational system contains the psychological processes that support these important interpersonal abilities. The relational system is responsible for determining the value (ranging from indifference to primary importance) and the general evaluative tone (helpful or unhelpful—scary or inviting) we assign to others and our social interactions. The relational system also helps us organize our interpersonal behaviors into a recognizable pattern or interpersonal style. This characteristic interpersonal style is often measured along the five-factor model (Goldberg, 1993) dimensions of agreeable–disagreeable and introversion–extraversion or the axes of the interpersonal circumplex (Wiggins, 1991), agency, and communion.

Theorists such as Sullivan (1953) and Kernberg (1996) have emphasized the interconnectedness and bidirectional influence of self and other mental representations. There is also emerging evidence from the neuroscience literature supporting the interconnection of self and other knowledge. Fisher, McCoy, Poole, and Vinogradov (2008) found that the prefrontal cortex supported both self knowledge (autobiographical information) and identifying another person's emotional state. Interestingly, in normal subjects, these skills were only modestly related to general cognitive abilities (verbal memory and intelligence) suggesting that specialized distinct cognitive systems give rise to these abilities. In normal development, the self or other systems mature in unison, achieving roughly equal influence in the overall organization of personality. However, in many pathological conditions, either the self or other system becomes overly influential and dominates personality functioning. Blatt (see Blatt, Besser, & Ford, 2007) has outlined the role of anaclitic (relational focus) and introjective (self focus) pathologies from the psychodynamic perspective while other theorists (Beck, 1983; Robins & Luten, 1991) identified similar concepts (sociotropy and autonomy) from the perspective of cognitive behavioral theory.

5. *Self-awareness and adaptation—the control and regulation system:* The final personality system proposed in the model is envisioned as an overarching supervisor and regulator of the other systems. The goals of this system involve ongoing self evaluation, behavioral regulation, and adaptation. This personality system actively monitors the inner and outer environments to adjust and regulate our behaviors, feelings, and goals according to ongoing feedback. This class of processes has been referred to at times as ego functions, psychological mindedness, or emotional intelligence (Slovey, Mayer, Goldman, Turvey, & Palfai, 1995). The goal of this system is to accurately evaluate the effectiveness of our actions, prioritize our motivations/goals, and anticipate future needs or threats.

This model envisions personality as the result of ongoing dynamic processes between these systems and external factors. Thus, the personality traits and other measured psychological variables that we observe are thought to result from the interactions of the systems previously outlined. Under certain conditions, processes across the personality systems are reliably activated in a coordinated and organized manner and give rise to specific psychological and behavioral response patterns (traits, disorders, etc.). The personality traits or psychiatric conditions that our instruments typically measure involve contributions from all subdivisions of the model, making them complex, broadband constructs. As such, a major advantage to using the model presented here involves the ability to decompose these molar broadband traits into the underlying contributions of the various personality systems.

Personality Focused Assessment and the PAI

In developing the Personality Assessment Inventory (PAI), Morey (1991) targeted a range of constructs relevant to personality, psychopathology, and the environment, making its scales and subscales compatible with multiple models of personality. In fact, as Table 12.1 shows, many of the PAI subscales easily map onto the personality domains outlined previously. In addition to locating the PAI scales within the model, Table 12.1 also provides descriptors of high scores. While this listing is not

TABLE 12.1   The Placement of Select PAI Scales in the
Trans-Theoretical Model of Personality Organization

Self-Awareness and Coping

Mean Clinical Elevation (MCE)	Distressed
INF	Confused or inattentive
ICN	Inconsistent
ALC	Using alcohol to cope
DRG	Using drugs to cope
ANT-Antisocial Behavior	Immoral
STR	Overwhelmed

Thinking (Quality)

SOM-Somatization	Unsophisticated
SOM-Conversion	Dramatic
ANX-Cognitive	Distractible
DEP-Cognitive	Dull
MAN-Activity Level	Hyperactive
PAR-Persecution	Deluded
SCZ-Thought Disorder	Confused
SCZ-Psychotic Experiences	Psychotic

Thinking (Content)

SOM-Health Concerns	Health problems
ANX-Cognitive	Worries
ARD-Obsessive-Compulsive	Environmental and internal disorganization
ARD-Phobias	Environmental threats
ARD-Traumatic Stress	Past hurts
DEP-Cognitive	Failures
MAN-Grandiosity	Future, grandiose fantasy
SUI	Death

Feeling

ANX-Affective	Anxious
ANX-Physiological	Tense
ARD-Obsessive-Compulsive	Constricted
DEP-Affective	Sad
DEP-Physiological	Lethargic/fatigued
MAN-Irritability	Irritable
PAR-Resentment	Resentful
BOR-Affective Instability	Unstable
ANT-Stimulus Seeking	Ready for action
AGG-Attitude	Angry

Self

NIM	Self with many problems
NIM, RXR	Self without problems
SOM-Health Concerns	Damaged self
DEP-Cognitive	Self without prospects

TABLE 12.1   The Placement of Select PAI Scales in the
Trans-Theoretical Model of Personality Organization
(Continued)

MAN-Grandiosity	Great self
BOR-Identity Problems	Unstable self
BOR-Self-harm	Intolerable self
WRM	Empathic caring
DOM	Assertive—agentic
Others	
ARD-Traumatic Stress	Hurtful
PAR-Hypervigilance	Mistrustful
PAR-Resentment	Resentful
SCZ-Social withdrawal	Uninterested
BOR-Negative Relationships	Unskilled
ANT-Egocentricity	Unempathic
AGG-Verbal Aggression	Aggressive
AGG-Physical Aggression	Threatening
NON	Unsupported
DOM	Controlling
WRM	Affiliative

Note: PAI subscale descriptions based on Morey (1991, 1996).

meant to be final or exhaustive, it adequately portrays the manner in which PAI
scales can be understood from the perspective of PO. For example, a high score
on Schizophrenia-Thought Disorder (SCZ-T) would suggest that the respondent's
thought quality is confused, and a high score on Aggression-Aggressive Attitude
(AGG-A) would suggest that the respondent often feels angry.

Indicators from other instruments can also be mapped onto this conceptual
structure. It can be particularly useful to link indicators of explicit and implicit
personality functioning using the five personality domains. For example, the
Rorschach Inkblot Method (RIM; Weiner, 2003) assesses more implicit aspects of
thought quality, thought content, emotional processes, self, and others.

Although it is not the purpose of this chapter to describe the RIM from the
perspective of personality focused assessment, it is notable that many of the RIM
variables map onto the personality domains of the model. For example, RIM
Comprehensive System (CS) Structural Summary domains (Exner, 2003; Weiner,
2003) easily fit into the major systems of PO outlined (e.g., thinking = ideation,
mediation, and processing; feeling = affect; self = self; others = interpersonal).
Integrating data about a patient's personality functioning across the implicit and
explicit levels is often more revealing than simply describing these findings from
the perspective of different tests, particularly when different sources yield apparently discrepant data (e.g., reporting that "the Rorschach suggested the respondent
was defensive while the PAI data suggested openness regarding personal limitations" provides very little useful information).

The benefits of using a personality model to guide the integration of assessment data is demonstrated in the following case description, focusing mainly on the integration of PAI and RIM data.

Mr. G: An Illustrative Example of Integrative Psychological Assessment The following case (which is a composite of a number of different cases) illustrates how using personality focused assessment helps organize and integrate data while maintaining a focus on the person as opposed to psychometric instruments or specific disorders. Mr. G was a 50-year-old divorced man with an MBA. He had had a successful but tumultuous career in finance until approximately 1 year prior to the evaluation, when he was abruptly fired. Since that time he had been unable to secure new employment and was under mounting financial pressure. He was also involved in a highly contested divorce that had been dragging on for more than 5 years. He had no significant medical illnesses or health concerns. He began seeing a psychiatrist who prescribed an antidepressant medication, but this treatment provided limited benefit. Mr. G was also not reliable in keeping his psychotherapy appointments. His condition continued to deteriorate and he was referred for a psychological assessment consultation. The referring psychiatrist requested help in understanding the nature of his depression, degree of impairment, and the extent to which personality factors might be contributing to his overall condition.

Behavioral and psychometric indicators of effort and response styles suggested adequate participation in the testing, although Mr. G demonstrated little interest in the testing process or findings. In addition, he quickly became frustrated on challenging cognitive tasks (e.g., Wisconsin Card Sorting Task) and he easily gave up. His affect was depressed and his speech and motor movements were mildly slow. His thought content was at times overly personalized and he frequently interjected irrelevant observations or personal history into his testing responses. For example, when asked to define "vacation" he replied, "Something I could have if I were working." While Mr. G's consultation included a clinical interview and a battery of psychological and neuropsychological instruments, in what follows we focus primarily on data from the PAI and RIM CS (Exner, 2003) to illustrate the integrative power of personality focused assessment. Where possible, scores from the RIM or PAI are provided to identify how specific interpretations were derived (Table 12.2 and Figure 12.2).

Self-Awareness and Coping Mr. G has adequate organized psychological recourses and skills available for coping with life's challenges (EA = 9.5), his history should evidence meaningful personal achievements and periods of stable functioning. However, at the time of the evaluation he was experiencing a significant increase in environmental stressors and emotional distress (D = −2; Adj D = −1; MCE = 59; STR = 55T), leading to reduced functional efficiency (current decrement in measured intelligence), inattentiveness (ICN = 64T), and disorganization (ARD-O = 38T). This situational stress also likely relates to his poor frustration tolerance (MAN-I = 69T). However, and despite this elevated stress level and diminished functioning, Mr. G appeared to have limited recognition that his problems might require personal change (RXR = 59T). Together, these findings

TABLE 12.2   Mr. G's RIM Rorschach Profile

Coping		Affect	Interpersonal
R = 29	L = 0.45	FC: CF+C = 1:5	COP = 0
		Pure C = 0	AG = 0
			GHR: PHR = 3:5
EB = 4:5.5	EA = 9.5 EBPer = N/A	SumC:WSumC = 5:5.5	Food =0
eb = 6:9	es = 15 D = –2	Afr = 0.32	Sum T = 0
	Adj es = 14 Adj D = –1	S =4	Human Cont = 8
		Blends:R =11:29	
FM = 5	SumC' = 5 SumT = 0	CP = 0	PER = 2
m = 1	Sum V = 2 Sum Y = 2		Isol Index = .21

Ideation	Mediation	Processing	Self-Perception
a:p = 8:2	Sum6 =4 XA% = 0.80	Zf = 22	3r+(2)/R = 0.31
Ma:Mp = 2:2	Lv2 = 1 WDA% = 0.73	W:D:Dd = 20:8:1	Fr+rF = 2
2AB+Art+Ay =7	WSum6 =15 X-% = 0.17	W:M = 20:4	SumV = 2
MOR =1	M- = 2 S- = 2	Zd = -1.5	FD = 4
	M none =0 P = 3	PSV = 0	An+Xy = 0
	X+% = .52	DQ+ = 13	MOR =1
	Xu% = .28	DQv = 1	H:(H)+Hd+(Hd) = 4:4
PTI =1 DEPI =7+ CDI =3	S-CON =6	HVI = Yes	OBS =No

Adapted from Exner, 2003.

point to a disruption in his higher-order psychological abilities to self-monitor and cope with stress, and the tendency to understand his current difficulties as out of his control or responsibility. Fortunately, it does not appear that he was using substances (ALC = 52T; DRG = 46T) or other criminal activity (ANT–A = 55T) to cope with his current distressing circumstances.

Thinking   Test data suggest that Mr. G is not psychotic (PTI = 1, SCZ-P = 50T), although the quality of his thinking is variable. He has adequate perceptual accuracy (XA% = .83) but is less committed to conventional behavior (P = 3) than is the average person. He is also prone to experiencing cognitive slippage (Wsum6 = 15). Therefore, despite having adequate reality contact, he may frequently behave in unconventional or unpredictable ways. Furthermore, he is ruminative (ANX-C = 64T), confused (SCZ-T = 67T), and disorganized (ARD-O = 38T). Cognitive difficulties appear to manifest most prominently in the interpersonal domains, where he likely has specific difficulties accurately perceiving and understanding the actions of others (M– = 2; WRM = 38T; ANT-E = 62T). He is preoccupied with thoughts related to personal threats (ARD-P = 62T; PAR-P = 60T). His thinking is overly complex, predisposing him to confusion and indecision (Blends = 11; SCZ-T = 67T).

Feeling   Mr. G has an unstable affective organization and is predisposed to mood dysregulation (DEPI = 7; BOR-A = 69T). He is currently experiencing extreme levels of painful affect (DEP-A = 85T; Sum Shading = 9), which he is unable to

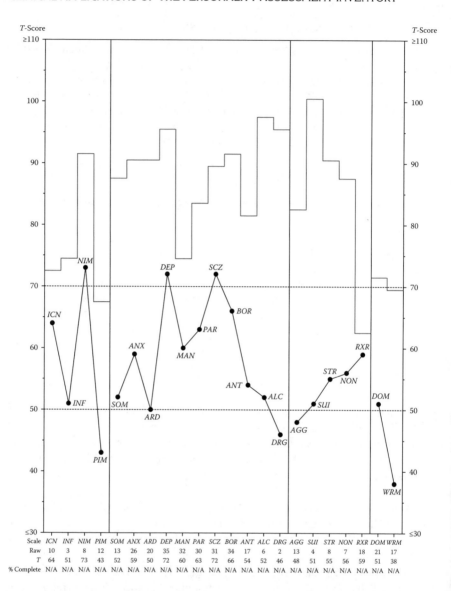

Figure 12.2   Mr. G's PAI profile and supplementary index scores. Reproduced by special permission of Psychological Assessment Resources, Inc., Lutz, Florida. Leslie C. Morey, Ph.D. and PAR Staff, Copyright by PAR, Inc.

process openly (C' = 5). Instead, his negative affectivity is likely experienced, in the forms of heightened irritability and hostility (MAN-I = 69T and PAR-R = 64T). However, he is not likely to be overtly aggressive (AGG-A = 51T). Overall, this pattern suggests that he does not have adequate ways to express or experience his emotions, leaving him very constricted (ARD-O = 38T) but tense (ANX-P = 62T), and defended against recognizing or attending to feelings. He relies heavily on intellectualization to minimize his experience of emotions (Intellectualization

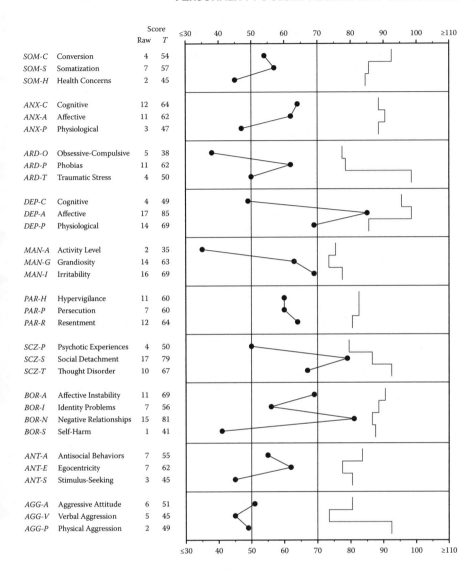

		Score		≤30	40	50	60	70	80	90	100	≥110
		Raw	T									
SOM-C	Conversion	4	54									
SOM-S	Somatization	7	57									
SOM-H	Health Concerns	2	45									
ANX-C	Cognitive	12	64									
ANX-A	Affective	11	62									
ANX-P	Physiological	3	47									
ARD-O	Obsessive-Compulsive	5	38									
ARD-P	Phobias	11	62									
ARD-T	Traumatic Stress	4	50									
DEP-C	Cognitive	4	49									
DEP-A	Affective	17	85									
DEP-P	Physiological	14	69									
MAN-A	Activity Level	2	35									
MAN-G	Grandiosity	14	63									
MAN-I	Irritability	16	69									
PAR-H	Hypervigilance	11	60									
PAR-P	Persecution	7	60									
PAR-R	Resentment	12	64									
SCZ-P	Psychotic Experiences	4	50									
SCZ-S	Social Detachment	17	79									
SCZ-T	Thought Disorder	10	67									
BOR-A	Affective Instability	11	69									
BOR-I	Identity Problems	7	56									
BOR-N	Negative Relationships	15	81									
BOR-S	Self-Harm	1	41									
ANT-A	Antisocial Behaviors	7	55									
ANT-E	Egocentricity	7	62									
ANT-S	Stimulus-Seeking	3	45									
AGG-A	Aggressive Attitude	6	51									
AGG-V	Verbal Aggression	5	45									
AGG-P	Physical Aggression	2	49									

Figure 12.2 (Continued.)

index = 7) and also externalizes his feelings (PAR = 63T; MAN-G = 63T) to a moderate degree. However, when his emotions overwhelm his defenses he is unable to modulate their expressions and he is prone to intense affective eruptions likely focused at others (FC: CF + C = 1:5; ANT-E = 62T; WRM = 32T). However, his willingness to admit to somatic difficulties (DEP-P=69T) may suggest an opening for clinical intervention.

Self Mr. G has a fairly stable (BOR-I = 56T) but complex identity. On the one hand, he has a chronic tendency to overvalue his personal worth and talents (Fr+rF = 2; MAN-G = 63T), yet he is currently prone to comparing himself unfavorably with

Supplemental PAI Indexes

Index	Value	T Score	
Defensiveness Index	1	38	
Cashel Discriminant Function	166.09	69	
Malingering Index	1	57	
Rogers Discriminant Function	0.21	61	
Suicide Potential Index	7	62	
Violence Potential Index	6	70	
Treatment Process Index	1	49	
ALC Estimated Score	—	55	(3T higher than *ALC*)
DRG Estimated Score	—	53	(7T higher than *DRG*)
Mean Clinical Elevation	—	59	

Figure 12.2 (Continued.) *Note:* These images have been reproduced with permission from Psychological Assessment Resources, Inc.

others, leading him to feel dissatisfied and disgusted (Sum V = 2; NIM = 73T). In addition, when he does introspect, he tends to ruminate about aspects of himself or his actions that he believes are undesirable (FV = 2; MOR = 1). Perhaps to minimize his painful self-criticism, he focuses less on himself and more on others at present (Egocentricity Index = .31). Consistent with narcissistic personality organization, he tends to externalize responsibility for his difficulties and he is not strongly motivated for psychologically based treatments (PAR-R = 64T; RXR = 59T), suggesting he would be reluctant to explore his contribution to his life problems. Furthermore, he is likely to more generally fail to see how others could be helpful in aiding him to get through his current difficulties, given very limited motivation for communion (WRM = 35T; ANT-E = 62T) and firm belief in his own abilities (DEP-C = 49T). Indeed, he typically sees others as most likely to cause him harm (ARD-T = 62T; PAR-H = 60T).

Others Mr. G has a hypervigilant interpersonal style (HVI positive; PAR = 63T). He is alert to possible threats to his personal safety and security. His suspiciousness makes it difficult for him to develop deep, smooth, or rewarding relationships (BOR-N = 81T; GHR:PHR = 3:5). He sees the world as dangerous and others as potentially duplicitous. Likely as a result of this view of others, he tends to be socially detached (SCZ-S = 79T) and his relationships are likely to be formal and superficial. Others may view him as reserved, aloof, or unsympathetic (ANT-E = 62T; WRM = 35T). He tends to guard his autonomy (S = 4) and to be less concerned than most people about the opinions of others (PER = 2). When his relationships do become intimate or emotionally arousing they are likely to be intense, unpredictable, and very conflicted (BOR-N = 81T). Given the extent of his relational difficulties, the development of more adaptive interpersonal capacities appears to be a primary treatment target. Ironically, this will be very difficult for a clinician, whose most powerful tool is his or her therapeutic relationship with Mr. G.

Summary Mr. G is experiencing significant emotional distress and life turmoil. Although he tends to minimize the severity of his current psychiatric symptoms, there is evidence that emotional problems are negatively affecting his cognitive efficiency. He is significantly depressed and situational stressors are compounding his mood problems. His thinking is mildly disordered, with perceptual difficulties most likely to occur in the context of his interpersonal relationships. He is hyper-vigilant and suspicious of others, and does not appreciate nor have the interpersonal skills to make use of social resources. He has limited ability to manage his feelings and tends to intellectualize and externalize his emotional reactions. These inefficient strategies lead to emotional dysregulation and cognitive slippage. Although his core self-image is narcissistic, he may be prone to episodes of low self-esteem. His tendency to externalize the cause of problems will make engagement in psychologically based treatment challenging for him. While the degree to which Mr. G's current mood symptoms are independent of his personality organization is not clear, treatment of his mood disorder will be complicated by personality factors.

CONCLUSION

The goals of psychological assessment should be to integrate data from multiple sources into a thorough dynamic understanding of how an individual functions in his or her life. Using a personality focused approach to assessment and the model of personality described in this chapter can help achieve this important goal. Furthermore, focusing our assessment efforts on personality moves us beyond the unproductive arguments about the superiority of one test over another and recognizes that data from different methods are necessary for generating an accurate picture of the person being assessed. The model of personality-focused assessment described here represents one method of integrating psychological assessment data that may complement other similar efforts. We believe that understanding assessment data in the context of a model of personality organization offers the potential to move beyond the poorly integrated and descriptive laundry list of psychological characteristics frequently seen in assessment reports and toward a more dynamic, integrated formulation that brings psychological data back to the person who was assessed.

REFERENCES

Ackerman, S. J., Fowler, J. C., & Clemence, A. J. (2008). TAT and other performance-based assessment techniques (pp. 337–378). In R. Archer & S. Smith (Eds.), *Personality assessment*. New York: Routledge.

Barrett, L. F., Mesquita, B., Ochsner, K. N., & Gross, J. J. (2007). The experience of emotion. *Annual Review of Psychology, 58*, 373–403.

Beck, A. T. (1983). Cognitive therapy of depression: New perspectives. In P. J. Clayton and E. J. Barrett (Eds.), *Treatment of depression: Old approaches and new controversies*. New York: Raven Press.

Blais, M. A, Hilsenroth, M. J., Castlebury, F., Fowler, J. C., & Baity, M. R. (2001). Predicting DSM-IV Cluster B Personality disorder criteria from MMPI-2 and Rorschach data: A test of incremental validity. *Journal of Personality Assessment, 76*, 150–168.

Blais, M., & Smith, S. (2008). Improving the integration process in psychological assessment data organization and report writing (pp. 405–439). In R. Archer & S. Smith (Eds.), *Personality assessment*. New York: Routledge.

Blatt, S. J., Besser, A., & Ford, R. Q. (2007). Two primary configurations of psychopathology and change in thought disorder in long-term intensive inpatient treatment of seriously disturbed young adults. *American Journal of Psychiatry, 164,* 1561–1567.

Buss, D. M. (2001). Human nature and culture: An evolutionary psychological perspective. *Journal of Personality, 69,* 955–978.

Campbell, J. D., Assanand, S., & Paula, A. D. (2003). The structure of the self-concept and its relationship to psychological adjustment. *Journal of Personality, 71,* 115–141.

Campbell, J. D., Trapnell, P. D., Heine, S. J., Katz, I. M., Lavalle, L. F., & Lehman, D. R. (1996). Self-concept clarity: Measurement, personality correlates and cultural boundaries. *Journal of Personality and Social Psychology, 70,* 141–156.

Davidson, R. J., Pizzagalli, D., Nitschke, J. B., & Putnam, K. (2002). Depression: Perspectives from affective neuroscience. *Annual Review of Psychology, 53:* 545–574.

Exner, J. E., Jr. (2003). *The Rorschach: A comprehensive system: Vol 1. Basic foundations and principles of interpretation* (4th ed.). New York: Wiley.

Fisher, M., McCoy, K., Poole, J. H., & Vinogradov, S. (2008). Self and others in schizophrenia: A cognitive neuroscience perspective. *American Journal of Psychiatry, 165,* 1465–1472.

Freud, S. (1923, English translation, 1949). *The ego and the id*. London: Hogarth.

Goldberg, L. R. (1993). The structure of phenotypic personality traits. *American Psychologist, 48,* 26–34.

Handler, L., & Meyer, G. J. (1998). The importance of teaching and learning personality assessment. In L. Handler & M. J. Hilsenroth (Eds.), *Teaching and learning personality assessment*. Mahwah, NJ: Lawrence Erlbaum.

Johnstone, T., Reekum, C. M., Urry, H. L., Kalin, N. H., & Davidson, R. (2007). Failure to regulate: Counterproductive recruitment of top-down prefrontal-subcortical circuitry in major depression. *Journal of Neuroscience, 27,* 8877–8884.

Kernberg, O. F. (1996). A psychoanalytic theory of personality disorders. In J. Clarkin & M. Lenzenweger (Eds.), *Major theories of personality disorder* (pp. 106–140). New York: Guilford Press.

Learner, P. M. (1998). *Psychoanalytic perspectives on the Rorschach*. Hillsdale, NJ: Analytic Press.

Mayer, J. D. (1998). A systems framework for the field of personality. *Psychological Inquiry, 9,* 118–144.

Mayer, J. D. (2004). A classification system for the data of personality psychology and adjoining fields. *Review of General Psychology, 8,* 208–219.

Mayer, J. D. (2005). A tale of two visions: Can a new view of personality help integrate psychology? *American Psychologist. 60:* 294–307.

Morey, L. C. (1991). *Personality Assessment Inventory: Professional manual*. Odessa, FL: Psychological Assessment Resources, Inc.

Morey, L. C. (1996). *An interpretive guide to the Personality Assessment Inventory*. Odessa, FL: Psychological Assessment Resources, Inc.

Robins, C. J., & Luten, A. G. (1991). Sociotropy and autonomy: Different patterns of clinical presentation in unipolar depression. *Journal of Abnormal Psychology, 100,* 74–77.

Schafer, R. (1954). Psychoanalytic interpretation in Rorschach testing. New York: Grune & Stratton.

Slovey, P., Mayer, J. D., Goldman, S. L., Turvey C., & Palfai, T. P. (1995). Emotional attention, clarity and repair: Exploring emotional intelligence using the trait meta-mood scale. In J. W. Pennebaker (Ed.), *Emotion, disclosure and health* (pp. 125–154). Washington, DC: American Psychological Association Press.

Sugarman, A. (1991). Where's the beef? Putting personality back into personality assessment. *Journal of Personality Assessment, 56,* 130–144.

Sullivan, H. S. (1953). *The interpersonal theory of psychiatry.* New York: Norton.

Surakka, V., Tenhunen-Eskelinen, M., Hietanen J. K., & Sams, M. (1998). Modulation of human auditory information processing by emotional visual stimuli. *Cognitive Brain Research, 7,* 159–163.

Wechsler, D. (1999). *Wechsler Abbreviated Scale of Intelligence: Manual.* San Antonio, TX: The Psychological Corporation.

Weiner, I. B. (2003). *Principles of Rorschach interpretation* (2nd ed.). Mahwah, NJ: Erlbaum.

Wiggins, J. S. (1991). Agency and communion as conceptual coordinates for the understanding and measurement of interpersonal behavior. In W. Grove & D. Ciccetti (Eds.), *Thinking clearly about psychology: Essays in honor of Paul E. Meeh* (Vol., 2. pp. 89–113). Minneapolis: University of Minnesota Press.

13

Therapeutic Assessment With the PAI

MATTHEW R. BAITY

The overall purpose of this book was to provide a forum for leading authors to present their acquired knowledge in a form that was amenable to teaching both general and specific features of the Personality Assessment Inventory (PAI). It is hoped that readers will be able to take away a broad scope of knowledge about the PAI and keep this book on their shelves as a reference tool when they have questions about certain clinical groups. In addition to this desire to provide information about profile interpretations and local norms for specific clinical populations, we also hoped to help readers think about how to use the PAI at an ideographic level. This chapter will focus on this latter goal by presenting a case in which the PAI was administered both at the beginning of treatment and a year into therapy. The profile will be interpreted both from the perspective of a psychologist knowledgeable about the test as an information gathering method as well as providing some suggestions about how to present and discuss these findings with a patient from a Therapeutic Assessment model (TA; Ackerman, Hilsenroth, Baity, & Blagys, 2000; Hilsenroth, Peters, and Ackerman, 2004; Finn and Tonsager, 1992, 1997; see also http://www.therapeuticassessment.com). In TA, patients are considered to be the experts on themselves, to have an acute desire to have their lens of reality confirmed, and to be inherently interested in seeking out personal growth. In many ways, TA is more of a healing intervention than a passive learning experience for the patient. Not surprisingly, TA contains many of the "common" or "nonspecific" elements of psychotherapy, including patients' desires to be accepted, respected, listened to, and given hope to overcome what Jerome Frank called the "demoralization" that develops as a result of being unable to resolve their difficulties on their own (Frank and Frank, 1991).

OUTLINE OF TA

Adopting the role as a therapeutic assessor is not the default position for many psychologists, perhaps due to the tendency of training programs that have adopted a medical model perspective in which the doctor is the expert and the patient is there to "receive" treatment. I teach my students using a metaphor from my own training: "You are not a GPS unit telling the patient where to turn, but instead are sitting next to them in the car with a roadmap, a highlighter, and a general sense of the best routes to take while you ask them where they want to go." This approach can be particularly effective with patients who tend to be more submissive or dependent because it places them in a role they are not used to, yet desperately want to have after repeated trials of unsuccessful relationships. The process of TA remains helpful whether assessment is undertaken to answer specific referral questions or used as a means for treatment planning. A general introduction to testing at the end of an initial session might proceed as follows:

> So we have spoken a lot today about you, what brings you to therapy, and how you would like to see your life change as a result of coming here. It has been very helpful in getting to understand the troubles you have been having and why you feel they are a part of your life right now [pause for comments from the patient]. To continue with this theme, I want to also offer you the option of completing a questionnaire called the Personality Assessment Inventory that I often use at the end of my first meeting with people to get to understand them even better. It will ask you a lot of questions about a lot of different areas that may or may not apply to you, but I think it could help us get a broader sense of where your primary strengths and weaknesses lie as well as develop a course of action for our time together. We can look at the results together and you can tell me what you think.

The point in this approach is to both acknowledge the patient's efforts in the face-to-face interaction and introduce something that may have added benefit for both the assessor and the patient (hence the use of the words "us" and "together" when information-gathering assessors might normally say "me" or "I") in helping to understand them *even better*. To return to the co-pilot metaphor, the assessor is saying "Now that we are here, I know that going in this direction has been helpful in the past. Should we give it a try?" Introducing testing in this way makes it an option for patients and gives them the power to decide as opposed to an obstacle or a step that must be completed. Once patients agree to complete the testing, as a way to begin the process of encouraging their involvement I ask them to think of a few issues or questions they would like to develop answers for with the test data. Many treatment-seeking outpatients seem eager to take this opportunity to complete the testing, as they are inherently interested in learning more about themselves; this is why they sought professional help in the first place. Inquiring about refusals or hesitations to complete the testing also has its uses. For instance, asking patients their thoughts about why they might not want to do any testing may give important information about how they process and manage novel information, as well as to give the assessor opportunities to dispel misconceptions about testing.

Test interpretation involves at least two steps. First, scale interpretations are done as a "blind read" as if there were no face-to-face contact with the patient, only the PAI profile. This can help to generate clinical hypotheses about possible diagnoses, obstacles to treatment, and risk assessment as it applies to the PAI normative samples. One reason to do this is it helps provide a perspective in the event difficult feedback is necessary (e.g., telling a patient who is in denial of his or her anger about an elevation on the Antisocial or Aggression scale) where one can say, "If I didn't know you at all and just had this profile, I would say that you really walk around with a chip on your shoulder, are more than willing to break a few rules or laws, and are quick to chew someone out when they cross you. The curious part for me is that this never came across in our meetings. What do you make of that?" Second, scales are interpreted in the context of the reasons patients presented for treatment and their stated goals for the assessment (i.e., the questions they wanted answered from the testing). The second pass through the data can help put a per-spective on why certain scales might be elevated (as opposed to only noting what scales are elevated) and to generate alternate hypotheses about profile configura-tions. Keeping the questions generated by the patient in mind is helpful in assimi-lating the information that will be presented to the patient.

Feedback is where TA really seems to have an incremental benefit over the more traditional information gathering model where patients are primarily told what their scale elevations are and what they might mean. Feedback from a TA perspective requires pre-planning and organizing data so information that may be new or difficult to hear is presented only after discussing those issues the patient is aware of or recognizes (Ackerman et al., 2000; Finn & Tonsager, 1992, 1997). Patients should be encouraged to provide their own thoughts after each piece of feedback is given (e.g., "What are your thoughts about that?", "How does that fit with how you see yourself?" etc.) as a means to further involve them in the process. This is not to say that TA excludes explanations of test scores or what a scale eleva-tion "means." In most outpatient testing situations, teaching patients about the test can include showing them the testing profile to help explain norms, t-scores, standard deviations, and clinical cutoffs. The PAI, in particular, lends itself espe-cially well to this procedure due to scale names that correspond to contemporary diagnostic constructs and the "skyline" that represents scores that are 2 SD above the clinical normative sample. Thus, a typical conversation about a Depression t-score of 75 might be:

> This line [point to t-score = 50] represents the average score of people who are in the community and not seeking treatment, whereas this line [point to t-score = 70] is the cutoff that is often used to indicate problems that are really interfering with someone's daily life. Scores that are above this skyline are unusually high even for people who are in clinical settings. Based on your responses, this score on the Depression scale [point to DEP = 75 on the pro-file] is above the cutoff of 70 and below the skyline. In other words, your score is right where we might expect for someone looking for therapy at an outpa-tient clinic, and suggests that your depression is really interfering with your life.

Approaching the interpretation in this manner helps to educate patients and normalize their feelings by contextualizing their difficulties in other populations. Showing the profile to the patients also allows them to see their other scale scores and ask questions about what they mean. Not only does this increase the transpar-ency of psychological testing, but it also opens up the possibility for generating other treatment goals or problem areas that the patient (or the assessor) might not have thought about. Personally, I have found this approach to be particularly effective in getting patients involved with the testing. The key point is to present the PAI as separate from the assessor or the assessment process itself, and emphasizing that scores were obtained by entering the patient's responses into the computer. All psychological tests are subject to measurement error and should be explained as such. This allows the assessor to wonder with the patient (remember the co-pilot metaphor) why a certain scale was elevated when he or she did not report feeling that way. In such cases it may even be helpful to review the individual items the patient responded to for that scale. Although engaging in this demystification process is an important step with most patients (especially suspicious or reactionary individuals) the assessor should determine the appropriateness of such techniques on a case-by-case basis.

The TA model requires a significant time commitment from all parties involved, as testing alone can be spread across anywhere from 3–6 sessions. Although taking nearly 2 months to complete a TA is certainly possible and provides a wealth of relevant clinical information and therapeutic benefit, it may not fit into every treatment setting. The economic status of many of our patients, the reimbursement schedules used by many third-party payors that have resulted in shorter treatment lengths across settings, and productivity-based pay often seen in clinics or medical institutions can reduce the length of time an assessor has to realistically work with each patient. These realities, though frustrating, do not render TA impossible. Just as we encourage our patients to generate alternate solutions when they face obstacles, the fundamental principles of TA can still be maintained in a customized or abridged procedure. Although not optimal, even using a TA model in 30-minute feedback sessions on an inpatient unit can have dramatic impacts on self awareness, focus on treatment goals, and instilled hope.

The following case explains how the PAI can be used in a therapeutic manner at the beginning and 1 year into psychotherapy. As the focus of the chapter is more on how the PAI can be used in a treatment setting with any individual as opposed to providing a specific psychological profile for the patient whose data will be presented (Jenny), the background and clinical information will be kept to a minimum.

CASE EXAMPLE—TIME 1

Jenny was a 48-year-old Caucasian female raised in a strict Catholic household. She was the youngest of three siblings who were all victims of verbal and physical abuse at the hands of their father, yet Jenny was spared from this treatment. She completed an associate's degree and got her real estate license in her early 20s, when she also met her husband at the office where both worked. They married shortly thereafter and had three children before her husband suddenly left the family to live with another woman from Jenny's office. She did not remarry and, with three children to care for and a full-time job, did not date. At the age of 46, as the result of high blood pressure, Jenny suffered a heart attack that left her incapacitated and unable to work for about 8 months. Jenny's middle son died in the hospital as a result of complications from a motor vehicle accident shortly before his mother's treatment began. This represented an important precipitant of her seeking treatment.

Likely due to her feeling of being ignored by her abusive father and the sudden ending of her marriage, Jenny had developed a very negative self-image and found it hard to be assertive. Although this seemed to be especially true in her relationships with men, she also had difficulties disciplining her children for fear they would no longer love her. As a result, Jenny seemed to have little control over her children's behavior. Her interpersonal style spilled into her work relationships, where she described having trouble both saying "no" to her coworkers and giving clients negative information (e.g., having house offers refused). She felt criticized by both her children and coworkers and had a chronic sense that she was being taken advantage of. Her lack of assertiveness left a lot of stress on her shoulders and she often ended up doing tasks that she did not want, or have time, to do. She stated that she could see herself being interested in dating men at some point, but was at a loss as to how to go about doing this and was afraid that men would become disappointed once they got to know her. The clinician conceptualized Jenny's case using Luborsky's Core Conflictual Relationship Theme (CCRT; 1984) model. CCRT includes an individual's (1) relational wish/fear, (2) the real or imagined response from others should the wish/fear get expressed, and (3) the response to self following the reaction from others. During the interview, the therapist developed the CCRT-framed hypothesis that Jenny has a deep wish to feel close to others but was afraid that others would reject or criticize her wish, so she ended up feeling worthless and resentful, and tended to withdraw from interactions.

Jenny was eager to engage in testing with the PAI. Although she did not generate any specific questions that she wanted addressed by the test, she expressed her interest in finding out what it said about her. Figure 13.1 shows the main clinical profile from Jenny at the beginning of treatment (Time 1) and Figure 13.2 is the subscale profile. Validity scales are all within acceptable ranges according to Morey (1996) and suggest that she was consistent in her answers (Inconsistency; ICN), able to attend to the task at hand (Infrequency; INF), and able to respond in an open and forthright manner (Negative Impression Management [NIM], Positive Impression Management [PIM]). Jenny's highest PAI scale scores were Anxiety-Related Disorders (ARD = 78) and Depression (DEP = 74) suggesting an individual who has, and is acutely aware of, a great deal of psychological turmoil and low self-esteem (see also the low score on Mania-Grandiosity; MAN-G). The combination of her high stress and feeling powerless to change her situation suggested that Jenny may have had some trouble engaging in treatment. Some difficulties in concentration are likely related to overall feelings of distress, which might make treatment planning with Jenny challenging as she may have had trouble articulating how she would like to change. Morey (1996) notes that this is a relatively common code type (2.5% of clinical sample) that is often accompanied by elevations on Anxiety (ANX) and Suicidal Ideation (SUI). Although her ANX scale was elevated (T = 69) her self-reported thoughts related to suicide were close to average in the community sample.

The next step in profile analysis was to review the subscale configurations starting from the highest scale score to the lowest. The ARD subscale configuration of

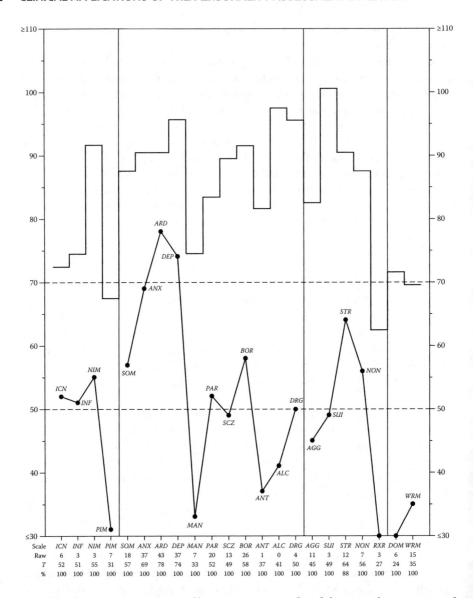

Figure 13.1   Full-scale PAI profile—Time 1. Reproduced by special permission of Psychological Assessment Resources, Inc., Lutz, Florida. Leslie C. Morey, Ph.D. and PAR Staff, Copyright by PAR, Inc.

low Obsessive-Compulsive (ARD-O), high Phobias (ARD-P), and high Traumatic Stress (ARD-T) point to someone who has experienced at least one distressing event in her life and thoughts of the event(s) continued to cause distress. Such people will go to great lengths to avoid situations, locations, or other stimuli that might trigger additional exposure. The Depression subscales suggest that, while Jenny did seem to have low expectations regarding her own agency (Cognitive; DEP-C, see also Dominance; DOM), there was a strong affective component to her presentation

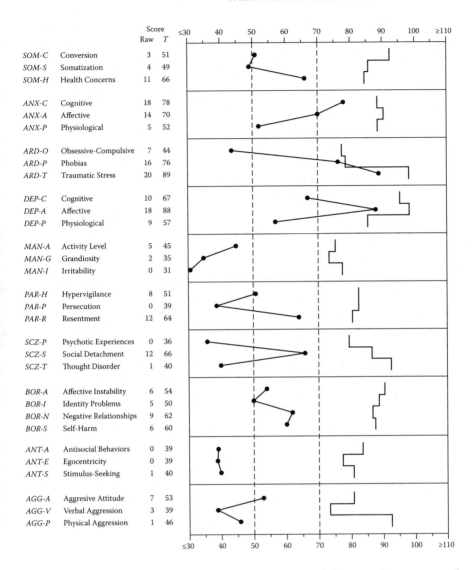

Figure 13.2 Sub-scale PAI profile—Time 1. Reproduced by special permission of Psychological Assessment Resources, Inc., Lutz, Florida. Leslie C. Morey, Ph.D. and PAR Staff, Copyright by PAR, Inc.

coupled with a lack of interest in potentially pleasurable activities (Affective; DEP-A). As one of the strongest indicators of current life satisfaction, an elevated DEP-A can also be considered to be a positive indicator of change (Morey, 1996). Morey also discusses how the self-evaluative component of the Mania-Grandiosity (MAN-G) subscale can provide useful information at the low end of the scale. At T = 35, Jenny may not have only felt inadequate, but this may be an internalized part of her personality. The high ANX-C (Cognitive), moderate ANX-A (Affective), and low ANX-P (Physiological) point to the fact that Jenny was a ruminator who tended to overanalyze her activities (or lack thereof), which often left her feeling paralyzed.

Her inaction would likely then feed into her low self-esteem and confirm her fears that she could not change her life. Despite her Somatic Complaints (SOM) scale elevation being below 60, her medical history warranted a review of the subscales. The isolated moderate SOM-H (Health Concerns) elevation suggested that Jenny was quietly preoccupied with the perceived complexity of her health status, which may also have been impacting her overall self-esteem. The moderate Paranoia-Resentment (PAR-R) and Schizophrenia-Social Detachment (SCZ-S) elevations have important implications when discussing the interpersonal scale configurations later on, and help to illustrate a volitional component to her detachment from relationships likely involving a smoldering anger that occurs when Jenny feels wronged by others. Perhaps a contributing factor to her isolation and resentment can also be seen in her moderate Borderline-Negative Relationships (BOR-N) elevation, where she thought that past relationships she had been engaged in were unstable or ended poorly.

With the exception of a slight elevation of the Stress Scale (STR), the treatment indicator scales of Aggression (AGG), SUI, Nonsupport (NON), and Treatment Rejection (RXR) did not indicate any "red flags" for treatment. Her very low RXR (T = 27) score suggested that Jenny was aware of the problems in her life and believed that she needed help, though she might not yet have been at the point of desperation (T < 20; Morey, 1996). The moderate STR elevation is very common in outpatient samples and points to certain situations in Jenny's life that were contributing to her overall level of distress. However, the average NON score suggests that she may have had sufficient social support that acted as a partial buffer against her situational troubles. From a TA perspective, the PAI is particularly useful, as it contains two bipolar interpersonal scales, Dominance (DOM) and Warmth (WRM) taken from the circumplex model of personality, that generally have the same means in nonclinical and clinical samples (Morey, 1996). When used in combination, these two scales form the four basic quadrants of an interpersonal style (High DOM, low WRM; High DOM, High WRM; Low DOM, High WRM; Low DOM, Low WRM), that can help the assessor tailor the feedback style to the patient. Jenny's low scores on both DOM and WRM suggested that not only was she interpersonally passive in relationships, but she may not have felt a need to be close to others (also indicated by her elevated SCZ-S score). She may have felt uncomfortable around people and been likely to opt out of social opportunities due to her anticipated discomfort. As pointed out by Morey, accompanying elevation on PAR-R with low scores on DOM and WRM indicate that Jenny may feel a certain amount of resentment when asked to do things that she does not want to do, thus decreasing her interest in pursuing new connections.

As stated earlier, the second pass through the testing data should keep the presenting problem(s) and goals of assessment in mind in order to help generate feedback style. If one was to group Jenny's issues together, three main areas seem to stand out: (1) the recent death of her son, (2) her low self-esteem, and (3) her interpersonal style. Generating hypotheses by roughly mapping the PAI findings in order of relevance to these three areas can further help the assessor organize the feedback and might look something like this:

1. Distress/Death of son
   a. ARD
   b. DEP
   c. ANX
   d. STR
2. Low Self-Esteem
   a. ANX-C
   b. DEP-C
   c. SOM-H
   d. BOR-N
   e. MAN-G
   f. DOM/WRM
3. Interpersonal Style
   a. DOM/WRM
   b. PAR-R
   c. SCZ-S
   d. ANX-C
   e. DEP-C
   f. BOR-N

As a general rule, recognizing patients' distress or discussing the main reason they are seeking assistance is the best place to begin feedback. This usually means explaining the highest clinical scale elevations first, as they often represent the area where patients are experiencing the greatest amount of psychological turmoil. In Jenny's case, the order would be ARD, DEP, ANX, and STR, with a stronger focus on those scales that were > 70. For the second domain, low self-esteem, a focus was put onto Jenny's cognitive signs of anxiety (ANX-C) and depression (DEP-C) first because she described her chronic worry and feelings of worthlessness in great detail during the interview. Using her own words combined with discussing the respective scale elevations could further validate her experience and act as an effective transition into explaining how her thinking style contributed to her self-image. The remaining scales (SOM-H, BOR-N, MAN-G, DOM/WRM) are ordered next because the extent of Jenny's awareness of how these areas might have contributed to her self-evaluation was unclear and it is important to begin with information close to a patient's awareness. The third domain, interpersonal style, can be helpful in virtually all psychological assessments, as it can represent how the patient approaches both relationships and more global obstacles. DOM/WRM scale combinations typically lead off in this discussion as they should reflect the patients' own views about themselves. In Jenny's case, PAR-R and SCZ-S came next, as they seemed to have particular relevance to her DOM/WRM scores, followed by those scales that had already been presented yet further contributed to understanding her relational pattern.

From here, feedback statements can be generated in order of how close each issue is to Jenny's conscious awareness. In the absence of patient-generated assessment questions, the simplest way to decide which testing feedback to give first is to look at what patients described as their reason(s) for seeking treatment, as this is an indication of what issues are of primary interest. As most patients are experiencing a significant degree of distress, this is typically a good starting point for discussion. As stated earlier, TA feedback should always include an open-ended question at the end of each point, such as "What are your thoughts about that?" or "How does that fit with how you see yourself?" in order to engage the patients in the process and allow them opportunities to get clarification. In situations where the information might be difficult to hear or the patients seem to be struck by the feedback, comments such as "What was it like to hear me say that?" or "Tell me what you are thinking/feeling after hearing that" can be helpful in that they demonstrate that the assessor is both attending to the patients and encouraging an open exploration of their experiences.

To return to Jenny's profile and knowing about her history and presenting problems, feedback would need to be generated with her low DOM and WRM scales in mind. How do you provide potentially negative information to a person who already did not have high self-esteem, was unassertive, and socially disconnected? The rule of providing ego-dystonic information first can be especially important with Jenny, as she is likely prepared to hear something along the lines of how her problems are of her own doing and if she would just stop feeling sorry for herself, she could make changes. Beginning with those issues that she may have little or no control over can be a very effective method to get her more engaged in the process. Regarding the first section of feedback entitled "Distress/Death of son," I would open the feedback with (1) a statement of the obvious and (2) potential contributors to her distress around this issue. For example:

> One thing that really came across in your responses is how much pain you are in right now and how much it is affecting your life [pause for comment]. In our first meeting, you described some horrible things that have happened to you and it seems as if memories of those events are still quite distressing despite your best efforts to get past them [pause for comment]. You seem to spend a lot of time analyzing and even worrying about these things to the extent where it can be hard to know what to do next [pause for comment].

Morey (1996) points out that while the ARD-T (Traumatic Stress) is a strong indicator of past trauma, it is not specific about the type of traumatic event. Given the recency of her son's death and severity of this event, an elevated ARD-T would be expected. However, her divorce and family abuse might also have been contributing to her responses. If Jenny did nothing more than acknowledge the accuracy of these comments, I might add another question such as, "What memories seem to be weighing the heaviest on you?" When in doubt, it is best to let the patient describe her thought process rather than make assumptions about what aspects of patient phenomenology are most likely driving scale elevations. The section entitled "Low Self-Esteem" might have a similar format based on Jenny's acknowledgment of her poor efficacy, but with an attempt to offer her some hope.

> In our first meeting you also described feeling ineffective in overcoming a number of obstacles in your life and this came across in your responses to the test items. You spend a lot of time thinking about your life, which I think can serve you well in therapy as you will be doing this quite often [pause]. Your struggle seems to be that each time you evaluate something, the outcome is

usually negative, perhaps often involving something you feel you should or shouldn't have done [pause]. You may be at the point now to where you *expect* things to go wrong and have a hard time making decisions about the next step [pause]. Many times when we expect something to turn out poorly, we start looking for those signs early on, find them, and focus on them even if there are also signs of more favorable outcomes. Therapy can be a place where you can take a closer look at your expectations, where they came from, and how they influence the choices that you make [pause].

Depending on Jenny's reaction to these comments, more specific information could be included in the feedback. For example, if she did not agree with her tendency to negatively evaluate her life and that it was her fault, the assessor could have asked her to explain it in her own words. This is also the part of the feedback where further inquiry into her perceived health status could be added. A self-perception that Jenny was medically unhealthy or with complicated health problems might have factored into her sense of self-worth, as she may have felt less of a person than healthier people. It would also be important to get her perspective about her stressful relationships with her children and coworkers and whether she saw any similarities in the way she interacted with them. Finally, inquiring about the ending of her marriage and her ensuing thoughts about that time in her life might have also provided important information about her relationship style, which was covered in the final section of the feedback, "Interpersonal Style."

> Overall, you seem to describe yourself as a passive person who finds it difficult to speak your mind around others even if you have something to say [pause]. This tends to not mix well for you when you are around people who are more assertive or bossy [pause]. I have a sense that this may contribute to your feelings of being ineffective or unable to change the course of your life [pause]. At times, you end up doing things that you do not want to do perhaps because it's hard to say no, and, like most other people, this leaves you feeling angry [pause]. Do you have any examples of this? [pause] Perhaps, related to your thinking style, which we discussed earlier, times when you feel wronged or put upon are "sticky moments." In other words, they are hard to let go of and you may find yourself resenting those people who have wronged you [pause].

The latter part of the feedback session can be used to offer hypotheses that are informed by, but not necessarily solely based on, the results of testing and interview. Jenny expressed a potential interest in dating men at some point, but her low WRM and elevated SCZ-S suggests that she is not interested in relationships and has voluntarily pulled away from interpersonal connections. Given cross-sectional assessment data, it is hard to know if her withdrawal is a reactionary state or long-standing trait. Two main approaches to addressing this apparent conflict come to mind and both can be used in the TA model. First, the assessor can generate his or her own thoughts about this, offer them to the patient, and ask for help in correcting any misconceptions. This procedure engages patients in a discussion about the results and encourages them to edit as they see fit. An alternate approach (particularly useful given treatment resistance) is to point out the discrepancy and ask patients to generate their own hypotheses. This latter technique relies on the TA assumptions that patients are the experts on themselves and have a desire for personal growth. Collaborative discussions of apparently discrepant goals or data can provide a wealth of information about the patient's self-awareness, investment in the assessment (and even therapy) process, and attitudes or events that might not have been discussed in the interview. Asking patients to help make sense of the testing results also places them in a position of authority, as well as making the assessor a true co-pilot in the feedback process as opposed to telling patients what the test says about them. After engaging in the co-generation of information, assessors can also include their own hypotheses to give an additional perspective for the patient to consider in making connections between more distal pieces of information. There are many ways to offer hypotheses to the patient. Here is one method to consider.

> [Assuming patient agreed with most of the information so far.] So, it seems as if you have agreed with most of the things we have been talking about today [pause]. There is one more piece that I would like your help with. In our interview, you mentioned that you could see yourself interested in dating again someday, which led me to think that you have some interest in relationships [pause]. However, your answers to the test items suggest that not only do you tend to be somewhat passive in relationships, but that you have intentionally pulled away from people and might even avoid them altogether at times [pause]. What I found myself wondering is whether you have never really been interested in relationships, or if this is something that has developed over time. I can offer some thoughts, but I am interested in how you make sense of this [pause]? [After patient gives explanation or doesn't know] I wondered if your experiences with relationships in your life coupled with your somewhat negative view of yourself and tendency to worry have had a cumulative effect. Perhaps, at some point, you decided that it was just easier not to be in any close relationships in order to protect yourself from future disappointment [pause].

Concluding a feedback session with information geared more toward a patient's relational pattern can often lead into a discussion about how patients see themselves in therapy. It can also (in cases where formal psychotherapy has yet to begin) provide a space to discuss expectations the patient has about the treatment process. At this point, the information from the feedback can be offered as a way to help patients generate their own goals for therapy. From Jenny's profile and presenting complaints, goals might have included (but not be exclusive to) reducing her level of distress, providing a forum for her to discuss her feelings surrounding the recent loss of her son, exploring contributing factors to her low self-esteem, and better understanding of how her interpersonal style might factor into her relationship struggles. Jenny agreed to these goals as a starting point and expressed a particular desire to discuss the death of her child and her relational difficulties. She entered into once-a-week therapy.

Although this chapter has focused on the potential therapeutic benefit of assessment, the PAI is obviously also useful for generating and testing diagnostic hypotheses. Jenny's data suggested the following diagnostic possibilities: Dysthymic Disorder, Generalized Anxiety Disorder, and Social Phobia, as well as Avoidant, Schizoid, or nonspecific personality disorders.

Time 2

Jenny attended a year of treatment before the re-administration of the PAI. As she described her desire to focus on the death of her son and her interpersonal relationships, these became the main foci of her treatment. She reported a decrease in her overall level of distress and a greater sense of who she was as a person, thus resulting in an improvement in her self-esteem. One piece of information that did not surface until after treatment began was that her relational struggles seem to be more specific to men in both the personal and occupational arenas. This helped to flesh out what might have been picked up by the ARD-Phobia subscale as a fear of getting close to men. Despite feeling better in general, Jenny continued to struggle in her relationships. Her passive nature did not seem to change much and her resentment toward others she felt had mistreated her (more pronounced with men) still appeared to be a contributing factor to her lack of significant attachments, despite her stated wish to be in a serious relationship.

It can often be helpful to refer back to testing data in therapy, as this keeps this information more accessible to and relevant for the patient and can facilitate discussions about additional testing if it becomes appropriate. The use of psychological testing *during* therapy can generate a great variety of reactions in both treaters and patients. Treatments that are at a stalemate where there is a lack of mutual understanding about the next step might seem like an excellent opportunity to seek a psychological assessment. However, some treaters can be reluctant to make a testing referral out of concern that it might show their patient or their colleagues that they are ineffective. In Jenny's case, retesting was used to update her overall psychological status (i.e., treatment outcome) and determine what additional treatment goals might be helpful. Although the therapist made it clear to Jenny that additional testing was not necessary, it was also emphasized how the original evaluation was helpful and how it might be useful to assess whether the profile had changed as a result of treatment.

The results from Jenny's second PAI can be seen in Figure 13.3 and Figure 13.4. The most striking feature of this second PAI was the drop in scale elevations for ARD, DEP, ANX, and STR, suggesting a general decrease, but not complete elimination of, her overall level of psychological distress. The subscales for ARD, ANX, and DEP (Figure 13.4) also showed a general decline. With the exception of ARD-P, each of these subscales was below 70T. Her ARD-T at Time 1 (T = 89) was nearly 2 SD above the clinical normative sample, yet returned to within an SD of the community norms at Time 2, indicating that her distress about the death of her son, one of her primary treatment goals, had significantly changed over time. However, the lingering elevation on ARD-P suggested that she remained fearful of certain (likely social) stimuli; even if she no longer felt the need to rigidly avoid them. Her moderately elevated ANX-C and ANX-A demonstrated that her ruminative worry had not completely dissipated. Although her anxiety was undoubtedly contributing to her moderate level of sadness (DEP-A), her feelings of being unable to change her situation dramatically improved from Time 1 (DEP-C = 52). Notice, however, that her MAN-G score had not changed, suggesting a more treatment-resistant (perhaps internalized) view of her inadequacies. Although there seemed to be clear-cut evidence that Jenny felt better about herself and her

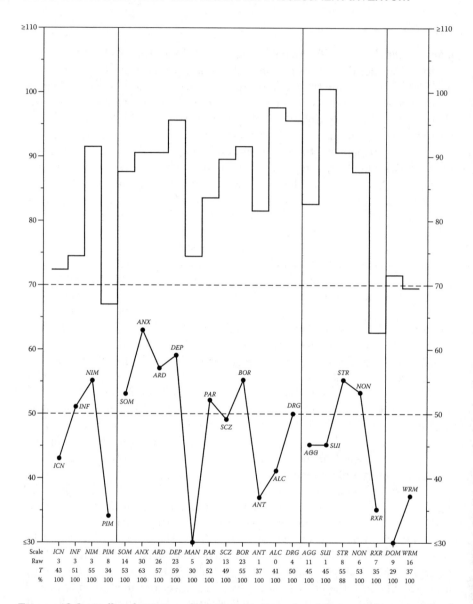

Scale	ICN	INF	NIM	PIM	SOM	ANX	ARD	DEP	MAN	PAR	SCZ	BOR	ANT	ALC	DRG	AGG	SUI	STR	NON	RXR	DOM	WRM
Raw	3	3	3	8	14	30	26	23	5	20	13	23	1	0	4	11	1	8	6	7	9	16
T	43	51	55	34	53	63	57	59	30	52	49	55	37	41	50	45	45	55	53	35	29	37
%	100	100	100	100	100	100	100	100	100	100	100	100	100	100	100	100	100	88	100	100	100	100

Figure 13.3 Full-scale PAI profile—Time 2. Reproduced by special permission of Psychological Assessment Resources, Inc., Lutz, Florida. Leslie C. Morey, Ph.D. and PAR Staff, Copyright by PAR, Inc.

situation on several fronts, the lack of changes in scales relating to her interpersonal style (DOM, WRM, PAR-R, SCZ-S, and possibly MAN-G) also warrants discussion. PAR-R and SCZ-S are more strongly influenced by generalized distress than DOM and WRM, so that a decrease in her overall level of psychological discomfort might have included at least a slight reduction in her resentment (PAR-R) and social detachment (SCZ-S). The absence of any change in these scales after a year of treatment suggested the possibility of persistent personality problems that

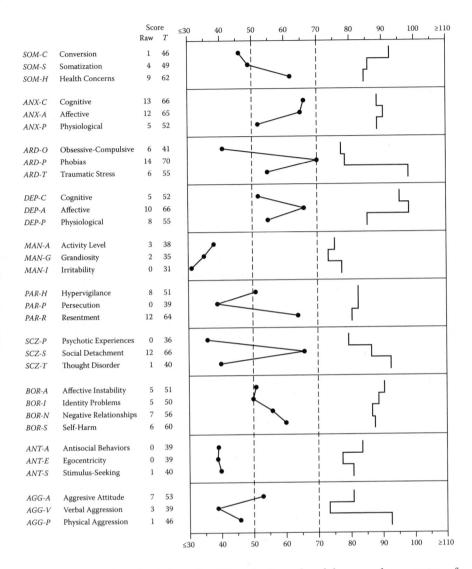

		Raw	T
SOM-C	Conversion	1	46
SOM-S	Somatization	4	49
SOM-H	Health Concerns	9	62
ANX-C	Cognitive	13	66
ANX-A	Affective	12	65
ANX-P	Physiological	5	52
ARD-O	Obsessive-Compulsive	6	41
ARD-P	Phobias	14	70
ARD-T	Traumatic Stress	6	55
DEP-C	Cognitive	5	52
DEP-A	Affective	10	66
DEP-P	Physiological	8	55
MAN-A	Activity Level	3	38
MAN-G	Grandiosity	2	35
MAN-I	Irritability	0	31
PAR-H	Hypervigilance	8	51
PAR-P	Persecution	0	39
PAR-R	Resentment	12	64
SCZ-P	Psychotic Experiences	0	36
SCZ-S	Social Detachment	12	66
SCZ-T	Thought Disorder	1	40
BOR-A	Affective Instability	5	51
BOR-I	Identity Problems	5	50
BOR-N	Negative Relationships	7	56
BOR-S	Self-Harm	6	60
ANT-A	Antisocial Behaviors	0	39
ANT-E	Egocentricity	0	39
ANT-S	Stimulus-Seeking	1	40
AGG-A	Aggresive Attitude	7	53
AGG-V	Verbal Aggression	3	39
AGG-P	Physical Aggression	1	46

Figure 13.4 Sub-scale PAI profile—Time 2. Reproduced by special permission of Psychological Assessment Resources, Inc., Lutz, Florida. Leslie C. Morey, Ph.D. and PAR Staff, Copyright by PAR, Inc.

had not been fully addressed in treatment. In any case, a clearer picture of how Jenny's interpersonal style impacted her relationships was very important when framing feedback from this second evaluation.

In cases of retesting with the PAI (or any measure that provides a visual representation of scores), showing the profiles from both assessments can be very helpful to demonstrate to the patient the changes, or lack thereof, produced by their responses. In fact, the PAI software allows the assessor to plot more than one set of scores on a single profile to further demonstrate differences. Here is an example of how this information might be presented and discussed with Jenny.

So here are your two test printouts. Your first testing is on the left and your most recent one is on the right. Just as a refresher, this line [point to T = 70 dotted line] represents scores that are at the clinical cutoff and this line [point to T = 50 dotted line] is the mean of the nonclinical norms. As you can see, your scores from this most recent testing have gone down in many places, which tells us that you are not as distressed by the issues that you first came to treatment with [pause]. How do you make sense of this change? [wait for patient explanation]. The biggest changes seemed to be with the distress surrounding the death of your son [point to ARD-T at Time one and Time 2] and your overall feelings of sadness [point to DEP-A at Time one and Time 2]—although you still may feel down from time to time [pause]. This would make sense as we spent a great deal of your time talking about your son and the impact that his sudden death had on you. Your general sense of worry has also decreased [point to ANX-C] but I imagine that you still feel it to some degree [pause]. However, unlike before, it seems as if you have increased confidence in your ability to make changes in your life [point to DEP-C; pause]. What do you think has brought about this change [pause for response]? There is a sense that you still have fears about specific situations that interfere with your life [point to ARD-P], but that you may avoid them less often [pause].

Discussing issues surrounding personality style can be somewhat distressing for some patients, especially when it appears as a more stable problem than symptoms of depression or anxiety. Knowing Jenny's personality style is passive and that she had a tendency to hold grudges, it was particularly important to pay attention to how this information is presented to her.

Now let's take a look at some of the scales that did not change very much. One of your other original treatment goals was to address the problems you have in relationships where you tend to be shy and avoid confrontation, but feel angry and frustrated when you end up doing things that you do not want to do. This frustration tends to stay with you and can develop into a grudge that you have a hard time letting go of [pause]. The more you anticipate interpersonal interactions to go this way, the more you tend to detach yourself from people. Do you think this might be a situation that you would avoid [point to ARD-P; pause]. Although this does keep you safe, I imagine that it can also be very lonely, seeing as how you have talked about wanting to date [pause]. The two main drawbacks with your approach is that it prevents you from meeting people you might like, and tends to further feed into your worries because you have no evidence that contrasts your negative experiences [pause]. Sometimes, this style is a by-product of psychological distress. The worse someone feels, the less they want to be around other people. As you can see, your own reported level of distress has decreased, but your relationship dilemma has not changed as much. How do you make sense of this [pause]? One possible explanation might be that, depression and anxiety aside, you have had a longstanding concern that you do not measure up to other people [pause]. In other words, even on your best days, you don't think very highly of yourself, and this feeling has been with you for quite some time [pause]. I worry that the more you hold onto that self-perception, the harder it can be to change who you are in relationships with even the most caring people [pause]. This does not mean that you are doomed in relationships, but I would expect it will take more work on our part in therapy to get at these underlying issues.

This last segment pertaining to her poor self-evaluation above and beyond her depression and anxiety seemed to be particularly unsettling for Jenny. Despite this issue's being discussed in her treatment, seeing the profiles and hearing the feedback in this session would later act as a catalyst for her to try something different. She agreed to remain in treatment with a specific focus on how she developed her negative self-views and to better understand how this attitude impacted her thoughts and behaviors when relating to others. Six months into treatment she was able to go on a few dates. Although a new committed relationship did not materialize and Jenny continued to be anxious and struggle with her self-esteem, she found these new experiences exciting and was hopeful about the future. Around this time, Jenny also discussed her interest in pursuing further therapy with a female therapist. This had come up at several points during the course of her treatment, but she was reluctant to pursue this topic. Her reasoning was that while she did not feel threatened or resentful of her current male therapist, she wondered if a female therapist might be able to provide a different perspective. Despite getting referrals, Jenny never acted on them for fear of "someone else having to get to know me," which also materialized into a discussion about not wanting to upset her current therapist. Thus, her renewed commitment to working with a female therapist was seen as a positive indicator of assertiveness and a willingness to explore new options. This time, Jenny followed through with her plan and was able to develop treatment goals that she would like to work on with her new therapist, to whom she transferred a few months later.

SUMMARY

Before summarizing this chapter, I would like to share a recent personal story. When my wife and I were expecting our second child, we went to our first 3-month sonogram appointment. Our first pregnancy was relatively uneventful so there were few concerns. However, the radiologist had concerns about the possibility of both genetic and cardiologic abnormalities, resulting in a frenetic rush to meet with a genetic counselor and scheduling a series of tests with very little explanation about false-positive findings. After waiting an exhausting couple of weeks to get the test results back, we were scheduled for a second routine sonogram that would also help to clarify any structural heart defects. The same radiologist entered the room with little more than an acknowledgment of our presence and no discussion about the previous exam or the potential anxiety it might have caused. After about 10 minutes of tension-filled silence while we watched him work, we had to ask *him* about his evaluation, which was relayed in a dispassionate voice without taking his eyes off the computer screen.

The point of this story is that an effective assessment (psychological or otherwise) is arguably more about the working relationship with the patient than the testing battery itself. The experience with the radiologist could have been dramatically improved had there been an acknowledgment of what we went through or even an explanation of what was being focused on in the appointment (even a smile would have done wonders). Psychological assessors with even the most sophisticated knowledge about testing instruments and pathology have an ethical responsibility to communicate results to patients in a language they can understand. This makes each assessment a unique and customized experience, and TA provides a framework to help reach this goal. The comprehensive and user-friendly nature of the PAI can make it particularly applicable to TA as both a measure of psychopathology and guide for developing treatment plans.

A wealth of nomothetic and ideographic information is presented in this volume from leading PAI researchers and innovators in the field of personality assessment. In many cases, information in each of the chapters has not been published elsewhere in aggregate form, if at all. Communicating these findings with the greater assessment community was indeed the primary goal of this book. The larger hope, as was intended by the various case presentations and the book title, is that the individual patient would not get lost in all the data and will benefit from the application of this information to his or her own life. As was hopefully demonstrated in this chapter, gathering information is a necessary, but not sufficient, step to providing quality personality assessments.

REFERENCES

Ackerman, S. J., Hilsenroth, M. J., Baity, M. R., & Blagys, M. D. (2000). Interaction of therapeutic process and alliance during psychological assessment. *Journal of Personality Assessment, 75,* 82–109.

Finn, S. E., & Tonsager, M. E. (1992). Therapeutic effects of providing MMPI-2 test feedback to college students awaiting therapy. *Psychological Assessment, 4,* 278–287.

Finn, S. E., & Tonsager, M. E. (1997). Information-gathering and therapeutic models of assessment: Complementary paradigms. *Psychological Assessment, 9,* 374–385.

Frank, J. D., & Frank J. B. (1991). *Persuasion and healing: A comparative study of psychotherapy.* Baltimore, MD: Johns Hopkins University Press.

Hilsenroth, M. J., Peters, E. J., & Ackerman, S. J. (2004). The development of therapeutic alliance during psychology assessment: Patient and therapist perspectives across treatment. *Journal of Personality Assessment, 83,* 331–344.

Luborsky, L. (1984). *Principles of psychoanalytic psychotherapy: A manual for supportive-expressive treatment.* New York: Basic Books.

Morey, L. C. (1996). *An interpretive guide to the Personality Assessment Inventory (PAI).* Odessa, FL: Psychological Assessment Resources, Inc.

Index